Here's what wine experts have said about *Vineyards in the Sky*:

Anthony Dias Blue, on CBS Radio and in a nationally syndicated wine column: *"This small-press publication is certainly worth tracking down....It is a gripping memoir that reads like a "major" novel....Following Prohibition and under the tutelage of Paul Masson, Ray championed the varietal concept. His commitment to this ideal made him the gadfly of an industry that packaged inferior blends with misleading labels. Ray insisted on producing pure varietal wines from premium grapes. It was this style of winemaking that would eventually bring California wines international recognition and adoration."*

Frank Prial, in The New York Times: *"... will fascinate anyone interested in the early days of the California wine boom. As words go, legendary is almost as overworked as gourmet, but if ever there was a legendary character in the wine business, it was Mr. Ray....He was an advocate of 100 percent varietal wines—all cabernet sauvignon or all pinot noir—long before they were fashionable."*

Herbert Engelbert, in "Time Out for Fine Wine," KFLN Radio, Philadelphia: *"You will want to read* Vineyards in the Sky!*... Martin Ray is still well-remembered among vintners and wine buffs. Eleanor Ray, his widow, and her daughter, Barbara Marinacci, have written a biography that is a fascinating history of a man and an era.... This is a full-bodied book, just like the man and the wines he made: 488 pages of tales that are stirring, comic, poignant, and tragic."*

Norman E. Gates, Grand Commander, Brotherhood of the Knights of the Vine: *"Good book—could not put it down!"*

Jeff Kellgren, in the Specialty Book Company wine book catalog: *"Martin Ray was a fascinating figure who embodied all the glamour and idealism of quality winemaking, and added another element—spirituality. He was definitely of the Romantic school of winemaking. His almost nightly dinners and parties were gargantuan, the decades of backbreaking labor he put into his wines were herculean, his dedication to the minutest aspects of quality was unquenchable, and he appreciated winemaking, and clung to it, as a supremely satisfying way of life. Indeed, to him winemaking was 'the good life.'"*

Maurice T. Sullivan, in The Wine Trader: *"For sheer entertainment and California wine nostalgia, I can recommend* Vineyards in the Sky.... *Anyone who has worked in the wine business in the last 30 years will delight in this book. We all k   ~out Martin (Ray) and his quest to make California wine labeling honest.... Eminen   historian Charles Sullivan consulted on this book and insures accura   ~ed to know about the California winery that entertained Charli   President Hoover, and scores of European nobility during   was largely a national embarrassment. Martin Ray set st   wines.... He was a courageous man of vision who left an   This is an important story, much of which has not been told be~.*

Tom Mudd, proprietor-winemaker, Cinnabar Vineyards, Santa Cruz Mount... vision, idealism, persistence, and hubris of Martin Ray were extraordinary. Eleanor Ra, captures it all as only a devoted admirer and eloquent author could. Three puffs for a great book about a real pioneer in the wine industry."*

Martin Mathis, proprietor-winemaker, Kathryn Kennedy Winery, Santa Cruz Mountains: *"*Vineyards in the Sky *gives the reader a glimpse into the spirit of the quintessential California winegrower—someone who lives and breathes winemaking at its finest. The history of the Santa Cruz Mountains in California is used to shed light on one winemaking family's achievement of 'the good life.'"*

Tony and Victoria Sargent, proprietor-winemakers at Rubissow-Sargent Winery, Napa and Berkeley: *"It's going to be a wine classic! It is so satisfying to read of a life in which so difficult a dream is pursued and realized despite all the horrendous obstacles in the path."*

*To the memory of
my beloved Rusty . . . of course*

Vineyards
in the Sky

The Life of Legendary Vintner
Martin Ray

by

Eleanor Ray
with

Barbara Marinacci

Foreword by Nathan Chroman

Published by
Mountain Vines Publishing, LLC
Aptos, California

Vineyards in the Sky:
The Life of Legendary Vintner Martin Ray
by Eleanor Ray with Barbara Marinacci

Published by:
Mountain Vines Publishing, LLC
PO Box 385
Aptos, CA 95001 USA

orders@mountainvinespub.com
www.mountainvinespub.com

Vineyards in the Sky: The Life of Legendary Vintner Martin Ray was originally published in 1993 by Heritage West Books of Stockton, CA.

Printed in Canada

Publisher's Cataloging-in-Publication
(Provided by Quality Books, Inc.)

Ray, Eleanor.
    Vineyards in the sky : the life of legendary vintner
Martin Ray / by Eleanor Ray with Barbara Marinacci ;
foreword by Nathan Chroman.
    p. cm.
    Includes bibliographical references and index.
    LCCN 2005938649
    ISBN 0974135704

    1. Ray, Martin, 1904-1976. 2. Vintners--California--
Biography. 3. Wine and wine making--California--
History.   I. Marinacci, Barbara. II. Title.

TP547.R39R38 2006   641.2'2'092
                             QBI06-600006

Contents

Eleanor Ray's

Acknowledgments

I AM GRATEFUL TO a number of people whose records, recollections, insights, and knowledge through the years have provided invaluable background information for this story of the life of Martin Ray, my late husband.

I am indebted to wine historian Charles L. Sullivan, not only for expansive and detailed history given in his book, *Like Modern Edens: Winegrowing in Santa Clara Valley and Santa Cruz Mountains 1798-1981*, but also for reading my manuscript for historical and technical accuracy. Telephone conversations long ago with both Nelty Lefranc Horney (daughter of Henry Lefranc, niece of Paul Masson) and Helen Barnett Fisher (girlhood friend of Adele Masson) provided insights into the Masson family. Mark Karakas of The Mountain Winery and Chateau La Cresta graciously gave me a tour of the much-altered premises that once belonged to Masson, then Martin Ray. Dora Moore Lipps and Joe Tarantino supplied helpful research assistance in the past.

I appreciate historian and publisher Sylvia Sun Minnick's enthusiasm in accepting *Vineyards in the Sky* as a project for Heritage West Books. My heartfelt thanks go to Nathan Chroman—lawyer and noted wine columnist—for furnishing the Foreword; to graphic designer Rudy Marinacci for doing both the cover design and line drawings of grapevines; and to Suzanne Goldberg for her production editing.

Others I particularly want to thank for their support and feedback during this book's long journey into print: my sons, Dr. Peter Martin Ray and Dr. Barclay Kamb; my daughters-in-law, Dr. Sara Fultz Ray and Linda Pauling Kamb; my grandchildren—especially Martin Forbes Ray, who wanted me to write the story as a novel. Special thanks also go to Mount Eden Vineyards' proprietors, Jeffrey and Eleanor (Ellie) Patterson; and to Rose Caglia, Martin

Ray's bookkeeper for many years. Also to Saratogans Willys Peck, Richard Tyrrell, Terry Cabrinha, Cecily Kyes, Josephine and Franc Fallico, and Ace Perry; and to Mar Preston and Marilyn Perzik of Los Angeles.

The photographs in the text come from my own collection, and include photographs taken of Martin and me by publisher Alfred Knopf. Available for queries and searches have been reference librarians at several public libraries in the San Jose area and volunteers at local historical societies.

Above all, I acknowledge the extensive assistance of my daughter Barbara Marinacci ("Bobo"), whose editorial and writing skills contributed greatly to assembling and publishing these reminiscences, both personal and historical.

Note to Readers: This biography has been partially dramatized so as to capture the spirit of Martin Ray's whole life. Basic information about winegrowing and winemaking, as Martin learned it as a boy, is provided in a narrative form. Some familiarity with each activity is essential in understanding the meaning of Martin Ray's lifework, and I did not take each reader's knowledge for granted. Names of particular individuals and organizations have been intentionally altered.

Foreword

by Nathan Chroman

THE LIFE OF MARTIN Ray, one of California's all-time great vintners, should be hailed with a vote of deep thanks by wine lovers and winemakers alike. His death in 1976, at the age of seventy-one, left a void as large as Mount Eden, where his beloved domain and mountain vineyards were located. This property is adjacently north of the old Paul Masson "Mountain Winery" vineyards in Saratoga, which Ray owned from 1936 to 1943, before selling out to develop an internationally acclaimed wine estate under his own name.

Martin Ray was a businessman of only thirty-two when he arranged to buy Paul Masson's holdings, thus fulfilling a boyhood ambition. When refusing his first offer, the French-born Masson had chided his protégé and friend: "I can't let you be a damned fool!" Soon enough Ray learned that the wine business was tough, particularly in the post-Prohibition years. But he persevered, and in time made a special niche for himself within the pantheon of great winemakers, not just in America but in the world.

For forty years Martin Ray held court in the foothills of the Santa Cruz Mountains that overlook the Santa Clara Valley. There he made some of California's greatest wines by following French *premier-cru* techniques in a successful American bid for equality with, even supremacy over, European wines. Yet except among the cognoscenti, Martin Ray's name and reputation by now have undeservedly receded, along with the availability of his wines.

To appreciate Martin Ray's contribution to the nation's evolving wine industry, one should be aware that, at the start of his vocation, making a commercial wine strictly from a fine-varietal grape—or, as in the current trend, from a deft signature blend of several prized varietals—were utterly fantastic notions. In the late '30s through the '50s the concepts had been made even more *outré* by the remaining wounds of Prohibition.

In 1939, Ray launched this country's first pure varietals, at prices four times that of other California wines. From the vintages of 1936, they were provided 100 percent from the varieties labeled on his bottles, such as chardonnay and pinot noir. Thus began the meteoric and oft-embattled career of this highly influential pioneer winemaker.

Most American vintners of the period were content to make wines from any grapes, or combinations thereof, so long as the wine was blandly palatable and easily salable. But not Martin Ray. He chastised contemporary producers unmercifully for having the gall to attach labels with varietal names to undistinguished wine blends, and then with greater gall sell them at prices in line with his own. The chastisement did not stop with a grower or two; he took on the whole of the industry in a personal crusade to curb the marketing of phony varietals. His sharp tongue, often containing more acid than his wines, spared no sacred "wine cows," including the then-powerful California Wine Institute, predominantly supported by large-scale producers.

Inevitably, Martin Ray earned a reputation for being contentious, but though he was often dubbed controversial, his wines were not. Indeed, many were hallmarks that other vintners tried to emulate. I doubt I shall ever taste better than his Pinot Noir 1960, his Chardonnay 1962, and his Cabernet Sauvignon Centennial 1952 (which he proclaimed the "greatest of all cabernets"). Not all his wines were great, but they were always interesting to drink—for he consistently *aimed* high, for absolute greatness. They possessed subtle nuances, character, and a style unmistakably their own, at a time when such qualities were scarcely valued in the wine trade. Furthermore, wines judged as disappointments or failures by enophiles may have become so under improper transportation or poor storage conditions. Yet Martin Ray risked damage to his reputation by always refusing to use the customary sulfur compounds to chemically disinfect and preserve his natural wines.

His wines were generally not for the neophyte, who needed to be introduced gradually to completely dry and full-bodied products. The reds required long-term aging and sometimes decanting, while the whites, having sat unracked on their lees for a season or more, and perhaps were unfined and unfiltered, often had sediment that would disconcert the uninitiated.

Martin Ray bottles traveled to retailers and customers in wood cases, as solid as fine mahogany and almost impossible to open—because that's how Martin believed they should be packaged. They also bore price tags truly astronomical in their day. But those who loved his wines, and knew the painstaking care he took in making them, gladly paid him his due.

The prices Martin Ray wines commanded, and got, raised delightfully chauvinistic ambitions in the industry, even as it tried to dismiss him as a gadfly and outsider in the Old Boy network. In the '50s and '60s many vintners, enologists, retailers, and wine drinkers began to rethink their ideas about the future possibilities of California wines. Today there is, of course, a long list of producers now bottling 100 percent varietal wines made from designated varietal clones grown in specifically named vineyard localities, the grapes often berry-selected during harvesting and fermented using handcraft techniques Ray surely would have admired. Many such bottles may indeed be worthy of the asked-for $30 or $50.

Martin Ray's life and work touched many people in the industry, directly or tangentially. On one occasion or another he either helped or fought with a variety of established or yet-to-be wine luminaries. His unwillingness to compromise his principles carried over into his personal relationships, which inevitably revolved around wines—his own or others'.

I sometimes suspected that Martin uttered diatribes in print and in person as much for the effect as for anything else. Many statements about his own creations sounded like self-serving puffery in sales promotion. Yet I as a wine lover, like so many others, would forgive all because he truly made great wines. Of them Julian Street, the much-revered author and wine authority of his day, said of Ray's first amazing wines: "They prove what California can do if it ever gets around to following the best practices of the finest vineyards.... He has made the best wines that have ever been made in the United States."

Unabashedly and unashamedly, I was, and remain, a Martin Ray fan. I still miss the rugged individualism, and the sometimes intemperate scolding which went with it, that were his alone. Both charming and bombastic, during his heyday Ray was a kind of self-appointed consumer wine advocate. He cussed out other winemakers because they didn't follow his own declared charter: a fine California wine must be vintaged wholly from the varietal named on the label. Indeed, he felt anything less was a compromise—to be banished from both Mt. Eden and consumer tables.

In *Vineyards in the Sky* Eleanor Ray, Martin Ray's widow, provides us with an engaging and insightful look at a remarkably charismatic man—unique in his own time and any other. This dramatic story of his entire life, from boy with a dream of a mountain vineyard to prosperous stockbroker to zealous winemaker-crusader, will convey to the reader a strong sense of the focused dedication demanded of an idealistic vintner. Those who have little acquaintance as yet with winegrowing will also learn, from the account of Martin Ray's own youthful apprenticeship, the basics of vineyard and cellar work. And those acquainted with Martin Ray or his legend will now see the human and personable aspects of his complex character, well rooted even before he chose to become a winemaker.

At the same time, this biographical memoir locates Martin Ray at the center of a fascinating period piece. His life, spanning the three-quarters of a century between its first and eighth decades, had as background elements the Prohibition and Repeal eras, two world wars, rapid technological advances, and other key socioeconomic and political forces—all of them shaping America's thriving wine industry of today.

Martin's own statement sums up his life and philosophy beautifully. "If you are looking for the finest life in the world, take up winegrowing," he said, "for it will provide and support a way of life like no other. . . . In winegrowing you have but one chance a year, and in an entire lifetime a winegrower has only a comparatively few vintages. There is no challenge like this and no greater satisfaction than meeting this challenge over the years."

Personally, I shall never forget my first visit to Martin, when I was a wine columnist with the *Los Angeles Times.* Due to a breakdown of our bus along the tortuous route up his mountain, I became separated from my friends and ventured forth alone. As I neared the top, I could see the strong, robust figure of Martin Ray standing tall and straight on his veranda. With two tall glasses of his Madame Pinot champagne in hand, he bellowed across the hills, "Come, Chroman, have a glass of my champagne . . . and live the Good Life with me!"

So *Vineyards in the Sky* is a delicious opportunity to glimpse, and for a few hours inhabit vicariously, the passion-filled world of the Good Life that was indeed Martin Ray's!

Los Angeles, California
1992

Preface

by Barbara Marinacci

VINEYARDS IN THE SKY, Eleanor Ray's dramatized life story about her husband, California winemaker Martin Ray, was initially published in 1993. In the years since then, it has earned a gratifying number of enthusiastic readers—some insisting that a wonderful movie could be made of its drama-packed pages. It has garnered numerous praises from wine writers, reviewers, and people in the wine industry, indicated by excerpts from their comments on the flyleaf. It is gratifying to note that items of information given in the book have been utilized, and duly credited, by a number of wine writers in both books and periodicals.

This third, somewhat revised and updated edition has been published by Mountain Vines Publishing LLC thirteen years after the book's first appearance.

During the early years after her marriage to Martin Ray in September of 1951, Eleanor Ray, who was my mother, worked on several versions of a novel that within its plot line often recycled colorful or dramatic stories that "Rusty" Ray had told her about his seven years as proprietor of the Paul Masson winery and vineyard property, as well as his connection with Paul Masson himself during his boyhood and in later years as an adult. Not surprisingly, the personality, opinions, and fighting spirit of the hero of her novel closely resembled those of Martin Ray.

Unable to interest publishers in her fictional work, Eleanor Ray increasingly devoted her writing time and efforts to publicizing Martin Ray's reputation as the maker of America's costliest, most elusive, and purest varietal wines. She did this through newsletters circulated among retailers and wine connoisseurs and letters written to special customers and friends. She also attempted to ghostwrite Martin Ray's "own" book, full of his uniquely adamant wine-connected opinions for an eventual publication that never happened.

Not long after her husband's death in 1976 Eleanor Ray began work on a memoir/biography of Martin Ray's entire life. It would include her own close friendship with him, begun long before their marriage (the second for both of them), dating back to their college years together at the University of Washington in the early 1920s.

Over the years the manuscript went through various incarnations, some even adapting scenes she had written much earlier for the unpublished novel. Before or after she submitted it to various publishers for consideration, she was inclined to either expand or shrink the tale of Martin Ray that she felt impelled to tell, thus adding or subtracting entire chapters. When photocopying became available, she had multiple copies made of different versions of her manuscript. She circulated several of these, whether with loose pages or in a bound form, almost like an underground publication—first among the people she knew who wished to know more about Martin Ray, or just about California wine history, and then among their like-minded acquaintances.

As my mother moved into her 80s, her hope of ever seeing *Vineyards in the Sky* in print began fading, along with the decline of her once-remarkable physical energy, social spirit, and mental acumen. By the end of 1989 it had become clear that she would soon need a live-in attendant, so I left Los Angeles and moved into her home on Rusty Ray's "Mt. Eden" in Saratoga, which commands a spectacular view of Santa Clara (or Silicon) Valley. By then almost thirty years had elapsed after Rusty had built this "chateau," originally intended for the pleasurable use of shareholder-members of Mount Eden Vineyards, the winegrowing corporation that he and Eleanor had founded—and ultimately lost (described at the close of *Vineyards in the Sky*). I soon decided to put my mother's manuscript into publishable form and then get it published within her lifetime. To prepare for this work, I enrolled in several courses on California wine history taught locally at De Anza College by noted wine historian Charles L. Sullivan, and I read a number of books and articles on the subject, most specifically about the long winemaking tradition in the Santa Cruz Mountains, which in the early 1980s became an official Viticultural Area (or appellation).

Having a long background in editing and writing books, which included often functioning as a "book doctor," I undertook the job of going through my mother's different versions of telling Martin Ray's life story and selected and arranged its many ingredients. I sometimes rescued pieces that she had discarded when trying to pare it down. (Some of them, rather oblique to wine history itself, were favorites of mine because they provided insights into MR's character and emotions, as well as suspenseful drama.) Also, to convey the essence of Eleanor Ray's ebullient spin on grape harvest time, I inserted, with a few changes, her delightfully spirited post-vintage report sent out long before as a memorable newsletter: "Martin Ray (with Ardent Friends) Races Storm to Bring in a Great 1958 Vintage."

Because I believed that my mother had taken prospective readers' knowledge of the basic processes of grapegrowing and winemaking too much for granted, I saw an opportunity to provide this information, mostly within the storytelling context that her fictionalizing approach had already established. (Memoirs, unlike formal biographies, of course often take the liberty of recapturing a subject's experiences through creating scenes and dialogue.)

Sylvia Sun Minnick of Heritage West Books in Stockton agreed to publish *Vineyards in the Sky:* The Life of Legendary Vintner Martin Ray. When the book went out of print in 2001, my editorial business, The Bookmill, published and marketed a new edition through a printing-on-demand setup with De Hart Printing in San Jose. A few changes had been made in the text and the book got a new cover using a painting by Rudy Marinacci of the chardonnay vineyard in front of the Rays' residence and the Santa Clara Valley below and beyond it. In 2004 Mountain Vines Publishing LLC, of Santa Cruz, California, took it over its distribution to wineries and the handling of online orders, and it is now the book's official publisher. The type for this edition has been reset, and a few changes were made in the text.

Martin Ray, I might candidly disclose, was never one of my favorite people. He and I never got along, to say the least, and frequently got into furious arguments when I challenged his strident assertions and objected to his behaviors. (I was of college age when I first met him and my mother married him, and in my own way I was already as much of a strong-minded maverick as he.) I must say, though, that by spending perhaps a year of my life in reworking my mother's manuscript, as well as learning a great deal more about wine history prior to the celebrated Wine Revolution of the 1970s, I began to understand, appreciate, and even respect Rusty far better than I could possibly do while he was alive—both as complex human being beset by genuinely deep, often contradictory feelings, and as an admired, even iconic figure among various wine devotées.

Since the time of close involvement with *Vineyards in the Sky* I have delved further into the recesses of MR's lifework and mind by going through in detail and then assembling his and my mother's extensive correspondence and other materials before turning them over in 1999 to Special Collections at the Shields Library, University of California at Davis, with its archive devoted to the history of the California wine industry. More recently I have been writing a series of articles about Martin Ray that are primarily based on his own correspondence: letters that are now the property of UC Davis but also, notably, the extensive, mostly long, and remarkable epistles that he wrote to wine authority Julian Street from 1939 until Street's death in 1947—fortuitously preserved before being turned over to Princeton University Library's Department of Rare Books and Special Collections. Unfortunately, most of Street's much-cherished letters to Ray were destroyed in a house fire in 1952. Since 2003 these articles have been published in installments in *Wayward Tendrils Quarterly*, a beguiling journal edited and published by Gail Unzelman of Santa Rosa, that is largely subscribed to by wine scholars and wine book collectors.

While going through many of Martin and Eleanor Ray's correspondence and other documents in the past years I have discovered that occasionally in this memoir/biography about her husband Eleanor either didn't recall or retell certain events correctly, or else Martin himself had changed the tale for storytelling purposes and afterwards stuck to the altered version, perhaps not even remembering the original occurrence. For instance, he had told Julian Street a somewhat different story than Eleanor tells about his dispute with André Tchelistcheff shortly after their meeting in 1939 or early 1940. Also, sometimes my mother located certain happenings in the wrong time period, creating anachronisms. One example is telling of the Streets' visit to Elsie and Rusty when they still lived in Masson's chateau; in actuality it took place in 1945, two years after their departure.

The most noteworthy example of an anachronism is her attributing to Martin Ray in his first vintage at Paul Masson, in 1936, the use of new French oak barrels for aging and even fermenting chardonnay, crediting it to his knowledge of traditional Burgundian methods, which he was determined to follow. In fact, he did not start doing this until the late 1950s—twenty years later, and somewhat by happenstance—and was pleased with the results of his discovery. But also he had been influenced by Eleanor's son Peter's reports on his observations when participating in a chardonnay vintage in Burgundy in 1957. Soon other vintners too began experimenting with the effects of new French oak in the making of fine wines, as well as multiple pressings of the pomace. Martin Ray, though, was seemingly the first winemaker to import new oak barrels from France in the postwar years, which he did in 1954.

This edition of *Vineyards in the Sky* remains mostly as it was at its first publication in terms of retaining Nathan Chroman's expressive Foreword, my mother's Prologue, and the main text. Some of the photographs have been changed, and new ones have been added. There are a few additions to the For Further Reading list. The Epilogue contains some updates toward its close, such as addtional news about the resurrection within the wine industry of Martin Ray's name in the Sonoma County-based winery owned by Courtney Benham. And coverage is given, of course, to Eleanor Ray's demise in April of 2000; by then she had recently reached the venerable age of 96, and lived to see the start of a new century. Unfortunately, though, by the time her book came out in 1993, she was unable to effectively promote it, as she would have done wonderfully well in earlier years, when she sometimes gave talks about Martin Ray and winegrowing before civic and other groups and even appeared in a televised interview.

I am now very grateful to the partners of Mountain Vines Publishing LLC—Ken Dawes and Casey Young, photographer and author of the attractive and admirable book *Mountain Vines, Mountain Wines* (2003): not only for adding *Vineyards in the Sky* to their as yet slim publication list, but also for devoting considerable time and effort in preparing the text for this new printing by using the amazing technologies of scanning and optical character recognition and redesigning the book's overall format. And special thanks go to Rudy Marinacci for designing the book cover. His painting is the view of Martin Ray's chardonnay vineyard as seen from the chateau he originally built for Mount Eden Vineyards, and of the Santa Clara Valley beyond and below it.

Barbara Marinacci
Saratoga, California
June, 2006

Prologue

L AST NIGHT A VIVID dream brought it all back to me. Martin, very much alive, came booming in from outdoors, where he'd been pruning vines. "It's here, our first real day of spring!" he exulted. "Gorgeous ... Madame Pinot, come out and sniff the air. Let's celebrate!"

Martin could explode *any* day into an event, blow it up larger than life. There were no so-what days for him. But topping them all for sheer excitement was the day when spring made its first appearance. Up here in California's Santa Cruz Mountains, spring sometimes arrives a few weeks ahead of the vernal equinox. The sun suddenly comes closer, shines brighter and warmer, and the air's rich with the pungent smells of newly generating earth—wildflowers bursting into bloom, foliage unfurling this year's greenery.

My dream's impromptu scene brought the past back into vibrant reality. Champagne iced for the great occasion. A large basket readied for a picnic, laden with favorite foods, and goblets tucked into white linen napkins. Calling friends to hurry up the mountain . . .

And here the dream began to replay an earlier era, before my life with Martin, but so familiar to me from his reminiscing. For a message went off to John Steinbeck, to come over after he stopped writing at two.

Then supper in the vineyard at sunset. Music—everyone singing, and perhaps somebody playing a flute or recorder. (In the later years, I'd be strumming my guitar.) A great gold moon rising close overhead. A gentle, balmy breeze.

After the guests went homeward, Martin stayed on with his dear little Madame Pinot (called so for her mad love of pinot noir), the two of them finally falling asleep on the fragrant carpet of wildflowers among the grapevines.

Of course I had conceded this romantic role to Elsie Ray in *my* dream! For to me she has always been the first and *the* greatest, hence the heroine of this sequence concocted by my nocturnal unconscious. In after years, when she had gone, it was I, the second Madame Pinot, who continued to celebrate spring's glorious arrivals in that same way with Martin Ray.

In the years since his departure, I know no one else who welcomes in the springtime—or for that matter celebrates any event, planned or spontaneous—with such marvelous élan. Now, my life with him sometimes seems almost a dream ... a splendid fantasy that lasted for a quarter of a century.

For what happier fantasy than this: to find some wonderful place in the country and make fine wines there, leaving the world behind—and preferably on a mountaintop, as Paul Masson did. This had been Martin Ray's own boyhood dream: to get that same mountain someday, and there make fine wines and enjoy the great life that went with them.

And he did. Martin Ray actually lived a real-life fantasy. I was fortunate to share it partly with him. Not that everything always went perfectly the way he and I wanted them to. Or easily: a winegrowing family faces constant challenges and uncertainties, and engages in physical labors of many kinds. Or that we ultimately triumphed over adversity, summoning up the Living-Happily-Forever-After conclusion of a fairytale. By no means! Still, the magic ingredients for a fantasy existence were amply there.

Nowadays many people who are wine lovers understand and share Martin's eternally young and idealistic vision. And a fortunate few—whether through persistence and hard work, the right connections with financial and property assets, or sheer luck—have realized their dreams of living on the land, in rustic simplicity or affluent elegance, all the while creating fine wines ... some of which may be recorded as great in the annals and lore of wine history, as vintages of Martin's have been.

But as Martin Ray was growing up and when he became a man, most Americans took no interest at all in wine. In fact, enough citizens were so averse to alcoholic beverages of any kind that their chosen legislators voted in National Prohibition, which took effect in 1920. The American wine industry, which had such promising beginnings in California, was thereby struck down. "It will take fifty years for American winemaking to recover," Paul Masson astutely predicted.

It was just as well that Martin had no crystal ball to consult at the time he bought the Paul Masson winery in 1936. Had he gazed into it, he might have despaired, and then abandoned his new calling. For the 1930s would belong almost exclusively to the bootlegger mentality, which continued to dominate the nation's trade outlets. Current dealers claimed that *no* wine was worth more than fifty cents a jug ... and that even if it were, in terms of labor and other costs, almost nobody would pay more than that. Moreover, the Great Depression still kept prices at rock bottom.

The American penchant for quantity, not quality, operated in full force in determining wine types and sales methods. At the same time there was an abysmal lack of know-how, for the long Dry years had prevented a whole generation of potential new wine-growers from getting technical education and practical training.

The "Wine Revolution" ushered in during the '70s and '80s—that growing boom in public appreciation of fine varietal wines and the focused, successful production and marketing of them—subsequently obscured the dark and difficult periods during and after Prohibition, from the '20s into the '60s.

In the post-Repeal generation that followed Paul Masson and his peers, those turn-of-the-century vintners, there were few champions of fine wines, winemakers who not only knew that California could match European vintages in quality but also dedicated their lives to proving it. Among them, Martin Ray for many years stood alone in refusing to compromise his principles for the sake of ever-expanding production and sales. He spoke out repeatedly against widespread wine blends fraudulently labeled and marketed as pure varietals.

Martin Ray could afford to remain "indomitable" (one of various descriptions of his character) because he was entirely independent from the industry's mainstream. Never a joiner of associations or a committee man, he didn't court favor from the corps of wine writers or professional connoisseurs. He avoided banquets and declined to enter wine-judging contests. Owning his own mountaintop, he had no need or desire to descend into the mundane world below him.

By the 1940s, with renewed prosperity partly brought on by a booming wartime economy, a few good people had come into the wine trade here and there. The majority of winemakers and wine drinkers, though, still judged no bottle worth more than a dollar, or a dollar and a half at most. By the 1950s the healthy economy in the postwar period pushed the going rate up a notch. But the mass-market distributors, and the wineries they served, argued vociferously that no wine in the world could or should sell for more than two bucks a bottle. Wine merchants, largely survivors of the Repeal era, agreed with them.

By the 1960s, however, retailers had mostly become a new and different breed. They realized that fine wines were no ordinary alcoholic product but occupied a high class by themselves. Often they themselves were connoisseurs, or at least had been educated about the fermented grape juice they offered for sale. They had many customers for whom price was no object; they needed only to find for them the best wines available, foreign or domestic.

During that beginning surge of public interest in wines, the vast majority of American wines could scarcely measure up to minimal standards for quality. Martin Ray's wines were a notable exception—so they would serve as models, as the highest benchmarks, for both established quality wineries and aspiring vintners. The latter, determinedly idealistic, harked back to the youthful Martin Ray of the dismal '30s and '40s.

Gradually, by the mid-1970s and the '80s, fine wines would begin reveling in their first American heyday. Oh, if Martin Ray could only have envisioned it at the beginning of his long and solitary crusade for quality! But perhaps he really did, for the grand vision sustained him throughout—though he himself had only a brief while to reap significant benefits.

In the forty-year span of his winemaking career, Martin Ray created some of America's greatest wines. But beyond that ephemeral contribution (for no wine lasts forever), Martin left a unique, invaluable legacy: his hard-fought, single-handed and single-minded campaign for quality. From the start, he knew that California vintners could someday make wines as good as any European ones. But first they would have to grow fine varietals, and not blend them out with lesser, cheaper, and more prolific grapes. So he stoutly insisted that our fine varietal wines, and their consumers, should be protected by a provision for specific *and verified* content labeling.

During Martin Ray's lifetime, his efforts within the bulk wine-dominated industry largely brought him ridicule and vilification. But what he championed, using his own lifework as prototype, ultimately came to pass. As a result, American varietal wines' prestige on the world market has skyrocketed, along with their prices—to challenge French wine supremacy successfully at last.

Thus Martin Ray led the way, as pathfinder for today's wine-growers. Partly through his dedication, it has become financially possible now for others, following in his footsteps, to dream again his dream of the Good Life—of making fine wines, even great wines. Though, as he put it before he died, that delightful dream is "just on loan, for a little while."

So what constitutes a great winegrower? Very importantly, he's creative, for great wines are the creations of artists, not chemists. He must be highly idealistic, yet with balancing practicality and a sense of orderly routines. He must have physical strength and a real love of hard work. He must also have patience. And he must be versatile, able to perform a wide variety of functions as needed.

Martin would say that above all a great vintner must care tremendously about anything and everything. And if he doesn't care almost madly (Julian Street called this "having the divine fire") about wine, he can never achieve greatness.

In accounts of American winemaking history Martin Ray's name isn't mentioned much nowadays, and sometimes not at all. During his lifetime, by refusing to play the necessary politics and public relations of the highly competitive trade, he alienated various influential wine writers and wine associations. They considered him obstreperous, difficult, arcane, a zealot, in his fight for authentic varietals—against the phony wines supposedly containing at least the required minimum (51%) of the variety so labeled. (And since the content was not checked, a wine might not even contain one percent of the claimed variety!) He also undertook another crusade: against the widespread use of grape concentrates that introduced additional sucrose into the fermentation process (now disallowed in making California still wines).

Martin's blasts against trade practices were heard but not heeded. So "controversial" was an adjective often (and still) used conveniently to summarize Martin Ray. But this wasn't because his winemaking techniques were experimental and dubious; they were classical, proven by time. He himself provoked controversies in his continuous, relentless war against the bogus "varietals" that damaged California's prestige on the world market.

Fortunately, many wine aficionados and winemakers have indelible memories. "The best wine I ever drank in my life was a Martin Ray . . ." some may still declare, fondly naming a particular varietal—pinot noir, chardonnay, cabernet sauvignon—or a champagne. And then grow misty-eyed at the very recollection of its full-bodied, 100-point splendor. Sometimes it was this glorious revelation of what a wine could be that launched someone else's dream of making wine. Others tell colorful tales, their own experiences or reporting another's, of a man already a legend in his lifetime, revered and loved by many, but despised by his adversaries. Needless to say, many such stories are embellished and exaggerated through time, even fabricated, and relayed third- or fourth-hand.

The Martin Ray I knew was a man, not a legend. As this memoir will reveal, I knew him from our college years together, long before we married. This book holds many remembrances of him. It also recounts a number of his own stories—as much as possible in the way that he himself told them. For Martin was a great raconteur as well as a great winemaker, as people who fell readily under his mesmerizing spell can testify. So that even in those parts of his life when I wasn't around him, I came to feel as if I'd actually been present, a witness to whatever had gone on. Accounts of events that took place involving Martin when I was not there to witness them therefore present his narrative and point of view, filtered through my own recollections of them. So they may be at variance with others'.

As an *Esquire* writer once aptly remarked about Martin Ray, he was the sort of individualist who is "always daring lightning to strike." Since he never hid from threatening storms, and sometimes even invited them, you can be sure that lightning figuratively struck Martin down many times. But he always managed to get up again to confront new challenges, new dangers. So life with Martin was exciting, never dull. It could also be nerve-racking at times, like moving along in the eye of a hurricane.

In the mid-1970s, while writing *Great Winemakers of California*, Robert Benson—law professor, noted wine writer, and wine consumer advocate—conducted in-depth conversations with twenty-eight of California's outstanding winegrowers. Among them were André Tchelistcheff, Robert Mondavi, and Joseph Heitz. He met with Martin only a few months before his death. By then, I was protecting Martin from most visitors, but Bob's interview-based project sounded fascinating to us. And in spite of badly compromised health, for several hours Martin somehow managed to tap a reserve of his once-renowned mental and verbal energy. "I found Martin Ray the most compelling of all the vintners," Bob has told me. "How could it be otherwise? He was a grand character."

If I succeed in resurrecting for you, dear reader, the dynamic essence of Martin Ray, so that he may sometimes visit your dreams as well, I shall rejoice. For through you, Martin and I will forever celebrate spring times and harvest times in our vineyards in the sky.

Eleanor Ray
Saratoga, California
1992

PART I

TIME FOR GROWING

1904-1922

1

The Trail up the Mountain

"A MOUNTAIN VINEYARD IS the most beautiful sight on earth!" Martin Ray always said.

He reached this conclusion early, as a boy of eleven years or so. During a spring day's wandering through foothills close to his home in Saratoga, he had followed a trail that ascended through brush and oak groves to a clearing high atop Paul Masson's mountain. He scrambled through a small opening in the wire fence that separated wild woods from the gently sloping vineyard property.

Entranced at the panorama before him, Martin quietly took it all in. Hundreds of grapevines stood in neat rows, each held against a heavy wooden stake, spilling fountains of green leaves upon the brownish-red, rocky soil still moist from recent rainfall. In the sky soft clumps of clouds scudded along, some lower than he stood now.

Wildflowers grew low to the ground among the vines, sending out tiny bursts of purple and red. Beyond this mountain the lower hills and vales nearby were vibrant with springtime yellows and greens of mustard and wild oats, annually renewing the distant heritage of Spanish rancheros who had started them in California as feed for their horses and cattle.

Far below him stretched the vast, soil-rich Santa Clara Valley with its patchwork coverlet of fields and orchards, some a dazzling white from the blossoms of apricots and prunes. Here and there small clusters of buildings were set down upon the land: farmhouses, barns and silos, watertowers, mills, villages. A clump of buildings jutted up in the distance; wider and taller than the towns, it would be San Jose—California's first civilian settlement, founded by Hispanic colonists in 1777, the year after America's Declaration of Independence.

Gazing northward, young Martin saw the shimmering blue-gray water of San Francisco Bay, with boats moving upon it and wharves and settlements lining the rims of its southern end. Eastward, the long, creased mountains in the Diablo Range, still green with spring grass, caught the midday sun and defined the far horizon. Closer to him, in graying layers stretching to the south as well as rising upward toward the west, lay the cool dark reaches of the Santa Cruz Mountains that he sometimes explored.

What a breathtaking sight! Paul Masson's mountain vineyard was so beautiful in the daytime. What could the nights here be like? . . . With tiny lights from farms like his grandparents' twinkling in the valley below, and a full moon shining down—

Then Martin recalled those long-ago evenings when his father angrily closed the draperies to stop his small son from further admiring the bright lights high up on that nearby mountain. The Reverend Ray likened the Frenchman Masson to Satan. For there at his winery intoxicating beverages were being made and consumed; disgraceful activities went on, such as dancing and noisy singing and lewd behavior. And though weakened by diabetes mellitus, Martin's father would somehow summon up enough energy to shake his fist in rage at the wicked winegrower high in the sky who corrupted all Saratogans by producing, consuming, and selling alcohol in their midst. As the town's Methodist minister, James William Ray was guardian to local citizens' immortal souls—and morals.

Even now, though his father had died five years before, Martin sometimes felt guilty when he pulled aside the curtains at his grandparents' home, to see whether Masson's lights above were beckoning to him again.

Paul Masson's vineyards in the sky had true grandeur. This was a king's domain. Martin wished he could look out upon this vista every day of his life. It was the only thing he had ever seen that he really wanted. Someday, somehow, he must have a place like this for his very own. . . .

Martin's reverie ended when he heard men's voices in the distance. Turning, he saw two men in work clothes coming slowly down several rows, headed in his direction. Occasionally they stopped to hoist up long vine branches and tie them against the stakes.

Was one of them the notorious Paul Masson? Rather than risk being caught as a trespasser out in the open, Martin ducked behind a large vine. As the men got closer, he heard them speaking in Italian. Cautiously, he peered out at them. And as it often did, Martin's curiosity now overcame shyness or caution. Obviously neither man was the dreaded Frenchman, so he came out of hiding.

The men at first looked startled, but then smiled when seeing just a boy. Smiling back at them, he asked, "Why don't you let the vines crawl along the ground?"

"If we don't tie them up, they could get broken by the wind or trampled by a horse pulling the cultivator," one man answered. He looked friendly as he approached young Martin. He had dark eyes, black hair, and a large mustache. "But what are you doing up in Mr. Masson's vineyards, boy?"

"I found a trail down below," Martin said, "and it came out here."

"Haven't you heard that Mr. Masson eats boys he catches in his vineyards?" The other man laughed.

Martin knew from a few boys who had ventured up here that the Frenchman was as fierce as the giant in Jack and the Beanstalk. "Does he?" Martin asked, aiming for innocence. "But I'm not doing anything! I just wanted to see the view from here. It's very beautiful. Do you get to look out at this all the time?"

"Almost every day. But it's not always so clear," said the man doing all the talking. "My name is Angelo. What's yours?"

"Martin. But everyone calls me Rusty," Martin said. Angelo glanced at his red hair, so Martin didn't have to explain the nickname. He had another question: "Why do you tie some of the branches up over the top of the vine?"

"See . . . they make a cage that protects the grapes from birds. Also, the leaves keep the hot sun from burning the grapes."

"Oh." Martin began thinking about how Paul Masson would make wine from these grapes—the wine that his father had hated. Martin wouldn't dare tell his mother about going up this mountain and seeing the splendid view.

"Does your family drink wine?" Angelo then asked.

"I don't think so." Martin often heard his mother talking about something called Prohibition that soon would come and save society from alcohol, which caused its worst problems. Actually, Grandmother Lovejoy drank wine, but she always called it her "medicine." Sometimes when Martin's mother gazed disapprovingly at her, she'd stir it noisily with a spoon.

"How are grapes made into wine?" Martin asked, curious.

"They have a lot of sugar in them. When grape juice sits around for a while, it starts to ferment."

"Ferment . . . what's that?"

"It's when grape juice changes because of yeast. Yeast is a tiny thing, like a plant, that is in the air and also lives on grape skins. You can't really see it with your own eyes, but you can see a bunch of it. Once Mr. Masson let me look at some yeast with his microscope."

"My grandmother uses yeast to make bread," Martin said.

"Yes, that's right!" said Angelo. "Wine yeast is just a different kind. It feeds on the sugar in grape juice and grows faster and faster. It turns it into alcohol. And gas bubbles too—carbon dioxide, like what makes your grandmother's bread rise."

"But if nature makes wine like that, why do people think it's so bad?"

"Some people think it's bad, maybe because they have seen others use it badly, like getting drunk all the time. But many good people, like my family and friends, drink a little wine with dinner. When we drink it we feel happy about life."

Martin thought about the temperance people his mother knew at church who wanted to have Prohibition so nobody could buy alcohol of any kind. Did they look happy? No. Mostly they seemed angry all the time—at least whenever they talked about evil "spirits," and how they should be outlawed.

"Maybe I'd like wine," Martin decided.

Angelo smiled. "You can try it someday, when you become a man," he said. "Well, Rusty, we must be going now to finish today's work. There are sixty acres of vines here we must look after. So run along!"

"But may I come back sometime?"

"Sure, come and see us again when we're out here working, and we can talk some more. You sure ask a lot of questions!"

"I could help you work too," said Martin. "I'm a good worker."

"It's a deal," said Angelo.

After that day, Martin sometimes took again the hidden trail up to Paul Masson's place. Only his grandparents knew he went up there. He'd tell them about how the vines changed as the weeks went by. But since he never saw Angelo, he didn't feel that he could enter the vineyard property.

One morning in late summer as he came up to the vineyard's edge, he saw a group of pickers moving along the rows and down the slope. They carried metal pails into which they set the grape bunches they rapidly picked, then emptied them into boxes placed out in the middle of some rows. As they picked, they sang songs together and shouted Italian words at each other above the vines. Since Martin couldn't spot his friend Angelo among them, he didn't walk out and ask if he could help.

"It's vintage time up there now," Martin's grandfather commented when he got the report of the day. "That's when grapes are picked and made into wine." He sounded rather wistful, as if he might have liked to be there himself, helping out.

Soon the wide-spreading vineyards on Paul Masson's mountain

turned from greens to autumnal colors. Yellow, scarlet, and golden brown leaves, bright in the slanting sunshine of fall, twirled in a warm breeze. The air smelled sweet, pungent, spicy—like fallen overripe fruit lying forgotten upon damp ground. Then came the winter time. The vines, stripped of their thick green summer coverings, now stood starkly upright in regimental rows—each dark, gnarled trunk an individual shape. The sharp wind blasted away at the vine branches. Some stayed safely tied to their stakes, but those that had broken loose got hurled about. The leaves, now sere and dusty brown, were blown in rattling heaps across the vineyard slopes. The valley below looked pale blue, hazy, cold.

The vines were resting now, Martin knew. Waiting for spring to happen again—like the fruit trees in his grandfather's orchard. He too was waiting, waiting to see Angelo again so he could go forth openly into the vineyard and learn more about this place and the work that went on here.

Then came the cold day in January when he saw several workers. Wearing knitted woolen caps and heavy sweaters, they were working on the vines, slowly moving from one to another. They released, then lopped off long branches and laid them neatly in piles. But other branches they clipped slightly and then bent into wide loops that they secured with metal straps onto the heavy wooden stakes, while fastening the thick main trunks themselves close to the stake. Each vine contributed its unique shape to the vineyard—a field of free-form sculptures made of twisting wood. The effect was strange but neat, since the vine branches no longer crawled all over the ground.

Unmistakably, one of the workers was the man Martin had been looking for. He ducked under the wire fence and walked over to Angelo. "May I help you today?" he eagerly asked.

"Hello, Rusty!" Angelo greeted him, beaming. "I was afraid we scared you away last summer."

"Oh no. I came up a few times but didn't see you until today. What are you doing now?"

"We are pruning the vines." Angelo continued his work as he chatted with the boy. "We do this to get them ready for the leafing out, which will start in early spring."

Martin said he knew something about pruning. Recently he'd been helping his grandfather prune fruit trees. "But why do you tie up the long branches like that?" he asked.

"That's how Mr. Masson wants it done," Angelo said. "He calls it 'basket pruning,' and says he learned it as a boy in Burgundy. When the branches—we call them 'canes'—are pulled up like this, they are out of the way of the plow."

"Most grapevines I've seen grow along wires," Martin said. He'd been studying vineyards down in the valley. "Why do these vines stand all by themselves?"

"Well, you're still full of questions," said Angelo. "Mr. Masson says that vines are stronger and healthier if they are planted like this, each one six feet away from the others, instead of being crowded together on trellises. And their grapes will be better too."

Holding up a thick branch with dark gray fibrous bark, he sliced it off at the trunk with his sharp clippers. "That was a bearing cane from last year," he explained. "Canes produce most of the grapes."

How could these dead-looking vines soon produce leaves and fruit? But Martin knew they would. So he asked Angelo to show him where they'd come from. Patiently, his worker friend showed him a vine branch with already swelling nodes with buds that would send out shoots in a month or two. Gently, quickly, he moved his hands along its length and suppled it at intervals so he could bend it into a loop, which he then secured against the stake with two metal straps. Another cane with smooth brown bark he then clipped off several inches from the base. A thinner one he lopped off right at the trunk.

"How do you know what to cut off and what to keep?" the boy asked, watching him closely.

"Ah, Rusty, knowing that is the real trick of pruning," Angelo said. "You must first understand how grapevines grow. You already know that pruning keeps fruit trees from making too many branches and leaves. You'd get too many fruits, and of poor quality—small, not very sweet or with good flavor. Grapevines are like that too. To get the best fruit you limit growth. The vines must also be trained with the future in mind. You decide what will be this year's bearing canes. But since they will be cut off next winter, as we're doing now, you have to plan for the following year's canes too." He showed the boy how he looked for strong-looking canes adjoining a new bearing cane, then sliced them off close to the trunk, after the second bud, so that they stuck straight out. "Some of these 'spurs' will become next year's canes," he explained.

When Angelo moved on to the next vine, Martin followed him, watching as the worker sawed off the whole top of a vine. "See how sickly looking the canes are?" he commented. "This way, the vine can start a healthy new top."

"Do you think I could learn to prune?" the boy asked.

Angelo grinned. "Sure, you're a smart young fellow. And you obviously have a mind of your own. Mr. Masson says this work is only for people who can make decisions quickly and easily—and aren't afraid to take chances either. Each vine needs its own special pruning and training. If you make mistakes, luckily they are rarely serious, for vines usually outgrow them, this year or next."

The man now reached into a bucket that held his tools and found an extra pair of clippers for Martin. "Work right along next to me," he said, "and you'll learn in no time."

At the end of the day's work, Angelo pronounced the boy an expert pruner already.

From then on, Martin frequently went up Paul Masson's mountain. Angelo and the vineyard workers always seemed pleased when this boy turned up to help. Like his grandparents, they enjoyed teaching him how to do things. And as he worked, Martin asked about their families and the villages they came from and about the foods they liked to eat. Mostly they came from northern Italy—Piedmontese whose ancestors, they said, had worked in vineyard lands for hundreds, maybe even thousands of years. "So California is the best place in America for us," they told the boy.

When pruning was finished and the vines were fast leafing out, Angelo happily put Martin to work at various tasks suitable for him. He snipped off the small shoots—suckers—coming from the base of vine trunks, sometimes below the soil, and yanked out or dug up weeds that would steal water and nourishment from the vines. He also helped load yellow sulfur powder into the spraying machines that the men carried up and down the rows, hand-pumping the handles as they dusted the leaves to prevent mildew from forming. ("Mildew ruins a crop in no time," Angelo said.)

And as the horse and plow slowly churned the vineyard soil, Martin walked ahead to pull any fast-growing canes aside, out of the pathway, or pick up large rocks and place them in piles to be gathered later and placed upon a horse-drawn sled.

"This mountain soil is very heavy," Angelo explained. "We have to loosen it up like this several times each year. If we don't do this, it will get hard like cement. Then the vines' roots could not breathe and drink." To him the grapevines were living and breathing creatures.

"But why does Mr. Masson have his vineyard here, in this rocky clay soil, instead of in the valley, where the soil is deep and rich?" Martin was thinking of the soft, smooth earth in his grandfather's orchard.

"He says this mountain soil is much better for producing his special wine grapes. Oh, the vines would like a perfect soil! But grapes have a stronger flavor when vines must work hard to get what they need for growing. Food, water . . ." Now that interested Martin: what was best did not come easily, then.

The boy was fascinated when he first saw Angelo taking slices one by one off young vines, selecting stubby stems from the bundle he carried with him, then deftly inserting them into sliced areas—each making a perfect fit. Afterwards, he tied tape around the joint.

"Why are you doing that?" Martin inevitably asked.

"This is field-grafting," Angelo explained. "We join a stem from a European grapevine with an American grapevine that's already rooted." He then told Martin how in the 1870s a tiny insect from America, a root louse or aphid called phylloxera, had invaded the vineyards of Europe and began killing off most of the vines. Soon it was ruining Californian vineyards too.

"Did phylloxera kill the vines on this mountain?" the boy wondered.

"Oh no! You see, by the time Mr. Masson planted these vineyards, using superb varieties he brought from France, he knew how to prevent that. By growing the European grapevine—Vitis vinifera is the species name—on native American rootstock. Because phylloxera just doesn't hurt it."

Martin enjoyed telling his grandparents about what he learned that day. "Now I know why President Jefferson couldn't ever grow wine grapes successfully at Monticello," his grandfather concluded. "The phylloxera latched onto the roots and just sucked them to death!"

When Martin visited Masson's vineyards again in early June, Angelo greeted him. "Look!" he said as he gently pushed aside some grape leaves on a vine. He revealed a cluster of tiny white balls on slim green stems. "These are grape flowers, the inflorescence," he said. "During the summer each will grow into a grape, with all of them making a bunch."

"And when will you pick them?"

"At the end of summer. When Mr. Masson says they are ripe and sweet enough."

"Can I help you this year?"

Angelo looked at Martin as if measuring his strength and determination. "We'll see. Mr. Masson does not like anybody getting in the way during vintage time. It is hard work. We start early and pick fast, before the sun heats the grapes."

Early one morning, as Martin arrived at the vineyard's edge, he saw the famous Paul Masson himself. For who else could it be? This man was big, powerfully built. Dressed in corduroy hunting pants tucked into high boots, he strode along swinging a shovel that he used now and again to check the soil's texture and chop at weeds. A wide straw hat jauntily topped thick, coppery hair that matched a deeply suntanned face, the cupreous effect further embellished by a bountiful mustache framing a firm mouth. A pince-nez dangled from a cord around his neck, and from time to time he placed it over his nose so he could peer closely at something on a vine.

Careful to stay hidden, Martin watched the winemaker's every move. He knew other boys who had hiked up here; when Masson spotted them, they were scolded and told never to come back. For Martin, that would be like Adam being banished from Eden by Jehovah.

Sometimes young Martin would gaze over the vines at the various impressive buildings beyond, on the crest of the mountain. Still feeling almost like an intruder, he had not yet dared to venture there. He was awed by Paul Masson's massive concrete house. Whenever he heard a worker saying something like "Mr. Masson is in the chateau right now," he'd picture the Frenchman seated like a king upon a throne in his formidable palace. For didn't that French word château mean "castle"?

"Mr. Masson's house looks like a big old church," Martin remarked to Angelo one day.

"Oh, that's the winery, not his house," Angelo corrected him. "But it does look like a church because after the big earthquake ten years ago destroyed St. Patrick's Cathedral, Mr. Masson brought its façade up here from San Jose and stuck it onto the front of his new cellar building."

"But then where is his ... chateau?"

Angelo pointed to a smaller, modest structure nearby, built on the hillside close to the winery. It seemed attractive enough, with walls of yellowish cut stone, large windows with small panes, and a long terrace overlooking the valley.

"He lives there?" Martin had somehow imagined a grander place.

"Oh no," Angelo said. "At French wineries, a house used for business entertaining is called a *château*. Mr. Masson only stays here occasionally, after a dinner that lasts well into the night. He lives with his family in a big home down in San Jose."

Martin hadn't imagined the Frenchman with a family. "Does he have any children?"

"Only one," Angelo answered. "A daughter named Adele, who's almost grown up now."

So Masson had no son, Martin mused. If he had, probably he'd have seen him up here by now.... Well, would he ever actually meet the winemaker himself someday?

Then came the warm afternoon in early summer when Martin, having scrambled up the steep trail, branched off onto a sketchy deer path for the first time. To his astonishment it suddenly emerged from a clump of trees close to Paul Masson's chateau itself. On the sunny terrace were about a dozen people—exquisitely dressed ladies and handsome men, like ones the boy had seen in picture books but never dreamed could actually exist. All laughing and talking, they sipped a golden fluid from fluted glasses that shimmered in the late afternoon sunlight.

So this was Paul Masson's notorious life of revelry that had so enraged his father, and now perturbed his mother and her friends! To Martin it made the loveliest sight imaginable ... happy people drinking wine made from those splendid vines.

What was this wine, anyway, that people could so despise it—or fear it? The chateau lights that his father had cursed in the night were beautiful. So were these people. And most beautiful of all were the green vines exuberantly thriving in the sunlight, in Mr. Masson's vineyards so close to the sky. Somehow his father must have been mistaken. The Holy Bible, after all, often spoke of wine. Jesus made it, miraculously, from water. And in the Book of Psalms ...

At that revelatory moment, Martin knew exactly what he wanted in life: not only those glorious vineyards in the sky, but this whole mountain existence. Just like the one Paul Masson was now enjoying—a world far removed from the valley below and its petty concerns. He would control this "Good Life" (for that is how he began thinking of it) himself, as Masson did—a monarch who owned his own special domain. With wonderful friends, much laughter and talk . . . and celebrated with glasses of that magical golden drink.

It was champagne they drank, the boy later found out. He also learned that Paul Masson's "champagne hour" usually capped his daily routines. (Eventually it would Martin's, too.) As the sun went down, all tensions and cares were cast aside as one hastened to the veranda to catch the sun's last rays in a champagne glass. With the sparkling wine's bubbles set ablaze, the day's events would take on a special glow when retold, relived, during this hour of enchantment.

On a fateful day not long afterwards young Martin, absorbed in helping the vineyard workers, was suddenly summoned forth by the sharp-eyed Paul Masson. "Hey, boy, come over here and let me look at you!" came the command. The Frenchman was staring right at Martin. Trembling inwardly, the boy stepped forward for the fearsome confrontation. He scarcely dared to move while Masson sized him up at close range.

And what would Masson have seen? A lad with tousled red hair and a freckled, squarish face, open and honest in expression. A pair of grayish-blue eyes that looked at you directly, without cringing or deception. A youth of just the right height and build, limber and strong, on the verge of puberty. A boy tentatively smiling, perhaps out of nervousness, to reveal the slight gap between his two front teeth that would always give him a winsome farmboy look.

Suddenly Masson smiled and said: "You must be the young man who likes our vineyards in the sky!" He approached closer and gave Martin's shoulder a mighty smack with his powerful hand. Though momentarily stunned by this attention from the great man, Martin took in those words of his. Vineyards in the sky: that was exactly how he himself thought of the place from the first moment he'd seen it!

"Sometimes I watch you from the chateau window," Masson went on. "My men tell me you are a fine young fellow who always asks questions about vineyard care and helps them in their work. That you are not like the usual trouble-makers who throw rocks and steal grapes. So they said that when I see you, I should not chase you away."

"Can I still come up here, then?" Martin dared to ask.

"Oh sure," the Frenchman said. He now rested a huge, work-gnarled hand on Martin's shoulder. "You can keep helping the men out here in the vineyard. If you want to hunt rabbits and gophers, I'll give you a nickel for every one you bring me. And at times maybe you can help me too—in the wine cellars up there." He gestured toward the big building with the cathedral-like entrance. "Would you like that?"

"Very much!" the boy said eagerly, curious to see what the winery looked like inside.

"Good. Well, come back soon to La Cresta!" Before now, Martin hadn't known that Masson's mountain property actually had a name.

Masson resumed his tour of inspection through the vineyard. But reaching the row beyond Martin, he turned around. "Tell me your name, boy," he demanded.

"Martin. Martin Ray."

"Ah, MAR-tan," Masson said approvingly, with the "n" sound oddly missing from the second syllable. "We have that name also in France. It is a saint's name. But I think you are not a little saint, eh?"

Martin grinned, knowing that his independent ways and daring adventures forever vexed his mother, who wanted him to be just like the goody-goody boys at her church sitting sedately in pews with their noses stuck in hymnals and prayer books. He wouldn't play with them. He much preferred the lively company of "bad" boys.

So that was the start of the long association between Paul Masson and Martin Ray. And throughout, Paul would always say Martin's name in the French manner.

2

Antecedents

Young Martin's eagerness to learn and to help out in vineyard and winery quickly endeared him to Paul Masson in that first summer of their association. The Frenchman had a deep and frustrated longing for a young successor to carry on his work and dreams into the future. Louise Masson was past childbearing age. Long ago Paul had given up hope for a son.

Whether fully aware of it or not, the winemaker searched for a son of his spirit—if no longer an actual son, then the appropriate protégé. The need for certainty in continuing on into the next generation and beyond preoccupies people as they grow older. Time begins to run down. There are vital skills and wisdom to confer, and the right person should be at hand to receive them.

More than most professions, winemaking traditionally is concerned with legacy. An intense and even holy dedication shared between father and son, master and disciple, has been crucial in the making of great wines. Priceless secrets must be imparted of an ancient art akin to both alchemy and sorcery. Land and vines require a special coaxing to produce grapes worthy of vintaging. A cellar full of beautifully crafted oak barrels, wine presses, and other equipment should be passed on to someone with appreciative knowledge of its contents' use and care. Vintages in cask and in bottle may need years of patient storage, aging them to perfection before release.

La Cresta, Masson's winegrowing ranch, was a place for work and also for entertaining famous and wealthy clients. Paul's wife and only child, Adele, did not come here. A son would have been a different matter, of course. So might the man that his daughter would marry—hopefully one with the potential for becoming a winemaker. After all, both Paul Masson and his own father-in-law before him, Charles Lefranc, had married winemakers' daughters.

Now young Martin Ray, a fatherless boy, right away adopted Paul Masson as a role model. He would always preserve Paul Masson as his primary example of manhood. Still a strong and vigorous man in his mid-fifties, the Frenchman took great pleasure in directing vineyard work, even in doing some of the manual labor involved. In addition to spending long hours caring for the wines he made, he put up buildings and fixed equipment, often relishing grueling and even grimy work.

Masson was also cultured; knew music, literature, art, the theater and dance. He was a spellbinding raconteur. He enjoyed fine cuisine along with the fine wines he always served. He had a sophisticated sense of salesmanship that adroitly persuaded people to buy his wines. He had his contacts in San Francisco's high society and in San Jose's exclusive St. Claire Club, where he, the "Duc de Cognac," had the reputation for being a lusty bon vivant who appreciated the company of beautiful women.

Mirrored now in a Saratoga lad were facets of Paul Masson's own joie de vivre.

A zest for life came spontaneously to Martin Ray, called "Rusty" by family and friends because of his red hair. He had lived ever since his father's death at his mother's parents' ranch near Saratoga. The town was on the far west side of Santa Clara Valley, at the base of the eastern slopes of the Santa Cruz Mountains.

Whenever he could leave farm chores and school classroom behind him, Rusty would venture out into the nearby wilderness of foothills and mountains, sometimes with friends but most often alone. His two older brothers seemed almost of another generation, with very different interests and values.

The hillsides close to the Lovejoy farm on Stelling Road presented the young explorer with a wild tangle of vegetation: manzanita shrubs with shredding magenta bark and leathery, gray-green leaves; tall madrone with slim, twisting bronze branches; huge liveoaks with long-stretching limbs that provided welcome shade; evergreens like pungent fir and spicy California bay laurel; buckeyes with tall white candle-flowers ending up as dark brown horsechestnuts so smooth to touch (treasures for a boy's pocket); the deceptively lovely poison oak with its shiny lobed leaves that turned flame-colored in autumn; lilac-flowering ceanothus, scarlet-berried toyon, and other plant habitants of the dense chaparral covering the steep, rocky slopes and narrow canyons, to withstand both winter downpours and hot dry summers. (Years later, writer John Steinbeck would dub this terrain "Rusty Ray country.")

Higher up in this coastal range and closer to the ocean were cool stands of tall redwoods and other conifers—so dark green and thick in places that in the distance the mountains looked almost black. Rusty liked to visit these forests on horseback, riding one of his grandfather's horses over narrow trails, most begun as deer paths and then widened by Indians traversing them on hunting or trading expeditions.

For a half century higher parts of the mountains had been strenuously logged, mostly for the Sequoia sempervirens, the coastal redwood that grew so abundantly. The supply of this durable and useful wood was considered limitless—easily replaced or replenished—and was treated accordingly. During his wanderings, Martin saw many ugly traces of clear-cutting, when an entire forest of ancient redwoods had been chopped down. Its timber giants were chained up and dragged down the mountainside to sawmills and railroads and freighters, leaving a vast graveyard of stumps.

Here and there in the Santa Cruz Mountains, settlers had moved into the meadowlands created by spoiled forests. They burned and removed the stumps, then planted fruit trees and grapevines—returning these areas at least partway to nature while making them economically productive. The farm families who lived up in these outposts led rustic lives. Cut off from the faster-paced, ever-advancing world below, they almost dwelled in an earlier era. Rusty liked to visit them and learn about their lives. Fruits growing here developed more intense flavors, they declared, not just because they grew closer to the sun, but also because the trees and vines worked harder to produce them.

Finding some heavenly spot, the boy would stretch out on the ground and lie there for an hour or two, watching the clouds and absorbing the aromas so distinctive of these mountain wilds. His grandmother always encouraged him to investigate and evaluate the sensory world around him. And so he did. In his pockets, for snack food during these daylong excursions, he carried collections of nuts, dried fruit, and other tidbits. He'd munch them reflectively, his palate even then intrigued by flavors and scents and textures, detecting which ones complemented each other. Unknowingly, he was already in training for a career that required extraordinary development of the senses, particularly those of smell and taste.

Having become a frequent visitor to Paul Masson's sky-high vineyards, Martin naturally became curious about what wine tasted like. Of course he never expected to sample it at home. Powerful and enduring was the Reverend James William Ray's hatred for alcoholic drinks in any form. His widow often had her tolerance sorely tested—living now with her three sons in her parents' household, dependent on their charity since the minister's untimely death in 1910. Her mother might set down a crystal goblet of wine for herself at the dinner table—an elegant tonic of medicine she shamelessly quaffed right in front of her three grandsons.

Sometimes when feeling poorly, Grandmother Lovejoy even sent her husband out into the night to fetch distilled wine—brandy—from a local vintner in Cupertino. When challenged by her temperance-minded daughter, she'd declare it was enough that, to keep peace with their minister son-in-law, they had given up making their own wines from grapes and other home-grown fruits and torn up their vineyard.

Martin's mother, Mrs. Eleanor Ray, long ago had taken the pledge to abjure forever alcoholic spirits, and persuaded both of Martin's teenage brothers to do so as well. Soon enough would come Martin's turn to take the vow of abstention. But how can someone give up something he's never even tasted—and have this mean something to God?

Martin's beloved grandmother would not dare give him a sip of the medicine she clearly enjoyed in spite of its wickedness. To do so would risk her daughter's fury, or heartbreak. But he could smell it, at least—in the bottom of her glass, and in Paul Masson's large wine cellar. The nose can pick up many of the nuances of taste. And wine smelled wonderful.

Like most children, Martin gleaned whatever information he could about his parents, whose marriage had created him. They had met at a Methodist revival meeting given in central California. A trio of Ray boys had come down all the way from Oregon. His mother of course fell in love with the most earnest one, a man already on a mission. James William Ray was going to be a minister. Serious and devout herself, Eleanor was certain to make a wonderful preacher's wife.

After their marriage, James took up his first ministry in the lumber town of Etna Mills in northern California. They had two sons close together in age. Martin came later—born on June 26, 1904. Their last child, a daughter, died in infancy.

In 1906 the Rev. Ray brought his wife and three sons to Saratoga, where he became minister of its Methodist Episcopal Church. The Lovejoys, influential in the west side community near San Jose where Melvin had served for years as a much-respected jurist, surely helped arrange this assignment, which would bring their daughter back to live nearby.

Perhaps the only closeness between father and his youngest son had come during the long walks they'd take together up Big Basin Way—a daily routine, weather permitting—to fill jugs with the mineral water from Congress Springs and take them home. The diabetic minister believed the iron and sulfur in it benefited his health. But then the walks ended. More and more, Martin's father took to his bed. Resigning from the ministry of the local church, he gave up on life. His death came when Martin was six years old.

Only many years later did Martin find out about the shadowy aspects, the human side, of the Reverend Ray. In some ways the ironic truth helped reconcile him to the father he scarcely could remember, in both home and pulpit, in any but harsh, forbidding ways.

"Despite his illness, your father could have lived much longer had he wished to," the minister's old physician told Martin long afterwards. "But he no longer cared to live." And he then told Martin of the amazing turn of events—confided in him decades before—that apparently had precipitated his father's rapid decline.

The minister knew and liked the priest who served at the village's Catholic church. Gradually a real friendship developed between them. They visited each other's parish houses and spent long hours discussing biblical theories and moral issues. The good priest loved his fine wines. Finally—incredible as it seemed—he persuaded the minister to share a glass or two of wine with him as they talked. He even managed to convince the minister that some Catholic principles might be valid.

The Reverend actually began to look forward to their convivial times together and seemed miraculously improved in mind as well as spirit. (Interestingly enough, in pre-insulin days dry wine was often prescribed for diabetics. It provided energy and nutrients without the sugar dangerous in that condition, and also helped reduce stress, another liability.)

But then guilt came to weigh heavily on the minister's soul. How could he actually enjoy taking a glass of wine, after all the years of denouncing alcohol to his own family and flock as that vilest of evils? No longer was he even certain of other beliefs he once had held so staunchly. Was the wine a means of revealing sacred truths heretofore hidden from his view and that of his religious denomination? Or had this wicked spirit simply seduced him?

Well, he simply could not go on preaching what he no longer firmly believed. So he left the pulpit. Now what was his purpose in living? Being ill and so despairing, he finally saw no solution to his hopeless dilemma other than to welcome death. It soon accommodated him, and he was laid to eternal rest in Saratoga's Madronia Cemetery.

The lives of the minister's bereaved family changed radically after his demise. Mrs. Ray and her three sons moved from a small house on Herriman Avenue in Saratoga to the Lovejoy ranch several miles to the northwest. Young Martin loved the wide-open spaces of the ranch, flourishing with vegetables in neat rows, an orchard, a large acreage of corn, and cattle raised for milk and meat. There were also the horses, for both work and pleasure, which Grandfather Lovejoy taught Martin to ride and care for.

Martin adored both his maternal grandparents. As role models, the Lovejoys made a durable imprint upon him far more positive than any conferred by his own parents. (Ironically, only in his utter dedication to the growing and making of fine wines would Martin later display his origin as a fundamentalist preacher's son. His zealous espousal of purist principles which brooked no argument, propensity for sermonizing, and charismatic skill in causing conversion experiences in wine initiates came from a conviction that he possessed the Truth, revealed to him in the holiest of moments.)

As Martin followed his grandfather around outdoors and in the workshop, he learned the traditional male spheres of work. But he took equal interest in the female realm of his grandmother. It was Mrs. Lovejoy who nurtured Martin's early faculty for tasting and smelling, so vital to a future vintner. She introduced him to the wonders of food combinations. And she'd take him on sniffing tours of the garden, pinching off bits of flowers, leaves, herbs for him to identify and compare. She would cut oranges in half, showing him how the fruit-half opposite from the stem is always sweeter. She'd demonstrate how fruits at different stages of ripeness hold strikingly different smells as well as tastes. When they compared the fragrances of various roses, Martin discovered to his wonder that the scent of rosebuds differed entirely from roses in full bloom.

Among Martin's many fond remembrances of his grandmother was her perennial interest in solving the intriguing mystery of a particular citrus tree. It bore golden fruits resembling oranges in shape but larger, more pale. For years the family queried all visitors. Was this an aberration of nature? Was the fruit safe to eat? Everyone, however, declined to taste it, for it might be poisonous.

Eventually, though, one guest broke into raptures. "Why, it's grapefruit—how wonderful! First time I've ever seen it grown out here." Mrs. Lovejoy was thrilled to know that this delectable rarity grew in her own garden. Every morning thereafter she reveled in a breakfast grapefruit. And Martin himself did so too whenever possible, continuing his beloved grandmother's tradition by becoming a devotee of that luscious, sweetly acidic fruit.

Grandmother Lovejoy took tremendous joy in other wondrous revelations she constantly uncovered in this rural environment so different from her well-to-do upbringing on the East Coast. And she was vastly proud of being related to fabulous Jennie Jerome of

New York City, the American socialite who had married England's famed Lord Randolph Churchill. Their son Winston was making a name for himself now, first as a journalist and then moving into British politics. He'd been in the cabinet initially as home secretary, but when war broke out with Germany in 1914 he became head of the Admiralty.

Mrs. Lovejoy avidly followed the news of the European conflict—made far more personal to her through this family connection. (Martin always would hold the eloquent, redoubtable, and sometimes pugnacious Winston Churchill as a prime hero, and savored reading his speeches and historical narratives. During the Second World War and afterwards he, like his grandmother before him, kept a proud eye on Churchill, cherishing his remote connection with Churchill on his maternal grandmother's family tree.)

Martin saw the beautiful Lady Randolph Churchill only once, when she paid a brief visit to her country cousin in California. A liveried chauffeur handed her out from a handsome landau heaped high with rich leather trunks. Graciously she pressed hands all around. Then she and Grandmother Lovejoy retired inside the house, where tea was served in the treasured silver tea service used only on the most important formal occasions. Everyone else had to stay outdoors and remain very quiet until the visitation ended. When Jennie departed, she left in her wake an unforgettable aura of beauty and regal opulence.

Mrs. Lovejoy persisted in maintaining special standards of living in her ranch home. Others in the family always filed off to church on Sunday morning. But not Grandmother. She made no excuses. Having God already in her heart, she didn't need anyone to preach to her about Him. She had a wonderful time while the rest of them were away, Martin discovered whenever he stayed home, too ill for churchgoing. She sang happy songs (rarely church hymns) as she polished her fine silver, or picked and arranged fresh bouquets. And as she prepared the family's Sunday dinner she enjoyed a glass of wine. Usually she squeezed in time for reading some fascinating book as she awaited the others' homecoming, stretched out comfortably on a couch angled into a corner of the ample kitchen just for that purpose.

Young Martin felt greatly honored when Paul Masson first asked him to assist in cellar work. "Come along, MAR-tan, you can give us a hand here," he said, summoning him into the winery. Martin loved the cool and damp premises, lighted by electric light bulbs, with stairways connecting the four levels of cellar floors, which descended in size from top to bottom as the structure was fitted against the steep hillside. The top floor was mostly used for storage of miscellaneous equipment and records. The lower three, Masson pointed out, reflected the transformation stages of grapes into fermenting wines, wines held in cask, and bottled wines.

On the third floor the winemaker and his cellarmen were busily emptying oak casks that they needed to prepare for new use during the coming vintage season. Using a pump, they carefully transferred wine from large barrels on the third floor down to casks on the second floor, through a long hose stretched down the stairway. They were "racking" the wine, Masson explained to the boy, assigning him to a position next to a cask on the second floor, where he would warn them as soon as the wine level approached the top.

Masson said that this process took last year's wine off its "lees"—sediment that had collected at the bottom of the barrels as the wine finished fermenting and began to age. The casks they were filling had recently been emptied and washed. The wine they once held was now in bottles, stored in tall wooden racks on the lowest level.

"But you don't bottle this wine now?" Martin asked.

"Not these red wines of mine!" Masson said. "They get better and better as they wait there in the wood. When we do bottle them a year or two from now, they will be further clarified. But then they will sit a year or two more, before we sell them. Aging makes these reds smoother, richer, more attractive to the palate. My whites, though, don't wait so long to leave the winery."

As Martin helped move and monitor the hoses, he tried hard not to allow a single drop of the precious wine to spill. Masson was noticing how the boy used his hands adroitly and painstakingly in doing various tasks, like drawing out wine samples for him into the fragile glass "wine thieves." Such skillfulness, unusual in most people, was remarkable in one so young.

"MAR-tan, where did you learn to take such care?" the Frenchman suddenly asked.

"I don't know," Martin said, unaware of having special deftness. But since Masson had commented upon it, he began pondering the matter. "Oh, I do know," he soon decided. "From my Grandmother Lovejoy." For surely the way he did things with his hands reflected her training. He had learned to show great respect for every treasure brought years ago from her home back East: fine silver, rugs, lamps, porcelain, books. Everything must be handled with a loving consideration.

Yet Mrs. Lovejoy was no fussy housewife: she moved in a far more elevated sphere in which great beauty was ever cherished and ingrained in her lifestyle. It was not enough just to own and admire something beautiful. You had responsibilities toward it.

Beauty's every aspect should be perpetually valued, maintained, and guarded. So when Martin touched any object or performed any task in Paul Masson's winery, he showed this same precise, vigilant respect that he had learned early and indelibly from his grandmother.

Mrs. Lovejoy's instructions were deeply instilled. The extreme precision in movement, cleanliness, and concern for care, already noticeable in Martin's early apprenticeship with Masson, later characterized his life as winegrower, marking not just his way with objects and actions but also his setting and holding to high standards. These doubtless contributed a crucial factor to his creation of great wines.

At the same time, young Martin excelled in the outdoor work that required effort from large muscles. He became a great help to his grandfather by taking over chores that his older brothers were avoiding or abdicating, being too busy with their school assignments and high-school social life. He even assisted his grandfather in building a big red barn for their livestock. (How proudly Martin showed it to me many years later! And it is still standing some seventy-five years after it was built, barely visible behind a tract of postwar houses. Always I must crane my neck to catch sight of this faded-red relic of his past as I drive along Stelling Road, my heart invariably saluting it with a sentimental thump.)

Paul Masson made sure to specially invite young Martin up to take part in his first vintage, which would accompany the harvesting of the grapes toward late summer. Knowing from the boy that his mother was an ardent temperance advocate, he made a helpful suggestion: "Tell your mother you will be spending the day with a farmer friend of yours who has a ranch up in the hills. Just don't tell her exactly what we grow here!"

"Well, I can tell my grandparents the real truth, anyway," Martin said. "My grandmother drinks wine."

"Does she? ... Well, someday I must send some bottles of my wines down, to see if she likes them."

Martin hoped that Mr. Masson wouldn't expect him to carry them. What on earth would his mother say or do if she saw him come home with several wine bottles tucked under his arm?

3

First Vintage

When PAUL MASSON'S VINTAGE time arrived in late summer, young Martin Ray was right there, eager to join in. He wanted to participate in both the picking of the grapes and the first "crush." Masson told him to try to arrive soon after dawn, before strong sunlight hit the mountain vineyards and the day's heat began.

As Martin approached him, Angelo took a small metal implement from a bucket. "This is a *serpette* or grape hook," he said as he handed the boy a sharp, curved cutting tool. "I will show you how to use it for picking the grapes." They stepped over to a vine so dense with canes, leaves, and fruit that the heavy stake supporting it was barely visible.

"Isn't this pinot noir?" Martin asked, recognizing the vineyard section that he knew particularly interested Paul Masson. The vintner from France already had told him that this red grape variety was the one most prized and widely planted in Burgundy, the province of his birth.

"Yes," Angelo said. "Pinot is our earliest wine grape to ripen." Handing a few grapes to the boy, he said, "Taste them!"

Martin's mouth puckered up, almost as if he'd sucked on a lemon. "They aren't really very sweet," he commented.

Angelo laughed. "They are still a bit sour," he agreed. "Or 'tart,' as Mr. Masson would say. That's the tartaric acid. He picks these grapes early to get high acid. For his champagnes. Like the *Oeil de Perdrix* that is so prized—and so expensive."

"Is that French? What does it mean?"

"Eye of the Partridge," said Angelo. "Maybe they have pink eyes!"

"But isn't red wine made from these grapes?" Martin asked, baffled.

"Of course it is! And Mr. Masson will make it. We are only picking some of the crop early. The rest will be left for a week or so to ripen more, until they have more sugar. But Mr. Masson always hopes they will keep their high acid too."

Martin remembered now that, when showing him around the cellars, Masson had explained how from some varieties of grapes, red and white, he made both the effervescent champagne and a "still" or table wine. ("But my champagnes are dry—not like the sickeningly sweet liquid with marble-dust bubbles, the foul wine concoctions that most Americans drink," he'd commented, concluding with an explosively disapproving "Bah!" And then Masson went on, "Because American-made wines are given French names—such as champagne, burgundy, chablis—winemakers like myself do the same, even though most are not the same as those made in France. After all, I must sell my wines to make a living!")

"Watch out for bees and yellowjackets," Angelo cautioned now, shooing a few away. "They collect juice from grapes where skins have been pecked by birds." He grasped a large bunch of indigo-blue grapes, each small berry swollen with fluid. "And be very careful as you cut," he warned as he demonstrated how a picker inserts and angles the serpette blade at the woody stem above the grape cluster before slicing it off. "Every year pickers get wounds, sometimes so deep a doctor must sew them up."

Holding the bunch in his hand, Angelo pulled off a few damaged or shriveled grapes before carefully placing it in a metal pail at his feet. "Mr. Masson wants his grapes as perfect as possible," he commented. "Now you pick a bunch too," he told the boy.

Martin followed exactly what Angelo had shown him. "Good," the man said. "Now just pick along with me." Several minutes later, before moving on to the next vine in their row, they emptied their grape-filled buckets into a wooden box. Other men were picking alongside them, in parallel rows. Soon the wooden box was filled, and Martin went to fetch an empty one from a nearby stack.

Masson himself now came along, standing tall on a slatboard sled and holding long leather reins attached to the horse ahead that plodded up and down the corridors between the vine rows. Two workers ran on either side, picking up boxes filled to their rims with grapes and setting them down on the platform in motion. "The grapes are taken up to the shady area behind the winery," Angelo told Martin. "They'd start to cook if left here on the ground where the sun will soon hit." Already the air was warm, and Martin's face was wet with perspiration.

As the sun had reached halfway to top of the sky, Masson shouted to the men to stop picking. "We have enough for the first crush!" he shouted. The boy ran up the slope above the winery to where the filled boxes had been placed.

"MAR-tan!" Paul Masson's voice rang out. "Go over to where those men are washing their feet. You do the same!" Martin saw two men who had removed their boots sitting on a bench next to a galvanized tub into which buckets of hot water were being poured. What was going on here? But Masson had delivered a command, and the boy obeyed. As he took off his shoes, he looked for guidance from the man seated next to him.

"Ah, Monsieur Masson honors you, boy, on this first day of vintage!" the man told him. "First, roll up your pant legs." He then handed Martin a cake of rough yellow soap and a brush. He had already scrubbed his own feet.

"But why are we doing this?" Martin asked, baffled, as he applied the brush.

The man laughed so uproariously that everyone looked their way. "This must be your first vintage. . . . We are going to trample the grapes!" he explained.

Trample the grapes? "Mine eyes have seen the glory of the coming of the Lord; He is trampling out the vintage where the grapes of wrath are stored . . ." Those starting lines from "The Battle Hymn of the Republic," which his grandmother sometimes sang, suddenly came to Martin. So that's what it meant. Only in the song it was God whose furious feet crushed the wine grapes.

Martin did as the others; slipped his clean feet into paper scuffs and shuffled over to the large concrete basin that sat alongside the winery, seeming to tilt slightly into it. Workers carrying boxes of grapes set them down next to it. "In you go, boy!" said Masson, his powerful arms lifting Martin up from under his arms and then carefully depositing him into one end of the trough.

"Wait until I tell you to start," the Frenchman said. He took a box loaded with purple grapes and poured its contents into the trough, then another and another. Onlookers cheered. A friend of Masson's took over now. Hoisting a box, he quickly emptied it into the large rectangular bin, and reached for the next one. Several more were spilled in afterwards.

A Victrola phonograph had been wound up and now a record put on. "Music for you to dance to!" Masson exclaimed. It was a tarantella, chosen to set a fast and furious pace for the vigorous exercise ahead. "Now step lively, you fellows!" he called out to Martin and his two companions.

Dancing about, Martin at first feared he'd lose his balance as his feet trounced the mounds of slippery grapes. He felt the grapes pop beneath his soles and between his toes. Hundreds of them, thousands of them. Juice squirted up from the bottom of the tank and washed over his feet and ankles. Still, though they'd been stomping around for some while, little liquid had accumulated below their feet as yet. "But where is the juice?" Martin asked his companion.

"Look!" the man said, pointing to a hole at the lower end of the trough. Juice, along with pulpy seeds and pieces of grape skin, poured down through it, heading somewhere below, into the interior of the winery. Martin wondered what was happening to it down there.

Another record playing. More treading and whirling about. Martin became breathless. What would his mother say if she saw him like this? He was afraid to look down and see both his pants and his legs stained with deep purple dye from the grape color. He'd certainly have to hide them from her, for how could he possibly tell her what he'd been doing? Her son, helping Mr. Masson make wine! Of course he would tell his grandparents, for they already kept his coming up here a secret. They knew he was safe and did not wish to disturb his mother.

Finally he dared to look. To his amazement, he saw his legs were not purple or red at all. Only wet and sticky. How come? "The color is only in the skins," the man next to him said. "See, the grape pulp is clear. That's why pinot noir can be used in making white champagne."

"Does Mr. Masson mash all his grapes like this when he makes wine?" Martin asked.

The man laughed. "Oh, this treading is just a ceremony, something Mr. Masson does at the very start of the vintage season—the way many European wineries do. As a boy Mr. Masson went to many a vintage festival in Burgundy where he trod on grapes. He says doing this reminds us how grapes were made into wine for thousands of years. And actually in places where modern equipment is not available, grapes are still crushed this way."

Martin now looked beyond the basin and noticed that wives and daughters of the Italian vineyard workers, and even some female friends of Masson's, had joined the scene at the outskirts. They were laughing and applauding, and some were dancing to the music.

"Stop now!" Masson's voice suddenly commanded as a record ended. "You women will please go down to the shaded area beneath the oaks, and start setting up the tables for our vintage *pic-nique*. The men will join you there for luncheon, after the crushing is finished."

Martin was glad to catch his breath. Getting out of the big basin, he rinsed his feet with a hose. The sun dried them quickly. While he put his shoes back on, he watched workers set a heavy wire-mesh screen partly across the trough's thick rim. Then a man with a flat wooden spade began lifting out the pulpy mass of trodden grapes. Shovelfuls were placed onto the screen until the trough was almost clear. Finally, after the screen was pulled all the way over the basin, men with large wooden mashers vigorously rubbed the solid stuff against the metal grill.

All the while, boxes of grapes were also being emptied onto the other end of the screen. Juice shot out on all sides as men attacked and squashed the grapes with wood paddles, pushing liquid and pulp through the huge coarse sieve. Now and again they'd scrape off the solid residue of brown stems and throw it onto a large canvas cloth, making room for more grapes to be processed. Occasionally this growing pile of residue was hauled away.

Martin, fascinated, didn't notice that Masson had come up next to him. "Boy, go down below now and see what is going on there," he commanded. Martin was happy to comply. On the third floor of the cellar, a continuous flow of almost transparent juice and darker, bluish grape skins came pouring down a metal chute. They fell into a large wooden cylinder set on a platform with wheels, standing taller than he. Its slim vertical slats, with narrow spaces between them, were held together by several iron bands around the circumference.

Sergio, an assistant cellarmaster, was standing on a ladder and with a long stick poked at the solid grape materials as they cascaded downward, directing them into particular areas of the press. "This is Mr. Masson's favorite basket press," he informed Martin. "He had it shipped from France many years ago, and so it came here by ship, traveling around the Horn of South America!"

Meanwhile, clear juice was spilling out through the side gaps and flowed down to the porcelain-coated metal base of the press. Two men took turns filling large pails at a spout at the bottom where the liquid gushed out in a small waterfall, emptying the contents into a large upended wooden puncheon open at the top, standing close to the wine press. It was much larger than a barrel.

"Mr. Masson designed his winery so that grapes can be crushed outdoors," Sergio told Martin. "The must then flows down by gravity to this floor, for the next stages of processing—pressing and fermenting."

"*Must?*" Martin wondered.

"That's the name for the crushed grapes—the pulp and skins and juice—that the wine is made from," Sergio explained.

Martin soon noticed that the flow from above was slowing down to a trickle. "You've come just in time, Martin," Sergio remarked as he climbed down the ladder. "We're going to press this first batch, now that the men have finished the crushing above. You can help work the press."

It took some while for Sergio and two helpers to adjust wood and metal gear pieces in a huge iron screw at the center of the basket press. Then he inserted a long iron shaft into a slot and began pushing the handle back and forth, forward and back. With each full turn, the huge iron ratchet on the thick threaded stem of the press propelled a heavy flat wooden disk farther downward upon the mass of grape skins.

"Your turn now, Martin," said Sergio, motioning toward the big lever. Martin had to walk almost on his tiptoes as he moved the rod to and fro: CLICK, CLACK, CLICK, CLACK. It got harder and harder to push it.

"Wait now!" said Sergio. He called for Mr. Masson. "Is this enough pressing?" he asked when the winemaker came.

The Frenchman dipped a glass cup into a pail of juice and held it up to the light. It was golden, with a slight tinge of pinkish orange. "Almost perfect," he announced. He looked toward the wine press and Martin. "Give it five more turns, boy," he ordered. Then he inspected the juice again. *"C'est bon . . . c'est fini,"* Masson pronounced.

Masson drank half of the beaker of juice and handed the remainder to Martin. "Drink up, MAR-tan!" he said jovially. "This is good for growing boys who cannot drink wine. Don't worry, it is not fermented yet, so your mother cannot put me in jail!" Then he was off again. The juice tasted both sweet and sour.

"But what about the crushed grapes left in the press?" Martin asked Sergio.

"Oh, they will keep oozing juice for an hour or two, ever more slowly, and we will collect it. But we will not put any more pressure on them. To get the special color from the skins for his *Oeil de Perdrix,* Mr. Masson combines free-run juice with a little that has had only a slight pressing. The remaining grapes will be pressed and fermented separately, to be added to some other kind of wine later. No good grapes are wasted here!"

"And what happens to the juice for the champagne?"

"Mr. Masson will add some special yeast to the must in the fermenter puncheon, to start the fermentation going fast. And from there it will be transferred to smaller casks, to go through the first fermentation."

Sergio covered the tank with a large cloth. "This will keep the flies out," he said.

Martin was swatting tiny fruit flies that buzzed around him, excited by the grape juice on his arms and legs. "What would flies do?"

"They could make the wine sick," Sergio said. "They carry bad germs, bacteria. The wine might end up with too much acetic acid—vinegar. Or something, anyway, that Mr. Masson would not want to put in bottles with his label. So he'd have to sell it cheap to some other winery."

"Later, of course, we will make a still red wine from the rest of the pinot noir grapes," Sergio went on. "Since the grapes will be riper and sweeter, the must will convert to a heavier wine—a still, table, or 'dry' wine—with more alcohol than champagne has. And it will be *very* red! The grapes are also handled differently then. We first crush the grapes directly into the fermenters, which are wheeled up and set under the chute. Not only juice, but also skin, pulp, seeds, and even some stems sit together for a week or more, fermenting, before we run the must through the basket press. By that time we are really pressing *wine* grapes!"

"Is that how you make white wine too?" Martin wondered.

"Oh no! White wine is made more in this way. We use white grapes, naturally. But the grape skins don't go into the fermenting vat. We only crush and press them, so that the juice alone is put into the fermenter. Sometimes Mr. Masson only wants the free-run juice by itself, without any pressing, to make an especially delicate wine."

Martin suddenly felt hungry. It had been a long time since his before-dawn breakfast. "Didn't Mr. Masson say there'd be a picnic?" he asked Sergio.

"Run along now, boy, and get something to eat before it's all gone!" Sergio said. "I will come down soon, so save some food for me."

Martin found the workers and their families seated at several long tables beneath some huge spreading oak trees. Arranged on the red and white checked tablecloths were large platters holding chunks of bread and cheese and sliced cold meats, dishes with pickles and olives, bowls of fresh fruit, and buckets of ice containing cool drinks: beer, wine, and lemonade.

Paul Masson came and joined them. He sat down at one end, at the space reserved for him. Martin was seated at his right. "You worked hard today, MAR-tan," he said, smiling at him and pouring him more lemonade. "You will sleep well tonight, eh?"

Martin did indeed sleep well that night, though his mind replayed some of the vintage experiences of the past day.

First, though, after he'd gotten home, Grandmother Lovejoy followed him into his bedroom and closed the door, to ask about his first winemaking adventure. "My goodness," she commented tersely after he described his grape treading, "I didn't think that wine was still being made with people's *feet.*" She stressed the last word in a clucking sort of way that showed her distaste.

"But that was only a ritual Mr. Masson does at the start of the vintage season," he assured her. He did share some uneasiness—though not about the grape-treading business. He was disturbed by the way the workers crushed grapes by laboriously pushing them through a wire-mesh sieve. Surely in this age of machinery more efficient methods would be available to vintners!

As his eyes closed and his brain began slowing down for a night of dreams, Martin vaguely recalled seeing some big old metal device of his grandfather's, pushed way back in a storage shed. Tomorrow, he'd ask him . . .

As soon as Martin awakened, he reviewed the exciting events of yesterday's harvest and crush, then focused on the thing that had bothered him: Masson's tedious and messy way of crushing grapes. He remembered now that his grandfather had a grape crusher but of course no longer used it to make wine. He'd brought this wonderful mechanism long ago from the East. It was so simple, so neat. You just turned a handle and all the grapes were crushed and cranked out, going in a stream into a barrel. Once his grandfather had even made grape juice with it to show Martin how it worked. But Martin's mother had been unhappy about that. Unless it was boiled and purified, grape juice, after all, would ferment into wine.

That crusher, Martin decided, was just what Paul Masson needed. So after breakfast, he asked his grandfather about it. "Mr. Masson's way of getting juice takes too much work," he said. "If you don't need your crusher anymore, he might really like to have it."

"Hmmm," said his grandfather, who had heard Martin's description of the crushing process. "Maybe, though, he wants to stick with the old French way of doing things. Sounds as if he might not use machines unless he *has* to." He saw Martin's disappointed look. "Yet it's possible he's never seen a crusher like mine," his grandfather continued. "Sure, I'd be happy to give it to him if he can use it."

So they pulled the wood and iron crusher out from under a pile of junk and then cleaned it up, all the while planning how they'd take it up the mountain in Grandfather Lovejoy's truck that afternoon.

Martin's enthusiasm had initially overridden any doubt he might have had about the crusher's acceptability. But as they drove up the narrow, twisting mountain road—Martin's first trip over it—the boy began worrying. The Frenchman, he'd already observed, didn't readily discard old methods for new. (This trait Martin himself would take on later as time went by.) So by the time he actually presented Masson with the crusher, he felt shy and hesitant.

Masson had been standing out in the winery courtyard as they drove up. "You must be the grandfather of MAR-tan," he said heartily as the two got out. "You are a lucky man to have such a boy around to help you all the time!"

"We brought this up to you," said Mr. Lovejoy, gesturing toward the crusher in the back of the truck.

Masson eyed the gift with tolerant amusement. "Wherever did you find this?" he asked, looking up and grinning. "I haven't seen one for some while."

So he already knew about such crushers! Martin's grandfather explained how he'd used it for many years, but no longer had a vineyard or made wine. Paul's eyes and hands, meanwhile, were examining the device. Was he remembering something from the past, or thinking of what he'd say to the boy?

"It's very handy for home use," Masson finally said. "But it grinds up the grape stems in the crush, as well as the skins. Stems contain a lot of tannin, which is strong and bitter in large amounts. So it can't be used in making fine wine. In fact," he went on, "various machines have been invented since this type was made, which crush grapes and take the stems out too. But most are big and noisy, with steam-driven engines. They don't do the careful job I want done with my grapes. That's why we still separate stems from skins and juice in the old Burgundian way. Doing the work by hand."

Seeing Martin's crestfallen look, Masson added: "Yet it was so thoughtful of you both to bring the crusher up here! Since you're not using it, I'll be happy to take it home. My wife and her sister, I am sure, will put it to good use. But wait a minute ..." He hurried off and returned holding several bottles of his wine. "Here's some good medicine for Martin's grandmother!" he said. As his visitors turned to go, he shook Grandfather Lovejoy's hand and gave Martin's shoulder a reassuring pat.

Interrupting the long silence on their drive down the mountain, Martin's grandfather said consolingly, "Well, Mr. Masson did say he was glad to have it and will use it. And I can't help but admire him. All that extra trouble he goes to, just to crush his grapes and remove the stems! No wonder his wines are so highly regarded."

Martin gave no reply. He felt embarrassed, chagrined. The gift had been so presumptuous!

From that day on, he often pondered the stem problem. Eventually his concern prodded him into designing a compact stainless steel crusher whose blades, electrically driven, tore stems from the grape bunches and shot them out the end, discarded from the crush. But by then he was making his own wine . . . and Masson no longer needed it.

In the next few weeks Martin kept very busy. Summer vacation would soon be over. When he started school again, he wouldn't have much time to assist his grandfather with ranch work. Or to hike up to Paul Masson's either.

4

Winemaker's Apprentice

ON A SATURDAY a month or so after the new school year had started, Martin returned to Paul Masson's mountaintop. The morning was almost half over when he arrived. Angelo was supervising workers who were handling the wooden boxes used in harvesting the wine grapes. They washed them down with a hose, scrubbing them with brushes, and then spread them out to dry in the autumn sunshine.

"Does this mean vintage is over?" Martin asked.

"Yes, we're putting all the boxes away till next year's harvest," said Angelo.

Martin, disappointed, regretted that he'd stayed away until today. Just then he saw Masson out in front of the winery, gesturing for him to come. Martin did so, running.

"Ah, MAR-tan, we have missed seeing you up here!" the Frenchman said.

The boy explained how he'd been busy at school; and before that, doing many things for his grandfather. "But maybe I can help today?" he asked.

"Of course. The cellars are full of new wines in different stages of fermentation. Come with me now and you will see them."

As they entered the large area on the third floor, Martin saw Sergio. "We have one more helper today," Masson announced. "And maybe for other days too. Sergio, please tell this boy what to do whenever I am not here. And tell him also why we do it. You know how he always wants to know *everything*."

Martin breathed in. The air was laden with powerful aromas that competed for attention and identification. He pictured ripe wild blackberries upon sprawling, prickly vines just waiting to be picked; bundles of just-mown hay stacked by the barn; his grandmother's kitchen at harvest time where she made jams in huge pots and prepared vegetables—peppers, cucumbers, beans, corn—from her vegetable garden; roadside stands next to orchards where racks of plums and apricots were drying beneath the blazing summer sun; moist, piney woods . . .

"What is that smell?" he asked.

"That, MAR-tan," said the French winemaker, laughing heartily, "is the smell of rapidly fermenting wine."

Masson picked up a short ladder and handed it to Martin. "Please carry this and follow me," he commanded. Then he took a long-handled tool with a small flat board attached to the end and walked over to a row of puncheons whose open tops were covered with crisply clean white cloths. He went to the first one and leaned the tool against its side. "Put the ladder down here," he ordered Martin. Then he pulled off the muslin fabric on top and laid it over the next puncheon, taking care so it would not touch the floor.

"These wines in these small oak fermenters are special ones, really for my own and my connoisseur friends' use," Masson explained, "so I mostly take care of them myself." He gestured toward some much larger tanks made of redwood. "The wines over there are for the public. They are blended reds. But mine, of course, are *pure* pinot noir—as befits a Burgundian!"

As soon as Masson lifted the cloth, Martin's nose picked up a pungent smell far more intense than the pervading cellar aroma. He coughed and then sneezed. Masson laughed. "That's carbon dioxide," he said. "It is very powerful in here right now; goes right up your nostrils. But you'll get used to it."

Up on the stepladder, Masson picked up the handle of his tool and thrust the squarish board downward into the tank. A loud swooshing and rumbling sound went on within, and suddenly a stream of red fluid shot up in the air. "I am punching down the *chapeau*—the cap," Masson explained. The exercise must be strenuous, Martin decided, for Masson grunted almost every time he pushed the implement downward.

"See how the level of the liquid sinks down as I do this?" Masson asked. Martin peered over the top. "We do not fill the fermenters much more than halfway. Otherwise the wine will spill over as the carbon dioxide expands it.... Just put your hand against the puncheon now, boy," he ordered, and when Martin did so he discovered that the wood there was as warm as if the vat had been sitting out in the sun all day.

"Feels like something is cooking in there, no?" said Masson. "And in a way it is. Cooking is a chemical process: heat from fire changes the texture and flavor of food. In fermentation, as yeast converts the sugar in the grape juice to alcohol, heat and carbon dioxide are produced. Both disappear when fermentation stops.

Only the alcohol and sometimes a little sugar remain to preserve the grape juice—in a very different form indeed."

"And what happens to the yeast then?" Martin asked.

"It quiets down and mostly dies off when the alcohol level gets high; also when the sugar is mostly used up, for sugar is its food. At this point we move the red wine out of the fermenter. White wines, made from clear juice and coming directly from the crusher and basket press, are fermented right in casks they will stay in for months. But the fermented red wine must from the fermenters is first put into the basket press. There we extract as much extra color and other substances from the skins as possible."

Masson stepped down from the ladder, replaced the fermenter cloth, and moved on to the next puncheon, where he began the same procedure as before—talking to the boy as he worked.

"But why do you have to push the cap down like that?"

"First, I am breaking up the solid material that rises and collects at the top of the must. It's mostly skins and pips. Punching the chapeau down mixes the skins back into the juice, putting stronger color and flavor into the fermenting wine. The action also releases carbon dioxide gas trapped below the thick cap, as you saw with that eruption. Actually, in some European wineries, workers still tread the cap—as you did when crushing the grapes."

Before putting the white cloth back on the tank, Masson rolled up his sleeve and dipped a tall glass vial down into the juice. After bringing it back up filled with blood-red liquid, he inserted a slim tube into it, and held it there with one hand while he perched his pince-nez against his eyes with the other. Then he scrutinized the numbers printed on the side. "This is a saccharometer," he explained. "It tells me how much sugar is left in the wine—and therefore how much alcohol is in it too. From these readings I decide when we should remove the must and press it. To get a very dry wine, I want to get close to zero sugar as fermentation is quieting down. This one is at 5, so I can estimate that we will press day after tomorrow, if the rapid activity is over."

"What would happen if you left the wine in the fermenter after fermentation stops?" Martin asked,

"It would spoil—get oxidized or, worse, take on terrible odors and flavors, or turn to vinegar—if left in the open air," Masson said. "That's as if the wine gets a disease. The carbon dioxide gas generated by the fermentation actually protects fermenting must. So when fermentation slows down, the new wine is more exposed to air-borne contaminants. The high heat in a strong fermentation, too, helps kill off bacteria that came in on grape skins, are carried by insects, or were on the equipment. Almost like sterilizing.

But there is always the risk that some bacteria remain, or will be introduced later. That's why, whenever we are handling it, we must avoid exposing wine to air for very long. And we always want equipment to be *very* clean."

Masson was already moving on to the next fermenter. "Can I try to punch down the cap on this one?" Martin boldly asked.

"Just stand on the stepladder!" said Masson. As Martin looked straight down into the vat, he saw a dry-looking, magenta-colored crust below him, several inches thick at least. Masson handed him the tool. "Push down slowly and firmly," he was told. Martin put his weight against the handle but met with strong resistance. "Just keep on," Masson said, "and try the edges first. Remember, this is hard work!"

Right then Martin broke through the surface and felt rewarded as a thin geyser of red wine shot up through the air at him, spraying his face and shirt.

"That's your badge of honor for the day, boy. But don't show that stain to your mother!" said Masson. "Give the shirt to your grandmother to bleach."

Fermenter by fermenter, Masson and his young cellar assistant moved around the cellar, taking turns punching down again and again in each cask until the entire surface was frothy with pink bubbles. Masson found other tasks for Martin to help Sergio with later. When Martin went home that afternoon he felt tired but happy.

Martin now began learning about the post-vintage care of wines. He was still too young to be entrusted to the actual handling of the wines on his own. But because of his obvious desire to learn more, Paul Masson provided various opportunities along with information regarding this cellar work. Step by painstaking step, Masson explained why he was doing what he did. "You will learn more from watching me than from reading any book," he told him.

"The first month or two after vintage is when most potentially fine wines are lost, in the cellar," Masson said. "A winemaker can use the best grapes, but if he doesn't take proper care of the juice made from them during the entire fermentation process, he might as well start with inferior grapes: for the product will be about the same."

Martin again saw the basket press in operation, this time when it was filled to the top with the red wine must removed from a fermenter. Pressure was applied until the ratchet handle would no longer budge. "Now you will see the *pomace*," Masson told the boy. The men removed the sides of the press to expose a hard round purple cake made of skins and seeds. They broke it up with shovels, and then placed the dry, crumbly chunks back into the fermenter.

To Martin's surprise, they then added many gallons of water and some sugar to it. "That's how we make a lighter wine for workers' everyday use," Sergio said. "There is still a lot of color and flavor in the pomace. The yeast starts acting right away on the sugar we added, beginning the fermentation all over again."

On his next visit Martin saw how Masson tended the red wine that had been put into casks after coming from the basket press. Martin stayed close to Masson so he could watch the vintner's every move as he talked. First Masson would remove the large wooden bung from the hole at the top side of each cask. He had wrapped small pieces of cloth around each bung, to absorb excess wine and keep it from spilling over. Frequently gas would be released explosively, almost like gunshot, with perhaps even a little wine shooting out too, which Masson would wipe from the barrel sides with a well-stained cloth. Then the winemaker would peer down through the large hole into the cask.

"For some while," Masson said, "fermentation still goes on in the casks, though much more slowly than right after crushing. Carbon dioxide continues to be formed, and the gas goes to the top of the puncheon. It can even push the heavy bung out if it isn't released! So every day at first we've got to remove the bung briefly. When the fermenting action is great, I may use wads of sterile cotton to plug the cask with my own special wines. With others we use glass 'air locks'—see them over there?—which let the gas out without letting air in. But I like this traditional way of doing things with my own wines. I want to *see* what's going on inside. And smell, too."

Masson picked up a small jug of wine he'd set down on the wood frame next to the cask. "Meanwhile," he said as he pulled out the cork and began pouring wine through a funnel into the bung hole, "the oak staves in the barrel are absorbing the water in the wine, with some evaporating into the air outside. In a cool, damp cellar like this one there's less evaporation than when casks are kept in a regular building, as many winemakers do. Anyway, the water absorption makes the wine level go down, and this becomes a special problem once fermentation stops. Want to guess why?"

"Air is at the top then?" Martin ventured.

"Right," said Masson. "As you know, air should not be in contact for long with wine, since it will oxidize the wine and even ruin it—turning it off color, giving it a flat or bad taste, perhaps making it vinegary if enough acetic acid is present. That's why the wine in casks must always be topped off."

"Is that what you're doing now? Topping off?"

"Yes. Adding enough of the same kind of wine to fill it up to the top." For each section of casks Masson would carry a different large glass container of wine, specially labeled. Sometimes he'd add only a few drops, other times almost a quart. Then, using a mallet, he'd bang the bung securely down again into the hole atop the cask.

"MAR-tan, you do now what I have just been doing," Masson said at last, handing him the mallet. "For someday—who knows?—maybe you will want to be a winemaker too!"

Martin grasped the mallet and, under the Frenchman's watchful eyes, commenced another facet of this early, hands-on training.

And later, when Masson declared some of the new wines ready for their first racking, Martin also participated in that procedure, which cleared the wine by removing it from its sediment, or "lees." To do this Masson tied a slim wine hose to a stick so that the end of the hose was several inches above the stick's end. By that simple method, when the stick was carefully lowered into the cask, the hose would not rest at the very bottom. Starting a small hand pump, Masson then transferred the wine into a newly rinsed barrel waiting nearby, where Sergio monitored the level, prepared to shut the pump down when it almost reached the top.

"And now, MAR-tan, how would you like to have a little taste of this wine you've been handling?" Masson asked over the hum of the pumping machine. He held out a goblet partly filled with wine that he'd poured specially for his young helper. He noted the boy's hesitant expression. But then, decisively, Martin reached out and grasped the wine glass by its stem.

"Swirl the wine around, then put your nose right down into the cup," Masson instructed him, "and sniff deeply . . . that's right! Put a small amount in your mouth and let your tongue roll around it, and carry it around your palate, to be absorbed. Sip more if you need it. Now try to push the aroma up into the nasal passages above your throat. Like this—" Masson took up his own glass and drank. "Ahhh," he declared. "The nose and the mouth work well together. Half of the real taste comes with the smell!" He looked at the boy. "Finally," he said, "you can *drink* the wine too"—which he demonstrated by audibly swallowing.

Martin had watched the Frenchman carefully, and now he tried to mimic what he had seen.... Was that warmly redolent sensation *wine?* He took another small mouthful and processed the scarlet fluid again. He smiled at Masson. "That tastes and feels wonderful," he said.

"It does indeed," Masson agreed. Then he was silent for a few seconds, "But I ask myself, MAR-tan, what will you do with all this knowledge of wine if the temperance people like your mother get their way and Prohibition comes? And come to think of it, what will *I* do?"

Martin could not offer up a single word.

"But right now, boy, we are about finished with our work today! And I am becoming powerfully thirsty. So after we clean things up here, why don't you come over to the chateau and take some refreshment with me?"

Since this was the first time Paul Masson had invited him over to his chateau, Martin felt both excited and curious.

"I call this my champagne hour," Masson said as the two of them sat down in chairs out on his sunny terrace on that spring afternoon. John, his accustomed helper, came out right away with a bottle of champagne already cooling in a bucket of ice, quite as if he did this every day Mr. Masson was here. He set the bucket and a tray containing a pitcher and two wine glasses on a low table next to Masson.

Martin, feeling privileged to be sharing the vintner's end-of-the-day ritual, watched Masson's every motion as he removed the heavy, dark green bottle from its bed of ice chips, wiped it with a white linen cloth, and then picked up a small tool with a slender steel blade and an egg-shaped wooden handle. With the bottle pressed sideways against his abdomen, deftly Masson slipped the blade under the metal clip clamped tightly over the bottle's mushroom-headed cork. "This is an *agrafe*," he explained as he began bending the clip aside. "It helps hold the cork in until one wants it out, as now." With the agrafe removed, Masson pushed his thumb hard against the top of the cork.

"Ready for the big bang, boy?" he asked. And then with his fingers he quickly twisted the cork around until it popped out, suddenly and resoundingly, shooting off across the terrace. Martin heard it bounce several times against the flagstones before coming to a rest. But his eyes were riveted on what Masson was doing meanwhile. As soon as the cork sped off, he had uprighted the bottle and pressed his thumb against the opening, to prevent the champagne from following the cork's trajectory. After a few moments he began filling a wide-bowled champagne glass with the frothy golden wine, set it down on the tray, and then turned to Martin.

"I am sorry ... I must not offer you any champagne," Masson said. "If your mother heard of it, I would get in terrible trouble! Of course down in the cellar you are just tasting our handiwork, not drinking socially. But we do have some lemonade for you." He removed some ice chips from the bucket and dropped them into a champagne glass identical to his own. "Even without champagne, the champagne hour should be conducted with due ceremony," he remarked as he poured some juice from a pitcher and then handed the glass to the boy, who watched tiny ice chips swirl within the fluted stem.

Then Masson picked up his own goblet and held it up against the sinking sun so the boy could see the champagne sparkle. He nodded his pleasure in seeing how the bubbles caught the light as they traveled merrily up the hollow glass stem. And finally he raised his glass and gently clinked it against Martin's.

"Well, here's a toast to the Good Life, MAR-tan!" Masson exclaimed. "Yours and mine. Wherever it may take us."

"Why do they call it a toast?" Martin wondered.

"It is an odd word," Masson agreed. "Actually, it comes from serving champagne in the old days, before its makers found better ways to disgorge yeast cells. Little bits of toast were passed around to put in the bottom of the glass before the sparkling wine was poured. The toast cleared the wine by soaking up the yeast flakes."

"I hope I can help you make champagne too someday," Martin ventured. "But Sergio says it's done at your San Jose building, not here."

"Well, boy, maybe we can arrange a trip there for you sometime," Masson said. Martin wondered how he might explain that excursion to his mother!

"Why doesn't this bottle have a label?" the boy asked.

"Wines I drink from my own cellar—'house wines,' I call them—often don't," Masson answered. "This champagne is three years old, and only now is it ready to be released for sale. Next week at our San Jose building we will label the bottles and put them in cases, then start shipping them out to restaurants and stores. And to many private customers too who buy directly from us."

"I also want to *drink* champagne someday," the boy ventured, gazing enviously at the gusto with which Masson emptied his wine glass and then refilled it.

"Not just make it, eh, boy? Oh, you will, you will," Masson assured him. But then a grimace came over his face, as it had briefly in the cellar, earlier. "Unless the temperance people have their way and get their damnable Prohibition all over the country," he amended.

"But I thought . . . Didn't the voters turn it down last fall?" Martin stammered, remembering all too well the church people's—including, of course, his mother's—ongoing crusade to vote Dry.

They were bitterly disappointed when Santa Clara County voters rejected legislation to outlaw liquor sales.

"They did," Masson said, "but that was the last election. And the Prohibitionists won't rest until they get their way. And it looks as if they might, with the Great War helping them!"

"How?"

"Well, the war in Europe has caused shortages of grain crops in this country. So the temperance folks want Congress and the President to pass a national law that forbids making or selling *any* beverages containing alcohol. Appealing to everyone's patriotism is just the latest tactic of those teetotaling moralists."

"But why would not making alcohol stop crop shortages?"

"Because corn and wheat and other grains, used in bread and cereal and many other foods, are sometimes grown just to make whiskey and beer. And though we are not in the war—yet—there's a shortage of foods, and higher prices now. America is exporting grain to the European nations too busy with war to grow crops. Prohibitionist politicians are saying that land should not be used to produce crops for nonessential products. They also declare that since distilled alcohol has important industrial uses, there would be more of it if people didn't drink it all up!"

"But what about wine?" Martin asked. "It just uses grapes. They aren't a grain."

"True enough." Masson sighed. "Wine can be distilled into brandy, but that isn't much good for industrial purposes. Or for drinking, either, the way the Americans make it—claiming it's like our French cognac!"

Martin now asked a question he'd wanted to ask for some while: "When are you going to visit France again?"

The Frenchman looked terribly gloomy. "Not until the war is over," he said. "It is too dangerous to take a ship there now. The Germans are now threatening to torpedo American ships, knowing many carry supplies to the Allies." His voice now came low and shaky. "There are major battlefronts very close to my home. I worry greatly about my family and friends there."

"Do you think that war will come here too, if we enter into it?" Martin asked. So many grownups talked of this. It was almost like Prohibition, with people taking up sides, for or against joining up with Britain and France and Italy.

"Not *come* here, anyway," Masson said, "because this country is far removed from the main action. And probably not right away, since President Wilson is trying to keep the United States out of a war that he says should not concern this nation. But Americans may go over there to fight the war. Maybe soon. Especially if the Germans sink an American ship."

Martin frowned. His mother feared that his two older brothers, Jim and Mel, might get drafted. Some of their school friends had already enlisted in the military service, now actively recruiting for the nation's likely entry into the European conflict. They were both about to graduate from high school, so something had to be done soon. She wanted them in college, not in a place where they might get killed. Both boys and their grandparents agreed that this was a good idea. And that, Martin suspected, would mean a big change in their lives.

Sure enough, Martin not long afterwards learned that his mother would be moving to San Jose—taking her three boys with her, of course. That night, after hearing the news, Martin lay in bed reflecting about how this change would take him away from the idyllic retreat created by his grandparents that had long given him a firm sense of permanence, of belonging.

He was grieving. Yet might he also welcome this dramatic change in circumstance? "Things seem to be changing faster and faster all the time," his grandmother often said, "and I can scarcely keep up with them!" With his appreciation for the past, Martin was different from his two older brothers, Mrs. Lovejoy sometimes pointed out. Mel and Jim were definitely inclined toward the new ways. In their generation, traditions and ideas and artifacts, once revered and passed on to one's children, were fast becoming outmoded. But she allowed, after all, that this was a new century and there were unlimited possibilities ahead. It was hard sometimes to know what to keep, what to discard.

"And what changes *you* are going to see in the years ahead of you!" Grandmother Lovejoy predicted. As he lay sleepless, he could almost hear her voice. These first two decades of the 20th century were times of rapid advancement in so many ways. Teachers talked of this in school, telling students to prepare themselves for amazing differences during their lifetimes. This would affect the jobs people did as well as the way they'd live.

New prosperity and now the war in Europe had sped up the pace in technological progress, constantly expanding uses for inventions developed and scientific discoveries made in the past hundred years. And the large farming community in Santa Clara Valley adopted and accommodated new developments as rapidly as possible. It was less than fifty miles from the sophisticated, prosperous, ever-expanding metropolis of San Francisco—that world port, a transportation and commerce hub, and West Coast financial and cultural center. So the latest material advances arrived apace in the whole area around San Jose.

Trying to get to sleep, instead of counting sheep Martin began listing changes that his grandparents had seen during their own lifetimes. Martin's head whirled now as he considered them: electricity for powering lights and machinery and streetcars; internal combustion engines fueled by gasoline and oil that moved automobiles and trucks and the airplanes that crossed the continent and someday would cross oceans; amazing, huge farming and earthmoving and construction equipment; telephones that enabled people to talk through wires; machines in the home that did domestic chores like laundering, ironing, refrigerating food, mixing, cleaning; phonographs and moving pictures for entertainment, and now even the wireless radio that somehow pulled sounds out of the air ...

What did such changes mean? Would they never end? Were they necessarily *better* than the old ways? Was there nothing in the world that would ever stay the same?

Now as he drifted into sleep, the image of Paul Masson standing on his terrace that day, holding a champagne glass up against the setting sun, came to him as a reassurance.

How had this change come about in Martin's life? Up to this time, his mother had never shown an independent spirit like his grandmother's. But now she did so. All her sons must get advanced education, she'd decided, and she would enable them to have it. Somehow. One thing was clear: they'd have to leave the Lovejoys' secluded ranch north of Saratoga. Mel and Jim were never attuned to the farm life anyway.

Martin's mother contacted the College of the Pacific in nearby San Jose. The respectable, Methodist-run institution was actually the oldest private college in California. Yes, she was told, a number of students needed board-and-room accommodations, since dormitory space was limited. Investigating, she found a large house for sale right across the street from campus. In these uncertain times, when war might be just over the horizon, money had become scarce. Only a small down-payment was required.

She talked now with her folks. Her father, she knew, depended on her boys to help him out with ranch chores. He was hoping they'd take over most of his workload before long. His doctor had begun urging him to retire because of a weakening heart. To the Lovejoys' great credit, they didn't try to discourage their daughter from her plan. They understood it was important for her, a widow, to start a new life now on her own, for herself and her sons. With her parents' financial aid she bought the house.

The Lovejoys' help scarcely ended there. They helped their daughter refurbish and furnish the house so their daughter could take in paying young boarders. Every week they drove over to San

Jose bringing fresh produce, milk, butter, and cheese. Her mother even baked pies and cakes to make the cuisine irresistible to hungry young male students. For the Lovejoys it was a full day's journey, going back and forth through the city's traffic, in which streetcars and automobiles and trucks with gasoline-powered engines were crowding out horse-drawn carriages and wagons.

So with her parents' immense support, Mrs. Ray's fledgling enterprise was off to a splendid start. A fascinating new life began opening up not only for her boys, but for herself as well. The house soon was lively with college students who brought welcome income as well as a new set of interests. Thinking of them all as "her boys," Mrs. Ray, like a second mother, proudly followed their progress in both school and social life.

She also made lifelong friends among the professors and their wives. She might even have remarried had she wished. But as she told the personable professor who was courting her, "My husband is waiting for me in Heaven. So surely you can understand how impossible it is for me to marry you."

Mrs. Ray's Methodist-based religion continued to dominate her life. But she now enjoyed the many educational lectures, exciting theater performances, and inspiring concerts offered to the public at the college. As did her three boys.

Martin quickly became reconciled to this abrupt change in surroundings. Just starting his teens, he took advantage of the stimulating new environment, developing a special interest in the music programs. In his first exposure to classical music he found a depth of enjoyment that would enrich his life ever afterward. Living next to the college, he attended not only concerts featuring famed musicians but also those of amateur musical groups.

His greatest enthusiasm came to center on the piano, especially as played by Howard Hanson, a very young man but already so outstanding that he headed the college's music department. Young Martin worshipped him. At night he'd climb up an ivy-covered building to look through the second-floor window and watch Hanson play in his studio there. Lost to time, he'd listen with mounting fervor. Sometimes Hanson would abruptly stop playing, bury his face in his hands on the keyboard, and burst into tears. Apparently he couldn't endure playing short of perfection.

This aim to attain absolute perfection was something Martin inherently understood. Because of his closeness to his grandmother as well as his association with Paul Masson, the boy continued to cultivate the aesthetic side of his nature.

5

The Frenchman's Tale

THOUGH BUSILY EXPLORING NEW facets of life in the bustling urban setting of San Jose, Martin forgot neither his grandparents on their Saratoga ranch nor Paul Masson on his winegrowing mountaintop. On many a weekend the young teenager took the "red car" to the end of the line and then walked the several miles to the Lovejoys' home. There he did as many chores as he could for his grandfather.

Whenever possible too, he scurried up the mountain trail he'd often traveled in the past, hoping to take part in some of Paul Masson's activities. He worked with even greater interest and enthusiasm than before, since the trip could no longer be easily and frequently made.

One Sunday at dusk, after leaving his grandparents' home, Martin was moving fast down the roadway toward the trolley stop. A large car came up alongside him and paused. "Is that you, MARtan?" a familiar voice called out the window.

Astonished, Martin turned and smiled. "Mr. Masson!"

"I thought that might be you rushing along—with your blue sweater and red hair. So I asked Burt to stop. Where are you going?"

"Back to our house in San Jose, on the red car," said Martin. "I've just left my grandparents' ranch."

"Well, I'm on my way to my own home in San Jose. Just like you. So hop in, boy, and we'll take you there." He opened the back door for Martin and then moved over, behind his chauffeur.

Martin climbed in, overjoyed. "Your home?" he asked, no doubt sounding bemused. Although he'd been told of Masson's elegant townhouse, he somehow never thought of his actually living there. Martin always pictured Masson in his mountaintop chateau.

Masson laughed. "La Cresta is where I work," he said. "And where I entertain people. Customers, friends, people important in the wine world. But I always sleep at my house in San Jose ... unless I have an important dinner that continues on into the late night hours."

"Where do we let you off, Martin?" Burt then asked.

"We live just across the street from College of the Pacific," he answered.

"Goddamn, I should have realized it before, boy. You live but a short distance from my house. Why, we could usually drive you home on Sunday night whenever you are in Saratoga that day."

So a happy new routine began for Martin on occasional weekends. During the ride to San Jose, Martin spent a half-hour with Paul Masson. He took great advantage of the opportunity to learn more about the man who was his hero. Frequently he'd succeed in getting the Frenchman to talk about subjects he'd often pondered but never had much chance to ask about until now. Also, as he grew older, Masson treated him less like a kid, more like a young man he could talk with about some real problems of past and present. And he knew that Martin always listened attentively to whatever he had to say.

Whenever Martin helped Masson in vineyard and cellar work, Martin inevitably noticed how the winemaker used swear words often and profusely. He became somewhat inured to frequent explosions, not only over things that had gone awry but also to stress certain points in arguments or even just instructions given: Goddamn it ... Jesus Christ ... God Almighty! and so on. Sometimes as Masson was swearing roundly, Martin considered how such profanities would strike his mother. Horrified, she'd of course judge them proof of the Frenchman's complete satanism. Not only did he brew alcohol, but he blasphemed the Deity and His earthly representatives.

One day in the cellar as Masson was cursing the temperance people who were succeeding in pushing through various anti-alcohol measures, he suddenly remembered that a boy was present—a boy whose father had been a minister. Perhaps he'd never heard language like this. Certainly not in his family home! "MAR-tan, I am sorry if my swear words offend you," he said. "I always use them to get someone's attention. Or when I am upset and angry."

Well, Mr. Masson certainly had a good excuse now for using the words, Martin told himself. He couldn't help but feel remorseful that his own parents had helped bring forth this climate of hatred against alcoholic beverages of any kind. And against this winemaker whom he greatly admired.

"I picked up the habit of swearing when I first came to America as a young man," Masson said by way of explaining his rich vocabulary of expletives.

"Oh?" Martin said. "How old were you when you came here? And why did you come?" The boy often wondered what Masson himself would say, but until now he had not talked about his past life in France.

"It's a long story. Do you really want to know?" the Frenchman asked.

"Of course!" said Martin, grinning.

"Then, boy, I will start telling you about it on our way home tonight." Masson acted pleased. Perhaps he wasn't often asked to talk about his background. And Martin was happy, for he welcomed any chance to learn more about his hero.

So during their next few trips together, Masson told his story. He and the boy sat side by side on the comfortable rear seat of his car while Burt the chauffeur drove Martin homeward.

"When I first arrived in California in 1878," Masson began, "I was a very young man, only nineteen years old." Doing some fast subtraction, Martin calculated that Masson would now be in his mid fifties.

"I'm from Burgundy, you know," his mentor went on. "In France we call it Bourgogne. That's where the best wine in the world is made—though the people of Médoc naturally insist their Bordeaux wines are better! . . . Anyway, the main business of the whole province is winegrowing. Beautiful vineyards grow right up the steep slopes of sunny hillsides—we call them *côtes*—toward forests and, beyond them, the sky."

"Like your vineyards now?" Martin asked.

"Yes," Masson said, "though these vineyards of mine are even closer to the sky. So they revel in glorious sunlight throughout the day."

"Is that why you put them there?"

"Boy, that is a later part of my story. Remember, you wanted to know why I came to California! And since that comes first, I will tell you about it first.... I was born in a village called Merceuil, near the city of Beaune, at the center of Burgundy. So I grew up surrounded by vineyards and wineries. But in the 1870s our vineyards began to be destroyed by phylloxera. Do you know what that is?"

Martin nodded yes. "The tiny root louse," he said. "Angelo told me."

"The root louse that had come from America!" Paul added. "Well, it was terrible to watch all those vines, hundreds of thousands of vines, dying all around us. There were few jobs available for young men—no future at all. I was full of energy and had such big dreams! I wanted to see America, especially San Francisco, where a relative of mine lived. We all believed that in California gold and silver lined the streets. So I borrowed enough money from my family to buy passage on a boat. And I stayed in this area for several years, traveling around, meeting other French people, doing odd jobs. I even attended college."

"You went to college in America?" Martin wondered.

"For a short time, right here in San Jose, at the College of the Pacific. I took business classes. And studied English too, of course. That is where I really learned how to swear—from the other students! I was so impressed with the forcefulness of their awful language. So I learned to use the words to great effect, especially when I went back to France, where I astounded everyone by tossing American profanities into the midst of my French!"

"You went back? Didn't you like it here?"

"Oh, I loved it! Especially the Santa Clara Valley, where so many French families lived because of the climate and the fertile soil, and because they all knew each other. They had started nurseries, bought land and planted orchards and vineyards, and were making wine. In fact, in those early years the best wines were made here! The North Coast winegrowing counties—like Napa, Sonoma—were barely settled then."

"Then why did you leave?"

"Because I ran out of money. Also, I was ambitious. In my family education was very important—one of my older brothers was a doctor, another a lawyer. I wanted to become a professional myself, but I wasn't sure what kind. And my family would lend me money for tuition at the Sorbonne in Paris, if I went there. So that is what I did. But then when I finished college, I still couldn't settle down. I told my parents, Goddammit, I simply have to go back to America! I was driving them crazy, so in a while they and a brother lent me more money, hoping that when I returned to California I would quickly make my fortune there and then pay them back. Because I was a Burgundian, winemaking already seemed the best possible vocation. But now I'd do it in America! Of course I headed straight for the Santa Clara Valley, for I knew that its land and climate were as good as in France's wine country, maybe even better."

"How long had you been away?"

"Almost five years," Masson said, "but most of the French people I had known in San Jose were still there. And they remembered me. One man gave me a job. Charles Lefranc. And that is how I eventually became a winemaker . . ." His voice drifted off for a while, and Martin knew he was musing about those years.

"I was hired to be useful around the Lefranc ranch. I was strong and not at all reluctant to pitch in and do whatever work was needed. So I did everything from blacksmithing—shoeing horses and mending metal tools—to pruning vines. And with my college education I could also handle correspondence and the account books. It made good training for me. Winegrowers must be versatile . . . skilled at doing many things. And willing to do them!"

"So this Charles Lefranc made wine?"

"Oh yes, he was a good winemaker indeed. I became his apprentice and learned all his cellar techniques. He had vineyards too, more than a hundred acres of them. They are still there, in the hills south of San Jose, near Los Gatos. Have you heard of New Almaden? They belong to my wife and her sister now, but I manage the business for them."

"But how—?"

"Well, you see, after Charles Lefranc died—he was killed suddenly, tragically, when trying to stop a runaway horse—I married his older daughter, Louise. They needed a man in the family who could take charge of things, make decisions. And I liked Louise. I followed an established tradition among the French settlers here. Charles himself had become a winegrower because he had married the daughter of Etienne Thée. Back in the early 1850s, just after California became a state, Thée had planted one of the first real vineyards in the valley. But he had no sons to carry on his work."

"And Mr. Lefranc didn't have a son either?"

"Oh, he had a son about my age named Henry. But he showed little interest in the ranch. However, after I married his sister in 1888, Henry and I became business partners, to continue their father's winery business. We changed its name to Lefranc & Masson. I didn't share in owning the vineyard property, though. New Almaden remained in the Lefranc family's hands; Madame Adele Lefranc inherited half, Henry got one quarter, and Louise and her sister Marie shared the remaining quarter.

"I was already determined to make much better kinds of wine. Especially I wanted to learn how to make good champagne in California. Any good champagne one drank here was imported, of course. It had to be brought over from France in bottles, shipped across the Atlantic and either put on railroad boxcars in Eastern cities to cross the continent or sent around the Horn to the West Coast. (What a difference that new Panama Canal is making now in shipping!)

"I was sure I could make my fortune in America with champagne. So during our long honeymoon in France I spent much time in Épernay, where cousins of mine were in the champagne-making business. I studied their techniques and bought a lot of special equipment to take back with me to California. Of course I was short on cash, as usual! But my family in Burgundy again helped me out with loans. Not only could I pay for my purchases, but I also was able to buy a beautiful home in San Jose as a gift for my bride. It was close to the Lefranc building, headquarters for our business, so I could walk to work."

"And did your champagne turn out as good as you wanted it to be?" Martin asked.

"Almost! But making any money from it was still in the future, because it takes at least three years to produce high-quality champagne. And I wanted to be sure that mine would be superb—far better than merely satisfactory—so that it would be greatly successful here. At least I realized early that I'd had beginner's luck: the 1888 cuvée was excellent, and then the second fermentation did not blow up most bottles!

"Blow up?" Martin asked in wonderment.

"Oh, champagne making can be dangerous!" said Masson. "I must tell you about it sometime. Anyway, in the meantime, I didn't just wait around. I was in charge of wine sales, wholesale and retail, for Lefranc & Masson, while Henry handled the vineyards and winemaking cellars for New Almaden. Business began booming, especially for the new label I initiated, which was called Lefranc & Masson."

"And did Henry like that?"

Martin's tale-teller paused for some while before answering the question in a way that would be suitable for the boy's ears. "No," Masson said finally, "not really. Frankly, Henry and I weren't getting along well. He got angry with me when his mother and sister, Marie—who has always been so close to Louise that they are practically inseparable—left the ranch at New Almaden and came to live with us in our town house. They liked the comforts there. And liked being able to visit with their friends. And of course were so near now to the shops and also St. Joseph's Church, where they went almost every day.

"But that wasn't all! Henry resented my criticism of the way he was making the wines. And perhaps even worse, he was jealous because my champagne quickly became a great hit and orders poured in from all over the country. Among California champagnes I had only one real competitor, Arpad Harazsthy's Eclipse. And that I soon eclipsed!

"Henry also envied the attention I was getting from publicizing our business far and wide, and accused me of acting as if I were the head of our firm. We had some noisy battles! In 1892 I offered to buy him out and, to my relief, he accepted. I found a few investors who enabled me to finance my own business, so by 1900 I changed the name of Lefranc & Masson to the Paul Masson Champagne Company. And because the firm had been incorporated originally by Etienne Thée, Charles Lefranc's father-in-law,

I could claim 1852 as its starting date. An early founding is a real advantage for enterprises with high-cost goods, for buyers naturally look for longevity and stability."

"And you didn't see Henry any more?"

"Oh, sure I saw him, because after all we were members of the same family. I continued to market the New Almaden wines he made. That was a continuing business arrangement. But then we got into fights over those too, because he began trying to make brandy and sherry and port—quite out of our family tradition and experience. He even started making champagne, probably just to annoy me. To my taste all his experiments were awful. Naturally I told him so, and he didn't like that. But after all I was the one who would have to market them!

"Moreover, Henry knew I wasn't happy with the wine grapes he produced at New Almaden. More and more I purchased grapes from other growers, particularly for my champagnes. But I still wasn't satisfied with their flavor or quality. So I intended to buy property of my own and raise my own grapes. And then I finally found exactly the area I wanted . . ."

"Your mountain place?" asked Martin hopefully.

"Yes. La Cresta," said Masson contentedly. "But it did not happen as easily as you might think! . . . Now, boy, I see that we are right here on your street. Your mother will be glad to see you arrive safely after your weekend with your grandparents. But don't tell her that you spent most of today with the notorious French winemaker—or that he gave you a ride home!"

Martin grinned as he opened the car door.

"So we must leave the rest of my story for some other time," Masson was saying.

"I want to hear it—soon!"

"It is a promise, MAR-tan," the Frenchman assured him.

When Martin next went up on Paul Masson's mountain, he was in luck. Mr. Masson told Martin he'd be able to take him home that night.

"You said you'd tell me how you got this place," Martin eagerly reminded the Frenchman as soon as he climbed into the automobile.

"So I did!" Masson remembered, pleased that the boy took such an unusual interest in his history. "If you remember, I searched long and hard for the right kind of land," he began. "The types of wine grapes I wanted would grow best in soil that was thin and rocky, with good drainage, and maybe with limestone in it like Burgundy earth—not rich and deep and heavy with clay, as the valley's soil is. The best grapes come from vines that are not well fertilized and watered, you know. Vines that have to work hard just to make a few grapes." Martin remembered that Angelo had said this too.

"And I also needed a special climate, different from the valley floor's, during the growing season—rather cooler so that when the grapes are fully ripe and sweet they will still keep the high acid so necessary in champagne and in the great still wines, red and white, of Burgundy. Actually, I hoped for land much like the famous côtes in Burgundy, sloping upward along sunny hillsides.

"For some years, whenever I could, I rode a horse around this county, up in the hills encircling the valley and also high up in the Santa Cruz Mountains where other people had orchards and vineyards; some were even making wines. I also scouted around in the Napa, Sonoma, and Livermore valleys, where various vintner friends lived, but I wasn't satisfied. And finally I found what I was looking for, in the foothills way above Saratoga, fifteen hundred feet high and more. These slopes face the southeast, receiving morning and midday sunlight but mostly protected from the hottest sun, the heat that cooks the grapes, in the afternoon. The hills are high enough above the valley to escape most of the fog that often sweeps in during the night from the ocean. Yet close enough to the ocean to get the cool nighttime breezes—though not so close that the vines would get washed out in heavy springtime coastal rains, or get cold and damp from summer fog. And the great oaks on the summit told me that the soil was good."

"So when you found the place you wanted, what did you do?"

"Well, I wanted a big spread, the whole mountain. But I found I had to buy the land piece by piece from different people who owned it. Much of it was wild, densely wooded terrain that would need to be cleared. It took a few years to put it all together. In 1896 I had been fortunate to get the vital part of the property from an Italian named Alessandro Rodoni, who was financially broke. There was a twelve-acre vineyard, and it had several small structures on it, including one he had used as a winery. That gave me a head start on winegrowing.

"It took even longer to clear the land for much larger vineyard areas. And what a job that was! In those days everything had to be done by human hands with tools and with animals hauling equipment. Such wonderful engine-driven machines they are making nowadays, that dig and push and pull! Anyway, we did it tediously with axes and saws clearing the trees and brush, and with picks and shovels hacking out the road winding up the mountain. Finally, after reaching the top, we had to excavate deep to remove the immense oak trees across the summit where we wanted the vineyards to be, and clear out the forests of madrones and bay trees too. The rocky soil, often with huge boulders, had to be broken up; then plowed again and again by horse-drawn scarifiers and plows to a depth of several feet, since pulverized soil was necessary for the young vines."

Masson paused while he wiped his face with a handkerchief. "It tires me out even now, boy, just to remember it," he explained. "But I got the work done. . . . And then for the planting! I was ready for it because on my last trip abroad I had brought back cuttings of France's great wine grape varieties. Among them of course were Burgundy's pinot noir and chardonnay—to be successfully grown in California for the first time, probably because they needed a Burgundian to do it!

"Those were the varieties I needed not only for making the French-style champagne cuvées but also for the great classic still wines of Burgundy, the red burgundy and the white chablis. Other vintners here claim to produce them, but they use inferior, ordinary grapes. They simply don't understand the necessity for planting top varieties, which not only are hard to grow but also produce sparsely. I also brought pinot blanc, a white-grape mutation of pinot noir that had recently been discovered in France. And other superb grape varieties that would make my vineyards in Saratoga outstanding.

"Most other winemakers for years had used the abundant mission grape, brought into California by the Spanish padres and Mexican colonists. The mission vine thrived everywhere, so to get the volume they were after they indiscriminately blended its grapes in with the superior red wine grapes imported later ... not seeming to realize, or even care, that they could make much better wine here in California. Well, at least phylloxera did California vintners and American wine drinkers a favor by destroying all those infernal mission vines along with the rest! ... Of course I drank many wines made with mission juice, especially in my youth. They were absolutely awful. Even a small amount of it could ruin a wine for me!" Masson shuddered involuntarily at the very recollection.

"I was already growing all my new grape stock in a large nursery, bench-grafted onto American rootstock—the Rupestris St. George that the French horticultural researchers judged the best. Most American viticulturists did not yet agree with them, so I was taking a big chance. But it proved right to do, because phylloxera hasn't come near La Cresta!"

"Why did you name it La Cresta?" Martin asked.

"I liked the sound of it as well as the meaning," Masson said. "In both Spanish and Italian it is like the English crest—meaning the top of a hill or mountain. Spanish of course was the first European language spoken here, so that was appropriate. But most of my workers, as you know, are Italian, and I knew the name would make them feel at home."

"Then after you planted the vines, how long did it take to make wine from them?" Martin wanted to know.

Masson eyed Martin sharply as their eyes met. "Being a winemaker," he said, "is not easy, MAR-tan. One must work very hard for success. And learn to wait, sometimes for years. You have to be very patient. Which is hard for me, since I am not by nature a patient man. . . . Anyway, it takes about five years for vines to come into good bearing. In the meantime, of course, I was continuing to make champagne and still wines—mostly in the cellars at New Almaden."

"But when did you start building the big winery?"

"I started planning it right away. I wanted to make it of concrete and stone so that it would not burn down, as many wineries do—ones made mainly of wood. I also wanted to make it look venerable, as if it had been here for a century. So I got fragments of the walls from the old Los Gatos and Saratoga Winery, and also hauled hundreds of wagonloads of coarse sand and river stones up here from nearby creekbeds. These were mixed with cement to form the walls. I planned to go four stories high, and did one floor at a time, gradually going higher and higher up against the steep hillside, until it was time to put the roof on.

"In the meantime, I was putting up my chateau, to use as a little home up here on the mountain, where I could eat meals, clean up after work, and take naps. I'd also use it for entertaining important customers and my winegrowing associates.

"But when the winery itself was finished, I wasn't entirely satisfied with it. Some greater *élégance* was needed in its appearance."

"Is that when the earthquake happened?" Martin asked in anticipation.

"Yes. Some of my friends actually accuse me of causing it!" the Frenchman said, laughing. "But I lost too much champagne in 1906 to merit that charge—hundreds of thousands of bottles, in my wine cellars at the Vendome Hotel in San Jose and in San Francisco's Palace Hotel. Yet I turned at least one part of the disaster to my advantage after I saw how St. Patrick's Cathedral in San Jose was almost utterly destroyed. The beautiful old sandstone façade lying amidst the ruins had once been part of a medieval church in Italy. It had been dismantled and shipped over here to adorn the new cathedral. But it would be of no use now to the church people, since the entire structure would be demolished. So I hauled it away in pieces to my mountaintop!" He paused. "It should last as long as my winery is there. And I am sure you agree, boy, that it makes a splendid effect."

"Oh yes!" said Martin. He was ready to pursue another story thread. "And what did Henry Lefranc think of La Cresta?"

"Well, by then, MAR-tan, he and I were barely on speaking terms. His life seemed much happier, so there was no reason for him to continue being envious of me. He had bought a house in San Jose, for he finally got married. And a fortunate marriage it was, to Nelty Delmas, the daughter of a prosperous nurseryman, Antoine Delmas. But he got so busy there in the city with real estate holdings and bank transactions that he hardly had time at all for the winegrowing business. I knew that he was getting into debt because he had mortgaged some of New Almaden's land. So finally I accused him publicly of mismanaging the family business and thereby defrauding his mother and sisters."

And what terrible trouble that must have caused, Martin anticipated to himself before Masson continued on. "Madame Adele Lefranc, the mother, was greatly upset, of course, at our perpetual wars. And when she died in 1901, Henry said I had killed her off! Her death made things even worse between us, because her estate—50 percent of Charles Lefranc's holdings, if you remember—was divided among her three children. With it, though, went various heavy debts and other liabilities that Henry had incurred. My wife and Marie Lefranc wanted me to take over managing the family business at New Almaden, which naturally infuriated their brother. We settled our problems at last by buying Henry out—taking over the vineyard ranch and assuming the estate's debts, and in exchange giving him full title to some land parcels. So that is why since 1902 I have been trustee of the Lefranc family holdings, including New Almaden."

"And what is Henry doing now?" asked Martin.

"Ah, MAR-tan, such questions you ask!" said Masson, almost sorrowfully for a change. "Well, Henry's story has a very sad ending to it, I am afraid. I was told that after getting rid of his responsibilities for New Almaden he quite enjoyed his life in town, completely free now from the wine business and all the problems of managing a vineyard estate. New interests occupied his time. And he and his wife had a baby daughter who was given her mother's name. But one day in 1909, when Henry and his family were trying out their brand new automobile, an trolley car hit them broadside. Only the child Nelty survived—though for a long while it looked as if she would be buried next to her parents."

"Where is she now?"

"Oh, Nelty lives with her maternal grandparents, and she's quite a treasure in the Delmas family. . . . But with Henry's death the Lefranc family came to an end. So I really have felt obligated to continue on with Charles Lefranc's winemaking traditions, which I got directly from him as his apprentice."

"But what about Nelty Lefranc?"

"Since she is a female, she probably won't be interested in winemaking. And the New Almaden vineyards are out of her hands anyway. Also, when she marries she will take her husband's name; so any son would bear that name, not Lefranc." He paused. "That would happen too, of course, with my own daughter Adele, the only other third-generation Lefranc descendent. Her children won't carry on my name either—that is, if she ever marries and has any . . ."

Masson's tone of voice sounded dubious and disturbed, so Martin refrained from any further questions for a while. He'd never seen Adele but heard she was in her mid-twenties, the right age to get married. Paul rarely mentioned her name. But then, he sometimes remarked that the womenfolk in a Burgundian winegrowing family didn't come into the winery, take any part in vineyard work, enter into business decisions, or even attend luncheons and dinners at the estate.

Martin wondered about this. He thought now about his Grandmother Lovejoy. An intelligent and practical person, how would she feel if not consulted about important business decisions? An expert in sensory detections and appreciation—but never asked to taste the new wines in the cellar and evaluate their qualities? A wonderful gardener—but not allowed to plant or train or prune vines? A marvelous cook—but not invited to select menus and prepare dishes for elegant meals? A gracious hostess—but kept away from the entertaining of well-to-do, cultured people?

To Martin such a situation was unthinkable. Women like his grandmother, American women, could have much to contribute to the winegrowing life. Well, if Adele had any spirit at all—and she was American-born—she would surely feel left out of the main part of her father's life, and be really angry. She was her father's only child. Should it matter so much that she was female? To Paul Masson it apparently did.

"Do your wife and daughter visit La Cresta?" Martin now asked, curious. He'd never heard of their going there, and of course had never seen them.

"No, neither of them ever comes up to the mountain. My wife, Louise," Masson added tersely, "is now a temperance person. A teetotaler, like your mother. And she's made my daughter one too. So they don't really approve of what I do—even though, ironically, their many comforts come not just from my work but also from the Lefranc family's vineyard property."

Now that was really unexpected! No wonder Masson often

seemed reluctant to stop his work and leave the mountaintop. . . .

Martin hardly knew what to say. But by then the automobile had pulled up at the curbside close to his home in San Jose.

6

Dry Years Coming

ALL DURING HIS CHILDHOOD young Martin Ray had overheard discussions, even hot debates among his relatives and other adults about temperance. For many people, however, temperance didn't mean moderation in imbibing alcohol; it meant total abstinence, applied to everybody else as well as themselves. As he now entered his teenage years, the topic of prohibition, along with the Great War, seemed ever present in all the grownups' conversations, reflecting each speaker's high hopes or dismal fears. Increasingly it appeared that nationwide, unrestricted freedom in the making and selling, buying and drinking of alcohol would soon end, as it already had in many local communities, even entire states.

Mrs. Ray and her circle of close friends connected with the Methodist Church were pleased as anti-alcohol attitudes and legislation fast gained ground everywhere. In April of 1917—Martin was then almost thirteen—the "Drys" got a special boost from the nation's declaration of war against Germany. Despite long efforts to avoid involvement, America's isolationism had finally run out. Restricting the production of spirits was deemed essential as a wartime measure to conserve grain and limit alcohol to industrial needs. Also, since many distillers and brewers were of German descent, it seemed only fitting to force them out of business.

Temperance advocates demanded the cessation of sales and consumption of any alcoholic beverages, including wine, even though it was made entirely from grapes, which were scarcely a staple foodstuff. Countering this campaign were many "Wets." Whether avid consumers or not, they disliked the prospect of legislation instituting a national prohibition, particularly as an amendment embedding it in the U.S. Constitution.

In many American households and social settings opinion was sharply divided between teetotalers and imbibers. Whenever

Martin's mother got together with her parents, though the Love-joys tried to refrain from conversing about temperance, almost inevitably the topic came up. And of course in her own home Mrs. Lovejoy continued to take her "medicine," a glass of wine, right at the dinner table, in front of her daughter and grandsons.

Concerned about how Prohibition would affect Paul Masson, young Martin often read newspaper articles and editorials. Usual-ly they were as biased on one side or the other as the grownups he listened to. Frequently he saw Masson's name mentioned, and took great interest in the Frenchman's eloquent and forceful defense of his product. The Saratoga winemaker had become a prominent anti-prohibition spokesman and leader, not just around Santa Clara Valley but statewide.

Young Martin could take a secret pride in Masson's political activism. He was being taken seriously now as a spokesman for the whole wine industry—portrayed in a wholly different light than in the society columns of local newspapers, where he was often presented not only as a colorful host, but also as a frivolous showman and notorious womanizer. Which was scarcely the seri-ous and dedicated winemaker whom Martin knew from his close contact. Yet the erroneous impression that gossip-mongers created and perpetuated of the scandalous Paul Masson was the one that the temperance people held.

It hardly surprised Martin that the vintner was devoting so much time and effort to trying to persuade the public and legisla-tors not to ban the making and selling of wine. His livelihood and way of life were both being threatened. But the man from Burgun-dy also fought for a principle: he believed that wine was a whole-some and indeed health-conferring beverage when used moder-ately. It was unfair to treat it like hard liquor, making it subject to the same fierce attacks by teetotalers and new official restrictions. The alcohol content in unfortified wines usually ranged between 8 and 15 percent, whereas distilled spirits contained some 40 to 45 percent ethyl alcohol.

Masson fought to educate the public in this matter, hoping that fermented drinks with low alcohol—unfortified wines and beers—would not go down with whiskey, rum, and gin if or when Prohibi-tion came. And up at La Cresta, Masson sounded out in increasing vexation about the militant teetotalers, to anyone within earshot. Martin realized of course that the Frenchman naturally worried about what would happen to his vineyards and winery—his whole existence here—if he were forbidden to make and sell wine.

Paul Masson explained to young Martin how the need to con-centrate on growing and conserving essential food products put added pressure on the national and state governments to outlaw beer-making and distilled spirits, which consumed vast amounts of grain. It was considered unpatriotic, un-American, not only to produce alcohol, but also to sell it or consume it. People who spoke out, as Masson did in support of winegrowing, could be called traitors.

For years, California voters and their legislature had resisted prohibitionists' pressures to ban alcohol statewide. But now community after community succumbed to Dry legislation as well-organized temperance groups utilized the state's 1911 "local option" measure to effectively outlaw local sales of intoxicating beverages. America's new role in the expanding war in Europe encouraged the public to respond more favorably to the louder call for temperance. The outcry for a total stoppage of alcohol production put Drys on the march in Santa Clara County, as elsewhere in California and throughout the nation.

"Those goddamn prohibitionists!" Paul Masson would storm as he spoke about the coming election in 1917, lacing his anti-temperance invective with a more than ordinary string of profanities. "They are completely crazy to try to prevent drinking alcohol of all kinds. Bah! When people want to drink, and drink to excess, no law will ever stop them. Whiskey and rum may be one thing. They tend to hit hard and make people foolish and irresponsible. But wine is entirely different—a moderate form of alcohol. It helps people relax and be merry ... to enjoy themselves and each other. When you drink it with meals, it aids digestion. Why, doctors even prescribe wine for all sorts of health problems, and to improve old people's blood circulation."

"Then why don't the temperance people just allow wine, if it isn't bad for people like the hard liquors?" Martin wondered.

"Ah, that's one of the problems I run into when I argue for keeping wine out of any prohibition laws. Unfortunately, a lot of Americans, when they drink wine at all, always want it sweet. Unlike Europeans, they have never learned to appreciate dry table wines. In 1890 the 'sweet wine law' was passed, which allowed winemakers to add tax-free brandy to any sweet wine. Spirits normally carry high taxes, but this brandy had none at all! When given a high alcohol content, the wine can remain sweet because its sugar won't ferment out. People often don't realize how strong this wine is. And since they like it, they buy it. Like candy! Many thousands of men and women have become drunkards because of this sweet fortified wine menace.

"Before the law was passed, sweet-wine production was less than a million gallons, but when the law took effect it almost tripled because of the demand, to almost three million gallons! And production skyrocketed from then on. Before that law, sweet wines made up less than a tenth of California's wine production. Ten years later, they were close to one-half!

"Of course I have always been appalled by these fortified wines—can't imagine why anyone would drink them. But the great demand pushed most winegrowers into making them. I really blame these sweet wines for destroying wine's age-old reputation as a healthful and natural beverage. Many people believe wine is always what drunken bums in the 'skid rows' drink because it's cheap and potent. They say wine is just as bad as liquor in preying on the poor and unfortunate. Teetotalers confuse the fortified stuff with decent wine, so are determined to put all wine out of existence! And though I give speeches and write articles defending wine, I am afraid we are losing the battle against those Dry crusaders."

"How many of these crusaders are there?" Martin asked.

"Hundreds of thousands of them," Masson said glumly. "And a great many are women. Like your mother. Like my wife." Then he ventured an ominous prediction: "They will doom the wine industry. When states like California began to let women vote, they really let the temperance cause move ahead fast."

"You don't think women should be allowed to vote?"

"Not if they are prohibitionists!" Masson loudly declared.

Not long afterwards Martin overheard a discussion between his grandmother and mother. Both were expressing hope that American women in all states would soon be guaranteed the right to vote through a proposed amendment to the Constitution. "And when we do," Mrs. Ray remarked firmly to her mother, "we'll get alcohol banned everywhere. And keep it so. Thank heavens California saw the light five years ago. Now we have a good chance to convert this county, the state, and even the whole country to temperance."

"Well," said Mrs. Lovejoy, laughing, "I guess my vote is always going to cancel yours out!"

But why on earth might women especially be prohibitionists? Martin, wondering, asked his grandmother later. She then provided some background history to explain how suffragist issues had invariably gotten connected with temperance. In the 19th century women's rights got linked with many other society-reforming programs. Since women weren't allowed to vote, they could not directly influence or enact legislation. More than men, women were closely connected to churches, and many promulgated the wickedness of drink. Traditionally the vigilant keepers of family well-being and morality, women were also more apt to be alarmed and harmed by household drunkards. Many a family—rich, poor, or middle-class—had been ruined by some member's alcoholism. "It's like a disease," Mrs. Lovejoy said. "And people can catch it from one another. In homes as well as in saloons."

Now in the second decade of the new century the Women's Suffrage movement was advancing arm-in-arm politically with Prohibition. "Many women eager to vote on this burning issue have now joined the ranks of the suffragists, who for almost a century fought an uphill battle," Grandmother Lovejoy told Martin. "Several generations of determined women, despite ridicule, condemnation, and physical abuse, have kept insisting on women's right to select political representatives and to determine federal and state as well as local laws. But unlike California, some states don't yet permit women to vote. So not just the public attitude must be changed. The Constitution itself definitely needs an amendment that will assure us full citizenship as voters.

"So it's only a question now which constitutional amendment will succeed in getting through Congress first," Mrs. Lovejoy concluded. "Women's rights or National Prohibition. . . . But as for our own city and state, those people—men and women—who want to be able to have a drink with alcohol in it had better go to the polls this November. And vote!"

To many residents' shocked surprise in that fall election of 1917, a majority of voters in San Jose—a notoriously Wet enclave—banned saloons outright, putting the city now on the "water wagon." Places where customers went mainly to drink, with or without socializing, could continue to exist only if they became restaurants and served complete meals. And then only beer and wine were permitted—those comparatively low-alcohol beverages. Now people who'd neglected to vote, having laughed at the possibility that temperance could possibly overtake their community, regretted their inaction.

Masson's vehemence grew terrible nowadays whenever he got onto the subject of temperance. He took it almost as a personal attack, an outrageous affront—particularly now that prohibition came to the community where he lived. "Next, voters will start regulating the clothes I wear and the food I eat and whom I will spend time with!" Masson stormed. "There is only one saving thing in this damnable new law, though. People at least can buy wine when they eat a meal in a restaurant. It should encourage wine sales. However, even that freedom will be removed if the Drys succeed in prohibiting alcoholic beverages altogether by getting a constitutional amendment."

"And what will you do if that happens?" Martin asked.

"I'll be damned if I know, boy! . . . But in the meantime, I am going to make wine. And champagne." The Frenchman's eyes scrutinized Martin. "MAR-tan," he suddenly proposed, "would you like to learn now how to make champagne? In the classic way as I do it—*la Méthode Champenoise?*"

"Sure! . . . Here?"

"No. At the Lefranc building on West Santa Clara Street. That's where I do the second fermentation and finishing. I ship from there too."

"When shall I come?" Martin was excited, for champagne to him not only symbolized utmost sophistication but epitomized Masson's career as winemaker.

"Next Saturday. By then the various wines to be used will be filtered and fined, removing all traces of sediments that would cloud the champagne, which must end up crystal-clear."

So early on the following Saturday Martin arrived at the Lefranc building's cellar.

"Good, MAR-tan, you have come just in time to help me prepare the cuvée," Masson said to the boy. "For this one I used just whites: pinot blanc, chardonnay, folle blanche, aligoté, burger ..."

"You mix them all together?" Martin asked.

"Oh yes. For my Blanc de Blancs champagne. During fermenting, after racking, and then when aging, they are kept in separate casks, just as if they were going to be still wines. Before I make up the cuvée, the mixture for each of my special champagnes, I taste each wine vintage separately. Then I combine them in particular proportions to capture the best characteristics of each variety and balance them with each other."

"Then will we bottle the champagne today?"

Masson smiled. "We have to arrange for the bubbles first."

"And how do you put them in?"

"Ah, MAR-tan, that is the great mystery and challenge of champagne making! Since you seem truly interested in knowing, you will have to see this process for yourself. There is nothing like learning through doing, eh?"

Masson produced a glass jar full of pure white crystals and set it down on his laboratory table. "Rock candy!" he said, handing a piece to Martin while popping another into his own mouth. He weighed a portion of it on a scale, then took it over to a large steel pail and dropped it in. Then he poured a kettleful of boiling water over the crystals. And handed a long wooden spoon to Martin. "Keep stirring the sugar until it all dissolves," he said.

"But what is this for?"

"You have a very important job, MAR-tan. You will be making the syrup for starting the champagne. First, after it cools, we will add to it a few gallons of white wine. Then it will all go into the cuvée, along with special champagne yeast. The new yeast starts working right away on the newly added sugar in this second fermentation, so bottling must be done very soon."

"So that's how you get the bubbles!" Martin said. "From the carbon dioxide ..."

While their young helper stirred, Masson and Sergio and several other workers readied the cuvée and the processing equipment. When Martin's job was finished, Masson asked him to inspect all of the heavy, dark green champagne bottles to make sure they were perfect, even without any scratches. "Otherwise they might break under the high pressure," he explained. Afterward, Martin helped wash out the bottles and set them upside down, to dry on racks.

Soon the bottling operation was in full swing. Martin stood by and watched the line. One person filled the bottle midway up its neck, a second person checked the level and adjusted it if necessary, a third pushed in a thick cork using a cast-iron corking machine, and a fourth applied an agrafe that straddled the cork and clamped over the bottle lip.

Masson showed Martin how to pick up bottles as they came off the line, set them temporarily in a basket, then carry them over to the tirage racks, where he would place them carefully on their sides.

"How long will they stay in here?" Martin asked as they worked together.

"Several years," Masson said. "This is the stage when things can really go wrong. Not many vintners produce champagne because it is a difficult and time-consuming process. And dangerous too! One needs to be a real master to know exactly how much syrup to add to the cuvée to achieve the second fermentation."

"But what can happen?"

"If you miscalculate the amount of sugar and have too little, you will not get the effervescence people want with champagne. But too much is worse, for the bottles will explode!"

Masson pushed up the shirt sleeves on both arms and displayed several scars to Martin. "These are some battle wounds," he said almost proudly, "which I got while learning to make my own champagne. Sometimes I had many explosions—like the battlefields now in France where mines are going off and enemy artillery is shooting. That's why men working around bottles with fermenting champagne should wear gloves and goggles, even a mask and a heavy vest."

"Do bottles still explode here?"

"Not often now, unless I start experimenting and vary my formulas, to see if I can get a different kind of champagne. And even if I don't change any ingredients, occasionally something will go wrong. Or maybe a defective bottle breaks from the pressure inside."

"What happens in the next stage?" Martin wanted to know.

"Let me show you, boy. After the wine in the bottles has finished the second fermentation, it is allowed to age some more. But see this—" He took a bottle from a long rack and showed it to Martin. "Notice that large indentation at the bottom? That's called a 'punt.' It strengthens the bottle and also lets you grasp it firmly with several fingers inside the dent." From another group of racks he pulled out a champagne bottle. "Now see that stuff inside the bottom? Those are dead yeast cells. If they were left in there, the champagne when it's poured will be cloudy, not crystal-clear as it should be. So the yeast has to be removed. But it has to be done without losing bubbles and wine. When the temporary cork is removed, they will come rushing out. Want to guess how we stop the bubbles?"

Martin thought about it for a while. "The yeast would have to be taken out all at once and very fast, and the bottle corked again right away," he ventured. "But how do you do that?"

"Come over here, MAR-tan," said Masson, ushering him over to a rack with two slanting vertical wooden boards with odd-shaped holes in them. The boards were joined together at the top, forming up-ended triangles. He then picked up several empty champagne bottles and set them into the holes. "Notice how they can fit in this rack at different angles, first almost horizontally and then more and more vertically. By gradually changing the angle of the bottles in the rack from horizontal to vertical, sediment will gradually end up in the neck, which by then will be upside-down. But it has to be shaken down from the sides, patiently, bottle by bottle. This process is called 'riddling.' Once or twice a day a riddler comes along, sticks his fingers into the punt of a bottle and shakes it sharply, then turns it slightly to the left or right before setting it back into the riddling rack. But when I said 'it' I should really say 'they,' because of course he does two bottles at once, using both hands, moving across and down each rack. In a few hours an expert riddler can do many thousands of bottles. It's an amazing sight."

"How long does the riddling go on?" Martin asked.

"Well, boy, for several weeks at least, sometimes a month or more. The champagne maker—and here, of course I am the chief—keeps checking the yeast crystals, and when all appear to be gathered together down in the neck, the champagne is ready for the final stage: disgorging."

"And that must be when you take the yeast out!" Martin said, intrigued.

"We put the bottles neck downward in dry ice, and when the 'plug' with the yeast in it gets frozen—it takes about ten minutes—the bottle is upended and we quickly open it, let the pressure of the carbon dioxide in the wine shoot the yeast plug out, add the *dosage* to finish it, then in the next second insert the final cork, using that old hand-corking machine over there that I brought long ago from France."

"What is that ... *dosage*?"

"It is wine that refills the bottle but also may add something: more syrup, maybe even a touch of cognac. Champagnes are classified according to a range from dry to sweet: from *brut* and *sec* to *demi-sec* and *doux*."

Masson then showed Martin a sample of the final product: a bottle beautifully labeled, with a foil wrapper all around the cork at the top, with the metal agrafe clamp securing it. "And now, MAR-tan, you know why champagne is so expensive when it has been made the right way!" he commented.

"I'd like to drink champagne sometime," the boy announced as he turned the bottle admiringly around in his hands. "Maybe some of this champagne we are starting to make today."

"And you shall!" Masson said. "With me, I trust. When you are a little older, MAR-tan, it will be ready for you."

7

Tasting the Wine of Life

FIFTEEN-YEAR-OLD MARTIN had never attended a wake after someone died, but he thought that the experience might be rather like the scene he witnessed up at Paul Masson's mountain. It was the autumn of 1919. Helping out with some cellar tasks, he couldn't help but notice how the mood of the place had turned tense and glum.

He knew why, of course: National Prohibition was now heading Masson's way. During the vintage period, when he came by several times, the boy had been acutely aware of a frantic effort to get as much wine as possible fermented and into casks before the whole operation might have to close down.

As Martin finished up the day's work, the Frenchman invited him to drop by the chateau for refreshments before going home. Soon he was sitting with his glass of lemonade out on the terrace. He listened while the winemaker gallantly tried to insert gaiety into his conversation with several male friends who had dropped by apparently to commiserate with him about his predicament.

"Paul, what will you do now that Congress has passed the Volstead Act?" one asked. "I know you hoped that wine would not be included in the restrictions."

Masson gazed silently over at his vineyards and, beyond them, down at the great valley of orchards and vineyards and ranchland below. There fingers of fog from the coast were inching their way through gaps in the dark mountains to the south. "I can always sell grapes to people who will make their own wine," he finally replied. "And who knows, maybe they will make ever better wine than mine! Though of course they would be jailed as criminals if they tried to sell it."

He now laughed bitterly. "Imagine what the French are saying these days about the unsophisticated and puritanical Americans! Well, now that the war is over, they will easily recapture their lost market here—though of course their wines will be contraband too, only for under-the-counter sales. And we were really starting to produce some fine wines here. . . ." At this he sighed with regret.

Martin knew that at the polls in last year's election California voters had again defeated a measure to institute statewide prohibition. But several months later, the state legislators, ignoring their constituents' mandate, decided to ratify the 18th Amendment anyway—thus providing the next-to-the-last vote needed for the two-thirds of states required for adding a new constitutional amendment. How Martin's mother had rejoiced!

So a few months from now, on January 16, 1920, National Prohibition was scheduled to begin. The Volstead Act would reinforce it through federal agents working locally. Actually, prohibition had officially gone into effect a half-year before this date. President Woodrow Wilson had earlier signed a wartime measure enacting total nationwide prohibition until the war was over. And though by now an armistice had been declared between the warring nations, the war was still not officially ended, since a peace treaty had not yet been signed. Officially, then, cessation of alcohol production had begun in July of 1919, this past summer. Winemakers like Masson, however, had mostly chosen to ignore it for the time being, still convinced that beer and wine making would be exempted. But their last remaining hope had just been dashed by the passage of the Volstead Act, over President Wilson's veto. California's legislators would not likely defy it, in spite of some vintners' lingering hopes.

No wonder Masson seemed to be at his own funeral! For in spite of the vintner's giant efforts to spare them banishment, wines were included on both the hit lists—one temporary, the other seemingly as permanent as the U.S. Constitution itself.

"Won't you at least be able to make wine for yourself?" one of the visitors asked Masson.

"Oh yes. The law at least will permit me to do that, as a private citizen. The head of a household can make up to 200 gallons—a generous enough allotment, to be sure. A thousand bottles a year makes about two and two-thirds bottles a day for home consumption. I shall try to live with that. But the parties ... ah, they will be difficult to handle. I must ration my champagne very carefully! No more than a bottle per day." He poured more champagne into his guests' glasses—but sparingly and even reluctantly, Martin noticed. He was already conserving the scarce supply.

"But how will you make a living here? Pay your expenses?"

"I must let many of the cellar and vineyard workers go, which will make us all very unhappy," Masson said. "I am hoping, though, that my champagne will bring in a little income. Friends of mine in Washington have succeeded, it seems, in getting me a special license to produce it. But strictly for medicinal purposes ... the only way I can remain legally bonded to make wine under my own firm's name. Of course some wineries in thick with churches have licenses to produce sacramental wines. It is too bad that I am not an avid churchgoer! A close friendship with priests would have been handy at a time like this. Now my wife—" At this, he stopped talking and sighed.

Martin felt deeply sad, witnessing this abrupt decline and probable fall of the Frenchman's great winemaking career in California, brought on by the National Prohibition specter. He also knew he wouldn't be coming around here much in the future. For what would there be for him to do?

Martin was still sitting there after the visitors had gone, when the autumnal sun slipped quickly behind the mountains to the west. The sky above was still bright, a pale turquoise, with streams of pink and violet clouds reflecting the hidden sun as it sank below the horizon, toward the ocean. Below them to the east, though, the fog had expanded and thickened. The valley was completely obscured by now, becoming a wide white sea upon which the last sunlight glinted. Here and there, nearby indigo hills protruded up through the fog like small floating islands. But the fog was creeping closer every minute, rising higher as it climbed through the canyons, toward La Cresta. Already Martin could feel wisps of damp chill in the air.

"Ah, MAR-tan, you remain here to keep me company!" Masson observed. After pouring more lemonade into the boy's glass, he sat down next to him. Apparently he still wanted to talk. "California vintners sold a lot of wine in the past five years, with the war in Europe cutting the importation of French and German wines," he mused. "I was so consoled when America got into the war, to spare my homeland from further destruction. But as a consequence, it seems we winemakers have lost our own separate war, just to stay in business!"

"Can nothing more be done to stop Prohibition from including wines?" Martin asked, feeling helpless in trying to console this man who always had seemed so strong, so invincible.

"I am afraid not. . . . Well, boy, at least I fought the good fight with all the weapons I had. Serving on state commissions and industry committees, giving speeches, writing articles, talking to politicians, journalists, influential people. For years. And I am very tired." His eyes sought the wild mountains above and beyond his premises. "Now that the Drys have won out, I perhaps should take to the hills. Maybe become a revolutionist, just to keep my land and way of life."

"Can I join up?" Martin asked. "I'd rather be here than any-where else!"

Masson's hearty laugh was good to hear. "Ah, MAR-tan, I hope I will still know you when you are a grown man! By then maybe this foolish Prohibition—they are calling it a 'Noble Experiment'—will be over. I could certainly use someone like you around here. Maybe when you finish high school, eh? Though I suppose you will want to go on to college."

To Martin that seemed a long time from now, though it was only several years away.

"And one of these years too I want to be able to share a bottle of my wine with you," the Frenchman mused. "In France, of course, even small children may have wine with their meals. But here, more than ever before, I would be committing some crime!"

Martin thanked him. "I'm looking forward to that day," he said. And he would—not only to drinking the wine, whether sparkling or still, but also to the privilege of sharing it with Paul Masson, its maker.

Actually, young though he was, Martin by now already had drunk some vintage Paul Masson wines. How did this come about? Down the street from his home in San Jose lived a German musician named Ed Schneider, famed in his day as a composer. And Schneider happened to have a son named Allen, just Martin's age. Additionally, Schneider reputedly had one of the town's fin-est wine cellars. While composing, he set a bottle of wine atop his piano and then would pour from it, taking long, meditative sips from a glass as his creative spirit soared.

The two boys became close friends. Martin often joined the Schneider family on picnics. His and Allen's role was to cool the riesling bottles in the icy waters of a nearby creek—winning a glass or two of these and other ambrosial wines as their reward. Head-ing homeward, they'd sometimes stop for a time at the Schneider brothers' ranch. To Martin this place, called Sans Souci, seemed haphazardly husbanded, especially compared to his grandfather's orderly ranch. So when he asked what the name meant and was told "without care," he was horrified that they actually would flaunt its lack of care on the big sign over the entrance gate!

Martin's favorite reminiscence of the elder Schneider was of the time when Sergei Rachmaninoff came to the college. Before the concert, the internationally renowned composer-pianist dined with his old friend Ed Schneider across the way. And of course they generously partook of the noble contents of the host's fabled wine cellar.

Everyone was assembled in the concert hall. But tension

mounted as Rachmaninoff did not arrive. Finally, after what seemed a wait of hours, down the main aisle came Rachmaninoff and Schneider, their arms entwined about each other's shoulders. They weren't actually singing, but there was a slight sway to their movement.

Then, to everyone's astonishment, when the celebrated Russian guest artist mounted the stairs to the concert stage, he failed to stop there, where the Steinway awaited him. Instead, he continued right on up the steps to a balcony high above, and there emerged, looking down on the audience with a happy, satisfied smile. Someone had to rush up and escort Rachmaninoff back down to his assigned place on the platform.

Martin always delighted in recounting this episode. And he said that, inebriated though he was, the great Russian gave a truly glorious performance!

Initially, Martin's friend Allen took no interest in his father's liquid treasures though he had free access to the wine cellar. Yet when Martin spoke excitedly of helping to make wine up on Paul Masson's mountain, Allen's interest flared. "My father has a lot of Paul Masson wines," he disclosed—and then invited Martin into the cool dark basement to see them.

Martin's friend launched the tour. First the German wines: the rieslings, rheingaus, mosels. Then on to the French: burgundies red and white; first-growth clarets in fabulous array. And, moving away from the European wines, viewing dusty old cognacs and rare single-malt scotches. Never having seen such bottles before, Martin was fascinated. He decided he should learn more about the rare alcoholic beverages they contained.

"But didn't you say he had some Paul Masson wines too?" Martin asked. It was worth a heap to Allen just to see Martin's face when he led him over to the place where Schneider kept his hoard of Paul Masson wines. He particularly favored them, his son said, for their supremely rich, unique flavors. Martin was knowledgeable enough to explain that their superiority was doubtless due to the great grape varieties in their blends, their mountain source, and of course superb winemaking.

Schneider had an amazing selection of Masson vintages, from years back. "Which one do you want?" Allen asked. "Just take your pick!"

Martin knew right off. "This old Paul Masson 1904 Burgundy," he declared, fingering a dusty bottle. "Because that's the year I was born." Besides, he knew that it was a splendid vintage; and so prized that even Paul Masson no longer possessed a bottle of it!

His friend was a tease. He removed two 1904's from the wine

rack. "If you can drink one without stopping, I'll give you the other one."

Easy, thought Martin—not having the least idea what he was up against. (After all, he'd only had sips of wine in cellar tastings at Masson's.) They carried the two bottles outdoors, and after the cork was pulled, Martin took a deep breath and began to drink. How astoundingly rich, powerful, spicy, those first swallows! Though overwhelmed at the flavors, he couldn't stop even to relish the wonders of this glorious wine—having to drink onward.

Almost at once it was too much to continue. But he simply had to earn that other bottle. When he'd finished half the bottle it was a wild struggle to keep on. Impossible ... he was gagging. But with fierce determination he gulped on, gasping for breath. And finally he made it—to the last drop, sediment and all. Then reeled, keeled over, and threw up. Staggering into the hot sunlight, he hurled himself down on the grass, his chest heaving. He didn't know it was possible to be so retchingly sick.

Allen was sorry it had been so bad. "Gee, I just thought it would be sort of funny," he said, gingerly handing Martin the coveted bottle. Martin clutched it savagely to his chest. By God, he'd won it, anyway—the rare Paul Masson 1904 Burgundy he'd so coveted.

By the next day Martin felt it was well worth it—a thousand times over. With a soft cloth he polished the bottle, fondly studied the old label, held the bottle against the light to exult in its heavy density, for not a glint came through the dark green glass. Now being the proud owner of this treasured bottle, he suddenly felt the loftiness of growing into man's estate. From now on, life was going to be different. And so it was.

To educate themselves further in viniculture, the two boys began lifting occasional bottles from the cellar. At the library Martin would look at the few books they had on enology, and surreptitiously read them there. He would not have dared to take them home with him, even if he hid them under his bed.

Occasionally Ed Schneider suspected that his store of wine was diminishing faster than he'd remembered it from his last cellar visit. "Say, are you two kids making off with any of my wines?" he'd ask. And they'd look at him blankly, in all innocence. He never could be sure, since the cellar was so extensive and he kept no inventory.

Because of his own experience—limited though it was—in Masson's vineyard and cellar, Martin already had some knowledge of what to seek when tasting and comparing wines. And drinking them. The drinking of wine somehow deepened the boys' perceptions and loosened their thoughts and tongues. As adolescents do, the pair held long philosophical discussions: What was the meaning of life? Of death? Is there an immortal soul? At the same time, Martin began verbalizing his dream of realizing his innermost ambition: someday owning a mountaintop like Paul Masson's, with vineyards in the sky. It went without saying that he would make wine there.

"Mountains must cost a lot of money," Allen said.

"I know," Martin replied. "That's why I must find a good way to make that money first."

Before long, the word spread around among the college students: those two boys across the street were a veritable goldmine of wines! So Martin and his friend were invited to many off-campus parties by their college acquaintances. Of course they were expected to bring along some bottles of wine with them.

As with generations of youths behind and ahead of them, rules about alcohol use were simply ignored. Did it matter that most of them were under twenty-one? With Prohibition here, illicit drinking seemed even more enticing. Some of these older fellows drank heedlessly and indiscriminately whatever alcohol came their way—which shocked Martin, especially if they did so with wine he'd brought.

Martin's exuberant spirit always made him a hit at these parties. Having been readily accepted by the college crowd and mature for his years, Martin really viewed himself almost as a college student himself. Already, he was bustling around with a variety of enterprises that brought in cash, which was not so much spending money as saving money.

And much faster than he'd expected it, the time came for his own college years.

8

Farewell to Boyhood

IN THE LATE SUMMER of 1922 Martin Ray began making his farewells to relatives and friends. Soon he would be going away, to register at the University of Washington. He'd decided that was the right learning and social environment for him. The Pacific Northwest had sounded to him like an open-minded, youthful place, still almost a frontier—and not at all subscribing to Bible-based rules about thinking and proper behavior. Surely it had room for a young fellow who had no money yet, but had plenty of energy and ambitious plans to get some.

His mother of course had wanted her eighteen-year-old son to stay at home and attend "her" college, a safely Methodist haven. Actually, the College of the Pacific was scheduled to move soon to Stockton, in the San Joaquin Valley. Firmly entrenched in the college "family" by now, Mrs. Ray planned to go with it to Stockton and set up another boarding house for students. So if Martin had decided to attend the college, he would be removed anyway from the Santa Clara Valley he loved.

Martin long had known that he should eventually get away from the overly religious atmosphere surrounding his mother, which always threatened to suffocate him. He'd never dared to tell her that, through the years, he often went up Paul Masson's mountain to help with the vineyard and winery work. (In his later years Martin purposely avoided any connection with Christianity, particularly Protestant fundamentalism, which he blamed for its negative influence regarding wine drinking and, in particular, for the destructive effects of Prohibition upon American winegrowing. His mother and brothers expressed their disapproval when eventually he became a winemaker, and refused to sample the wines he proudly made.)

As for Martin's grandparents, life for them hadn't been as full or happy ever since their daughter departed with her boys for San Jose. Her intended move even farther away, to Stockton, came as a real blow. Melvin Lovejoy's heart condition was becoming disabling. Hired help was costly, and in any case it wasn't a permanent solution—as passing on this ranch and this way of life to grandchildren would have been. Whatever future dreams and plans the Lovejoys had once harbored seemed doomed.

Throughout his high school days Martin had come as often as possible to assist his grandparents. But they knew that, like his older brothers, he aimed for college—and doubtless a profession removed from farming. If Martin had wished to become a rancher like his grandfather, things might have worked out very differently for them. (For a while longer they struggled to make ends meet. Finally selling the ranch, they moved to a small house in nearby Los Gatos, where they spent the remainder of their years.)

For the past months Martin had been busy—first finishing up his high school classes, then working at summer jobs close to home, earning money to pay the first tuition installment and also sustain him in his first weeks on his own at the university. Once in Seattle, he would get part-time employment.

Martin, who hadn't been up to La Cresta for some while, kept putting off his parting visit to Paul Masson. He knew the winegrower was coping nowadays with the disastrous effects of Prohibition on his business, and there wasn't much for Martin to help out with.

Of course the chateau and vineyard ranch high up in the hills still occupied the heart of Paul Masson's life. In past years, the French winemaker's blazing social life, recounted by journalists, had tantalized innumerable readers with descriptions of glorious dinner parties given up at the winery—meanwhile dropping names and innuendos about former occasions too. But gone now—perhaps annihilated, if indeed he ever fully existed (for Martin had never really seen him)—was that legendary bon vivant of yore.

Last time he'd been up there, Masson's mood had been doleful. Unable to lift his spirits, Martin felt awkward and depressed. He also suspected that more than Prohibition was bothering the vintner.

With only a few days left before his departure, Martin, having borrowed his grandfather's car, finally made his way up to La Cresta. It was late afternoon. There in the cellar he encountered Paul Masson busily directing his men in preparations for the oncoming vintage season. Masson seemed delighted to see him—though he eyed Martin's jacket and pants dubiously.

"No, Mr. Masson, I've not come to work today!" Martin said.

"Though I wish I could. I've just come to say goodbye."

"Goodbye?"

"I'm going off to college in a few days. To the University of Washington."

"How wonderful!" Masson exclaimed with a nostalgic look in his eyes. "Sometimes I think my years at the Sorbonne were the happiest in my life."

Perhaps, Martin figured, he was contrasting his carefree student days, when he possibly envisaged a glorious future in American winemaking, with the misery brought on recently by Prohibition.

"Let us walk together over to the chateau," Paul proposed, taking Martin's arm. His pace was much slower than his accustomed stride when Martin had first known him, and his breath seemed labored. "The sun is still too hot," he commented as they reached the house. "We will go inside."

Entering the spacious livingroom, Masson motioned toward a chair where Martin was to seat himself. "Excuse me for a moment, MAR-tan," he said, "while I get a bottle of champagne so we can suitably celebrate your becoming a college man!"

Martin remained standing, however, while awaiting the Frenchman's return. His eyes roamed over the room, noting the various views from windows, looking at mementos on tables and shelves, at art work upon the expansive walls. He was particularly interested in a large, elegantly framed photograph featuring a bevy of attractive girls arrayed in Parisian-style, turn-of-the-century garb and poses. At the center was a vivacious brunette, obviously the leader of the group. Now who might they have been in Masson's life? For surely there was some reason for them to be featured thus in his chateau.

Martin was still examining the photo when Masson returned with two glasses and a champagne bottle resting in a bucket of ice. After Masson set things down, he began twirling the bottle around to cool it quickly. "Well, I see you have an eye for female pulchritude, eh, MAR-tan?"

"Who are they?"

Masson laughed. "The Floradora girls. That one in the middle is Anna Held. Have you heard of her?"

"I don't think so."

"Well, in her day she was a famous performer. She sang and danced and acted all over America."

"And you knew her?"

"Oh yes. A little. Sooner or later I probably met all French people well known here! She first came to San Francisco years ago. That's when . . ." His voice trailed off, and Martin caught a reminiscing twinkle in his eye.

Then Masson laughed. "So you never heard the story about how she took a bath in my champagne?"

"Did she really?"

"That's what a lot of people seemed to think," he said. "And I had no reason to persuade them otherwise. It made good publicity for me, certainly. . . . Ah, MAR-tan, those were the glory days in the wine business!" exclaimed Masson, his face animated in reverie.

"So what happened?"

As he talked, Masson kept twisting the bottle around in the ice. "Well, Anna Held already was renowned for taking milk baths. So after she tasted some of my champagne at the Palace Hotel, she told people she was going to get me to give her a bath in it. The ultimate honor, I guess." He shrugged with amusement. "Later, she sent me this photograph of her troupe. And now when visitors see it here, naturally they ask me about that bath." He grinned at Martin. "I just smile and say nothing. Keep it a mystery. It adds spice to my reputation as a notorious roué."

"But wouldn't it be an expensive bath? And an awfully cold one too?" Martin asked.

"Yes! Too cold even for a hot day in San Francisco—even if the champagne wasn't iced," Masson said. "Which reminds me . . ." He removed the champagne bottle from the bucket. "Now, MAR-tan, I want you to see the label on this bottle." He held it out. A Paul Masson brut champagne, which meant the driest one, Paul's favorite ...

Could it be? "Is this the one I helped mix the rock-candy syrup for a few years ago?"

"Yes, it is. I made a special note in my cellar book reminding me to serve you some when it was ready. We disgorged and bottled it a few months ago. So you have come visiting at a good time! And now, MAR-tan, since finally you are about to drink some champagne with me, I expect you to open the bottle."

He handed Martin a white linen handkerchief and the agrafe opener. In the past seven years Martin must have seen Masson open up a few dozen bottles. Always he had watched him closely, memorizing his every move. He felt a bit nervous now as he took the tool with its small egg-shaped wooden handle and carefully yet quickly pried off the clamp while pressing the thick cork firmly with his left thumb. The cork, released, shot out into his palm, cushioned from its impact by the cloth, which also absorbed the explosive spray.

In less than a minute Martin had their glasses poured. "You are a champagne sommelier already!" Paul complimented him as he was handed his glass.

"I had a good teacher." For a few moments Martin held the glass up to the west window, silently admiring how the bubbles caught the afternoon light.

"Let us toast your new life at college," Masson now proposed as he touched Martin's glass with his own. After they seated themselves, Masson gave Martin a searching look. "So, boy, what do you plan to do with your university education?"

Martin paused for only an instant. "Find some way to make money. And then buy a mountain like this one. Like La Cresta."

Masson's face took on an odd expression, as if he didn't know whether to feel flattered or challenged. "But what need do you have for a place like mine?" he asked.

Martin never had thought much about a need, practical or otherwise. It was the ambience of a separate existence, a dedicated way of life, that attracted him ... as well as the wide perspective it provided on the world below.

Suddenly the telephone rang. Paul went to answer it. During the next five minutes or so he only mumbled a few words now and then while the caller talked at him, perhaps even ranted—for at times his eyes would roll and he'd hold the receiver away from his ear.

While Masson was on the telephone, Martin pondered his last question. This mountain he so loved—and in fantasies wanted for his very own: Did he really have any need for it ... or some other spot resembling it? Not now, certainly. He wouldn't be able to make a living in a place like this.

He well understood how Paul Masson needed his mountain for reasons quite different than mere money-making. Maybe this was what his question really meant. Masson certainly exulted in the physical work he did here in both cellar and vineyard. And then, of course, there was the scintillating social life the Frenchman had carried on over the years at this place, with its fabulous view of valley, bay, and mountains. . . .

"Goddammit, Adele, I can't listen to this anymore!" Masson suddenly shouted into the telephone mouthpiece. "I have a guest here!"

What was Masson's daughter saying to perturb him so? Martin often had wondered about his relationship with her, along with all aspects of his life, both private and public. Gossip had it that his home life through the years with a teetotaling wife was dismal, compared with the life he lived up at the chateau. To keep the spirit of romance alive, Paul had spent time with other women. Workers sometimes had whispered to Martin about seeing certain things go on.

But Masson had a Catholic marriage, designed for eternity, as well as a French marriage, arranged for practical purposes as a merging of business interests. To end it and marry again, partly in the hope of begetting more children would have been impossible at that time for a man in Masson's social class and business position. Anyway, Masson might now be too old and impatient to easily undertake raising a son (if he had one) and training him to be his successor. The right son-in-law would be a godsend: and he would have to come through Adele.

Masson finally banged the black metal earpiece into its cradle against the wall. "Damnation!" he said, clearly upset by the phone conversation.

"My daughter will be the death of me yet. . . . Oh, MAR-tan, let us go out to the veranda now that the sun is leaving. I do need the fresh air."

Martin picked up the champagne bottle and glasses. After sitting down in a wooden chair outdoors, Masson wiped his brow with a handkerchief, then sighed. "Adele is not good for my blood pressure," he commented. "My doctor tells me that I should not allow her to bother me. He thinks she does and says things just to upset me. Tells me I should just let her do whatever she wants, as long as it isn't too crazy or dangerous. But that I should never pay for anything beyond the monthly allowance I give her."

Martin didn't know what to say. Except there was something he'd been wanting to ask about: "Didn't Adele get engaged a few years back? Whatever happened?"

Masson winced for a second, then remembered the champagne glass that was at his side. Gratefully, with a shaking hand, he took a few sips, then plunged into telling Martin a history of his troubles with his daughter. Once in a while Martin offered a question or comment, just to show sympathetic interest. But mostly he just sat there and listened.

"People have always said that Adele strongly resembles me. If so, this is an odd thing, since she has always been so close to her mother, never to me. But I think they mean in our temperaments. She is determined, stubborn, quick to get angry. And passionate. Yes, she has my passion! But unfortunately it took a peculiar form when she was in high school. She decided she wanted to become the bride of Christ . . . to enter the convent and be a nun! That is what comes of going to an all-girls' parochial school. That and having a mother and an aunt who spent half their lives on their knees, in church, praying. She'd already taken vows as a novice before I heard of this. Naturally nobody had bothered to consult me about the matter: they knew very well what I would say! I was enraged and marched over to the parish house, where I had a great row with the priests. They sent me to the convent to see the mother superior, and I started in all over again, accusing them of seducing my young daughter, who was not old enough or worldly enough yet to know what was best for her life ahead ..."

Paul stopped for a moment to catch his breath. Martin sat on the very edge of his chair, fascinated—imagining how it would have been for those hapless nuns and priests to confront Masson in his fury!

"Well, the mother superior relented when she realized that I might make a public scandal out of the situation. I took Adele home with me. She wouldn't speak to me for weeks. A few times I invited some fine young men I knew to the house, for family dinners. My wife ordered me to stop, saying that Adele intended to adhere to the vow of celibacy she had taken as a novice. You can damn well imagine the bloody hell I raised then with the Catholic hierarchy in San Jose! They had taken my only child, and doomed her to a life without marriage or children. The priests of course told me how my behavior mortified both Louise and Adele. What right had I to blight my daughter's happiness in being married in spirit, if not in name, to the son of God? I had a father's right, I told them, and I was more father to her than they were, absurdly calling themselves fathers when they had no actual children of their own! And again I forced them to back down. They told Adele then that she was released from remaining celibate.

"My daughter had grown into a lovely young woman—with her curly dark hair and brown eyes. To try to make her happy I bought a house at Pebble Beach, with a glorious view of the ocean. I encouraged her to take art classes and other courses to keep her busy and help her meet other young people. And then her good friend Helen Barnett introduced her to a cousin visiting here from the South. It was love at first sight for both her and Lloyd, I heard! For the first time I could remember for a long time, Adele seemed really happy with me as her father—I, who had stopped her from becoming a nun!"

"And did you like Lloyd?" Martin asked.

Masson shot a fierce look right into Martin's eyes. "If Lloyd had been my own son, I couldn't have loved him more," he said. Which meant that in Lloyd he had found just the right person to help him in the business and ultimately succeed him.

"They got engaged only a few weeks after they met. When things are right, sometimes you move fast! I decided to suspend my rule about having family gatherings up at La Cresta, and put on a splendid engagement party for them, with all our friends and relatives attending. Louise even allowed me to serve champagne!" For a few brief moments Masson was quiet, with a smile on his face, happily immersed in the memory of that brief time of promise.

"Then Adele had the physical checkup that her mother thought she should have before the marriage. She wasn't sick. But the physician found signs of renal tuberculosis—a severe and chronic kidney disease, he said. He warned Louise and me it might be fatal. And he told Adele she'd never be able to live a normal life. Saying she wanted to be fair to Lloyd—for she should never risk having children—Adele decided to break off the engagement. When I heard of this, I got very angry. 'Wait!' I said. 'Maybe the doctor is wrong. Maybe you will get better.' But Adele has always been headstrong. She told me it was the only thing, the right thing, to do. And she reminded me that it was her life after all, not mine."

"So how did Lloyd take this?"

"Well, he was in such distress that he went off right away, joined the Air Corps, no doubt hoping to go to war and get killed! . . . Meanwhile, Adele spent many months in bed rest. Her Aunt Marie helped to build up her strength by administering formerly forbidden sherry and port. Miraculously, in about a year Adele's good health returned. Another physician told me later that her kidney ailment must have been misdiagnosed, for she would have died from what her doctor said she had!"

"And did she contact Lloyd then?"

"She wanted to. And she asked Helen to give her his address. Up till now she'd told Helen not to say anything about her cousin because the subject pained her so. Now she got a terrible shock: Lloyd recently had married.

"She told us only that she was taking a trip with some friends for a few days. What she did, I heard later from Helen, was get on the train to Alabama. When she arrived there a few days later, she took a taxi at once to Lloyd's new home. There at the door she handed her former fiancé a very expensive painting of a Carmel seascape, a vista they both had loved. 'Here's my wedding gift to you, Lloyd,' she said. 'I hope you will be very happy.' And then she rushed back into the cab and rode away."

Martin sat there, wordless, waiting for more.

"She wasn't home for long before she went off again, this time in her car and not saying anything to us beforehand. I received a long-distance phone call . . . from the Tiajuana police. She had crossed the border heading for God knows where in Mexico. For traveling companions she'd taken several of her cats—with no provisions at all for them. The car was a mess, and so was she. They put her in jail. 'Loco—crazy!' they kept saying to me. I had to go down to get her and bring her back."

"Is she all right now?"

"The doctors say she will never be—how did they say it?—'quite right.' That I should expect her sometimes to do strange things, say strange things. That there's not much any of us can do except be kind and patient and loving. And firm too, when necessary."

"And—she's still in her twenties?"

"Yes. I guess she lives quite a bohemian life in the city these days. Perhaps she enjoys herself. I doubt that she will ever marry now. But does it really matter, eh, MAR-tan? With this damnable Prohibition likely to go on for many more years, what could I pass on of much value to a son-in-law, to a grandson or two, except for my land? The winery and the winemaking business itself are of negligible worth nowadays."

Martin had noticed how Masson's agitation after concluding his conversation with Adele began to subside as he drank his champagne. By now Martin had refilled his glass several times, and his host had become quite calm.

"There's something incredibly soothing about champagne that makes the unacceptable more bearable," Masson remarked, as though reading Martin's thoughts. "It has become a great consolation to me during this whole Prohibition madness, as well as with all these problems with Adele!"

"And you can make champagne legally," Martin commented. Which meant Masson would always have plenty of it on hand.

"Oh yes, as a medicine for sick people!" Masson said heatedly. "For people with sore stomachs. For pregnant ladies. And for people with certain nervous conditions . . . like me! But it is only obtainable through doctors' prescriptions—and sold at pharmacies.... Is that any way to be a winemaker?"

Masson sighed. "There are no more Anna Helds asking for champagne baths, to be sure. The fun is all gone now. Of course I cannot publicly entertain customers as I used to. I would be considered not only an immoralist, but possibly a criminal as well!"

"But you still give dinner parties here, don't you?"

"Oh, now and then. But MAR-tan—" he looked at his young friend rather dejectedly—"you must realize that Prohibition has broken me. And of course I am growing old."

"Old?" . . . Doing some fast calculating, Martin figured Masson would be in his mid-sixties. That was still far from antiquity.

"Old in spirit now, certainly, because of this infernal temperance craze that has afflicted America. At least the federal government allows me to carry on part of my business. My firm has the only license to make champagne—but solely for medicinal purposes, as the permit states. If selling champagne to the public were easier, I would have a monopoly! Friends of mine in Washington just wanted to make sure I could keep on with my Oeil de Perdrix and the other sparkling wines they crave."

"But what do you do with the rest of your wine grapes?" Martin wondered. For Masson had many acres of grapes not used in making champagne.

"Well, it is amazing. So far I have been able to market them in advance, with contracts at good prices, to distributors in the East and the Chicago area. They ship them out on railroad cars and sell them—often right off the boxcars!—to people with permits to make wine in their own homes."

"But who are they?"

"Oh, many thousands of ordinary people who use wine as part of their daily diet. A lot of them are foreign-born—southern Europeans especially, like Italians. The government figured that since this habit was part of their culture, it was possibly harmless to them. So it gave them permission to make wine legally, but only for family use. Since they have to apply for permits, they can be watched by the enforcement agents. The head of a household can make up to 200 gallons a year. But he cannot sell any, even to friends."

"Do any home winemakers buy grapes directly from you?" Martin asked.

Masson gave a wry smile, which Martin didn't understand until he listened to what the vintner said next. "Sure they do. And some of them are former workers here. You remember Angelo. He helps take care of my vineyards in exchange for so many tons of grapes. Of course he gets many more grapes than the quantity he needs to make his 200 gallons. I don't ask him what he does with the rest. He may sell grapes to other people. Or he may even do some bootlegging himself—making wine on the sly and selling it to other Italians or outsiders who have heard he has some."

"But can't he get in big trouble doing that?"

Masson shrugged. "Maybe. Maybe not. But if he's doing it, it's on a small scale compared to what others are doing now. Bootlegging and rum-running are becoming highly profitable businesses. They can buy off many of the 'revenooers' who start investigating them. . . . Ah, MAR-tan, this Prohibition that your mother was so eager to have is corrupting the morals of America, instead of stopping people from drinking!"

Martin nodded in agreement. He was certainly seeing this within his own college-age crowd. "But what about other wineries? How can they keep going now?"

"Many have simply gone out of business. Ones with their own vineyards can at least sell the grapes, as I do. But some wineries are doing all right because they legally make and sell wine now for sacramental use—for the churches that use it in communion services, and in Jewish synagogues too. Not only wineries run by religious orders can do this, but also some secular ones—like Beaulieu in Napa, owned by my friend Georges de Latour. Other wineries can survive by making wine under contract for licensed ones."

"But are there enough religious groups that need wine to keep them in business? The Methodists I know don't use wine; they use grape juice."

"It would shock good Christian teetotalers to know how many religious groups have started up since Prohibition began," Masson observed with a smile. "Anyone who calls himself a minister can easily get a whole congregation of worshipers! And he can use his own livingroom as the church."

"But at least it sounds like you're conducting a paying enterprise here on the mountain," Martin said. "Which at first you were afraid you couldn't."

"Oh yes. It keeps the warehouse and office in San Jose going too." Masson's eyes swept over the vineyards below the veranda, and when he looked back at Martin his eyes were sad. His voice came slowly, painfully. "It just isn't the same, though. I cannot make all the still wines I used to make. To sell legitimately, anyway. Of course I always save some of my best grapes and make a small amount of wine for my own and my friends' use. I must be careful doing this, because inspectors are always coming by to check the cellars and count up the gallons of wine kept in cooperage."

"Do you think Prohibition will go on for a long time?"

"The Drys are stubborn," Masson snorted. "They think people will get out of the habit of wanting alcohol after a while, when it becomes increasingly difficult and costly to get it. They don't realize yet that Americans don't want anyone ever to tell them they can't have or do something. Especially their government. In fact, if someone prohibits something, they feel they must get it or do it! And they will, somehow. Even if they have to pay big prices for it from gangsters, risk going to jail, paying a fine ... or getting sick and maybe dying from it. There are also many people who simply want to drink alcohol—any kind of slop! We tried hard to warn voters and politicians about this, saying that our beneficial wines should be kept legal and available ..." The Frenchman's voice drifted off.

Martin wanted to get Masson's opinion of a growing aspect of this Prohibition era. "What about the bootlegging and gangsters you mentioned?"

"Well, a lot of people are getting rich—some very rich—from dealing with contraband: making, smuggling, transporting, or

selling alcohol. Prohibition is creating a whole new class of criminals." He said the last word rather ominously, and Martin felt a
sudden chill.

"Like what is being called 'the Mafia.' It's a wide and tight ring
of international crooks and killers. This Prohibition has played
right into their greedy hands." He looked straight at Martin. "And
sometimes I have to deal with them myself. That is what has become of the worthy profession of winegrowing!"

Martin drank the last of the champagne in his glass. Its bubbles had long since fled. He'd overstayed his visit, but sensed that
the vintner had needed to vent his feelings.

Martin stood up and looked toward the ink-blue mountains
beyond, silhouetted by the orange-red sky of approaching sunset.
Masson too arose and came to his side. As the sunshine departed
from the terrace, the air had become noticeably cooler. Martin
noticed that Masson was starting to look much older. His torso
was heavier than before. But it wasn't time that was aging him so
much as Prohibition. Surely the Frenchman sometimes felt utter
loneliness and a sense of futility.

Martin felt Masson's gaze upon him. "Well, MAR-tan," the
vintner said, "you still haven't told me what you would do with a
mountain like mine."

Martin gazed down at the valley, where the last rays of the afternoon sun spotlighted different patches of orchards and fields in
varying hues of green, golden, brown. "I'd live on it," he said.

"Even if you couldn't make wine?" Paul sat down again, heavily.

Martin looked directly at him. "Oh, I wouldn't want it now. Not
with Prohibition on. But someday . . ."

"Then make a lot of money first," Masson advised. "Land costs
much more than it used to, especially when men got it free just by
homesteading."

"I plan to be a millionaire by the time I'm thirty," Martin said,
smiling.

Masson chortled. "I will bet on you, boy!" he said. "MAR-tan, I
mean. For you are now a man, yes?"

He stood up—a signal for his visitor to go.

"Don't go off yet," Masson said. "We will go to the winery and
get a few bottles of wine for you to take with you," he proposed.
"They will provide the proper start for a man's collegiate career."

Accompanying Masson into the dark, cavernous cellar, Martin was struck again by how quiet and empty the building had
become. It used to be a hive of activity throughout the year—especially during the vintage season.

Outside the winery, Martin set the box of wine that Masson

had prepared for him on the ground. Then he held out his hand to his boyhood idol. "Goodbye, Mr. Masson," he said with a catch in his throat.

"Paul," the older man corrected him after he hugged him. "From now on, just call me Paul."

Martin was off. Going down the path, he heard Paul calling after him: "Be sure to come and see me, MAR-tan, next time you are home."

Martin wondered when that would be. Not soon. Seattle was far away.

PART II

SUNLIGHT AND SHADOWS

1922-1936

9

The World Beyond the Valley

THE CAMPUS AT THE University of Washington changed forever the moment that flame-haired lad with the happy grin arrived there in September of 1922. My own destiny would be shaped even more, in the days to come, by his energy and dreams. Even more so, in the years ahead—a half-century of them!

"That's Rusty Ray, from California—the one everybody's buzzing about!" a girl whispered in my ear as we stood together in registration line. She nodded her head toward a spot behind us.

For Northwesterners like me, the very name California held a special magic. So my eyes at once followed my new acquaintance's admiring gaze. I saw a young man about my age, wiry and tall, his face alight with enthusiasm, his hands making lively swirls as he talked. Occasionally he ran fingers through his sunstruck red hair as he topped off something he was saying with a rippling laugh. And when he laughed he showed flashing white teeth, the two front ones slightly parted, giving him a wonderful Tom Sawyerish look. So fresh-spirited, ingenuous, engaging ...

Like everyone else, I was at once enchanted. And I didn't even know him yet.

Well, it wasn't surprising to hear later that by nightfall he'd been pledged Deke, a top fraternity. And the next day he'd landed a job on the university's magazine, *The Columns*, to help pay his way through college. Afire with new ideas, Rusty Ray in a month was its new manager—virtually running the magazine.

And working on that magazine was how I first met that fascinating dynamo, Rusty Ray. Having literary and journalistic aspirations, I joined *The Columns'* editorial staff. I'd gone to a girls' prep school in California and had spent time in the Bay Area. These experiences helped create a friendly bond with Rusty, for I could readily tune in on many of his background stories.

Early on, he told me of his ambition to buy someday a mountain all his own, back in his home state—he already knew the exact location—and make superb wines while living there. Of course that clinched it: here was my dream man, with a sky-high dream!

But I already knew it was futile to keep my eye on Rusty Ray, though continued to anyway, along with many other girls. He was so confoundedly busy he had no time left for romance. He had so many deals going on that he could scarcely even attend classes.

Having figured out how to turn the monthly publication into a big product, he went to see the campus's business manager and asked for an incentive contract giving him all profit above a certain point—if anything above that possibly could be achieved. Unhesitatingly this officer granted him the contract, since the magazine never yet had earned a profit. He didn't know Martin Ray's business acumen and powers of persuasion.

"Don't bother with one-shot ads," Rusty instructed his student crew selling advertisements on commission. "Get yearly contracts, nothing less. They're just as easy to sell as a single ad. And really go for the big national firms, not the hole-in-the-wall shops that can scarcely afford the tiny ads the mag's been running. That way, we'll shoot sales up a thousand percent!"

Shortly the magazine's size exploded from a paltry two dozen pages or so to almost a hundred, with whopping full-page ads, largely from national corporations. And profits shot high above the contract level. From the financial headway Rusty was making, it looked as if he'd soon have money enough to buy that mountain he wanted!

Rusty Ray's limitless instinct for enterprise branched out in other ways as well. He organized several profitable theater program publications and got students to sell ads for him. He set up lottery candy boxes in sorority and fraternity houses. Something new and fun for us, they made big hits—and proved highly remunerative for him. He got whatever clothes and shoes he wanted free from the best stores in Seattle, just so he'd wear them and set campus fashion trends.

(Those who knew Martin Ray at college were unlikely to ever forget him—and afterwards they told tales to others of his amazing doings. Years later, someone in a social group was recalling college days. When Martin happened to mention that he'd been at U.W. in the '20s, the fellow was all agog. "Say, you must have been there at the time of the fabulous Rusty Ray! Did you ever know him?")

The lingering nick in my heart was somewhat smoothed over by my coming to know and like Rusty's pal and roommate, Walter Kamb, the magazine's editor. (As the two prospered, they soon were living in a choice apartment just off campus.) Stories Walter wrote were being published in affiliated college magazines around the country, giving him an aura of success and prestige. Walter's humor, having a savvy, satirical twist, made a hit in college circles. He played his role of Big Man on Campus to the hilt. His ego needed this boost of admiration: a thick veneer of sophistication and intellectualism hid his fear of being seen as a country bumpkin.

For I was gradually uncovering the insecure young man hidden behind the smooth surface, and felt privileged to be trusted enough to be shown the deep shadows there. Walter poured out tales of a miserable boyhood spent on an isolated farm. His immigrant parents hadn't appreciated his unique talents. They made him pick peas and carry slop to the pigs and couldn't understand his desire to go away to college. My sympathy surged out to him in waves, and in my presence he brightened, abandoned his biting cynicism, and miraculously emerged with a touchingly wistful glow. His need for attention and affection seemed insatiable—he'd surely starved for them as a child. And he convinced me that only I could satisfy it.

It was terribly flattering and romantic that Walter so needed me. Whereas the sunny, buoyant Rusty Ray needed me like a fiddler needed two bows!

We became a companionable trio. Often after working together into the night in putting out the new edition of the magazine, we'd go to some gathering spot close to campus—most likely a hangout where booze was served without any fuss to students. For those of us under twenty-one, there was no need to produce fake ID cards: after all, drinking in public had become illegal at any age.

Up here in the Northwest, Prohibition was regarded mostly as a nuisance to be ignored. Liquor flowed freely from the obliging underworld: bourbon, scotch, gin, beer, liqueurs. But wine? If Rusty asked for some, he was told that nobody drank it. He doubted that most residents of Washington state even realized that such a thing as wine existed. Later on, though, he found sources for reasonably drinkable wines made by Italians who lived in the Seattle area and sold homemade wines to friends of friends. But those dives that catered to the university crowd did not stock such products.

At the local night spots we college students tried out all the bootleg liquors urged upon us. They didn't taste good—and sometimes even made us sick. But knowing no better, we accepted them, preferring them mixed with sweet, fruit-flavored beverages and ice.

As with much else, Rusty Ray was an exception. Having already been introduced to the world of fine wines, he couldn't endure the revolting drinks the rest of us consumed around him.

He drank beer—poor but bearable. His sidekick Walter, though, drank everything, making wry faces and amusingly disdainful remarks all the while. As for me, I fiddled with the array of proffered drinks, taking a mere sip or two between dances. I went there, wherever it was, to dance. I loved dancing, and gave the drinks little thought.

By now it was becoming apparent all over the nation that Prohibition had spawned a monstrous rebellion. Traditionally free-spirited Americans didn't like being told they couldn't do something—even when their own elected representatives had voted for this new law. So what better way to protest than to simply ignore it, even defy it? Young people are inclined to challenge vested authority anyway.

The inevitable result was that traffic in all alcoholic beverages got delivered straight into the hands of the unscrupulous greedy. Mobster cartels were after money and power, and to get and keep them, such people did not hesitate to bribe, threaten, cheat, rob, blackmail, kidnap, maim, and kill.

The situation constantly worsened. Nobody could have become more alarmed than my idealistic mother, Ina Phillips Williams, a renowned suffragist who was one of the first women elected to the Washington state legislature. Wanting to close the unsavory saloons that had degraded and bankrupted family life for uncounted years, she had fought hard to bring on Prohibition. As a powerful public speaker, she helped the temperance crusade succeed in the Pacific Northwest. Determined to save millions of homes from the disaster of alcoholism, she was now in for a disillusioning experience.

From the sidelines Mother watched her four college-age daughters drink horrifying bootleg liquors with their friends. Our behavior, she knew, was being repeated across the country during these jazz-paced, raccoon-coated, Roaring '20s years. Nobody really enjoyed the contraband drinks. Yet for all but the rich there was little else but these frightful concoctions. Mother became so disturbed at seeing us drink such awful stuff she feared might be lethal that on at least one occasion she actually helped two of my sisters make gin in our bathtub back in Yakima. It might taste harsh, but at least it contained no poisonous ingredients!

Sometimes Rusty, brooding over his tasteless beer, would begin rhapsodizing to us about the glories of fine wine—and his dream of making great wines someday high on a mountaintop of his own in California, like Paul Masson. Then an impatient Walter might laugh and cut in, "Come on, Rusty, let's stick with the real world!"

I often marveled at how these friends could be so compatible and competitive at the same time. In many ways they had opposing natures. Rusty had a relentless business drive, yet in person was amiable and gentle-natured. Priding himself on his creative literary prowess, Walter styled his hardboiled manner after the newly popular tough-guy detective heroes. Somehow, though, the combination made effective teamwork.

Rusty put up with Walter's kidding. How could he make the rest of us understand about wine? We hadn't experienced what he had. He also came to realize that with each passing year of Prohibition, an ambitious dream like his was becoming more difficult to maintain.

Martin Ray learned more about the dismal prospect confronting winegrowers when he received indirect news of Paul Masson. It came about this way: U.W.'s President Henry Suzzallo had heard of course of the phenomenal Rusty Ray from California. He asked him to drop by his office for a chat and was astounded at the young man's potent organizational drive. Dr. Suzzallo was equally fascinated with Rusty's ultimate life objective: to make fine wines in a place much like Paul Masson's.

So on a trip south to the Santa Clara Valley, Dr. Suzzallo searched out the French vintner at his mountaintop ranch. He admired both the wines and the man who made them—so nobly enduring the blows delivered by the 18th Amendment. On his return to campus, he sent for Rusty, to report in detail about his visit to Masson.

Busy in his enterprising new life at college, Rusty inadvertently but inevitably had put distance between his current life and his past one. He hadn't made time to write to Masson and keep a correspondence going, as he'd intended. With so many irons in the fire at all times, he didn't go home for vacations and holidays, as other students did. His mother, anyway, had moved to Stockton along with the College of the Pacific.

So Rusty was eager to hear what Paul Masson was doing these days. Dr. Suzzallo had both good news and bad. Paul Masson had bought a very elegant home on 13th Street, in San Jose's fashionable Naglee Park area. The owner of this Maybeck-built house, a recent widow, knew that her friend Louise Masson adored it—and was unhappy over the commercialization of her own neighborhood. Sensitive to Paul's pinched financial plight because of Prohibition, she sold her home to him at a bargain price.

Dr. Suzzallo hadn't seen the house, but Masson's description made it sound marvelous. Bernard Maybeck's design had supposedly been inspired by photographs of a mansion on the Italian-Swiss border. The house, though, had Maybeck's customary

touches—the outside circular stairs, planter wells, many balco-
nies, and a livingroom with ceiling-to-floor windows of colorful
leaded glass that caught the sunlight in jewel tones. Rusty enjoyed
picturing Paul Masson living in this fairytale dwelling and hoped
it was lifting his spirits at this trying time in his life.

Then the bad news: Masson was having a tough time maintaining his business, despite the license to sell champagne as a
prescription elixir. Increasingly, sinister elements entered into and
then pervaded the wine industry. Big-shot bootleggers were taking
over the market.

Through East Coast brokers Masson still shipped wine grapes
in boxcars for purchase within railroad yards. But the high prices
that wine grapes commanded at the start of Prohibition began
to plummet as more farmers and speculators around the state
planted grapes. These low-quality and high-tonnage grapes made
far better long-distance travelers than Masson's thin-skinned,
tight-bunched, superb varieties. So Masson had been financially
pressured into grafting many of his vines over to such "shipper"
grapes—a decision he loathed.

Masson had complained in confidence to his visitor that he
knew all these worries were undermining his health. "And frankly,
Rusty, he seemed older to me than he says he is," Dr. Suzzallo
concluded. "I'm afraid Prohibition may kill your friend off, one way
or another."

As Martin listened painfully to this disclosure of woes, he
pictured Paul as he had seen him last, his sturdy figure standing
in an eternal pose—against the backdrop of the vista seen from
La Cresta, with the green expanse of vineyard at vintage time,
foothills and valley stretched out below, the vast blue sky vaulting
above them. He wished to God he might get through college sooner,
so he could go back to California and hopefully be of some help to
Masson. But such sentiment wasn't realistic. After all, how could
he ease the winemaker's situation? Only an end to Prohibition
would do it.

Rusty figured on recounting at dinner that night all he'd
learned about Masson's predicament, banking on Walter and me
to be sympathetic listeners. He furnished a special treat: Dr. Suzzallo had brought back for Rusty a bottle of Masson's burgundy,
made mainly from his pinot noir grapes, a gift from the winemaker.

"Just remember, this table wine is very 'dry,'" Rusty cautioned
us. "It may taste almost sour to you at first, particularly because
you're used to those sweet drinks made to mask those godawful-
tasting spirits."

Rusty expertly twisted the corkscrew to remove the cork and

happily poured the precious wine into the glasses he'd set before us. As we picked them up, he proposed a toast. "To Paul Masson . . . and the end of this damnable Prohibition!" We clinked our glasses with his.

Walter took the first sip and then another. "Wow!" he said. "This is powerful stuff!"

Rusty shot an irritated glance Walter's way. It was clear he didn't appreciate having the word "stuff" applied to Masson's wine.

"What did Dr. Suzzallo have to say about Paul Masson?" I asked Rusty.

"He thinks that if Repeal doesn't come before long, neither Paul nor his business may survive!"

"Not much chance for Prohibition to end, though," Walter remarked after he'd downed another mouthful of wine.

Rusty set his own glass down and just stared at him. "Why not?" His right hand moved onto the wine bottle as if to guard it from Walter.

"Too many people in positions of power have a good thing going for them with this Prohibition thing," Walter went on. "The nation's economy is booming with all the fast and loose big money around. Do you think people with the real power will easily let it go?" The expression on Walter's face deliberately turned tough, and he made sure that Rusty's eyes were upon him. "Anyway, when—or if—Repeal ever comes about," he announced, "nobody in his right mind would want wine. Whiskey and gin pack the real wallop. And that's what drinkers are after."

Then seeing he had hurt his friend—and he did cherish him— Walter hastened to relent. "Oh, I know how you feel about wine, Rusty. To you it's greatly romantic. Drinking it. Even making it, for God's sake! But as for getting into it as a business, to make any money from it . . ."

"Wait!" Rusty protested hotly. "I've told you often enough that I don't think of winegrowing primarily as a business. It's a way of life. And that's what I'm really after."

Walter's mouth screwed into a dubious pucker, as it did whenever he heard Rusty expressing idealism of any kind. When the two of them talked intensely of various money-making schemes they'd do together, he vastly appreciated Rusty's imaginative capacities. But this was different. He felt excluded, with a potentially lucrative future livelihood threatened.

"Well, Rusty," Walter said after draining his glass, "let's have some more of that priceless wine of yours now—and see if it's worth your dreams of glory!" Almost reluctantly now, Rusty wordlessly refilled our glasses.

"Most people would have to really educate themselves in learning to like a wine like this," Walter remarked. "And that's too much like work." He looked directly at his friend. "As you often say, if one has to work, he might as well make a lot of money at it. And you do want to make money!"

"Right," Rusty agreed. "But I was talking about making money as a means to an end. Making money by itself is no life. What kind of life can we buy with the money we make? That's what we must think about, both of us, for the future." Already he assumed I was going to marry Walter, for the matter of my earning a living wasn't included.

Silently now, we picked at the meal on our plates and finished the bottle of wine. Graduation would be looming up in less than a year, and each of us had a lot to think about.

Rusty stopped talking to us about his winegrowing dream. Walter must have thought that Rusty at last had become the complete realist he needed him to be, now and in the future. The two of them worked remarkably well together in making the college magazine a continued great success. Rusty's entrepreneurial skills depended on having a creative managing editor who'd maintain quality and readership interest. And Walter was a good editor as well as writer.

I sometimes wondered whether Rusty knew at all the Walter I knew, deep under that façade of callousness and pseudo-sophistication. It was a shell that protected his vulnerable interior. But so reticent was I about sharing this secret that I never spoke of it to Rusty. Men, I suspected, might never again respect or even trust a friend whose weaknesses were revealed, whether by himself or someone else. And just as Walter needed Rusty to focus on business deals, I would need Walter to make a success of his life—if indeed I married him.

Thus I never found out, till years later, that Rusty had a similarly sympathetic insight into the nature of this man who had gained our affection. In fact, like me, Rusty thought that he alone really understood him. Rusty had come to value Walter more than any friend he'd had before now, so he accepted and accommodated his various oddities, as close friends do. He also thought that I, an early "liberated" woman, might not choose to cast my lot in life with a man with a split personality, whose sensitive interior in time could burden me emotionally. As Walter's trusted buddy, he couldn't honorably say anything to me that would reveal his concern.

Meanwhile, I was sure that Walter's psyche was my exclusive province. I would rescue him from the brooding sadness of his early life and lead him forward into bright happiness. I felt flattered that I alone knew of his singular vulnerability. And always I was elated at those rare times when he dropped his reluctance to display his true feelings, saving them as secret treasures to unveil at supreme moments.

Walter and I decided to get married after graduation. I cherished the note he had written to me after our engagement, expressing his deep devotion.

> Dear One:
> I want you to know why you are so special to me—the only one in the world I feel this way about. Everyone else is a challenge to me. I have one urge: to pass them, show them up, destroy them—so that in the end I, I alone, can go on before. But, dear, I don't feel this way at all about you. You're completely apart, a goddess to me, whom I adore and cherish. And I will follow after you always. Promise me this, my precious one, that you will never, never let me catch up with you, that you will stay forever ahead. You must. I need you so much to worship, to light my way.

The indelibly premonitory warnings in these lines did not strike me at the time. Such as the frightful insecurity that propelled him to put others down in order to bolster his own frail ego. (He obviously would consider even Rusty an adversary.) But with my love and support, I knew, he'd outgrow that urge toward constant ruthless competition.

And as for Walter's urgent need to worship me: could that be such a bad thing? Yet when I showed the note to my best friend—who was to be maid-of-honor at our wedding—she startled me with her question: "So what happens if he gets the idea that he's caught up with you?" I had to laugh. She was always one to conjure up a fly in every honey jar.

Rusty, naturally asked to be Walter's best man, dutifully accompanied us to my home town to be part of the festive wedding party. But he was clearly impatient to be off to California, sometimes finding the pre-wedding dallying irksome. But the day finally came. And a charming wedding it was, in Yakima's small Episcopal church.

My parents hadn't really been eager to accept my wedding plans. "Why the big rush?" they'd protested before finally giving in to the inevitable. But my father kept a dear sense of humor about it despite all the solemnity, right up to the church door. As the wedding march struck up, he and I were about to enter and walk down the aisle, my arm on his. And suddenly he proposed, "Let's just disappear—run around the corner!" He had a twinkle in his eyes; perhaps he still harbored some hope that even at the church door he could divert me. (In hindsight, I recall that my normally taciturn father took an obvious liking to the best man but grumpily discounted the groom.)

At the ensuing reception, Rusty got away from us the first moment he could. "It's goodbye—just for now," he told Walter and me, embracing us both at the same time in his wide arms. "We'll get together again. Somehow. In California!" he then called out exuberantly from the window as he went on his way in his little blue Ford coupe.

I was surprised to find myself in tears. How close, almost inseparable, we three had been through our college years.

"I miss him already," Walter said, aware of this sudden large void in our lives.

10

Career Trials

AFTER MAKING A QUICK visit to his mother in Stockton in that early summer of 1926, Martin Ray sped off in his little Ford to the Santa Clara Valley. While staying for a few days with his grandparents in Los Gatos, he made a special trip over to Saratoga to visit Paul Masson at his mountain winery.

No more was La Cresta a place of bustling activity. In the wine cellars he broke the hollow silence by calling out for Paul. But only his voice came back to him, bouncing off the cold concrete walls. Finally Sergio appeared—older, grayer, stooped. "Mr. Masson is up at his chateau," he said after happily greeting Martin. "His doctor says he must not do the heavy work here anymore."

When Martin rang the doorbell, another person so familiar in his past let him in. Dear John Bussone! He gave him a sentimental hug. "Mr. Masson is napping," Masson's longtime factotum whispered. "Please seat yourself, Martin. I'll bring some wine for you to drink while you wait for him to wake up." It seemed like the hushed house of an invalid.

Drinking the white table wine that John had served him, Martin felt apprehensive. Perhaps he should not have come. Sometimes it is better to hold in one's memory the image of a hero at his prime.

But then Paul Masson walked slowly in. And when Martin saw the warm smile of delight on his face and felt that outstretched hand—its skin still leathery and seamed from a lifetime of work—he knew why he had come. This man had meant as much to him as any father could have. And all the respect, warm rapport, and potent influence were still there, just waiting to be revived.

"MAR-tan, my boy! You have come back at last to see me! How long has it been?"

"Almost four years, Paul. Four long years."

"And are you rich yet?"

Martin laughed. "Not yet, but I have strong hopes." He mentioned some of his financial successes during his college years.

"Ah, MAR-tan, what brilliant things you could do with a business like mine if we did not have this Prohibition thing upon us!" He spat out this hated word as if it were rancid on his tongue. "John, please bring me some of the wine that our visitor is drinking!" he ordered. Then with a naughty expression on his face, he told Martin, "Dr. Beatty tells me I must drink at least a quart of liquid each day. He does not specify what kind of liquid." And he laughed heartily at the joke he was putting over on his physician.

As Martin chatted with Paul about the difficulty of getting decent wine in Washington, he noted the Frenchman's corpulence and pallid skin. Did he no longer go out into the sunshine? He also saw that whenever Paul's face dropped its animation, he had an abstracted or even melancholic look.

"So how are you, Paul, really?" Martin dared to ask. "Dr. Suzzallo gave me a rather disturbing report a while back. Not just about your business, but indirectly about your health too."

"Well, boy, I am not as young as I used to be, that is certain. Oh, I am not an old man yet! Only sixty-seven. But my heart does not pump as well as it should, so the doctor forbids me to go up stairs—which means I cannot go down them much either. So that usually keeps me out of my cellars, of course. And I am supposed to stick to a rigid and very dull diet because of my high blood pressure and a touch of diabetes. Though of course sometimes—" he grinned at Martin wickedly—"that is simply impossible for a Frenchman."

"And how are the champagne sales going these days? Enough to keep you financially afloat?"

"They alone could never support this place and pay for family living expenses," Paul said, sighing wearily. "And since my champagne can only be sold in pharmacies for medicinal purposes, I've had a hell of a problem from the start. Naturally I had no sales contacts with druggists around the country. Fortunately I finally found one good agent who takes care of all these sales for me, telling people completely ignorant about champagne about how to handle it properly. But there are far worse characters than druggists that I have to deal with, believe me!"

As he talked about his business problems, Masson became increasingly agitated. He constantly rubbed his hands together, massaging the joints of his fingers that looked swollen and painful—arthritic.

"Criminals, you mean?" asked Martin.

Masson gave him a piercing look. "Yes. Some even wearing government uniforms! They can make good livings from looking the other way whenever people operating illegally—the whole bootlegging bunch—pay them enough. Those fellows often come snooping around here and at our San Jose warehouse and office, trying to catch us doing something against their rules. And of course always find something not to their liking. So to save my skin I must buy them off with cases of champagne."

"How awful!" Martin said—though he was scarcely surprised. No wonder Masson's health had deteriorated under such constant stress.

"And the grape that was going to be my salvation," Paul went on, "has ended up almost destroying me with problems."

"Which grape?" Martin wondered.

"MAR-tan, do you remember the one with such intense red juice that it looked almost black? Look—" Masson reached into his vest pocket and took out a fountain pen. Then he found a piece of paper, wrote his signature upon it, boldly and fluidly, and handed it to Martin. The ink was such a dark crimson that it was almost black.

"This is actually wine made from my *salvador* grape—that's Spanish for savior. Before Prohibition I had only a small block of it here, and some over at Almaden too. But my Italian workers who began making wines themselves discovered that only a little added to white wine would turn it a deep red. Many bootleggers, you may know, happen to be Italian. Their families traditionally know how to make wine, blend it, and fix it up if it's defective. And now they often know how to sell it surreptitiously. Well, to these Italian bootleggers a wine is not wine unless it is red."

Martin knew this well from his own wine-buying experiences in Washington.

"Also, you probably remember," Masson went on, "white wines are more difficult to make than red ones. So much more can go wrong. Besides, you can't make as much from the same quantity of grapes unless you ferment the skins within the must before pressing. But best of all for the bootleggers, they can mix a gallon of salvador juice to ten of water, add several pounds of sugar, and—*Voilà!* they have a bonanza in bootleg wine. So . . ."

"Everyone wanted your salvador grapes," Martin supplied.

"Yes, when the news of what they could do got out to the bootleggers around the country, demand for them became fantastic, much greater than I could supply. That first year, East Coast dealers bid such high prices that I shipped most of them out, but right away got into such trouble everywhere that I decided to give it up as too risky. I soon found out that just growing them became a life-threatening hazard. A couple of gangsters even came up here and tried to get me to tell them exactly where my salvadors were. Of course I said I had no idea, since I was not the vineyard manager. But they knew I knew. And that was just the beginning of the trouble ...

"Rival bootleg gangs began roaming through my vineyards here and the ones over at Almaden, searching for the salvador vines and getting into fights with each other over who had the right to steal my grapes. There were ugly scenes, I can tell you, and one man got killed. I began patrolling the vineyards myself. Someone even took a shot at me—and just missed."

"Really?"

Masson rose to his feet as if the effort taxed him, and then slowly walked over to a sideboard. He came back with a hat, handing it to his visitor. "Look at this, MAR-tan!" he said. "I keep it to show the sort of danger Prohibition has dumped on my doorstep."

Martin examined the beige felt hat, gingerly touching a singed edge of a hole at the crown. How often he'd seen Masson wearing it: out in the vineyards as he worked, or riding home in his car. "My God, Paul!" he could only say, horrified. "That shot might have killed you. And is this still going on?"

"Well, after that incident I hired armed men to keep thugs from stripping my vines clean, here and at Almaden. But I can't keep all the thieves out, even with round-the-clock guards. For it is no longer just grapes at harvest time they are after. They got smart and started going after cuttings. That way, any time of the year, they could graft onto vines that had no value to them, or root the cuttings themselves, and begin to grow their very own salvadors. Actually, the vines appear resistant to phylloxera, so a year can be saved if they are started on their own roots."

"I hope the champagne part of your winegrowing is safer and easier on you," Martin said.

"Christ Jesus no!" Paul protested vehemently. "Not that I've been shot at over it—yet. But because champagne is such an expensive wine, a luxury item, it is much prized by criminals. They get paid a lot if they can obtain it. We have had holdups at the San Jose warehouse. Truckers are afraid even to load cases for delivery."

Just then John came in with a tray. On it sat two wide-bowled glasses with hollow stems, and a tall dark bottle with a cap made of gold foil. "I brought this in honor of our visitor," John explained. "It is already iced."

Paul Masson Champagne. Martin gazed happily at the once-familiar wine label he hadn't seen for all too many years.

"Oh, for the love of God, let's have the champagne!" Paul Masson cried out.

How marvelous it was for Martin to hear these very words again, said with the same gusto as of old, in spite of everything the winemaker had been enduring.

After his troubling visit with Paul Masson, it took some hours for Martin to regain his buoyant spirits. By the next day he braced himself and set forth on his objective: to find some magazine or newspaper he might manage or even acquire. Drawing upon his excellent experience with *The Columns*, he'd then build it into a lucrative venture toward his ultimate goal—that mountain of his own, Prohibition or no.

In the following few weeks he canvassed the San Francisco Bay Area, probing into several likely publications—weeklies and monthlies, and one bimonthly—known to be seeking new management or buyers. But none of them seemed suitable for Martin's enterprising talents.

Coming back from our honeymoon, Walter and I expected to hear something from Rusty about his activities, reflecting his usual high-spirited and entrepreneurial nature. But no word was forthcoming—indicating that he was encountering difficulties. Rusty, we knew, never liked to acknowledge any problem if he had one, and certainly wouldn't want to pass it along. Meanwhile, Walter took a job on a Northwest publication. Starting our post-college life together, we were a happy pair.

Finally one day we received a cheery letter from Rusty. First, he informed us he was calling himself Martin to new people he was meeting, now that he'd left the campus and was back in California doing serious job hunting. He then reported a chance encounter with a friend of his from the past. He'd known Corky Chapman from his years of associating with College of the Pacific students in San Jose. Even in college days Corky was always self-confident, knowing exactly what one should do about any problem and how to do it. It helped that he was older than the other students. Now he'd developed into a rumored genius of sorts, the kind of fellow who knew everything and everybody and cultivated wide connections in the business world.

It was a great break, Martin said, to run into Corky at this particular time, when he was feeling so frustrated over not turning up any hot prospects. Hearing what Martin searched for, Corky told him that his finger was on the very pulse of Bay Area publishing. He'd check around and provide Martin with just the right situation. They'd meet next week, when he'd tell him how to proceed in his ambition to take charge of some publication. In the meantime, he was actually flying off for some deal-making in New York—derring-do that greatly impressed Martin. Only recently had small, fledgling airliners begun transporting hardy travelers to and from airports sprouting up in far-flung major cities across the nation.

So writing us now, Martin sounded elated about his much-brightened future back in California—since Corky could always be depended on for supplying sharp and practical ideas. He'd let us know as soon as possible what transpired. For he knew that Walter and I hoped he'd land a top-level position in a publication that the three of us could work on, as we'd done so successfully before. Or find one we actually might buy.

As an upshot of Martin's next meeting with Corky Chapman, one evening we got a phone call from him. He needed a fast decision: a letter would be too slow. First off, for background, he reported that Corky had given him a rundown on what he'd discovered. "I've been looking over the entire publishing scene here," Corky had said, "and I know precisely the magazine you should have—one that'll have a great future in your hands. *The Talisman.* It comes out of San Francisco, of course. And it's one of the oldest magazines in California. Once it was tops, but it's not much now. Definitely a lack of creative energy there! But it has a marvelous potential in these booming times in The City."

Martin somehow had missed that magazine entirely in his search for a possible acquisition. Strange. But Corky had commented on its poor publicity and distribution these days. So Martin was grateful for Corky's tip. Furthermore, his well-connected friend had assured him of help in getting a lot of advertising. "It's a cinch," he'd said. "I can put you in close touch with all sorts of important contacts. You'll make a whopping fortune out of it, for you've already proved you have the know-how."

Martin had jumped into it, making an appointment with the owner and publisher, a Mr. Harriott, for the next morning. Sitting by himself in the waiting room, he leafed through the latest issues of the magazine. Corky's assessment had certainly been correct: it wasn't much—drab looking and dull reading, with the possible exception of a long gossip-mongering column that Martin didn't bother to read. He then looked at gilt-framed covers of issues out of the past century that hung proudly upon the walls.

The Talisman definitely had potential, he decided. He knew he could rouse great attention by putting new vitality into this long-established magazine. For starters, it had a valuable and venerable founding date to lend prestige—1852, only two years after California achieved statehood. And its respectable enough circulation of 6,000 was printed on the masthead.

Finally Martin was ushered into the large, oak-paneled office of a silver-haired older man with a benign countenance. He didn't look capable of exerting much effort in improving his publication.

In fact, the whole office suite—dusty, quiet, antiquated—seemed preserved in a moribund condition, still encased in the 19th century. An elderly, stiff-limbed secretary was the only staff person visible. Here, if anywhere, was a crying need for the new generation's drive, imagination, and business acumen!

Martin soon learned that Mr. Harriott lived in the Santa Clara Valley. It turned out that he had even gone to high school with the elderly man's daughter! This gave him immediate rapport with Mr. Harriott. Which made it almost like dealing with a father.

Yet when Martin sounded him out about selling his publication, Mr. Harriott seemed far from eager. He had a strong sentimental attachment to it, he explained, so had never even thought of selling it. But perhaps he should consider it. His health was no longer excellent. "Give me a little time to think on it. Maybe you could come in tomorrow. . . ."

Next day, Martin met with Mr. Harriott again. As before, the owner stressed his reluctance to sell out. But after Martin told him how he'd build the magazine into something very special, something its former publisher would be proud of, the owner finally agreed to sell. "I know the magazine will prosper under the guidance of a bright and experienced young man like you," he said, smiling benevolently.

The price Harriott asked for was not exorbitant. But how much down payment? He wouldn't be too demanding, he said. A mere $10,000 would suffice. However, that amount, trifling to Harriott, seemed a fortune to Martin. With tremendous effort he had managed to save half of that. But Mr. Harriott wouldn't budge a bit. So their deal was off. Martin left, badly disappointed, for he'd expected to have the magazine tucked into his vest pocket by now.

Later, it occurred to him that by some off-chance possibility Walter just might come up with the additional $5,000. Then they would own and operate the magazine jointly. Walter of course would be wonderful at building up the editorial part of the magazine, making it strongly appealing to advertisers as well as new readers. And Martin thought of columns and features I might write for it too.

But Martin also knew Walter. No way would he have any savings to tap, even though he'd profited well on their business ventures in college. Walter always spent everything that came his way. ("Save?" he'd say as though the very thought was preposterous. "Just have to earn more. That's the only way to stay ahead of the game.")

So after much internal argument, Martin finally did phone us that night. And told us about the great possibilities for us all in *The Talisman* ... if Walter could put down half of the $10,000 needed. Could we get the money together somehow?

Walter and I, already afire to go to California to live, saw this magazine as the predestined chance for us to be a threesome again. So feverishly we went to work to raise that second $5,000.

Why shouldn't I ask my father? Of course he was conservative about spending, even tightfisted. But he had a good business sense and obviously had liked Rusty. So I telephoned him and told him excitedly about this marvelous opportunity. Just as I feared, he dismissed the whole plan as unsound, and strongly advised against our getting involved. Moreover, he distrusted all Californians—though he'd made an exception when he met Rusty, I remembered.

We had better luck with Walter's father, who as a hardworking farmer had managed to salt away some cash. Told about the long-established magazine and our great plans for its future, he said he'd lend Walter the needed money. And got his bank to wire it to Martin the next day.

So Walter and I packed our possessions in a flurry and set off to California—to the San Francisco I already adored. Nothing in the future ever had seemed so exciting to me.

A joyful reunion it was, for the three of us, in San Francisco. For the occasion Martin had managed to get a bottle of Paul Masson champagne—and with all the trouble of obtaining a doctor's prescription, it made quite an investment. We celebrated at the small apartment he'd found on Russian Hill. He'd even located a flat for us close by.

Corky lived in the vicinity too, so Martin had asked him to join us. The four of us had a genial dinner together. Corky told fascinating stories of San Francisco's past and of various colorful people he knew, whether achievers or eccentrics, artists or bankers. He gave us an exhilarating view of the kind of life we could fashion for ourselves here. Walter took a special liking to him from the start. Already we felt quite at home in that most glamorous of cities.

By now Martin had settled the deal with Mr. Harriott, and we quickly took over the magazine's office. Since the entire operation was in disarray, we spent many hours bringing order out of chaos. We couldn't imagine how the magazine had functioned at all.

Martin had left the office rearranging to us, for he had to launch his drive to acquire advertising from prominent businesses in the area. He returned late that first day, perplexed. The firms he had initially contacted had never heard of *The Talisman*, though it had been published in San Francisco for almost three-quarters of a century. This created a different problem from the one he'd confronted with the U.W. magazine. There, at least, if firms didn't know the magazine, they at least knew the university behind it.

Now Martin began the necessary next step: searching out and talking to firms that sometime in the past had advertised in the magazine. An occasional ad manager recalled an ad or two. But there was no spark of enthusiasm in the voice.

To make a strong start for the revitalized magazine, Martin must establish at least a few substantial accounts to provide credibility to the whole venture. So he phoned Corky. Now was the time he needed his influential contacts, so he could get the ball rolling.

At the moment, Corky was much too busy to talk. But he did briefly caution him: "Rusty, I can't really do anything until you've made the right initial start. Hook the smaller fish now. Then I'll help you land the big ones."

Corky's desertion gave Martin a bad jolt. So far he'd proven all talk and no help. Later, if things went right, he wouldn't really be needed.

So Martin went back to phone calls, to pavement pounding and cooling his heels in waiting rooms. As a seasoned salesman, he increasingly realized that something had to be wrong. How could a magazine with a sworn circulation of 6,000 be unknown to so many ad managers in mid-town firms? Sure, this wasn't a big figure, but it could represent a sizable segment of the business-related population in the Bay Area. Most were doubtless "upper crust" subscribers whom advertisers courted. Still, Martin rarely spotted *The Talisman* on magazine racks and newsstands, underscoring poor distribution efforts in the past.

Martin, baffled, now investigated the circulation files. He came up with a real shocker. Actual paid-up subscriptions numbered a measly one hundred! The whole deal was now thrown into a lurid light. What maelstrom had he gotten us into? The monstrous fear lay not so much in the low subscription figure but that the 6,000 circulation figure had been faked in the claim printed on the masthead.

Feverishly searching further, Martin found evidence that in past issues of the last years no more than a thousand copies had been printed. If so, how many had been actually sold? he wondered.

He saw he'd been foolishly unwary in accepting Harriott as a man of honor. Before signing the proprietorship transfer papers and making the down payment, he should have insisted upon going through detailed records.

In great alarm, Martin now phoned Corky to relate his frightful discovery. Corky was irritable. "For God's sake," he barked at him, "take it easy!" As he'd told him, the magazine was currently at a low ebb. So what if Harriott had fudged a bit on the claimed circulation figure? Or maybe he just had not gotten around to revising the correct figure of the past. Martin should accept the situation as a challenge. Instead of panicking, he should put zeal into hoisting the actual circulation into a figure that would impress the publishing community and have advertisers pounding at his door.

Martin then called Mr. Harriott. Naturally he expressed surprise at Martin's revelations. Surely he was mistaken. If Martin checked into the matter more carefully, he'd find that claimed number accurate. Martin didn't like the icy tone of his voice. Something was very wrong here!

But Martin persevered, determined to win out somehow against the dismal odds. Day after day, he kept on soliciting ad accounts. And when occasionally he did contact a firm that knew of *The Talisman*, the remarks he heard made him uneasy. Nothing specifically critical. But how to interpret certain veiled comments to the effect that this magazine wasn't what it should be? In any case, persons on the other end of the dialogue were unwilling to get their firms involved, ever or again, in spite of the change in ownership.

Martin was shaken. Great God, was there actually something sinister about the magazine?

Finally he encountered a real estate broker who spoke frankly. "Want to know the real truth, Mr. Ray?" he asked. "Harriott turned that fine old publication into nothing but a blackmail sheet." Martin, reeling with shock, hastily took a nearby chair. So that was the substance of the monthly gossip column he hadn't bothered to read!

The broker was a handsome man, but with his jaw set now he looked startlingly pugnacious. "I happen to know because Harriott tried it on me. He phoned to say he'd caught up with something in my private life that he knew I'd want to keep quiet. If I'd pay—and he named a staggering sum—he wouldn't publish the item in his magazine. But he had the wrong man when he picked me. I refused to go along with his blackmail ploy. 'Publish what you damn please!' I told him; 'I can take care of this myself.' And I did."

So Martin and Walter had been conned by an expert schemer—a horrifying experience for two young fellows just starting out on their own! Martin saw only too well how he'd been enticed into Harriott's trap. He realized it came partly from having known the man's daughter. In high school, she seemed to embody all female virtues.

So what could we do now? Martin decided that we should at

least try to retrieve the $10,000 down payment before calling it quits. But how? Working on the problem non-stop, he came up with the solution: we would put out a big special edition of the magazine, packed with advertising from all over the Bay Area. And make enough profit from this one expanded issue to recoup the down payment and make something from our investment before walking off into the sunset. . . .

He even figured out a theme to promote the edition as a collector's item. They'd call it the "Carquinez Bridge Issue," to memorialize the new steel bridge just being completed in 1927 to link the East Bay area with the north counties, across the Carquinez Strait, where the Sacramento River flowed into San Pablo Bay.

Miraculously, the idea took fire. Martin now rounded up tremendous sales in advertising space from all around the San Francisco Bay area. Meanwhile, Walter and I fattened the issue up with all kinds of special features. We'd get back our precious ten thousand for sure!

And when the magazine came out, it made a big hit on the newsstands and with columnists. We even began wishing we could stick with it, since we had already radically, and successfully, changed the magazine's image and reputation.

The advertising receipts were pouring in. That's when Harriott appeared at our office. Only Martin was there at the time. Incredibly, the former publisher demanded all monies taken in as his proper due. Apparently the shrewd schemer had seen through our plan: having learned by now about the magazine's shady past, we'd be taking flight after retrieving what we had initially given to Harriott.

Martin, his blood boiling over such evil trickery, told Harriott exactly what he'd found out about him and his blackmail sheet. We were cutting off right now, and would not turn over a single cent of this money that we, not he, had earned. Harriott should be plenty satisfied with the $10,000 he'd tricked us out of.

Harriott's face hardened into a sinister mask—hardly the visage of the amiable and genteel fellow of the earlier negotiations. "Every cent that comes in here is mine. Or else I will really fix you. Do I make myself clear?" His narrowed eyes glared at Martin.

"You can't threaten me like that, after what you've pulled on us," Martin said. "I'll take legal action. I want to see what a judge and jury do with a cheating blackguard like you!"

Giving Martin one final look, Harriott departed.

The situation was appalling. Fortunately, Martin told himself, we'd already paid off all the printing costs, so no money was owed to creditors. Enraged, Martin phoned Corky to let him know the outcome of this magazine venture he'd so highly recommended.

After hearing just a few words from Martin, Corky exploded. "What do you expect? You're chickening out of a deal. Do you actually think Harriott would let you out without paying him for all the trouble you've caused? You just used the magazine to make a big flurry . . . and now you're dropping it back into his lap." Refusing to listen, he hung up on Martin.

Martin sat there, stunned, He'd have to seek a lawyer at once, not only to take the business dispute to court, but also to advise him regarding Harriott's implied threat to kill him. So he got up and charged out the door, greatly perturbed.

A half-hour or so later, the middle-aged lawyer was drumming his fingers on his desk as Martin went into details of the story. Suddenly he interrupted. "Young man, I must warn you now: This is no idle threat. I happen to know a lot about Harriott. If you fight that man, he can and will have you bumped off. So I advise you to get out at once . . . even though you lose everything you've put into the business."

He looked intently but kindly at Martin as he spoke further. "Better to be alive and broke than dead. Just move on now. Put it behind you as an invaluable lesson. For never again are you likely to be victimized in business. What you've learned from the whole wretched experience will assure far greater success for you in the future."

That night Martin told Walter and me of this succession of scenes. We too felt shattered. It was almost impossible for us—naive young products of university life—to believe that a whole community of intelligent people would knowingly tolerate the presence of such a rank villain!

In spite of what had happened, Walter still maintained a friendly association with Corky Chapman. He told me he did so not just because he liked Corky, but he also valued Corky's wide business and social contacts—which could prove useful in the future.

Yet whenever Walter mentioned Martin's name in his presence, Corky would cut him off. He clearly blamed Martin for making a fiasco of what might have been a highly promising enterprise for the three of us. Once, when Walter began telling him of what both the realtor and lawyer had said of Harriott, Corky blasted forth with a final denunciation: "Martin was foolhardy from the start. He should have checked in advance to find out if anything was wrong with the deal. But he had the temerity to blame *me!*"

Astonishingly enough, not long afterwards it did pay off for Walter to have kept his friendship with Corky. Dashiell Hammett had begun earning enough from writing detective stories to consider leaving his advertising manager position with the Albert Samuels jewelry firm in San Francisco. Hearing of this through one of his many connections, Corky arranged for Walter to meet Hammett. In the following week Walter took over Hammett's job.

Sometimes the two of them lunched together. (Actually, Walter lunched while the late-rising Hammett breakfasted.) And because I occasionally joined them, I too came to know Dashiell Hammett. I was especially impressed by his breakfasting upon pigs' feet!

By now I'd found an interesting job too, as a personnel officer at the Emporium department store in downtown San Francisco. So Walter and I soon shed the magazine debacle with all its anguish. Walter never did repay the money borrowed from his father, but Rusty eventually did so himself, since he felt he'd gotten us into the bum deal.

Martin did not shake off that profoundly traumatic "learning experience" as easily as we had. And he still had more to learn from adversity.

11

Into the Fray

AFTER TAKING SUCH A blow in the journalism world, Martin wanted no more of its unsavoriness—ever. But where to turn? One thing was certain: he must find a trustworthy route to making money. A well-established firm far beyond any question of solidity and repute. He would work *only* for such a place.

So he pondered this premise. What was the top prestige name in the world of high finance? Decidedly, the august investment firm of J. P. Morgan. For him its fiscal integrity stood apart from all others in America as though possessor of a glorious, ancient lineage.

He must go then to New York City and work for J. P. Morgan—none other. But how could he get there? After the magazine plunder, he had scarcely any savings left. He did have his old Ford coupe, which he'd sell for whatever he could get. And so he did.

Then he counted all the money he had. Just enough for a ticket to New York and for several days' subsistence until he'd get his intended job. But he could make it. Risky? Of course. But he was always convinced that if you wanted something enough, you must be willing to take risks to obtain it.

So he caught the next train to Manhattan. The morning after his arrival, he hastened to Wall Street. Suddenly, from across the street he sighted it—the impressive entrance to the banking house of J. P. Morgan. He stood there gazing at it, feeling intimidated. Finally with a tremendous shot of courage he rushed across the street, dodging taxicabs, and stepped up to the imposing door. There he made himself and his purpose known to the uniformed guard who opened it.

"No, you may not enter," he was told crisply. "We do not receive people here for employment interviews. Only clients are permitted to come in." Whereupon the door closed abruptly.

Stunned, Martin stood there for a moment. As he walked along

Wall Street amid the rushing throng of New Yorkers, he slowly collected himself. What would he do now? Send a letter. No time for that. But he might try to call them. Yes, that was it! He found a phone booth, dialed the J. P. Morgan firm's number, and asked—in what he hoped was an authoritative tone—to speak to their personnel director.

It worked! He was connected. And it turned out that the personnel chief sounded wonderfully human. Martin told him briefly how he'd just come all the way from San Francisco for this one objective: to work for J. P. Morgan. And he added enough background color to intrigue the man.

"Do come in to meet me," he urged Martin. "I'd like to talk with you. I'll send a runner to the door to let you in."

And that's how Martin got an interview with the personable personnel manager at Morgan. He had to tell the young, red-haired fellow from the West Coast that when the firm hired newcomers, which was rare, usually they were sons of important clients—who well might pay for this initial banking experience rather than be paid.

As they talked, though, the humane executive grew so interested in this ambitious and energetic lad from California that he said he'd really like to have him come and work for them. He would make a concession: pay him a nominal sum. But he added a realistic caution: Martin would simply be unable to live in this costly city on that stipend unless he had an outside income. Did he have one?

Of course Martin did not. So he had to decline the kind offer.

The man was disappointed. "But I'll tell you what I'd do if I were you," he said, brightening. "There's a young brokerage house out in San Francisco that's doing a top job. It's called Blyth & Company. You should go right back there and get a job with them. It would be a splendid opportunity. You're just the sort of fellow who would go far with that firm."

The man got up and held out his hand to say goodbye. "Do keep in touch with me, Martin. I'll be eager to hear of your progress all along the way." (And they did correspond over the years. Martin was always grateful for such excellent advice given at a crucial point in his life.)

But getting back home turned out to be another horrendous experience. First off, Martin didn't have a ticket back to San Francisco. After all, he'd arrived in Manhattan intending to land a job right away with J. P. Morgan. He had only enough money to get by for a few days. And already he'd run up hotel expenses. He called the railroad station and learned the cheapest fare to San Francisco, then counted his cash. He would just make it by leaving at once

... and skipping out on his hotel bill. (He could—and did—repay them later.) Not a cent remained, though, for buying any food to eat all the way across the continent. Could he go through with it? He'd never experienced going without food for more than one meal, and this trip took almost five days! But being an indomitable fellow, he made a quick decision—and caught the train.

Later, when remembering that trip, Martin could never decide just which day without food caused him the greatest torment. Each held its special agonies. By the time the long trip was half over, he was getting numb to his ever-weakening yet still ravenous state. On the following day, he found it almost impossible to walk steadily toward the men's room. But he made it there. And glory be to God! There on the ledge sat a big fat apple—the most luscious sight he'd ever seen! He grabbed it and was about to take a bite when a small boy emerged from the tiny toilet compartment. Martin panicked, for the apple was surely his.

"Here, let's play catch!" Martin found himself desperately proposing. Smiling, summoning up what little energy remained in him, he tossed the apple carefully into the boy's hands. "Now throw it back, like this." He had to show him. The boy laughed, delighted to be playing a ball game on the confining train.

"Whoever drops it loses it," Martin then announced. And of course the boy soon missed. "So I get it!" cried Martin happily. He began devouring the apple at once—all the while keeping up comments about the art of catching. Noting the boy's beaming face as they left the room, Martin couldn't help but wonder whether the apple actually had been left by someone else.

Anyway, he felt that the apple had saved his life. For the food energy from it enabled him—barely—to step off the train, unsupported, onto the platform and then make his way into San Francisco.

Martin knew that, once back in town, he could count on us to revive him with food and affection. But dreadfully weak, and lugging his weighty suitcase, he found it almost impossible to walk up the ever-mounting heights to our Russian Hill place. The only thing that kept him going was the prospect of the joy he'd feel when we'd open the door and he could fall into our arms—saved!

That evening, I was frying chicken in our apartment kitchen, with the door closed to keep smoke from the livingroom. Corky Chapman, here to have dinner with us, was telling some tall tales to Walter in his usual theatrical way. Through the closed door and above the kitchen noises I heard his voice suddenly raised to a high pitch. Evidently he'd reached the dramatic climax to his story. "You good-for-nothing! So you've turned up again like a bad penny! Nobody wants you here. Get out!" And then I heard a door bang somewhere. I wondered vaguely what all that was about, but was too busy cooking to give it further thought.

By the time I emerged from the kitchen with the serving dishes, Corky's story had ended. Only then did I hear that Martin had come. Corky bragged how he'd blasted him and ordered him out.

Rusty here—and sent away? He deserved a warm welcome from us, always. (And of course at the time I knew nothing of his starvation ordeal.)

I was outraged. "I don't care what your relations are with Martin," I stormed at Corky. "You have no right to send him away from *our* home! Please leave at once." So ended my own dealings with him, for all time.

"But where's Rusty? Where could he have gone?" I demanded now of Walter. I was furious at him too for permitting Corky to push our friend out into the night. "He may have nowhere to go, since he gave up his apartment when he left for New York. Something went wrong there for him. That's why he's back." I slipped on my coat and headed for the door.

"Don't be an idiot," Walter said. "He left at least fifteen minutes ago. It's dark outside. He could have gone in a dozen different directions. But wherever he's gone, he'll make out. He always does. So he won't need you mothering him!"

I was too angry to be fully rational. "Did Rusty get to say anything before Corky slammed the door in his face?"

"He yelled, 'Go to hell, both of you!' Is that any great solace to you?" Walter was again a college boy hiding behind the sardonic face. I knew he'd been shocked by Corky's behavior, but things happened too fast for him to come to his senses and intervene. So now he hid his shame by acting indifferent.

I rushed out the door and automatically ran over to Rusty's old quarters—for where else could I look? Thick fog enveloped Russian Hill. His place, when I got there, was dark, deserted. It had been madness to hope I'd find him there, maybe sitting on the entrance steps. Madness altogether to go searching for him through the foggy night.

I collapsed right there on the steps myself. Desperate, frustrated, I began to cry as I banged my fists on the brick steps, absurdly calling out, "Rusty! Rusty!" Only the moaning foghorns answered, far below on the bay. Where oh where could he have gone? Deep within me I was certain he was in dire distress. And had come to us, his best friends, for help.

It was a long time before I learned what had actually happened to Martin that night. After his experience at our place, we hardly expected him to have anything to do with us again. So we did not see him for some while.

It took months before Martin could bear to recollect any part of that trying week in his life. After being turned away at our door, he made his way downhill slowly, step by step, in a state of shock. He was so weak that the effort of carrying his bag threw him off balance. He staggered and fell. There he lay, so spent and shattered that he could not move, even when he tried.

A policeman driving a patrol car spotted him and picked him up. The officer at first assumed he was intoxicated, probably from boozing in a local speakeasy, and planned to deposit him at the drunk tank. But as Martin managed to mumble a few words of his story, the officer realized something was awry and took him instead to an emergency clinic. There he was hospitalized. Given nourishment, after a few days of expert care he was almost back to normal.

But the demoralizing experience of that night remained perhaps the darkest disaster of his entire life. Famished, exhausted and disoriented from days of traveling, and deeply disappointed over his failure to get the job he sought, he had come home—to be verbally assaulted by an enemy and then virtually turned away by his closest friend. This physical collapse would make him vulnerable to future stresses.

But Martin Ray was still a young man. Twenty-three years old, he had a full life ahead of him yet, beckoning him forward. His resident resilience rebounded with his physical recovery. He lost no further time in looking up Blyth & Company—that successful young brokerage firm so highly recommended by the J. P. Morgan man.

He entered a firm vibrant with activity, buzzing with highly charged young executives whom he liked at first sight. And they liked him too. He told them right off how highly the Morgan executive had recommended their company, which greatly pleased them.

They explained to Martin that they dealt only in blue-chip securities. Nothing less. And they themselves backed certain bond issues that met their standards. This Martin Ray who had just walked in their door, with his intelligence, energy, and winsome personality, seemed definitely created to be among them.

So he was hired and put to work at once. The initial training period had him studying securities, in all their forms and ramifications. He loved it.

Martin Ray found Blyth & Company all that had been described, and more. Everyone in the brokerage firm was doing well indeed. Just being part of such a successful business increased his self-confidence, his stature.

This brokerage career, Martin now realized, had been the right place for him all along. He had simply taken a few side trips before finding it. Here was the position, the work, in which he could make the kind of money he would need to buy that mountain world he aspired to have someday.

After emerging from a concentrated learning phase, Martin was ready to sell bonds. Selling, of course, had always been his forte. He had a natural gift for it, though he often claimed to dislike it. So in no time he was outselling most other bond salesmen around him.

The firm then appointed him to serve as their representative in the San Jose area. That's when he actually began living in the grand old Vendome Hotel. It was an incredible attainment for a lad who'd grown up in the Santa Clara Valley, revering from afar this palatial hostelry.

Martin considered the Vendome the essence of luxury. So did all the other brokerage-firm salesmen who lived there. Since they had practically taken it over, inevitably it reflected their fast-paced lifestyle. Every night was a celebration, differing according to their mood, what was going on in town, or which of them had pulled off the most stupendous deal of the day—in which case he footed the hefty bill. And each salesman had a rotating collection of attractive girlfriends.

A few women who held prestigious jobs in the business world were Vendome residents too. For instance, Elsie Bauman Howell. She was an executive secretary with the most time-honored title company in the entire region. Charming, sexy, beautiful she was, and with something more—terrific character, which lit up her face and expressed itself in the way she moved.

Elsie was the only woman who'd ever instantly attracted Martin Ray. But she showed no interest at all in him. How could it be that no mutual attraction caught fire, he pondered—when he felt so powerfully drawn to *her!* Twice he tried for a date, but was put off. Yet she clearly didn't dislike him. She seemed as much at ease with him as with anybody else. So what was the problem?

"Elsie Howell?" one of Martin's friends said when he asked about her. "You might as well give up trying. She's our virgin queen, you know. Has no intention of getting married, ever. So she makes a point of avoiding any man who appeals to her."

"But she's such fun!" Martin protested. "And is so attractive. What's her prejudice, anyway, against marriage?"

"Nobody has yet been able to figure it out. And believe me, the best of us have tried. Elsie just won't discuss it, even with the other gals."

Martin heard that each day huge bouquets arrived at Elsie's

hotel suite—plus boxes of chocolates, exotic fruits flown in from Hawaii, and so on. Apparently all came from a suitor she didn't consider a threat, a wealthy, older bachelor type who didn't care for the married state himself. The man also obtained orchestra-seat tickets to whatever concerts, plays, and ballets Elsie expressed an interest in, escorting her to all such events. They both liked the arrangement fine.

"Well, I'll be damned!" Martin muttered when he heard of this association. It made him all the more determined to break down Elsie's barrier against him. Unlike the other salesmen, Martin wasn't much of a wild-oats type. For the first time in his life he felt like getting married—with Elsie Howell his choice for wife. And no other would do.

After pondering the problem from all angles, he decided his best hope was to put on such a rush courtship that she'd be swept off her feet and married to him before she quite realized what had happened. So he sketched out a wonderful plan in his mind. But was delayed in launching it because Elsie Howell's firm sent her to New York for several months. His impatience as he awaited her return was somewhat abated by several distractions.

Walter came to see him. Since the ugly incident with Corky, Martin had seen both of us at a few gatherings with mutual acquaintances, where the two old friends somehow eased back into conversation. But this was their first one-on-one meeting in many months.

Walter had become increasingly restive over his advertising job. It was all right, but lacked the glamorous appeal and big income he'd heard Martin's work gave him. Martin had even been profiled in the business news as a new sales phenomenon. So Walter was thinking . . .

By now Martin had put aside the hurt and anger he'd felt over Walter's passively allowing Corky to yell and throw him out. His friend just didn't have a fighter's makeup. Many wonderful things had happened in his own life since that dismally low point. So Martin was cordial, treating Walter as though nothing ever had gone amiss between them.

Yes, said Martin after they'd talked together. Walter might well fit into the brokerage business. So he accompanied him to Blyth & Company's headquarters in The City and introduced him about. Walter soon joined the firm. After the customary study period, he began the actual bond-selling and discovered he not only did well but liked the work very much indeed. As his old friend Martin had thought he would.

Walter's new association with Blyth & Company was but one of the happenings in Martin's life that occupied him during Elsie

Howell's absence. A momentous event that deeply concerned him in that same period did not involve Martin directly. It was something that took place on Paul Masson's mountain.

On April 5, 1929, as he emerged from the Vendome, Martin glanced as he always did at the newsstand's offerings. He was shocked at several newspapers' bold headlines. "NIGHT RAID AT MASSON WINERY!" Martin quickly picked up several different papers.

"Funny that the papers just got around to writing about this now," the newsboy commented as Martin paid him.

Standing right there on the sidewalk, Martin scanned the articles. Wines at Paul Masson's mountain winery had been stolen during the night of April 1—several days before. Only yesterday was the story released to the press by the local U.S. attorney's office. The G-men had wanted to keep it quiet while they sought the culprits. But no one as yet had been apprehended.

Masson himself had been interviewed too—though he sounded reluctant to say much. Apparently a gang of desperados had spent a whole night on the premises, "ransacking Masson's collection of rare wines and spirits." Something was wrong here: Martin knew of no such collection within either the winery or the chateau. Paul normally kept prized wines at his home, bringing them up to La Cresta as needed.

Of course he knew Paul was always worrying that something like this would happen to him. Several weeks earlier, Martin had invited his old mentor out to lunch at a wonderful small French restaurant in San Jose, which permitted Paul to bring in his own wine.

Martin again had been alarmed at signs of Masson's continuing poor health and increasingly agitated condition. "You need some relief, a good rest away from Prohibition, Paul. Why don't you take a trip to France?"

Paul looked at him darkly. "Why does everybody want to me leave town right now?" he asked angrily. Martin wondered whether this "everybody" was primarily Mrs. Masson urging a vacation trip to Europe. "Certainly a change of scenery would be good for me," Paul went on in a tired voice. "The people I must deal with get worse all the time. You cannot imagine now terrible they are!"

Martin had seen enough of what was going on everywhere regarding the illicit traffic in alcohol to realize that the winemaker was bound to be at the nervous edge of a great deal of criminal activity. "All around me in the Santa Cruz Mountains are moonshiners and bootleggers," Masson complained. "And rumrunners hang out in coves all along the coast. Every man carries at least one gun. I hear shots all the time, even near my house in San Jose. What do those damn temperance people, surrounded by drunks and gangsters and dead bodies, think of their Noble Experiment now?"

For a while that day the two men discussed the dangerous absurdity that Prohibition had become. The San Jose area, renowned as a region of high liquor consumption in the pre-Prohibition past, made enforcing the Volstead Act notoriously difficult. Nine years into the Dry period, city backstreets harbored hundreds of speakeasies; rural communities sheltered bootleggers of wine and spirits. It was simple to find purveyors of any desired kind of imported alcohol—so long as you paid dearly for it. Prohibition was not so much ignored as openly defied.

How could law-enforcement agents possibly be effective in the midst of the public's wholesale rejection of the 18th Amendment? "Revenooers," the hapless federal agents on the scene, pitifully understaffed and grossly outnumbered, often succumbed to bribe-taking. An "If you can't lick 'em, join 'em!" attitude prevailed among the local police and sheriffs' departments. The monies coming from the contraband traffic grew ever more huge. Even the local Lincoln dealer was in on it, producing a custom-made fleet of bootleggers' cars with heavy-duty back springs and specially constructed trunks that would hold a dozen cases of liquor bottles or wine.

"Well, Paul, at least making champagne legitimately keeps you safe from the worst gangsters," Martin ventured.

"Safe? *Safe?*" Masson's voice got shrill. His large hands were trembling almost violently as he rubbed his swollen, arthritic knuckles. "MAR-tan, if you only knew . . ."

Now carrying the newspapers with him into his office nearby, Martin sat down and reread their stories about the armed robbery. That ominously incomplete sentence of Paul's echoed back at him. If he only *could* know what Paul was keeping back from him: he was sure that would provide the clue to the recent raid.

Martin mentally summarized the articles' reports. Eight burglars impersonating federal officers, wearing uniforms and badges and carrying firearms, had invaded La Cresta in the early evening. They had cut the phone lines at the foot of the mountain before driving up that narrow, twisting road. Ten Masson workers, gathered together at dinnertime, were taken captive and kept indoors, under guard, for hours in the kitchen.

Meanwhile, the thieves went about their work. First they ransacked the chateau, then they broke the locks on the winery and removed wine barrels and perhaps other things. Apparently hoping to find hidden treasures, they had even taken axes and crowbars to floors and walls in the chateau. Before going away, they had released, unharmed, the winery employees. When they went off, they took not only some wines and liquors, but Paul's gun collection and even some furniture. And since their own two trucks couldn't carry all the loot, they'd loaded up Masson's Ford truck too and gone off with it.

Masson hadn't been there at the time, safe in his San Jose home. But next morning, as soon as he learned of the heist, he'd hurried up his mountain to survey damage and missing goods. Then he began detailing some of his losses and estimating their value. He initially estimated that the value of the stolen goods might exceed $100,000.

The crime was under full investigation, reporters had been assured by the U.S. marshal's office. But why not the county sheriff's office too? Martin wondered. Well, apparently G-men were handling the case because Masson contacted them first; the hijack involved a federally bonded winery and the robbers had impersonated federal officers.

Martin wondered now what he could do to help Paul out. He might at least provide companionable moral support to the troubled winemaker, whose mountain sanctuary had been invaded by reckless crooks. So right away he phoned Paul at his home and asked to visit him.

"Ah, MAR-tan, that is so very kind of you! But I feel right now that I should stop talking about this to *anyone*. The whole incident is getting so mixed up in my head, and all those reporters are driving me so crazy I cannot even leave my home." His voice sounded unusually tired, perturbed, strained. Martin did not want to push himself upon Masson, who was obviously still in shock.

In the ensuing days Martin read more news stories about the heist at the winery. Some of them smacked of sensationalism, and of course there were the usual mentions of past flamboyant doings on the Masson mountaintop. But he noted how the facts and figures in the case kept getting revised. The value of the stolen goods went from a high of $400,000 down to a mere $7,000 or so. Finally reporters on the track of new leads and information, obviously frustrated, abandoned their efforts. There was little further mention of this story—which initially had been featured on front pages as the most sensational Prohibition-connected event in the whole Bay Area.

Well, Martin, still curious, would have to wait until Paul Masson felt like talking to him about it. Then he might learn about what had really happened on the night of April 1st—April Fool's Day.

Soon, to his vast relief, Martin could set aside as a major concern in his life this latest calamity that Prohibition had visited upon Paul Masson. For Elsie Howell had come back from New York.

12

Commitment Making

ON HIS WAY TO work one morning, Martin Ray ran into Elsie Howell at the Vendome Hotel's entrance. She looked more ravishing than ever. Holding his verve in firm control so as not to scare her off, he casually asked about her New York stay. What all did she do? See any plays and musical shows? This led to a lively conversation—and in the midst of it he suggested that they have a quiet dinner together that night so he could hear more. He knew a quaint little French restaurant way out in the country she might like . . .

And Lord be praised, she accepted! He then asked if she could make it early. They'd start before sunset, so on the way he could show her vineyard slopes all lighted up by the setting sun. That caught her enthusiasm. She'd love to see all that—especially after the concrete and steel, big-city scenery of New York.

Great God! Well, here was his chance at last to initiate wooing. Yet the world was now spinning round so fast Martin couldn't remember the big courtship plan he'd worked out in detail before she went away. It was to be a rush affair, anyway ... he was going to sweep her off her feet. That seemed like a terrific plan at the time. But now, just how to implement it?

As the hour approached, he kept turning the bottle of champagne being cooled on ice. Then he decided on two bottles. It was a tight squeeze to get them both in the bucket, but he managed. Take it easy, he kept reminding himself. If she saw him excited like this when he picked her up, she'd stay home. And that would end it all.

Elsie was ready, wearing a smashing white sports ensemble that made a dramatic contrast to her shining dark hair and bright red lipstick. She broke into a happy laugh when she saw the two champagne bottles. "What, one for each of us?"

"Just wait till you see the vines all caught up in that sunset glow," Martin said. "With a glass in hand and that view, the champagne just disappears!"

His lighthearted remark was put to the test after they'd driven toward Almaden Valley and stopped where the Lefranc family's old vineyards spread across the hillsides. They sipped champagne as they walked among vines whose spring-green growth cascaded down like thousands of small waterfalls. They finally found just the spot for maximum view of the oncoming spectacular sunset and viewed it together in silence, witnessing a phenomenon so eerily beautiful that any words of theirs might disrupt its sheer magic. The last rays of the sun as it slipped behind the hills caught all the vines in pure gold, lit them for a few brief moments, and then were gone.

"Martin, you were so right—that whole bottle just disappeared!" Elsie marveled as they returned to the car.

"We'll have the other one on our way home," Martin promised as they set off. "Same place. But we'll see it differently when it's alight under the full moon!" Even the lunar schedule was cooperating with his now-remembered plan.

They drove through a twisting canyon where some battered relics of the historic New Almaden Quicksilver Mine were still visible in this small southern cup of the much bigger valley. Having sometimes explored the area as a boy, Martin pointed out features of this once valuable site, whose importance was near forgotten now. Here, cinnabar deposits that rivaled Spain's yielded the mercury essential in extracting gold dust from the crushed ore of the Sierra foothills as well as silver from Nevada's rich mines. Elsie was intrigued with this evidence of Martin's wide-ranging knowledge. And she had thought him only a brokerage rep!

And then they dined at a charming and secluded old Gallic restaurant that somehow had survived the years of boom and bust among the local residents. Now it was known mostly to epicures, who might drive long distances to revel in its delectable cuisine and quaint atmosphere.

Elsie's customary reserve seemed to have relaxed—partly due to the champagne, no doubt. Martin also had brought wrapped in brown paper a bottle of good French claret, which the waiter now discreetly opened and poured into their glasses. They lingered over their dinner. Elsie told Martin enthralling stories of her New York stay. Not chatter but delightful vignettes of her observations of life there, each story with some special appeal.

When it came Martin's turn to talk, he discovered that Elsie was the best listener he'd ever known. She listened attentively to all he said, her lovely face showing genuine interest. She also reacted with keen sensitivity to both his story of the Paul Masson hijacking and his speculations about it.

How in the world, Martin asked himself, was it possible that a woman so entrancing not yet been captured by some eligible man and carried off? Had there been no one so determined as he? Martin recalled his intention to move fast and catch her before she realized she'd be caught. Yet he knew he risked total loss if he dared that.

On their way home they did stop at the same place in the vineyards. The scene was wholly changed now as moonlight flooded the vines, dazzling their lush new growth with pure silver. The champagne in their glasses had turned from gold to silver, too— pure magic, Elsie said.

And suddenly Martin's impetuosity burst its bonds. Tossing his glass into the air and giving hers a flip at the same time, he caught her up in his arms and kissed her passionately. Wrenching away from him, Elsie slapped his face sharply. "No!" she exclaimed. Then seeing his stunned, hurt look, she apologized. She really did like him, but had reacted out of impulse. It was too difficult to try to explain. Her lower lip trembled.

Knowing she was upset now and in a quandary, Martin caught her to him, this time with a tighter grasp. Brushing aside her attempted protests, he kissed her even more ardently. It felt wonderful, especially when he sensed that her defenses were crumbling. Then he released her gently.

He was sorry for his persistence, he said. But he was truly in love with her, had been for some while, and wanted to marry her. For she was the only girl he'd ever wanted so, in all his life. And he went on to say he couldn't help but feel she actually had responded to his love but just wouldn't, or couldn't, admit it.

Elsie was at least honest enough to confess that she did find him most appealing. But that was the trouble. She simply could not permit herself to fall in love and get into marriage.

"And why not, for the love of God?" Martin insisted. "What's so great about staying single and being alone for the rest of your life? Let's talk this out honestly. I want to understand why you're so dead-set against love and marriage. I intend then to knock down every argument you may have! Because I love you madly and am going to marry you, whatever you think now. See?"

By this time they could even laugh at each other's absurdity. So they'd become intimate friends of a sort. After they got back to the car, Martin with compassionate stubbornness tried desperately to persuade Elsie to be absolutely frank with him—as he always would be with her, he promised. Couldn't she explain to him why she so absolutely ruled out matrimony? For she must have a valid and poignant reason.

The appeal to honesty and frankness was important. For she did want to tell him. But didn't know where to start. "I just paid far, far too high a price in reaching for love," she finally said. "I've buried that need deep inside somewhere. So deep it's gone now. And I don't wish to recall it ... can't speak of it." She fell silent. Never before had she ever tried to tell anyone about it.

He reached over and gently patted her hand to encourage her to go on.

It all began like this, Elsie told Martin. It was toward the end of springtime. About to graduate from high school, she was excited over plans to start college in the fall. Then one day, out with a girl-friend and her older sister who attended Stanford, she met Sonny Howell, the university's much-idolized track star. She fell in love, head over heels, at first sight. She was so surprised and excited when he telephoned, wanting to go out on a date. For she was so much younger and more naive than his Stanford crowd.

They had several dates. She could hardly believe her good fortune when he told her that for him as well it had been an instantaneous love. Then the day came when he simply said, "Say, let's get married!" Of course it was a madcap idea. But to her it seemed out-of-the-world wonderful, this so-casual proposal.

Why not marry, really? Sonny was the most exciting man imaginable—sophisticated, older by a few years, a sure winner. Everyone would envy her. She told herself that she didn't need all the fuss over wedding plans other girls and their families went through. Having each other was everything. So, riding on this spur-of-the moment impulse, they found a minister willing to marry them on the spot.

Since Sonny had to run in tomorrow's big race at the intermural track event that ended the season, their real honeymoon would have to be postponed for a little while. That day Sonny seemed to be coming down with a cold, but this too hadn't fazed the two young hotheads so much in love.

After the brief ceremony, Elsie phoned her mother to say she wouldn't be home, then to tell her what she and Sonny had just done. Her mother, shocked, said she should have waited—at least for a reasonable period—before taking a serious lifetime step like marriage.

Well, that step was now taken. "Just think, we've done it ... eloped. It's real!" they congratulated themselves gleefully as they registered as man and wife at a local hotel. They had to be close to Stanford for the next day's race.

Now, as the elegant wedding-night dinner they'd ordered came to a close, Sonny's oncoming cold suddenly seemed awful. He was coughing—a deep, rasping sound. His throat was sore and his eyes were red. Scared, Elsie suggested they postpone their being together that night. He should go home, get medication, and go right to sleep. He had to be in top condition for tomorrow. But Sonny wouldn't consider it.

When they got back to their cozy suite, Sonny's coughing fits worsened. Elsie, alarmed, ignored his protests and phoned the desk clerk. A doctor came. He took Sonny's temperature and examined him carefully. Then he told Sonny to check into the hospital at once.

But Sonny refused to listen, was angrily against it. He knew that, once hospitalized, he wouldn't be allowed out the next day. And damn it, he was going to run! So the doctor treated him as best he could. Painted his throat. Supplied ample aspirins and a codeine cough remedy and other sedatives. He instructed Elsie to watch him closely all night and phone him if there was a crisis. He'd return in the morning.

So Elsie spent her whole wedding night administering various medicines, keeping the feverish Sonny covered while he tried to throw off the blankets, watching over him with mounting fear. When the doctor came, he sternly forbade his patient to run that day. But fiercely determined as well as doped up with medicines, Sonny was beyond any appeal to reason. He got out of bed and dressed himself. Assuring Elsie he'd be all right, he drove them both to the stadium.

And run Sonny did. Terrified, Elsie watched him circling the track. Again a winner. She should have felt proud, thrilled. But instead she saw her young husband crumple just beyond the finish line.

Sonny was rushed to the Stanford Hospital. His parents were already there at his bedside when Elsie arrived. He had pneumonia, she was told. When the parents heard that Elsie had just married Sonny, they were enraged. How could she do this to him—especially just before this crucial track event? And of course they blamed her for the dangerous condition he'd developed the night before as well as his collapse after the race.

Elsie's new in-laws still treated her contemptibly even after the doctors announced Sonny was afflicted with an infection far deadlier than pneumonia: tuberculosis. Probably he had been harboring the disease for some while, they said. The Howells simply refused to accept the diagnosis. How could Sonny, with his healthy good looks and rosy cheeks, possibly have had such a serious affliction? And to Elsie herself this prior condition did appear highly improbable.

After some weeks of expensive treatment, the hospital transferred Sonny to a nursing home, for extended care. His parents indignantly refused to pay any of his many bills for hospital care, doctors, lab tests, the sanatorium, medications. Since Sonny's sickness was all her fault, they declared—and, anyway, she had married him—certainly all debts were her responsibility, not theirs.

Elsie found a job at once so she could start paying the enormous bills. She gave up any hope of ever getting a college education. She never spoke a word of complaint to anyone. It would only have made her situation seem worse, she felt. She'd always been a happy, self-confident person. And by forcing herself to cultivate patience, acceptance, and serenity, she managed to rise above her problems—above feeling resentful or depressed. She just quietly went on working and paying bills, and her calm demeanor and intelligent application enabled her to achieve success in the business world. Despite her secret tragedy, her life actually was good.

She visited Sonny regularly in the nursing home, always bringing little gifts to cheer him up. But there was always a terrible tension about these visits. For, as the doctors warned her from the start, if she had any regard for her own life she must never allow any kisses, let alone close embraces, between them. This wouldn't be easy, they said, for TB patients tended to be abnormally ardent—though sexual activity might kill them off.

The doctors' warnings proved apt. Elsie quickly developed ingenuity in escaping her young husband's frantic grasp. To be absolutely safe, she usually asked a nurse to accompany her. Sonny, resentful, accused her of not loving him. There were bitter confrontations. And actually by this time they did seem total strangers. They had nothing in common to share. It was clear they had never really known each other.

Elsie continued unfailingly these tense visits. In time they became merely routine duty, her responsibility. Sonny lived on for several years, and his death at last released her. Paying off all his bills took her a long time, but she did feel good about having done it. Since then, every day of her life was joyful. And all her own, with obligations to no one.

Yet, said Elsie now, the whole experience had been mystifying, devastating. How could it have happened? From just a sudden infatuation, her first. And she'd paid the price of her youth as well as lost the opportunity for college. . . .

Elsie felt she'd told Martin enough of her tale. So she asked whether he could now understand how she might vow never again to fall victim to love.

Martin took her in his arms and held her closely, stroking her dark hair. "What a brave girl!" he murmured as he kissed her cheek. After such an appalling story, what more could be said?

As they drove back home, Martin felt that a close bond had been forged between them—whatever might come of it later. "I think you gained far more than you ever lost, by such an ordeal," he finally said thoughtfully. "You developed a tremendous strength of spirit. It illuminates your face—shines in your eyes. That's what gives your beauty its unique quality."

His words comforted and reassured her. And when they arrived back at the Vendome Hotel and he said goodnight at her door, he gave her a parting kiss and an endearing hug—without paying a penalty this time. Elsie even agreed to have dinner again with him the next night. Two nights in a row—unthinkable for her!

"Early again?" he asked. "If it's all right with you ... I have another astonishing sun-struck sight to show you."

The next afternoon—again with iced champagne—Martin headed the car toward Paul Masson's mountain. Masson probably would not be around, but Martin knew he wouldn't mind his showing Elsie the view from the premises.

They drank their champagne on the terrace as the sun began dipping in the sky behind them. Though she'd grown up in the valley, Elsie had never seen such a glorious panorama. The whole of the Santa Clara Valley was spread out below them to the east in the vibrant springtime green of orchards fragrant with the pink and white blossoms of apricots, peaches, and plums. The blue expanse of San Francisco Bay glimmered in the north.

As they raised their glasses, the champagne bubbles danced in the sun's last brilliant rays. A luminous golden glow soon enveloped the scene. Then suddenly the sun was gone, leaving the mountain and entire valley in one vast indigo-colored shadow.

"But look!" Martin cried, waving his hand toward the line of mountains on the other side of the valley. Miraculous! Whereas all else was darkened, the sun still painted the entire Diablo Range in an incandescent pink, intensified in contrast to the deep blue-shadowed valley below. "I call it our alpine glow," he said, awed as much as when he first saw the sight as a boy. As abruptly as it came, the light went out. That magic show was over. But Martin had other marvels still in store.

While they ate the tasty picnic supper Martin had brought along in a basket, Elsie asked, "Do you have nights like this all the time?"

"That's my main objective in life," Martin said, laughing. But in a moment he grew serious. "One thing is certain. Every day and night will be as wonderful as this when we're together."

And then he confided to Elsie his lifelong dream: to own a

mountain world all his own just like this one, with vineyards growing far and wide over the slopes, and there to make great wines as Paul Masson did. That had been his aim ever since he was a boy, coming up here. He had witnessed, even experienced then, the kind of life possible at this place.

"How extraordinary, to have a dream like that!" Elsie exclaimed, her eyes opening wide as she regarded him in a wholly new way. "And here I thought you just wanted to be the world's most successful stockbroker!"

By evening's end Elsie surely must have wondered what spectacle Martin would conjure for the next night to possibly match these two. For she'd actually accepted the third date in a row, shattering all her set rules!

Certainly Martin was doing some creative thinking. He had to. This third night must top them all. It took hours of preparation, for Martin was taking no chances. And as always, but more than ever before, he aimed at absolute perfection.

Again they set off in late afternoon. But now Martin turned the auto toward the East Bay, heading for Berkeley. He hoped to capture the most spectacular sunset yet. He had in mind a certain hill from which one could look straight out through the Golden Gate. (No tall orange bridge with towers and spans was there yet to cross that great open gateway of incoming sea.)

Fortunately for him, the fickle spring weather was fully cooperating with his plan. "This is the evening of the supreme light," he announced tantalizingly. "Not sunlight, not moonlight, not starlight. You'll never guess, but wait till you see it!"

He'd timed their arrival perfectly. Enormous sweeps of rainbow colors made a vast arc high over the entire western sky, beyond the two sentinels guarding the Golden Gate and reflected upon the Pacific's waters below.

"Fabulous!" cried Elsie as Martin poured their champagne. They drank of its golden nectar while she absorbed the magnificent sight. The brilliance of the colors lasted through their champagne tryst.

"But all that still isn't the supreme light," Martin then said. "This light glows for you alone . . ." And as he said this, he opened a little leather jeweler's case and set it in Elsie's hands. Lights from a thousand stars seemed to glitter from a great square-shaped diamond, most beautifully cut, crowning a gold ring surrounded by an array of lesser diamonds, exquisite against a black velvet setting.

"Great God Almighty!" Elsie gasped, overwhelmed by such dazzling splendor. "Now I'm sunk," she murmured to herself as an afterthought. Spellbound, she gazed at the ring while Martin slipped it on her finger. "This really does it," she had to admit, laughing then at the way he'd worked it out until by now all her opposition seemed undone. As if by magic—which it was!

"Now," said Martin, "the supreme light after all is but a guide to the supreme adventure that awaits us. For that, of course, we'll have to drive on to Reno. To be married. We're partway there already. So let's go!"

Elsie sat there—stunned by that gorgeous diamond ring on her hand, enraptured by the view of the splendid sunset now fading into pastels, and half-mesmerized by the champagne that always made everything seem so wondrously perfect. Most of all she was enchanted by Martin's magicianship. By his uncanny ability to master-mind this brief, incredible courtship to the point of no return. What a powerful force he was! For a woman who had been so long alone, that was reassuring.

For a moment she could say nothing. By the time she finally recovered her composure, she laughingly said: "Martin, do you know the only really fitting remark for me to make right now? The one gasped out to Sherlock Holmes by the skilled marksman he'd surprised and cornered ... 'Oh you, clever, clever fiend!'"

The remark called for an endearing off-to-Reno embrace. So with much gaiety—and without Elsie's ever having to agree in words—they sped through the soft evening light toward Nevada. Which didn't seem far, in their happy state.

"I brought a suitcase with everything you could possibly need for the time being," Martin remarked, taking his eyes off the road for a moment to glance at this beloved companion at his side.

"Oh yes, you would, you would!" she agreed, laughing. "But how could you know I like only one kind of toothbrush? And hairbrushes with real bristles, not some synthetic kind?"

He chuckled triumphantly. "Easy. I had your room-maid check vital stuff like that. And I duplicated all of it."

"Oh you clever, clever fiend!" she repeated softly. By now her head was nestled cozily on his shoulder.

And thus Martin and Elsie arrived in Reno late that night, to get married.

They returned from their honeymoon to astonished friends. Elsie's intimates couldn't believe the news. They'd never heard of Martin Ray. Nor had Martin ever mentioned the name of Elsie Howell to us. And of course Martin's stockbroker pals at the Vendome reeled. How could he win over the virgin queen, who'd been absolutely unassailable?

The newlyweds' first concern was to find a suitable house.

Luck was with them. They discovered a quaint English-style cottage set within an old-fashioned garden. Right off, Elsie admitted she knew nothing at all about cookery. Martin was amazed. He assumed everyone learned to cook at an early age, because he did. As a small boy he'd followed his grandmother about the ranch kitchen, and she—of course a highly gifted cook—let him join in all her culinary projects.

So Martin now had a great time turning out delicious meals. First his bride watched, then helped, and gradually began taking over doing many things herself. Their joint cooking sessions were an entirely new kind of adventure for them both.

They invited Walter and me to come down from San Francisco and have dinner with them. Eager to meet Elsie, I accepted enthusiastically. And was captivated not only by her unique beauty and charm, but also by a quiet self-confidence that gave her a "lady of the manor" quality.

After dinner, Elsie and I were talking as we sat near a window facing the street. I noticed her eyes following a car that drove slowly past the house. Her conversation faltered, though she quickly picked up the thread. Before long the car passed again, slowing as before. This time she jumped to her feet, saying she wanted my ideas on redoing the guest bedroom, and we moved off. Naturally I wondered what was brewing, to cause her such concern.

Later I learned that the car passed and repassed all night long. Its recurring headlights worried Elsie and she couldn't sleep. She knew well whose car it was. The car belonged to Trevor—the socialite bachelor who'd been sending all the flowers and luxury items that had filled her suite at the Vendome. The one who'd always escorted her to whatever events she cared to attend. Doubtless he was shocked at the news of her sudden marriage. And bitterly resentful. But she didn't like his odd way of showing it.

Elsie didn't want to disturb Martin about this problem. She kept hoping the annoyance would cease, and it did when morning came. By then she had decided she must tell Martin. But what would he do? She had so hoped to avoid any turmoil. When she finally talked to him about Trevor's strange behavior, Martin said it was too bad she hadn't told him when it first started, rather than worry herself sick over it in secret.

"You say he always prides himself on being the perfect gentleman?" Martin asked.

"Yes, that is the very essence of Trevor."

"Well, in that case, I think I know how to deal with him," Martin said. Thereupon he sat down and wrote a brief note to Trevor, appealing to him, as one gentleman to another, to desist in annoying them. His strategy worked. Elsie's jilted admirer never harassed them again.

After that first dinner with Martin and Elsie in San Jose, the four of us had frequent evenings together, at their home or ours. Often we women chatted while the men inevitably discussed brokerage matters.

Martin found companionable satisfaction in our foursome, as if we were an indissoluble unit. Walter, however, wasn't so enthusiastic about it—probably because he was jealous. Something got nipped from his ego, for until now he'd considered Martin his own personal monopoly, a reinforcement to his faulty self-esteem. He couldn't help resenting that Martin had taken on a wife—who clearly came first with him now.

Moreover, Elsie's self-assurance, underscoring Walter's own uneasy confidence, threw him on the defensive. Walter countered by making gratuitous references to our college life together, as if to emphasize her lack of a college education. And he'd drop advice on books she should read, as though leading her toward an acceptable level of culture. (Later, to his chagrin, he learned she'd read twice as many books as he ever had!)

Elsie's brown eyes revealed how she took note of Walter's every offense, while choosing to disregard them—for now anyway—as due to some unfortunate ego problem. So the atmosphere remained congenial and happy enough when the four of us were together.

In that summer of '29 Blyth & Company decided to move their salesmen around. Martin, now the brokerage firm's top salesman, was summoned back to San Francisco, where he'd handle some of the biggest accounts. Thus Martin and Elsie were uprooted from their first little home, to take up residence in The City.

At the same time, the firm asked Walter to replace Martin in the San Jose area. So we two couples exchanged locations. Though I'd always loved San Francisco, this move from fog to country sunshine seemed wonderful. We rented a house too, so I could garden!

Walter also liked the change. He soon was doing well with the brokerage accounts he'd taken over from Martin. He joined the country club—began to play golf and make friends. Happy over his new interests, I took up country-clubbing with him. This was Walter's golden period—when he cast off his shadowy dissatisfactions and seemingly found life almost as good as others did.

13

A Broker's Universe

WHEN THE SUMMER OF 1929 was in full swing, Martin made a date to come down from San Francisco to visit Paul Masson up on his mountain. "I'm bringing someone I'd like you to meet," he said. "My wife!" Martin wanted Elsie to get to know his boyhood idol. He was also hoping to learn more about that mysterious winery heist in April.

As the afternoon sun dipped low enough for shadows to appear on the terrace, the men sat down after Martin had pulled over a chair for Elsie that provided her with a view of the vineyards in summer's full growth, and the great valley lying far below and beyond the slopes.

"So this is the lucky lady who caught MAR-tan!" Paul said after pouring the just-opened bottle of champagne. As Martin distributed the three tulip-shaped glasses, Paul gazed at Elsie carefully in undisguised approval, giving a hint of his past proclivity for female charms.

"It's the other way around, Paul," Martin said. "I caught her. She gave me a difficult chase, but she sure is worth it!" His eyes met Elsie's and they laughed.

"Here's to the two of you . . . may you enjoy a long and happy life together!" Paul proposed, raising his champagne glass.

"To our Good Life!" Martin echoed as the three goblets touched and gently tinkled.

For five minutes or so they talked of this and that, nothing consequential. Then Martin couldn't hold himself in any longer. He leapt right into the matter that still perplexed him. "Well, Paul, what really went on up here that night?"

Paul, uncomfortable, looked down. "It is all over now, MAR-tan," he said. "Why bring it up?"

"Because at our luncheon, before this happened, I got the uneasy feeling that someone was trying to force you to go away. Paul, if you have a business problem, maybe you can tell me about it. A friend who knows what really went on may be able to help you if more incidents like this occur in the future."

Paul glanced questioningly at Elsie. "You can say anything you wish in her presence, Paul," Martin assured him. "We will both keep it just to ourselves."

"Then let me tell you about it," Paul said, audibly releasing his breath. Getting to his feet, he paced up and down as he related the story.

"Sometime in March a fellow named Asona—you know, the federal marshal appointed to supervise Prohibition enforcement in this area—dropped in on me up here. 'Mr. Masson,' he said gravely, 'I came to warn you about what I just learned from an undercover detective. A gang plans to raid this place early next month.' He saw my quick alarm, and he added: 'Evidently we're dealing with a group out of Chicago.'

"Hearing that Al Capone's mobsters were involved in a scheme connected with me and my winery of course practically paralyzed me. The local bootleggers I've been able to withstand. But when a ruthless band of thugs like the Mafia steps in, I want out! This is the one thing I've dreaded most through these wretched years.

"Asona then began getting chummy. 'Paul,' he said, 'this gang thinks you keep your finished champagne up here. But I know it's cased in a San Jose warehouse.' Waiting for what might come next, I began getting very nervous."

As Masson paced around, continuing his tale, his steps quickened, his breath became labored, and his voice climbed higher, almost shrill. "Asona stuck his face next to mine and told me, 'These fellows will get very angry after breaking in here and finding no champagne. They may take other stuff, but won't get what they're really after. Naturally they'll soon find out it's all in your warehouse, so will go and get it there.'

"'But since you now know from the detective that the gang is going to come here,' I argued, 'surely you can find out exactly when ... and arrest them in the act!'

"He said, 'I can't do that, Paul. The Mafia would kill my undercover man as a stoolpigeon! And I need him around, to get really important information for us. So to stay out of their clutches, you've got to ship your champagne out at once!'

"But I haven't sold the finished champagne yet!" I protested.

"'Ah, Paul, you see I can take care of that,' he assured me. 'You'll just turn it all over to me for safekeeping. My men will pick it up and get it off your hands. Record the transaction as an operational transfer. My office, of course, can easily handle all necessary official paperwork. So it shouldn't really cost you much to keep the Mafia out of your business.' As he said this, Asona kept grinning at me!

"'But that's ... ' I was afraid to say the words extortion or blackmail to a U.S. marshal.

"'Regard this only as an accommodation to protect you,' Asona said smoothly to me.

"He then said that it would be best if I went away: 'Take a long trip and spare yourself discomfort,' as he put it. Because any investigation into the break-in at the winery would be hard on me. I balked at being told I had to leave town, and said so. 'Well, then, make sure you stay far away from here starting on the first of April, if you want to avoid getting hurt,' he told me.

"What could I do, MAR-tan?" Paul asked, seating himself now and looking at Martin almost beseechingly. "I told him to come and get the champagne. But at least I did not run off, like a coward." He sank back in his chair and gulped down a little champagne before he continued. "So the gang did come, as you know. They made a big mess here. We had a lot of trouble cleaning it up. Newspaper reporters and the police hounded me for days, wanting to know this and that. But Asona told me himself that I did not dare mention what he'd said about the Mafia. 'They could work on you next time, Paul,' was how he put it."

Martin finally spoke up. "But Paul, it doesn't figure right."

"Eh?" Paul leaned forward, all ears.

"I've read and reread all the news reports I could get my hands on. Some reporters think there's a mystery here. I suspect there is, too. And I think I know what's behind it. Nothing of real value was actually taken away, right? There was mention of old sherry, brandies, and liqueurs—stuff I know Henry made long ago that so angered you and which you considered worthless. But no mention from the employees held hostage that the robbers were actually looking for champagne. Then think of all those costly cases of champagne Asona removed from your warehouse! He really stole them, didn't he? For obviously he didn't intend to pay you for them. You were to think he was doing you a favor. So to back up his warning to you about a heist, he sent underworld friends of his up here to break in, harass your employees, and truck out some odd stuff. He staged the whole event. It was complete fakery! He told reporters whatever got into the papers, and he controlled what you said too."

"But how can he do this when he is a U.S. marshal?" Paul protested, which caused Martin to laugh. "This is Prohibition, Paul. Anything goes!"

"Just a moment, MAR-tan, I want to show you something!" Paul said. He went into the house and soon returned with several slips of paper clipped together. He handed them to Martin. Scribblings on different kinds of paper were signed by women unknown to Paul. Both contained warnings. One said that if Masson hoped to survive he must be "extremely careful"; she had just heard some strangers say they "plan to get you."

"Paul, these are fakes too," Martin said. "I'll bet you anything that Asona wrote these up to keep you scared, so you'll be fearing the Mafia's next move!"

Paul collapsed back in his chair. "Maybe so," he said. "But I can't be sure. So I must keep Marshal Asona supplied with champagne . . . because he says he'll make sure I am well protected!"

"I'm sure he will," Martin agreed with a wry grin. He could see, though, that Paul remained greatly agitated. Just talking about it all had stirred up a storm.

Martin was scarcely surprised some days later when he learned that Masson had persuaded his wife and sister-in-law to trade their Almaden property for a large tract of land near Gilroy. This unloading at least relieved Paul from the double burden of directing two separate winegrowing establishments in an era increasingly dangerous to vintners.

Martin Ray's daily brokerage life revolved in a strikingly different way than Paul Masson's world. He encountered no apparent dangers. All in a seemingly serene arrangement that accumulated ever more profits for his clients—and healthy commissions for him—as the stocks-and-bonds market went up, up, up. Blyth & Company was doing so well, in fact, that the San Francisco firm decided to promote Martin Ray to the sales manager position, certain that he'd stimulate sales to even higher levels for the entire sales force. It was crucial to have a master strategist at that post.

Naturally Martin was greatly pleased at the new honor bestowed on him. He called his first meeting of all area salesmen for the afternoon of October 24, 1929. Thursday would be a big day for him, and he had lined up key points for the pep talk he'd give them. He had to get down to the office just before the New York Stock Exchange opened, three hours ahead of California time, to be up on the latest action and prices. So he arose well before dawn.

He couldn't believe the news as it came over the wire. The market was plunging drastically, going all to pieces. Terrible panic ensued in the East, with brokerages' floor traders dumping tens of thousands of stocks and bonds at rock-bottom prices just to save themselves and their clients from total disaster. The tidal wave roared westward across the continent, by tickertape, radio, telegraph, telephone.

The worst calamity of all time had hit the stock exchange. Utter bedlam ensued among brokers and clients in the sales room as they watched the numbers plummeting downward. There'd be no sales-pep meeting today, Martin realized. And got to work at once monitoring the accounts for which he was responsible. When the head of Martin's firm came in, he canceled all organizational changes until the market recovered. So the former sales manager was shifted back to his old post.

The market would soon rebound, everyone said. But it didn't. In fact the first precipitous price drop on "Black Thursday" seemed minuscule compared with the freefalls that followed, one day after another through the next weeks, as brief respites gave way to new selling panics. Everything simply went to hell on the Exchange and its intricate network in cities around the country. Millions of people who had been rich on paper suddenly found themselves penniless. Or, worse yet, if they'd bought "on margin," owing many thousands of dollars.

In shocked despair, some ruined speculators leapt out of windows in tall buildings. Martin himself had to forcibly prevent a woman, a complete stranger, from jumping to her death. Looking dazed, she'd wandered into his office and walked toward the open window. Since she was a heavy woman, it was all Martin could do to grab her in time, then escort her to the hallway and call for others' help.

Still new to the brokerage business, Walter was simply immobilized by the disaster. He took to his bed, unable to function for several weeks, saying he was despondent over the terrible losses sustained by his clients. But I knew he was bemoaning the cruel personal fate that had enticed him into the lucrative brokerage business, then utterly stranded him.

Meanwhile, well seasoned in the business and an optimist by nature, Martin carefully considered the portfolios of all his clients so as to move fast and salvage whatever they could. Clients often blamed the firm, not the salesmen, for whatever losses they'd taken from their investments. So Martin realized it was vital to keep in close contact with them in this agonizing period—providing supportive sympathy, even if he was helpless to save the bulk of their assets. During this stressful time, while helping to smooth over their relations with Blyth & Company, he developed lasting friendships with clients.

Gradually the stock market settled down. Once he saw that the Crash hadn't put a permanent end to his job, Walter revived and returned to normal. Much to his surprise, clients were eager to reinvest whatever funds remained to them. For since prices were at a low ebb, the word got passed around that this was the greatest of "bear market" times—a terrific opportunity for investing at bargain-basement prices. So business began to pick up remarkably.

Now, whenever our foursome got together for dinners or weekend outings, Martin invariably launched into a subject of immense importance to him. He knew that individual clients disillusioned with the big, well-known houses they'd dealt with in the past felt inclined to desert them in favor of small brokerages that would give their precious funds more personal attention. "Think of the tremendous advantage we'd have now if we had our own small firm!" he'd say.

But Walter wasn't enthusiastic. Why take the risk? Both of them were doing well financially and without any of the worries or responsibilities of ownership.

So the debate went on between them for over a year before Walter finally agreed to Martin's plan of launching their own company. He'd seen by now that as successful brokers they would be insulated—thus far, at least—from unemployment and other miseries that beset many Americans during the economic collapse brought on by the Crash of '29.

Martin proposed that each would bring in half the capital needed to start the new business. Most would be obtained from select clients. Lining up this financial backing would require months of effort, Martin said. So they set a date when the total funding amount would be escrowed. And on that day, with their firm launched, they'd turn in their resignations from Blyth & Co.

In the meantime, Elsie and I were talking of the future in a different form. We wanted to found two families for the years ahead, not a joint business concern. We decided to try to have our babies at about the same time.

Walter didn't hear about this distaff plan until the day I happily told him that our baby was on its way. He was far from delighted. "You certainly picked one hell of a time to have a baby . . . just when we're about to go into business for ourselves!" he growled. Elsie was disappointed over not getting pregnant too on our prearranged schedule. Now my baby would come first.

For some inexplicable reason I became deliciously obsessed with the hope of having twin boys. For me, that would be the greatest possible achievement! In my mind's eye I imagined them in tiny yellow shorts. I bought twin baby outfits of everything. Then an x-ray let me down, clearly showing but one baby. Evidently either the film had been mixed up with someone else's or had missed something—for, to my immense joy, the very twin boys I'd dreamed of arrived in mid-December of 1931 as my supreme Christmas gift! Fraternal twins, they were named Walter Barclay and Peter Martin.

My husband, in his dry-humor vein, remarked that a couple

of fellows were about to move in on him for lifetime support. But Martin Ray went into rapturous excitement over their birth—wired everyone we knew in the Northwest, and newspapers as well.

Walter couldn't be located on the day we were to leave the hospital, so Martin came rushing down in his car to transport us home. Walter arrived later. He stood looking down at the boys in their cribs as if he still didn't believe such a thing could happen to him. "This is so typical of you," he finally said. "You couldn't be satisfied with just having the usual baby like anyone else. No, you had to make a big production of it—a superstar performance, turn the world upside down, by having twins!"

Dear Walter, I told myself . . . still with the same satirical humor of our college days masking his deep feelings. Of course I knew he really thought that having those twin boys was as miraculously wonderful as I did.

Martin's continuing drive to line up clients' funds to back the new brokerage firm was bringing gratifying results. A month or so before the deadline he had almost all the agreed half of monies assured. So he was growing impatient with Walter, who in turn showed annoyance whenever Martin inquired about his progress. "Don't worry, I'll have my half ready in plenty of time," he said.

Martin had become good friends with the brokerage's sales manager, Gerald Scott, who shared his concern over clients' continuing to pull away from the big, established firms like theirs. One day Martin hinted at maybe starting a small new brokerage of their own. Gerald jumped at the idea. "I'm with you!" he declared. "Just let me know when you're ready to go, and you can count on me to join you." That was a welcome development. A dynamo of energy with plenty of good contacts, he'd prove invaluable to the fledgling business.

Hearing that Gerald would be joining them, Walter rallied perceptibly. He began to work more at rounding up investors. But he still didn't like being asked about it. Knowing his secretive nature, I felt sure the requisite backing was already well in hand; that he would just quietly come up with it at the scheduled day.

Finally that day arrived. As planned, Martin—with the new venture's wheels already in motion—told the sales manager at Blyth & Co. that he had just resigned. Did he still intend to join them? Gerald remained enthused over the new brokerage. Well, then, now was the time for him to resign, Martin said; Walter too would be turning in his resignation.

Martin then rushed off to handle some legal technicalities of the corporate founding. When he came by the office later, Gerald called him in. "Can't join you, Martin. I'm terribly sorry. When I told the boss I was leaving, he made me such a big offer I couldn't turn it down. But you'll still go through with it?"

"Of course," Martin said. He was badly disappointed, though, for success with the new business would have come faster and easier with this man aboard as a partner. But he and Walter could manage on their own.

Busy with other errands, Martin wouldn't be around to see Walter when he came in to tell the firm's executives that he was leaving. But as prearranged, he and Elsie were to come down to San Jose for dinner with us that evening, to celebrate the start of their new company. Walter could tell him about it then. And they'd also review the total funds accumulated from their various backers as well as their own cash reserves.

When the Rays arrived, of course we first had to toast the new firm in champagne—Paul Masson's champagne, which Martin in his usual custom had brought along, iced and ready. I thought Walter seemed unusually taciturn, whereas Rusty was bursting with excitement. But I reminded myself this was typical of the balance in their temperaments, which had served them well for a decade in various joint ventures.

Before going over all the details of the new business, we decided to sit down to dinner. To make conversation, Martin asked Walter how his resignation was taken by the firm's top brass. At this, Walter visibly paled, then said, "Well . . ." and added nothing more.

"Well—what?" Martin demanded, alarmed by the guilty look on his partner's face.

Dropping his eyes, Walter finally said, "I'm not going."

Martin leapt to his feet. "Not going! Jesus Christ, Walt, what kind of creature are you: a man or a rat?"

Walter, still looking down at his plate, shrugged his shoulders dejectedly and tried to explain this desertion. "They told me we couldn't possibly make it, with the Depression deepening as it is. I already knew they'd persuaded Gerald to stay, and figured we didn't have a chance on our own." For once, he used his paterfamilias status as a handy excuse: "After all, Rusty, I've got a family to support here!"

Elsie realized the terribly precarious position Martin was in now. Stunned for the moment, she went completely out of character when she offered the only words of compromise I ever heard her make: "Martin, would they take you back if you talked with them?"

Martin turned his fury now on his wife. "Take me back!" he shouted. "I'd never try to slink back like a whipped dog! I am starting this new business, and if nobody joins me I'll just go it alone." Whereupon he threw down his napkin and stalked from the room.

Elsie ran after him. Violently ill, he rushed to the bathroom. She helped him and finally calmed him down enough to walk him into our guestroom, where he collapsed on the bed. She stroked his forehead. "Of course you're so right to go ahead," she said soothingly. "Never turn back! I know you'll make a great success of it."

Knowing that Martin had episodes of dangerously high blood pressure when under great stress, Martin's doctor had prescribed sedatives to be taken in emergencies. Elsie always carried some in her purse, in case of need in subduing an overwrought condition. She gave him one now. And gradually Martin relaxed into a deep sleep.

When Walter and I got up in the morning, we found Martin and Elsie gone. Needless to say, the incident and their departure signaled a final parting of the ways between Martin and his old friend. Walter wouldn't speak at all about the whole issue, and I didn't press him.

We saw nothing of Martin and Elsie for months. But we read in the newspapers of Martin Ray's phenomenal success with his new San Francisco-based brokerage firm. Ray & Company had become the talk of Montgomery Street. Walter remained edgy and unhappy about the subject. However, he seemed to be doing well enough in his bond-selling job with Blyth & Company. So no complaints there.

I was enveloped by my own blissful world at home. I had one glorious time with my twin toddlers. I suspected Walter felt jealous—left out of the picture he'd never yet tried to be in. Evidently some shy reluctance or awkwardness, even resentment, prevented him from joining us in our fun as the twins learned to walk and talk, and developed distinct personalities.

Meanwhile, Walter threw himself into all sorts of activities: golfing in the daytime with clients, both current and prospective, and in the evenings nightclubbing and hobnobbing with local bigwigs, some known to be unsavory, involved with underhanded and lucrative Prohibition-era deals.

I managed to think up excuses for Walter's fooling around on his own. After all, I didn't wish to join him, even if invited. As a farmboy he had missed out on the fun of adolescence by slaving out in the fields and barnyard. So he was desperately trying to make up for it now. Anyway, I told myself, it was all business-connected somehow.

It seemed a shame, though, that despite all his running about, he really didn't seem to enjoy himself. One afternoon he came into the garden where the little boys and I were playing ball. For a moment he stood there glaring at our happy scene, then snapped angrily, "I wish to God I could enjoy anything as much as you enjoy those children!" And he stalked off. Poor Walter . . .

I was both surprised and pleased when Walter told me one day that he'd be joining Ray & Co. Almost a year had passed since its founding ... and the friendship's concurrent rupture.

I learned much later—not having heard a word of this from Walter—that all these past months, he and Martin had been contending against each other for desirable accounts. By now he'd lost most of his best clients to Martin's Ray & Co. So one day Walter dropped by to see Martin. He wasn't shown directly to the exit door. Grudge-holding wasn't part of Martin's nature: he was much too busy with the present. He greeted Walter genially.

"I guess I'm ready to join up now, Rusty," Walter said in a calculatedly offhand way. Of course he wanted in, now that the new firm had proved a great success! Yet Martin didn't remind him of his desertion at the risky start.

Walter was still his good friend of college days, whose underlying insecurity he'd always understood, eventually forgiving its manifestations. After all, he reasoned, Walter did have a growing family to support, including his little namesake, Peter Martin.

So all he said was, "I'm glad you're back, Walt. Sure, I'll let you have an equal partnership, just as it was supposed to be." So once more the two old college pals began working together, now in their own company. Walter covered the Peninsula–San Jose area, while Martin focused on The City and the East Bay.

These were the early to mid-'30s, the bottomed-out Depression years, when it often looked as if the whole nation would go under. Nevertheless, in the San Francisco Bay area and elsewhere, a few small, innovative, high-energy brokerage firms—not the old giants—actually managed to function quite profitably. Despite hard times, there was money around that sought strong and sturdy investment opportunities. One of these winners was Ray & Co.

Walter and I remained in San Jose, moving from smaller homes to ever-larger ones. He made more and more money, with the pace and quantity increasing geometrically after he joined Ray & Co. The surplus income exaggerated Walter's attempts to enjoy himself. He seemed almost frantic. As soon as he came in the door at home, he wanted out—to go off and play. All his nighttime revelries with dubious companions multiplied. He naturally justified them on the grounds of "spending time with clients." And so they were—these high-living, fast-spending princes of the tail-end of Prohibition era: well-to-do professional people like doctors and lawyers, and the flashy gamblers and bootleggers providing suitable entertainments and refreshments.

Walter even toyed with gambling, adding to his spendthrift losses. Savings? As before, he didn't know the word. He made it clear that the money earned was his, not mine, so I had no right to criticize how it was spent. Didn't he provide me with nursemaid, housekeeper, cook, gardeners?

What on earth else did I expect from him? he asked, irritated. What indeed? And he from me? Well, I felt that I was still "lighting his way," as he'd pleaded for me to do in that treasured note written before our marriage. To my mind, creating a great family life surely was projecting a high-powered light into the future. For him—for us all. In time he'd appreciate that, I knew.

And since I felt no family was complete without a daughter, ours became filled on that lucky day when a baby girl, Barbara, arrived—an adorable babe the twins immediately began calling Bobo. The nickname stuck. She blossomed into a firm-minded character from the start, capable of holding her own against the mighty twin combine, no small achievement.

So now we had an enchanting, complete ménage. Though Walter still couldn't tune in on it. But then neither did he seem to enjoy the nightly escapades he grasped at with such frenzy. I became increasingly concerned. Could the hard surface of the shell that both hid and protected his sensitivity be somehow invading his inner self?

The cynical wry humor was ever present. Whereas it once was droll and impersonal, it now had a malicious edge to it, as if he hoped to transfer his own misery onto me. Oh, I knew he cared for us, under that impenetrable surface! But no longer was I able to reach him. Yet my sympathy went out to him still, as it had when I first heard about his miserable childhood.

Meanwhile, Martin never forgot, as his firm brought him gratifying earnings, that all his assets would be used eventually to acquire the life he wanted. And then he could withdraw from the money-making rat race. He'd never lost that dream of a mountain world where he'd make splendid wines. And in sustaining that boyhood fantasy, he had kept in touch with the aging Paul Masson.

Martin was already readying himself for this future to be explored as soon as Prohibition ended. He and Walter had been buying wines and liquors from foreign ships that docked out in the bay. The wines of course were for Martin—Burgundian and Bordeaux chateaux greats; whereas Walter bought whiskeys exclusively, particularly scotch, despite Martin's urging him to educate his palate to appreciate fine wines. We drank such wines, at least, whenever we had dinner with the Rays.

Martin determined that now Walter was back in partnership

with him, he too could be in on that way of life, if he wanted it. He saw our two families as an indissoluble unit, forming a sturdy dynasty in a splendid winegrowing domain. Occasionally he reminded Walter of this intention. He was hoping to halt Walter's propensity to let money slip through his fingers even faster than he made it, as if there were no tomorrow.

"What, you still have ideas like that?" Walter inevitably would scoff. As he did one day at lunch in 1932. I'd joined them for a change, and just sat back and listened to the debate. "Those vineyard-owning plans of yours were college-boy notions, Martin. Get realistic! How would we make any money at winemaking? Do you really think that Prohibition's ever going to end? It's been too much of a good thing for too many people." Certainly it was greatly profitable for Walter's shadier clients.

"Well, the tide's really turned toward Repeal," Martin said. "Don't you read the papers at all?" He rummaged through his briefcase. Pulling out a folder, he showed some articles to Walter. "Here's the Hearst chain's contest for 'The Best Plan to Repeal the 18th Amendment.' And a big blast from Nicholas Murray Butler of Columbia University—the scholars are in this too, you see—saying you can't enforce conflicting laws, and Prohibition conflicts with the whole body of the Constitution and the Bill of Rights."

"Oh, nuts to that stuff!" Walter commented, pushing the folder aside. "All the churches full of God-fearing, booze-hating people are still behind it, anyway."

"But they aren't!" Martin protested, retrieving his folder. "See, here's a statement from the Federal Council of Churches. Their leaders are now admitting that Prohibition works against the very ideals that prompted the law. So you see, Repeal's going to happen. Sooner than you think—especially if that fellow Roosevelt gets in."

"So what?" Walter argued. "How will that make winemaking a smart business to be in? Who wants wine, anyway? There aren't many people like you. I've never understood why you think it's so terrific." He shook his head. "What's wrong with sticking to what we're doing? Making great money, instead of trying to make great wine and losing money!"

"I told you back in college, Walt, and I'm telling you still, that with me money's just a means to an end. As it should be with you, if you'd stop to think about it. Making money is no life. But we need it—and need to save it—to buy the kind of life we want for our futures."

"What's the point in saving money? We simply should make bigger money, much more than we're making. Then this saving thing can take care of itself. And the future will decide what kind of life we can afford to buy..."

Martin looked at him closely. "Walt, you'll never see the day when you make so much money you won't find ways to spend it all." His voice got sharp. "And here's another thing to think about: we won't be able to keep on forever making the big money we're making now. So we should play it for all it's worth, while saving toward our big objective. And plan for a good life ahead that we can buy with whatever assets we've got."

"Then what will happen to the brokerage?" Walter protested.

"Oh, we can keep it going if we want to. As a source of income to help sustain us. For I don't think of making wine really as a business. To me it would always be a way of life. And think how wonderful it will be for your kids. And Elsie's and mine, when we have some."

Walter actually began to look a bit interested, as if Martin's eloquent conviction was mesmerizing him.

Then Martin's face suddenly brightened into a wide smile and his eyes sparkled. "Know what, Walt? I'm going to find a giant bell—something that looks like the Liberty Bell—and take it up to Paul Masson's, so we can ring in Repeal when it comes." He gave a hearty laugh. "I'll get up early that day to celebrate . . . and wake up the whole damn valley with the bell!"

"You're the wildest optimist I've ever run into," Walter said sardonically. But he too was smiling.

14

Ringing in Repeal

MARTIN RAY'S PROPHECY CAME true. After FDR became the new president, the politicians jumped on the Repeal bandwagon ad events moved fast. Prohibition was axed. In the San Jose area, low-alcohol wine and beer became available. Now the sole delay was final ratification of the 21st Amendment, which would nullify the 18th and thus legalize Repeal nationwide.

Paul Masson and other vintners still remaining on the local scene in the Santa Clara Valley began to refurbish their wineries by readying their cooperage, buying bottles, and preparing for the vintage ahead. It required close planning, new investments, taking risks—for with wine, particularly red wines, the payoff might be years ahead. They figured that Repeal would take place before the end of 1933.

As he'd vowed, Martin went to work right away on securing a big bell to ring in Repeal. It took many months for a friend of his in the Northwest to locate one of those huge old-time bronze bells, but he finally got one. An old schoolhouse was being torn down and replaced by a modern structure. So the giant bell, brought in by a team of oxen sixty years earlier, used for calling children to school, had been retired. Martin's friend bought it at an auction and shipped it down to him.

The bell's great weight created a problem: finding a trucker who could haul it up the Masson mountain and then hoist it into its new, specially built frame. Also, because Martin intended it as a surprise, this had to be done when Paul Masson was not there— right before Repeal took place. He managed to do this undetected because he knew that Paul did not intend to visit his mountain on the targeted day. Thus the mammoth bell was settled into a dramatic niche all its own at La Cresta, just ahead of that monumental day, December 5, 1933.

By phone, Martin was keeping close track of Masson's activities through John, his long-time helper. He would be spending the day before Repeal at his San Jose home, which had become a great comfort to him as he grew older. Almost two years earlier his wife, Louise, had died, but her sister, Marie, remained to provide part-time company. Daughter Adele was long gone, spending most of her time now either at her Pebble Beach home or hanging out with bohemian artists.

Masson's daily routine, in fact, differed radically from that of his earlier years. Paul attributed these changes to Prohibition, but of course his advancing age coincided with it. Physical labor was out for him now, so he had to be content with supervising. He usually went to his chateau in the late morning, checked around the premises. At one o'clock he ate lunch, then took a nap. He'd be driven back home by dusk. The lights that had sometimes blazed all night on his mountaintop were no more. So if he gave one of his wondrous (if rare) midday dinners at the chateau, they'd end by late afternoon.

Checking now with John, Martin heard that on the eve of Repeal Paul became increasingly excited over the coming epochal event. He had declined attending the town's big Repeal celebration, for he knew it would turn into a rowdy, spirits-drinking affair, with fine wine having little or no part in it. He'd really like to greet Repeal from his mountaintop, he decided—looking at his vineyard and stately winery, freed at last from the absurd restrictions of Prohibition.

Departing from his usual routine of morning visits, on December 4th Paul had asked his chauffeur to drive him up to his ranch in late afternoon instead. He'd have a quiet supper, then sleep overnight once more in the ranch house that he called his chateau.

Somehow Martin had known it would be this way. That Paul Masson couldn't possibly awaken to the day of Repeal anywhere but on his mountain, among his vines.

Imagine Paul Masson's surprise, before dawn the next morning—the morning of Repeal—to be shocked from quiet sleep by ungodly shattering blasts from a bell somewhere very close, on his own mountain. The bell rang joyously, exuberantly, insistently.

Wondering what the devil, Paul hastened to the window. He looked toward the winery and saw, to his amazement, there in the dim light of a brightening sky, his young friend Martin Ray—yanking on a rope and ringing the most stupendous bell he'd ever seen! Paul fumbled hurriedly into his clothes. Outside the chateau doorway, he stood there, transfixed.

The resounding peals, ringing in Repeal, rent the air so explosively that they would certainly be heard far and wide across the valley. Yet despite their deafening power, the deep voice of this particular bell seemed incredibly sweet. What a glorious hurrah for the end of Prohibition!

The thunderous music held prodigious joy for Paul Masson. But for him there were undertones of wistful regrets too in the clangs detonating and echoing down the mountainside—regrets for the utter waste of thirteen years lost to the making of great wines, time that a winemaker could never regain. For Masson, these had been the prime vintage years of his maturity, when his skills were at their peak.

But he shouldn't let such regrets disturb his day. Good fortune had finally returned. He could make wine now not only for himself but to be released again to the world.

Martin was continuing to clang the bell with wild abandon. Elsie, who was with him, had retreated a distance from that ear-splitting noise. Now Paul himself approached, and Martin moved out to hail him. And though he had released the thick jute rope, the bell clanged on, its huge tongue still banging insistently against the bell's heavy bronze interior, its roar slowly diminishing.

"Happy Repeal, Paul!" Martin and Elsie called out to him. Martin embraced his old mentor. "This is our special gift to you, Paul, to commemorate your great day of freedom," he said.

There were tears in Paul's eyes. Daringly, he went forward to examine that marvel of a bell. Martin had mounted it in a handsome and sturdy metal cage that stood six feet above the ground. Paul expressed astonishment not only at its size, but also at its elegantly curved lines. "And see the size of its tongue!" he exclaimed, bending over to look up at the inside of the bell. "It's so heavy they had to place guards to protect the inside, where the clapper strikes."

Paul found the plaque telling of the bell's origin: the Gould Company in Ithaca, New York. A long way away, he observed. "Yes," Martin said. "That apparently was a main source for those old-time American bells."

"Well, this is the masterstroke to ring in Repeal!" Paul said, beaming. "How did you think of such a thing? And then find it?" So Martin had to tell him of its history, which delighted him.

By this time a handful of employees came running. Remaining with Masson throughout the dark Prohibition period and residing here, they too had been awakened by the sonorous booms. Paul told them to take turns in ringing the giant bell. "We will certainly put to shame all those church bells down in the valley!" he declared.

Just then John came down from the chateau, quivering with excitement. "Oh by golly," he cried, his voice unsteady, choked with emotion. "When I hear that big bell I really know it is true. Good old days return now, no?"

"Yes, John, we made it!" said Masson, putting a large hand fondly on his shoulder. "I always said Prohibition was so absurd that damned if I'd ever let it outlive me," he said. Then he turned to his visitors. "We will start celebrating right now," he proposed. "John, please bring up some champagne. We will drink it before we have our breakfast."

The bell still sang, for the workers were ringing it now, greeting with cheers its booming blasts. "And John!" called Masson. "Make sure the men take some of the good red wine for themselves. A gallon each. And tell them to eat a big dinner with their families, to celebrate."

The bell's loud clangs softened as children took over. A ranch truck, a Model T, roared up the driveway and stopped in the yard. It was Angelo. He leapt out when he saw the bell in action, waving a newspaper.

"So that's where all the racket is coming from!" he cried. "It boomed like thunder down below. Everyone jumped into their cars and started honking!" He ran over to Paul Masson to hand him the newspaper. "Look, Mr. Masson. In big letters it says REPEAL!"

Paul stared at the long-awaited headline and then glanced at the rest of the article as the others looked over his shoulder. Then he sighed: "At last!" He was thinking of his many winegrowing friends who had not survived to this day of Repeal. Some had died; others, growing discouraged, had abandoned the art and trade of the vintner.

Masson looked off to the rolling hills below, tawny in the dormant wintry landscape, and farther away to the far-flung valley, each nearby farm visible and familiar to him in the sharp, clear air of this December morning. All the fine vineyards below were gone. Just to think, at one time there were over four thousand acres of grapevines in the West Side alone—Cupertino, Campbell, Saratoga, Los Gatos.... But now the fertile land was mostly devoted to prunes and apricots. Worthy crops, but not for wine.

He turned from the view. Martin watched Paul, sensing what he was feeling. He hoped Masson wouldn't focus on all that he had lost, but seize this day in gratitude, as the start of a new era—a time of renewed promise. But of new effort too. And was old Paul up to the challenge ahead? For he'd grown stout, stiff with arthritis, and had a faltering heart . . .

John couldn't have appeared with the champagne at a more auspicious moment. Standing out on the terrace, with more than his usual ceremony Paul Masson pried up the metal agrafe and popped the cork. Beyond them the great bell was still pealing. And just as the sparkling wine was being poured into the three waiting goblets, the sun came rising in all its glory over the Diablo Range and spilled into the valley—a perfect symbol for the dawn of a new age for winemakers.

All three raised their glasses and touched them together lightly to produce that lovely silvery plink of pure crystal. And as they drank the zesty, golden champagne they felt their spirits leaping high. Here today, Elsie and Martin poignantly realized, they shared with Paul Masson an important transition in history.

Repeal was being celebrated in all manner of ways all over the country that December day in 1933—whether feted noisily as the dramatic end to the long Dry period, or greeted with relief that the government had finally recognized that its great experiment in regulating human behavior had been an ignoble, even calamitous failure.

Most people in the reviving wine industry figured that nirvana had arrived with Repeal, that from now on they'd have no more problems. As with most things, this new era wouldn't turn out as ideally as anticipated. But it would take time for the sober realities of Repeal and the grimly enduring aftereffects of Prohibition to put in problematic appearances.

So it was well that the bell Martin Ray gave to Paul Masson rang out with such joyous hopefulness on Repeal morning. For dark days and trying years lay ahead for each of them. At that time too my own life would take a drastic turn.

But before any of this went on, Martin came up with an interesting idea—which he proposed during one of our frequent get-togethers. "I've been wondering whether Paul Masson is really going to be able to revive his once-thriving wine business," he speculated. "He's seventy-five now, and his health and strength are questionable. My impression too is that he doesn't have reliable managers and assistants to handle everything that needs to be done in reactivating the winery. And fixing up the vineyards, too."

"So you're thinking he might be interested in selling out," Walter commented in that tone of voice he usually used whenever Martin spoke of his dreams of wine—sardonic, impatient, patronizing.

"Well, as I said, I've been wondering ..."

"Then what are you really saying, Rusty? Do you want to buy him out?"

"I do think it would make a strong investment opportunity for Ray & Company," Martin said rather formally, though his enthusiasm showed in both his voice and face. "Since you're a partner, Walt, you'd have to agree to my approaching Masson—probably through some intermediary."

"He might sell out cheap, since you say Prohibition really hit him hard," Walter said. "And surely he realizes he's too old to make a good go of it now. But why pay an agent's commission if you could arrange your own deal straight out?"

Martin paused and looked at Walter as if he could scarcely believe what he'd heard. "Because I might not get anywhere with Paul if I did that. I've never heard of him negotiating deals directly—certainly not with friends. So I'd have to handle it very carefully. . . ."

Walter snorted. "If he's so evasive, how did he get known as a shrewd businessman?"

"Frenchmen have a different style in doing things."

"But someone else could get to him while you're still just waltzing around."

"Then you are interested in getting into it too?" Martin asked, trying to pin Walter down.

"Maybe. If I don't have to risk my own shirt," Walter said. "The property must be worth something, even if the wine business is not."

"That mountain of Paul's is only part of the attraction," Martin said. "Remember what I've said about the way of life that's possible there?"

"Well, in all your years of talk, I've never been able to picture it for myself," Walter said.

"Is there some way we both could actually see the place?" I now asked Martin.

"Of course! . . . Why didn't I think of that before? Sure, I'll arrange with Paul for the four of us to visit up there soon. Maybe this weekend." Martin beamed at me. This plan was the best way to get Walter to understand what he'd been trying to tell him for so long.

Next day, Martin phoned Masson to ask if he and Elsie could bring up two of their closest friends, a couple. For just a short visit, he assured him. They'd pick up some gourmet picnic fare from a local delicatessen for an informal luncheon out on the terrace, to share with him.

Paul said the coming Saturday would be fine. And that he'd be happy to join them at around noontime. Of course he would supply the wine for the occasion. In the morning he'd be busy in the lower vineyards, so if they came early, Martin could show his friends around the premises.

That's how it worked out that Walter and I, with Martin as our eloquent and knowing guide, first saw the wonders of Masson's mountaintop—its magnificent views as well as the glorious vineyards and the stately winery building with its four floors of cellars. Walter was obviously captivated by La Cresta, almost in spite of himself. And we were both bowled over when Martin, at the end of the tour, led us over to the northeastern edge of the vineyard and pointed over at an undeveloped ridge. "If we owned this property," he said, "you could build a house for yourselves right over there."

"I'm beginning to see what you love about it here," Walter admitted. Hearing this, I felt a rush of hope that living in a spot like this might utterly transform my husband, releasing that hidden inner self, the sensitive country boy I'd married but had scarcely glimpsed for years.

We set out the smorgasbord luncheon casually on the blue-and-white checkered tablecloth Elsie had brought. Soon Paul arrived. After briefly greeting us, he sat down on a bench to shed his boots and don leather slippers. Then he tossed aside his wide-brimmed straw hat.

John arrived at once with a damp linen towel for Masson's use in wiping his hands. "And John," the Frenchman said, getting up and moving toward the table, "please bring out that selection of wines I chose for my friends here!" He sank his heavy frame into a redwood armchair at one end of the table, his customary place as lord of the manor. His eyes settled upon the enticing array of foods Elsie had arranged before him. "Well, MAR-tan, you didn't tell me you were planning a feast like this!" he exclaimed, smacking his lips in anticipated pleasure.

John came out with four bottles of wine—two red and two white. Masson pointed out their differing qualities and vintage years. After the wines were poured—each of us had four glasses for tasting—Martin proposed a toast: "To your continuing Good Life, Paul, and the many splendors you have created here on your mountaintop!"

Masson raised his glass with us, then relaxed back in his chair and drank of his wine, sighing with enormous satisfaction. "Ah," he exclaimed, "this is the only life to live! Eh, MAR-tan?" Martin just grinned in happy agreement.

I'd been curious, I confess, about whether Masson, having once had a somewhat rakish reputation, would show in his advanced years any of these attentions to Elsie and me. He made no attempt to charm us, as if barely noticing our presence. He concentrated on addressing our spouses as he talked. Afterwards, Martin explained that Paul's own wife never came up here.

Walter and I sat back and listened to Masson and Martin converse. Paul seemed tired, yet somehow his powerful presence naturally dominated the scene. By carrying forward the thread of conversation, Martin inspired Paul to furnish some delightful recollections of him as the boy who virtually grew up under his watchful eye. "What do you suppose would have become of you if it hadn't been for my wicked influence?" he asked jocularly. "Probably you would be a teetotaler like your mother! Maybe even a minister of the church—" And at this he gave Martin a sly look.

Walter kept pouring the wines into his glasses, enjoying this ample sampling of Paul Masson wines made during Prohibition years. At the same time he watched Masson closely, clearly impressed with his forceful personality. Since I knew he liked to speculate about how people got the way they were, he must have decided that Masson came from aristocratic stock whose wealth and property were seized in some political upheaval in his homeland. "What was your family history?" he finally asked the Frenchman.

"Oh, the Massons are basically of Burgundian peasant stock," Paul said.

"But the French peasants aren't educated, are they?" Walter wondered.

His face showing sudden outrage, Paul flared up. "What are you talking about? I have a degree from the Sorbonne! One of my brothers is a doctor, the other a lawyer . . . and my parents are scarcely illiterate! Do you think America is the only nation that offers opportunities in education to its citizens? Almost anywhere, people with intelligence and ambition can rise above provincial roots. And just where were you educated, young man?"

"At the University of Washington, with Martin," Walter mumbled. "I meant no insult, believe me, Mr. Masson. My own parents are farmers." His apology seemed to mollify Paul, who quickly went on to another topic.

After an hour or so, the food had been consumed and the wines were gone. It was time for Paul's afternoon nap, Martin knew, and he signaled this to us by starting to gather up our picnic leavings.

Masson got up and walked with us over to the terrace steps. For one last time Walter and I took in the amazing panorama, picturing to ourselves how it might be to live up here—maybe at a not too distant time.

"Well, this is really a great place you have, Paul!" Walter remarked. Then impulsively he ventured it: "Say, if you're thinking of retiring, how about selling it all to our company? Martin, you can be sure, would take the very best care of your vineyards and winery."

Masson drew himself up sharply at the very suggestion. His

heavy jaw quivered as he made a quick response. "No!" he burst out. I will never sell. Never!" Then he added, "How could you ever entertain such a preposterous idea?"

I glanced at Martin. He looked shocked himself that his partner—full of wine and unaccustomed enthusiasm—could jump the gun like this, completely heedless of Martin's having emphasized the need for a cautious and discreet approach.

15

Transitions

NOW THAT PAUL MASSON had been tipped off about Ray & Co.'s interest in buying his property and business, Martin realized he'd have to lie low for a while. Again he forgave a blunder of Walter's. He was pleased at least that his taciturn friend was attracted to the mountain and the possibility of our living there someday. With such a goal in mind, Walter might finally begin to change his big-spending lifestyle. But he soon saw this as an unrealistic hope. If there were any changes, they invariably went in the wrong direction.

Martin began to realize, and then admit to Elsie, that he'd made a bad mistake in admitting Walter into his company. A sound brokerage firm had no place for an unstable partner. He now drew up a tight plan to double-check every move of Walter's that involved Ray & Co. But nothing quite solved the basic problem of Walter. It was evident that Walter would never capably handle a lot of money—not just his own, but other people's. Having it on easy tap went to his head.

Personal intrigues proliferated within and outside of the office. Violations in proper procedures exploded at every turn. Accounts got overdrawn. ("Oh, Rusty, calm down! I'll put the money back tomorrow," Walter would say offhandedly.) Showoff machinations with clients backfired, and Martin learned of them sometimes too late for them to be rectified. And there were blatant affairs with a succession of secretaries, which offended Martin. (I kept a naïve blinder on against suspicions.)

Whenever Martin confronted Walter about such matters—and increasingly he did so—Walter criticized him for being too fussy, puritanical, and demanding, as well as abrupt, unilateral, and dictatorial in decision making. But the fact was, Walter couldn't be trusted.

Martin didn't tell me of such things, for he knew I was worrying already about my own situation with Walter. One evening I had confided in Martin and Elsie. Walter's large income was undermining our marriage, I told them. Earning so much money hadn't soothed his deep insecurity at all; it merely exaggerated his need for admiration and envy. And it enabled him to fool around nightly in dives with dubious companions, while footing the bills like a big shot. And though indulging himself, he seemed maddened over not enjoying anything at all, really.

Still having deep sympathy for Walter, I attributed all his frantic running around to a holdover unhappiness from his childhood. I truly felt that he'd outgrow his insecurity in time if I could only be patient and understanding. I'd also been brought up to believe in personal freedom and that people had no right to *own* someone else. Yet at the same time I believed in mutual fidelity in marriage. I wanted to trust Walter, but . . .

"Trust!" Martin burst out. "That's nuts! More husbands are lost through trust than all the distrust in the world. The women who hold onto their men never let them out of sight." Was he right?

Walter had often complained of seeing me always with some baby in my arms. He wanted a wife to have fun with, he'd said. Which showed he felt excluded and deserted, I now realized. So after my talk with the Rays I decided to change my domestic habits. Asked to play golf with him, tried to join him whenever he went out in the evening. But he didn't like that either. "Why don't you quit trying to follow me around?" he said irritably. "Let's face it: you don't fit in where I go. Just stay home and enjoy your own kind of life."

If trusting that my husband would eventually gain equilibrium was my Achilles heel, firm loyalty to an old friend and business partner proved Martin's Waterloo. Walter's offenses mounted and intensified, followed by more confrontations, contrite promises to reform, then another misdeed. Martin's energy was increasingly consumed in trying to maintain a control system. He felt like a police officer.

Martin often felt the blood pounding in his head. His doctor warned him of his ever-mounting high blood pressure. Try to take it easier—much easier—he advised. Go on a long vacation, far away from stressful work. But Martin couldn't, of course, for that would mean leaving Walter in charge of the brokerage.

Elsie, greatly worried, kept insisting that Walter was the chief cause of Martin's hypertension, whenever Martin attributed it mostly to the fast-action selling of stocks and bonds in these roller-coaster Depression years. Finally, after the latest incident with Walter, Martin finally decided he'd have to end it with his errant partner. Push him out of the company. Tomorrow. And for ever. He knew the loss of income would mean hardship for me and the children, but it simply had to be. His own survival was at stake.

As he drove homeward through The City's heavy traffic, all of a sudden a sharp, terrible pain seized Martin at the back of his neck. It was all he could do to concentrate on driving. He narrowly missed a few collisions. If he could just make it home . . .

Coming in the door, he frantically asked Elsie to get some champagne right away. He sank down on the sofa. When Elsie brought in the chilled bottle, he struggled to get up, then barely managed to open it. As he poured the elixir into their glasses, Elsie searched his face for clues to his high-strung yet exhausted condition. He was like a taut violin string that might snap any second. Once he relaxed a bit with the champagne, she'd ask him about whatever had happened . . .

"It's so hot in here!" he said, taking an urgent swallow. "I had a terrific pain at the base of my head, driving home. Almost didn't get here." In an instant, Elsie knew something was very wrong. She felt his forehead. Blazing hot. He didn't look like himself. His eyes . . .

Suddenly Martin dropped his glass, clutched at the back of his neck, and collapsed on the sofa. Elsie tried to rouse him, but he had blanked out—unconscious. Panicky, she phoned the doctor. When he came, she described what she'd witnessed and told of what Martin had said of an earlier pain while driving home.

He'd been under continuous strain at work for a long while, the doctor reminded her. "It may be a stroke," he said, "though that's very unusual for someone so young. He's only thirty! Still, I'd been warning him that his blood pressure was getting perilously high …"

Helpers were called in to move Martin gently to bed. There he was given various medications. "Maybe it's a temporary spasm of some kind, and he'll just sleep it off," the doctor said hopefully.

Martin slept for twenty-four hours. When he awoke, he was obviously still in great pain. And he could barely move or speak. The doctor came again and declared he must be hospitalized at once. His condition indicated something far more serious than overstress. At the hospital, heavily sedated, Martin slept another full day. Elsie remained at his bedside throughout, except for taking brief breaks. Inevitably she recalled those young years when she sat next to her bedridden first husband as he was slowly dying.

By the third day Martin came partially out of his insensible state and opened his eyes, only to drift off again. Physicians meanwhile put him through various tests: lifting his eyelids to shine lights into his eyes, pricking his skin with electrode probes, banging his legs with rubber hammers. They determined that he probably had suffered a stress-induced, massive occlusion within the brain that caused widespread cerebral nerve damage, to an extent as yet unknown. A neurologist, keeping him eased under light sedation, watched him closely. Martin was partly paralyzed and might never fully recover, he now told Elsie. The best care for him involved complete rest.

After some days, Martin finally regained consciousness. He seemed to recognize Elsie, who had been intermittently trying to coax him into awareness. He smiled at her, made a great effort to speak. But when he moved his lips he merely mumbled. The devastating stroke had ravaged both his memory and ability to speak. For a while, his legs appeared useless, but slowly they began responding, first to neurological tests, then to physical therapy. Day by day, he continued to improve. Ever so slightly.

Amnesia and aphasia, along with partial paralysis of the lower limbs, the neurologist declared. His prognosis was scarcely encouraging. Of those who survive extensive nerve-center brain damage involving loss of memory and speech, he said, few can ever regain comparative normalcy. However, Elsie could hope. . . . But he shook his head dismally and conclusively.

For weeks, Martin's recovery remained uncertain. But Elsie was with him almost constantly, giving quiet and strong encouragement. Apparently, at least, Martin's tremendous willpower hadn't deserted him. He finally managed to say a word now and then that Elsie could understand. But all his thoughts seemed blurred, turned in fuzzy circles. Then, after many struggles and very slowly, he began to make thought connections. Yet he still could remember nothing.

At long last Martin was in stable enough condition to be cared for at home. To assist her, Elsie hired a live-in nurse. Martin was noticeably more relaxed there in their apartment. But was as weak as a baby. With Elsie's help, though, he could now get to the bathroom himself—for him an immense, symbolic advance toward recovery and self-sufficiency.

Martin's doctor wanted him to soak daily in warm baths. As he lay there inertly in the tub, Elsie sat close by, saying simple things to him quietly, asking simple questions to elicit some response. Very gradually, with her loving encouragement, he began to connect present with past. To remember a few things. She would then repeat what he remembered, making slight additions to expand memory associations.

From then on, Elsie saw constant improvement in Martin's ability to speak and recollect. But he still had no strength, and at the least effort would break into a sweat. He had survived the worst part of his total collapse. But would he ever regain normal functions and revert to his vigorous former self? Or be able to work again? Elsie hated to face these questions. There was so little to encourage her.

Elsie now asked the neurologist whether Martin might do something further to pull himself out of this helpless state and come back to the world again. Though the physician still seemed pessimistic, he proposed that Martin start to get physical exercise now, as fast as his body would permit it. Actually, what might help him most would be to get out of The City. If he led a quiet life out in the country, he could find suitable outdoor activities. Why not relocate in some secluded place down in the Santa Clara Valley, where Martin had grown up?

Right away Elsie went off to look at places. She found a charming old house in a woodsy Los Gatos setting and immediately rented it. Once ensconced there, she encouraged Martin to start taking little walks along the peaceful rural road, all by himself. On his first walk, after only a few paces from the house he broke into a sweat, went so limp and tired he scarcely made it home. There he fell heavily on his bed and slept for eight hours.

But Martin persevered, and each day got stronger, could walk a bit farther. Finally he began to look forward tremulously to these daily walks, when he quietly communed with nature and for a brief while depended on no one. But he knew he had to progress beyond these strolls. What else could he do to bring back his strength?

Then Martin remembered Grandfather Lovejoy saying, "There's nothing better than an axe to free your mind and tire your body so you can relax." At his ranch he had taught young Martin how to split and chop up tree limbs, laying them into neat piles for firewood.

Martin decided this work would be his next physical challenge. So he had some rough tree limbs delivered, along with a new double-edged axe. As he ran his hands over the shiny new blade, his face lighted with the most exciting challenge he'd felt since his illness.

Initially it was almost more than he could do just to lift the axe by its handle. And the first time he gave it a few swings he was drenched with perspiration and had to take to his bed for hours. But gradually his strength increased. He could chop wood for ten minutes . . . then half an hour. He found great satisfaction in the growing stack of wood as well as in the bright heat they generated in the fireplace.

This simple work renewed not only his energy but his confidence. After an hour of woodcutting, Martin first would rest, and then ponder how to enlarge his sphere of activity further. Gradually he undertook ever larger projects in both house and garden. Now what other things might he dare think of doing?

Then one day Martin, in wonderment, halted all this pondering. How could he have forgotten it? *The mountain*—that great dream he'd harbored since boyhood of acquiring a world of his own like Paul Masson's, and creating glorious wines there! Over the past year that dream had somehow been wiped from his memory. But now, by God, he would get it back! One of these days he'd go up and see Paul Masson. Talk to him; find out how his revived business was doing since Repeal. But not quite yet. Paul should not see him in his present weakened state.

After moving to the country, Martin had been referred to a psychiatrist at the Stanford Medical Center who specialized in treating patients with central nervous system damage. Some were shell-shocked veterans of the Great War. Thus Dr. K. V. Francis had begun to help Martin immensely at this stage of his recovery.

After examining Martin and researching his medical history as well as talking with Elsie, Dr. Francis concluded that Martin had been pushed into dangerous hypertension for years. Dealing constantly with many demanding situations and contradictory variables finally led to a near-total shutdown of mind and body. The equivalent, he suggested, of living in the trenches, under frequent and heavy bombardment, for months or even years. Martin's high-stress brokerage work had been a significant factor, yes. But he also considered the brief collapse Martin had suffered some years before, after returning from New York—when, famished and exhausted, he was stunned by Corky's insults and his close friend's rejection. Somehow this experience could have harmed his nervous system, predisposing it toward some future breakdown under extreme stress. True, Martin ostensibly had coped well with the shock and aftermath of the stock-market Crash, but doubtless they took an inner toll. Then the tension generated by his partner's perpetual misbehavior provided that final, catastrophic catalyst.

Dr. Francis avoided the deep analytic probing of the psyche that Sigmund Freud was pioneering. He knew Martin could never endure such long-term and rambling couch talk. Instead, he gave Martin simple, practical instructions that enabled him to avoid stress and confusion by always handling everyday problems as they came up. Among other admonitions, Dr. Francis impressed upon him the absolute necessity to simplify every thought and move in his life.

Thus Dr. Francis tailor-made his treatment for Martin. "If you have two problems," he'd tell him, "you *must* put one aside. This may sound easy, but it isn't. Keep it constantly in mind. For, around other people, you can be bombarded with a number of ideas all at once. Arguments too, of course. Protect yourself always against them. Consider but one single thought, one problem, and set all the rest aside for a time ... or forever, if need be."

By applying Dr. Francis's concise directives, Martin began making a remarkable recovery. Elsie was greatly impressed with his rapid progress, and decided she should know every nuance of Dr. Francis's method, the better to protect her husband's vulnerability to stress in the future. So for months she had individual sessions of psychiatric training—which proved immeasurably helpful. By learning how to spot all manner of potential problems, she could avoid and thereby prevent most complications and chaotic scenes from ever getting close to Martin.

I saw Martin briefly toward the end of his long convalescence. He looked perfectly normal to me. Walter and I had not been allowed to visit him either in the hospital or later at home. Doctors' orders, we were told. Walter seemed relieved to accept it at that and therefore did not push to go in. (I suspected at the time, of course, that Elsie had alerted physicians and hospital staff to the necessity of banishing any stress or annoyance, which Walter, above all others, could have embodied.)

Fortunately, Martin's expensive medical care and sustenance were largely paid for by a health insurance policy, supplemented by savings he had accrued from years of hard work. So the Rays did not depend upon income from the profits at Ray & Company— where Walter, as the other senior partner, was now at the helm, at its main office in San Francisco.

Martin, perforce insulated from business concerns by his illness, first had no ability and then no inclination to question what might be going on during Walter's stewardship. As he emerged into improved health and mental energy, he persuaded himself that this take-charge opportunity was exactly what Walter had needed to prove his mettle under fire. For if something had gone badly awry, Martin surely would have heard of it by now. . . .

During the long year of Martin's hospitalization and recuperation, to me Walter appeared more responsible, far less restless and rebellious. He often stayed for the whole work week in The City now, coming home to San Jose on weekends. And then he didn't run off to nightclubs. Nor was he so apt to criticize or ridicule me. To be sure, he was still remote, disclosing little of what he really felt about anything. Like Rusty, I believed that the unexpected responsibility of directing the brokerage firm benefited him, and that he was at last growing out of his chronic adolescence.

But how we were both fooled, Martin and I!

One day Martin, accompanied by Elsie, finally made a brief

visit to the office in San Francisco. This trip was regarded as therapeutic—an encouragement for him to progress further in getting back to work of some kind. No one was expecting him there. And when he quickly reviewed the records of the past year, he experienced a real shock. During his long absence Walter had never made a single day's profit for the firm from stock and bond sales!

Martin uncovered this and much more. To sustain himself in his accustomed high-living style, Walter had dipped heavily into company funds. One means was through a new double-signature resolution card at the bank, on which he had forged Martin Ray's signature to pair with his own. Or rather Walter's new secretary had forged it. This duo of embezzlers had set up living quarters together in a nearby hotel suite.

Furious but struggling to hold onto calmness through a steely composure, Martin summarily ordered these two crooks out of the office—implying that Walter would face lawsuits for both the signature forgery and his misappropriation of corporate assets.

This quick end of the partnership, a godsend to Martin, simultaneously spelled the end of my marriage. For Walter came home and, giving no explanation, swiftly packed up some clothing in suitcases, cleaned out the liquor cabinet, and departed—evidently heading south to evade arrest.

A shock, yes. But after several days, when I finally realized he had probably gone for ever, an enormous weight was lifted from me. For years I had been vainly trying to prop up a dispirited person's morale, and becoming victimized in that very role. I'd never realized how heavy that burden of caring had become. So gradually I began to feel as light as air. I felt a surge of new energy toward creating a future on my own.

Even the staggering financial problems I faced somehow got converted into challenges. For Walter had left the children and me with few tangible assets and no provision for support. At first I assumed he'd made some arrangement for Ray & Co. to provide me with regular payments. I'd been told nothing of his theft of Ray & Co. funds. Knowing of his touchy condition, I avoided bothering Martin now with my personal concerns. But I did talk with Elsie. She hadn't heard that Walter had left me and tried to be sympathetic. But her proper role was to protect Martin. She informed me that Walter was no longer connected with Ray & Co., had left deeply in debt to the firm and definitely under duress. So I could not look to the company for any support. She advised that if Walter was not sending me support payments. I should take legal action at once.

(None of us knew where Walter had gone. Months later I found out that he lived now in Hollywood. Obviously fearing forgery and embezzlement indictments, he and his female accomplice had fled there together. So Walter at last was pursuing his originally intended vocation of writing—screenwriting now. And eventually he married this woman who, he'd told friends proudly, threatened to kill him if he ever went back to his wife or had an affair with any other woman. So Rusty had been right. Walter couldn't respect a wife who accorded trust while granting him unsupervised freedom!)

I couldn't afford to hire either a lawyer or a detective. I quickly realized that I had no time to brood in despair or to rage over abandonment. Nor could I succumb to a paralyzing fear over being a single parent wholly responsible for raising three small children during the Depression years. I had to get a job to support us, and fast. Few if any jobs would be available to me now, at the nadir of the Depression. So I knew I'd have to *invent* a job for myself—somehow, somewhere. I decided that advertising was the proper place for me.

So I went directly to the advertising manager of the Emporium, the big San Francisco department store where I had worked years before. I told him I thought they needed a good new copy editor for their ads—which, I claimed, lacked customer appeal. Probably as a kind but easy way to dismiss me, he said, "Well, just take some of our ads home, and tell me later what you'd do with them."

Actually nothing was *wrong* with their ads, I saw when I looked at them closely. But since I was desperate, I managed to find them faulty, some even ludicrous. Fresh ideas rollicked through my head. So I wrote the manager an amusing letter detailing my critiques of the ads, and then replanned them. When next I dropped in to see him, he almost threw his arms about me. I'd made myself a job!

But before starting work, there were things to do. I must move to The City to be close to my job. And get a housekeeper to care for the children. Not to mention find a house to rent at no more than $25 a month—all I could afford on a monthly salary of a mere $125 (which I was lucky to get, at that). Until my job began I was broke. I sold off everything I could for cash: all our elegant household furnishings. And even my car. It did hurt to sell the mellow-toned Mason-Hamlin grand piano, but its heavy weight for certain would crash through the floor of the absurd little clapboard farmhouse I'd found right in the heart of San Francisco . . . yes, for $25 per month!

The Matson Line Roths had their famed "Why Worry Farm" down the Peninsula from me. Now I had my "Why Not Worry Farm." I loved that laughable little dilapidated house more than any other place on Earth—a precious haven, and all our own!

From then on the children and I had a great time of it. (I told this tale in my book *We Kept Mother Single,* published in 1951—so no more about all this.)

One bright noontime on my lunch hour, as I was dashing through San Francisco's Union Square, I ran smack into Martin Ray! Of course we fell into each other's arms like the long-lost friends we were. Martin looked wonderful—the same old vibrant, sunny Rusty Ray I had so cherished since our college years in Washington.

"Let's have lunch together!" he proposed, happily relieved to see me thriving on my own out in the world.

Months had gone by since we'd been in contact. Why? Because I had been so devilishly busy fixing up our lives since Walter's departure. And Martin and Elsie had no idea where I'd disappeared to.

I told him about my job, the children, and our little "Why Not Worry Farm." He was delighted at my ability to treat the crisis in my life as an adventure. As I talked, though, I could tell that Martin was palpitating to tell me *his* exciting news.

He ordered champagne. Paul Masson champagne, it was. "So very much has happened," he began. "You haven't heard? But where shall I start? Because there's so much to tell . . ."

"Start right at the beginning," I urged. "And don't leave out a single thing!"

And this is how I learned that Martin Ray had entered an exciting new phase of his life.

PART III

INTO SUMMER GLORY

1936-1941

16

Buying the Dream

Here is the story Martin Ray told me during our champagne lunch together, that day we'd met serendipitously in San Francisco:

When Martin felt he'd recovered sufficiently from the invalidism that had lasted a year, he went up to see Paul Masson on his mountaintop. As they'd done so many times before, the two old friends took a bottle of champagne out on the terrace. Heartily they toasted the occasion of their meeting for the first time in more than a year.

Paul quickly noticed that Martin was sipping the sparkling wine gingerly, as if rationing himself. "What are you doing, MARtan? You look like an old lady with a cup of tea!"

"It's awful, I know, Paul. But the doctors say I shouldn't have more than a touch of alcohol, if even that, for a while longer."

"Bah!" snorted Masson. "My doctor has been telling me for years not to do this and that. Almost anything good, in fact. Not eat cheese, not have sweets, not put cream on anything. With Louise gone now, he has appointed himself guardian of my health. He really tries to push me around. But he would never dare tell me that I couldn't have wine! Anyway, I don't pay much attention to what he says. And here I am, still going strong."

Masson sat in his chair in the sun, rubbing first his knuckles, then his knees. Martin knew all too well how Paul conducted his life. Forget special diets! He'd seen him make a simple supper of cubes of dry French bread, then pour on whole cream—but virtuously top it all off with a bit of milk. For years he'd had circulatory problems: a weakening heart, hardening of the arteries, high blood pressure, plus diabetes onset. But at least he'd made it into his mid-seventies.

Recently Martin had heard reports that in the two years since

Repeal Masson was not regaining the prosperity his prestigious winery had enjoyed before Prohibition. Doubtless the lingering economic depression was partly to blame. But Paul did look old, tired, frail. Would he ever consider retiring? Martin, however, vividly recalled the vintner's fierce response when Walter had asked him whether he'd sell out. Though circumstances change. Maybe in the past year, fighting an uphill battle at his advanced age, he'd looked at the possibility of unloading his corporation. Which would be Martin's chance to buy the place he so loved.

Now, too, Martin really *needed* the mountain and the way of life it offered. From his sessions with Dr. Francis he knew he must end any daily involvement in the high-pressure brokerage scene, with its constant competition and conflict.

If Masson was considering selling, surely he'd want his vineyard and winery to belong to a man he trusted, knowing that his traditions would continue on in the care of someone he himself had educated in winegrowing techniques and values. A stranger would have entirely different notions.

The conversation was edging in that direction when Paul began complaining bitterly about his problems. Prohibition had ruined his vines and cellars, and had also wrecked the market for California wines. With Repeal, wine connoisseurs could again buy European wines over the counter; why should they buy American wines sure to be inferior? And those many Americans who out of desperation had drunk bootleggers' swill wanted nothing more to do with wine now, thinking that was how it would always taste! In the meantime, wineries had popped up everywhere, flooding the market with hastily bottled, frightful concoctions made for quick profits. Few people bought them.

"We barely climbed out of Prohibition and now we are in another wine depression—the worst yet!" Paul exclaimed in utter disgust.

"Paul," Martin finally got up the nerve to ask, "have you given any recent thought to selling your property and business?"

The Frenchman quickly turned on him, irate. "Sell this mountain? Never!" he thundered, glaring at Martin as though he were a thief. Only *he* had the skills and knowledge to tackle the complex work involved in rescuing the Paul Masson Champagne Company, he declared. Anyone else would make a mess of it—and fail.

Martin had learned early never to argue with Masson, to challenge any statement of his. A virtual potentate on his mountain, he would not abide being crossed. Ever. So he said nothing and simply let Paul rant on.

"But those problems you complain about, Paul, constitute the very challenge I want!" Martin at last dared to assert.

"You? *You* want to buy me out?" Paul looked at him almost contemptuously. "Well, forget it," he said.

They spoke of other things for a while. As Paul began to calm down, his manner toward Martin mellowed, and he became kindly, almost paternal. "Anyway," he said, "you know I'm devoted to you, MAR-tan. So I can't let you be a damn fool." And if Martin insisted upon getting into the winegrowing business at such a desperate time, *this* was what he should do. . . .

Masson got up from his chair and walked toward the edge of the terrace. "Start out fresh," he advised Martin, who had come to his side. "Buy that wild mountain just north of my land." He gestured toward the other side of the little canyon between the two hills. "It's actually the other half of this mountain, which county maps call Table Mountain. See ..." He pointed to a high ridge in the northwest, far above where they stood. "The two top ridges actually join at one point at the very crest, two thousand feet high."

"You would pay far less for undeveloped land," Paul continued. "Don't buy a place like mine! The land will be eroded—spent. Neglected during Prohibition because vineyard owners couldn't afford to keep many skilled vineyard workers. The vines that produced fine wine grapes will be old and diseased, or dead. In any case, badly pruned for years. Or grafted over to the shipper and juice grapes the bootleggers wanted."

Martin saw he couldn't persuade Paul to see things differently. Not today, anyway. After departing, he of course continued to ponder the matter. His heart and head remained firmly set on acquiring Masson's developed vineyards as well as the winery business with its all-important, established name and prestigious lineage. He had the drive and vision to make a success of it, though it might take years of exertion.

How would he find a way around Masson's objections? Martin talked in confidence with Masson's banker. He heard from a banker friend that a $50,000 bank loan was coming due; the bank was concerned that Paul would be unable to meet it. Then Masson might have no other alternative than to sell.

So armed with that knowledge, Martin decided to approach Paul again, hoping that in the meantime he'd been reconsidering both his situation and Martin's expressed interest. Maybe the banker would have prodded him too. But when he brought the subject up again, Paul flew into another tirade.

"Why do you persist in being such a goddamn *idiot!*" Masson stormed at Martin. He paced back and forth in utter vexation that Martin would have the gall to introduce that noxious topic once more. "You have no idea of what you would be getting yourself into!" he said, once he seated himself.

"My vineyards are a disaster and must be replanted," he intoned in a weary voice. "The cellars need complete overhauling. And what is worse, much worse, any taste that the American people were developing for fine wine has been utterly destroyed. And it will take fifty years—half a century—to bring it back!" As he looked at his visitor in a penetrating way, his face bore an intense expression of pity and scorn. And vexation beyond endurance. "MAR-tan, do you really think that *you*, with no experience in these matters, could turn this place around and make it thrive again, when I cannot? *Mon Dieu!*" He had again worked himself up into a state and was almost yelling as he banged his walking stick upon the floor.

"I'm sorry I even suggested it, Paul," said Martin, shocked at the old man's rage.

Paul finally grew calmer. "Just remember my advice to you last time we talked of this," he said. "That's what *I* would do if I were a young man like you."

But Martin Ray never gave up easily on any plan or dream of his. So he resorted to a go-between. Going through an agent might be his only hope for making a deal. Visiting a local realtor who knew Paul Masson on a friendly basis, he spoke of his desire to acquire both the Masson land and winemaking business. The broker told Martin what he'd learned over the years: Paul held the Old World view, that a gentleman didn't conduct direct business negotiations himself but left transactions to an agent. So he'd be glad to represent him.

The broker then went to Masson and made a good offer on behalf of an anonymous third party. Though reluctant, Paul at least heard the man out. Said he'd think it over. There were more sessions, and more sessions beyond those, with the price and stipulations escalating. Behind the scenes, Martin directed every proposal.

All to no avail. "He refuses to sell, that's all there is to it," the broker always reported. "But he *has* to sell!" Martin would retort, and then think up some new plan of attack.

Paul kept stalling. Yet at last he gave in. The explanation was that his doctor insisted that he sell. But this was after setting a price almost prohibitive for Martin, who had wanted to finance the deal all by himself. But at least he could meet it by bringing in some trusted old Ray & Co. clients as co-investors. It was that important to him.

And who was the unnamed buyer? Masson finally asked when the time came for going into escrow. "He almost blew his top when he heard who it was!" the broker reported afterwards to Martin. "He was trembling violently with shock. 'MAR-tan Ray?' he shouted. 'For the love of God, why didn't you tell me that to begin with?

So he thought that through you he'd get around me!'"

Still, Masson's expression had shown a touch of amusement. "I should have guessed all along that scamp was involved in this," Paul had said. Then he'd fumbled in his pocket to draw out a tiny silver cognac flask and raise it to his lips. "But it's unthinkable—unforgivable!" the Frenchman declared. Kindly but determinedly he dismissed the agent. So the set deal was off.

With his dream aborted just before realizing it, Martin decided that backing off and biding his time might yield a solution. Days passed, then weeks. What if someone else bought the place, now that Paul was willing to sell? He grew desperate with a renewed determination. By God, he'd drive up there on the mountain and confront Paul Masson for one last time . . . even though it risked ending their friendship!

He'd make it seem offhand, casual. Paul was probably still angry with him. But once they got together, if Martin handled it just right, he just might be able to smooth things over.

Martin took some peace offerings with him up to La Cresta—insurance that he'd at least get a civil reception. Plump, wonderfully fresh artichokes from Castroville, wild mushrooms just picked in Santa Cruz, and those *andouillettes,* the sausages that Paul so prized, from the only butcher around who could still make them.

Paul greeted Martin cautiously, carefully. But when he set his eyes upon the andouillettes, he couldn't hold out—and exploded with enthusiasm. After that it was as if there had never been any trouble between them. They talked and laughed together as Paul described in his colorful way various happenings on the mountain. Neither mentioned, of course, the hapless deal.

And then Paul asked him to stay for dinner. They'd of course have the andouillettes. Happily, Martin accepted the invitation. They relaxed with their champagne out in the afternoon sun, then had a delicious meal and several bottles of wine. Paul selected one bottle for himself and kept it close to him—his daily wine quota, as he'd promised his doctor.

Martin drank more than he intended to of Masson's enormous reds—some pinot noirs he'd vintaged during the Prohibition years. He began to feel giddy. Then he threw caution to the winds—but eased into that forbidden subject by aiming at it obliquely.

"Wouldn't we have fun, Paul, if we could carry on here like this far into the future—enjoying life to its fullest, the two of us together? Nothing would really need to change. You could remain as president. We'd give great dinners up here with all our friends ..."

"Dinners?" At this Masson's eyes watered with sudden pleasure. "Yes, yes!" He straightened up and his eyes held such fire that he no longer looked old and infirm. Martin caught a flash of the powerful figure he had first seen as a boy—the boy who long ago had clambered up the trail to Masson's mountaintop. To those vineyards in the sky, where a Frenchman kept the lights blazing all night while he entertained the social elite of San Francisco, the politicos, artists, actors and actresses . . .

"Ah yes," Paul was saying dreamily, "we might have many fabulous dinners together. An endless series of them. I'd come to know all your friends, and you'd know mine." Then he halted. He stared off into the distant hills, and when he spoke again his voice was dispirited. "But I don't have many friends left anymore. They are mostly dead now. Most people I knew in the wine business are gone too—left it during the Dry time, or ended up in jail, if not in the grave."

"But I have friends, Paul, and they'll be your friends too," Martin offered.

"MAR-tan!" began Paul in sudden inspiration. "Is it possible that you know any young French couples? How I long to hear the melodious sound of my own language again at the dinner table."

Paul didn't realize that he had played right into Martin's hands. Martin was well prepared for this. "As a matter of fact, I do!" he replied. "I know two very attractive French couples. In the restaurant business. They are connoisseurs of both food and wine." As he proceeded to tell Masson more about them, Paul leaned forward, hungrily intent on his every word.

Delicious and mischievous memories twinkled in Paul's eyes as he relived in memory the essence of all the great dinners held at La Cresta through the years, vibrant with gaiety, flirtations, splendid attire, cultivated conversation. Could such times possibly return again for him through his young friend Martin? He sighed. "Maybe—" He wavered just for a moment. "It is an idea, MAR-tan. ... I think I like it. I *do* like it. Let us just leave it there, and enjoy our dinner now."

With gusto and relief the two men leisurely drank their wine and ate their meal, knowing the matter had been settled between them. The only time Paul mentioned it was when they were about to say goodnight. Paul suddenly dropped his voice.

"Now, MAR-tan," he said earnestly, "one thing is important. I trust you don't intend for your wife to live up here. For us Burgundian winemakers, that is like fouling one's nest. This life at the mountain ranch should be yours alone—for doing the hard work, yes, but also for entertaining very special clients. My wife and daughter were rarely permitted to set foot here. Nor did I allow the ordinary residents in the valley to come up and visit, as they often asked to do. This was my domain—mine alone. The women in my family had their beautiful home down in the valley to keep them happy. It was a perfect arrangement. And so it should be for you as well."

These words hit Martin like a bucket of cold water, but he said nothing in reply. Of course Elsie would live up here with him in the chateau! But to pipe up in protest, saying that things were different in the U.S., might well jinx this now amicable deal, which had been impossibly difficult to negotiate. Let the French have their customs. Once here, Martin would establish and maintain his own.

That little dinner for two was a historical milestone. From then on, Martin and Paul reveled in a succession of magnificent dinners at the chateau—celebratory transitions into the change in owner-ship and residency. Their pleasure was vastly heightened by the rare French wines Martin had been accumulating in his "treasure trove" collected since Prohibition times.

And from the start, without saying anything to Paul, Martin made it clear that he fully intended for Elsie to be always present as reigning hostess. She did so with such warmth, charm, and *élan* that Masson was inescapably enchanted. Indeed, he seemed to for-get entirely about banning wives from the chateau life.

The broker representing Martin and Paul's lawyer and banker took care of all details in the sale of Masson's large acreage, his cor-poration, winery business, and wines. Amazingly, this all went on without either of the principals ever speaking of it to each other.

Both were present, naturally, at the lawyer's office to sign the final documents. There Paul made one last shrewd Burgundian move. Martin had taken up the pen to affix his signature when Paul said in an offhand way, "MAR-tan, I have one more little thing . . ." He looked up. What the devil?

"See this small area here on the other side of Pierce Road?" Paul handed Martin a map with a spot he had circled. "Many years ago, the road ran below my property. It crossed a wooden bridge, which in time became too rickety to support the weight of four full pun-cheons of wine en route to town. So I made a deal with the county. I deeded them a right-of-way across my property for them to build a new road higher up, which wouldn't require a bridge. That change in the road cut off this section from the rest of my land. . . . Now, MAR-tan, I am so used to having a place in the country to drive to every day. So I would like to keep those few acres, and maybe put up a tiny house there. The land will be of no value to you. There are just a few old prune trees on it."

Martin looked up, quizzical. Why hadn't this matter been brought up before? "How many acres are there, Paul?"

"Why . . . fourteen, I believe." Masson glanced at his lawyer, who nodded agreement.

Scarcely a minuscule property, Martin told himself. But certainly considering the total size of the La Cresta ranch, 185 acres, sixty of them planted to vineyards, they seemed a trivial amount. Also, wouldn't it be nice to have Paul close by part of the time?

"Okay, Paul," he agreed. The lawyer had already prepared the release papers for him to sign.

Another item struck Martin oddly. The lawyer reported that Adele Masson, having learned of the impending sale, insisted on a codicil that would grant her the right to come to La Cresta at any time and there sit upon a certain large rock. Paul looked embarrassed, even pained, over the very mention of his daughter's strange demand. Since Masson's own lawyer maintained that granting this access might cloud the title, Martin simply refused to honor the request.

That afternoon Martin and Elsie took a drive to look over their new domain. On the way, they wanted to see the fourteen acres they'd given up so readily. They were astonished to find them on an enchanting hillside—with a perfect exposure and slope for a vineyard.

"That wily old Burgundian!" Martin commented. All they could do now was laugh at being taken in. Yet Martin suspected that had he refused to turn over the property, the whole deal might have fallen through. He couldn't have endured that! And Paul surely had been counting on this.

"Well, he kept a gorgeous plot of land for himself," Elsie agreed. "But it actually makes me happy to know he still owns a piece of his old ranch."

So, elated that their destiny was determined now, the new owners drove up the narrow, winding road to their newly acquired mountain. They strolled around the premises, champagne goblets in hand, admiring the grand vista that now was theirs. And as they moved hither and yon, Martin kept scouting for Adele's mystery rock.

It was a crisp March day, yet a glorious fragrance wafted about, creating an atmosphere Mexicans call *la prima primavera* (the first spring)—an early and deceptive "false" spring. Buds and fresh green leaves were popping out on the vines spread out on all sides of them.

This joy in possessing the mountain of his dreams Martin long had anticipated. A relaxing, salutary interlude like this was essential before plunging into the hard work that lay ahead.

Now what was it Paul Masson had tried to warn him about ... being a damn fool?

17

Challenges Unbidden

ALMOST IMMEDIATELY, MARTIN RAY began paying a higher price than he'd anticipated for his mountaintop dream. First off, he was smacked in the face with an alarming situation.

All Paul Masson wines were customarily bottled, cased, and sold not from the mountain cellars but from the old Lefranc building in San Jose. At the time Martin bought the business, Masson maintained an office there. Over the years, by conducting all business from his city headquarters, he was able to keep his mountain estate as a pleasant retreat, free of any contamination from trade contacts.

Martin Ray soon discovered that the Masson company was in jeopardy because of its modus operandi at this very building. Making several inventory checks, Martin was struck dumb to find that several hundred cases of champagne simply had disappeared within a few days. Immediately he called in a detective to conduct a 24-hour a day surveillance from a room located across the street. He hired another to pose as a new employee.

The two detectives soon provided abundant evidence of thievery. Every night a truck or two would back up to the freight door and load champagne. For years, it turned out, the cellarmaster had been paying his bills with cases of champagne. And his personal taste ran into high expenses: for instance, he'd just acquired a Packard car in exchange for a hundred cases of champagne.

As for the workday in the warehouse, the investigator there observed this daily routine: Right after checking in, the cellarmaster and his cronies would open a bottle or two of champagne and sit about for the first hour or so exchanging stories about the previous night's escapades. Then they'd do a few chores. At about 11 o'clock again the man would say, "Well, fellows . . ." That was the signal to start popping corks again, so as to be pleasantly exhilarated by noon, at which time they knocked off for a two-hour lunch break. After several hours of leisurely afternoon work, they'd gather once more for a round of champagne to build up a suitable mood for that evening's adventures.

The in-house detective also found the answer to one of Martin's puzzlements. While cleaning out Paul Masson's office so as to make it his own, Martin wondered why so many large paper bags were crammed into drawers in a big cabinet. He couldn't get a satisfactory answer from Paul's secretary. She was remaining there to help Masson gather up his papers but also assist him whenever he came by, as he still did out of long habit. The detective enlightened Martin now: not a single employee—including this secretary—left the premises at night without a bag bulging with wine bottles!

Martin was horrified. How long had large-scale rip-off been going on? First Prohibition had bled Masson nearly dry. Then, when his fortunes should have upturned with Repeal, his trusted employees were busily undermining any chance for financial recovery. Without Paul's awareness or suspicion, they systematically drained him financially by stealing his wines.

Doubtless the period that encouraged lawlessness made this internal chicanery seem permissible. Apparently the workers expected to continue on this way, despite any change in command. They didn't know Martin Ray. Within thirty days all employees had been fired. All wines were transferred to the mountain winery, where he could keep his eye on them. From now on, shipping would go out directly from La Cresta's premises.

So Martin had this problem firmly in hand, at least. But hardly had he finished dealing with it than another crisis hit.

For years Paul Masson had marketed all his wines through one wholesaler, a good and longtime friend of his. All through Prohibition the man had sold only the champagne, but after Repeal he could offer Masson's full line of wines as they began to be released.

This arrangement for handling distribution was ideal for Paul, freeing him from direct contact with anyone else in "the trade." Periodically, the two men met together over a glass of champagne at the St. Claire Club. While Paul told his friend what wines he could have and at what prices, the wholesaler took notes. Then the gentlemen dismissed crass business matters so they could enjoy their foods and wines together.

Martin saw no reason to change this amicable situation. But suddenly this wholesaler dropped dead of a heart attack. As Paul Masson's sole sales representative, he was thus Martin's only direct "customer." A complete stranger took over in his place. And from that day Martin received not a single order. Here he was, with an overhead of $5,000 a month—formidable in those days—with but one client. Who wasn't buying.

When Martin telephoned him, the man coolly told him that he would give him an order for 500 cases of champagne—if he'd take a price cut of 25 percent. "Damnation," said Martin to himself, knowing he was cornered. He had all these terrific expenses. He'd have to take the cut. But he felt furious and apprehensive.

Sure enough, when the next order came up for discussion the wholesaler demanded a deeper cut. Martin told him frankly that he couldn't cut his prices further and stay in the quality wine business. He had hoped to reason with the fellow. But he was abruptly informed that if he didn't wish to supply him on that basis, plenty of others would.

"For your information, Mr. Ray, Masson is no longer one of the few bonded wineries in California, as it was during Prohibition," the man went on. "You're but one in hundreds! Every ex-bootlegger and his brother are now in the wine business—and they're offering me all the wine I can take, at next-to-nothing prices." Then, dropping his voice, he added, "However, if you meet my price I can make it worth your while. I can sell all the champagne you can turn out. Any amount of it. You'll make up for your price-cut on volume."

Martin explained that his business never could be a volume operation. His production was limited to the grapes grown in his own vineyards. He also wished to maintain high quality in his wines—impossible in a big-volume operation. But the wholesaler cut him off. "That's your problem, not mine. It's yes or no, Mr. Ray. You work with me or you don't."

Having put it crudely that way, he made up Martin's mind for him instantly. "No!" Martin said decisively. Then, after ringing off, he sat there for a long time, stunned. He'd cut himself off from his one and only customer! He'd have to start from scratch on sales, a hellish position for a newcomer—and right in the midst of a terrible wine depression. But by God he was right, he reaffirmed to himself. Never again would he deal with such a man.

Wistfully he thought of Paul's "talking it over" with his gentleman friend over a glass of champagne, letting him know what wines he could have. No more! Prohibition had spawned a different race of tradespeople, with tough, often criminal backgrounds, and no appreciation of fine wines—including their monetary worth. For the love of God, how could he work himself out of this impasse?

Just then the phone rang. And who should it be, at Martin's lowest hour, but former U.S. Marshall Asona—who wanted six cases of champagne delivered to his home by that night.

"Is this an order?" Martin asked, remembering all too well what Paul had said of this man. Silence. "You're paying for them?"

Asona was indignant. Of course he had no intention of paying for them! Masson always furnished him with all the champagne he needed. Martin informed him that Prohibition had been over for three years now. Hadn't he heard of Repeal?

The man then said, in a tight voice, that Martin would find it worth his while to furnish him with the sparkling wine. He just might do him a "favor" someday . . .

At this Martin blew his top. "If I ever need a favor from you, I'll be in one hell of a shape!" he shot back at him. And hung up.

That did it. To calm himself, he went outdoors. He paced up and down. As he looked out on the wide valley below, slowly a sense of peaceful purpose began to infuse his spirit. He had never shied away from challenges, but always met them head on.

He needed that resolve. For don't calamities come in threes? The following one was certainly the worst. And was predetermined before Martin Ray even took over the Paul Masson winery.

Over the years, partly under Paul's guidance, Martin had developed a good palate. Still, when it came to paying a large sum for the Masson wine inventory alone, with most of the wines still in cask, he knew it would be unsound to rely on his personal judgment alone in appraising the wines. He'd be biased toward having a favorable opinion of them. But more crucially, his ability to judge wines admittedly had declined during his illness, when for so long his doctor had prohibited all drinking. Even now, he could safely drink only infrequently and abstemiously. And keeping one's palate sensitive required daily drinking of the best.

So Martin concurred with his banker's opinion: it would be foolhardy to risk a heavy investment in Masson wines without getting advice from an acknowledged expert. Since the banker suggested the well-reputed E. R. Morris, Martin contacted him. He would be paid a substantial fee to taste each wine and also make a chemical analysis, which his firm was equipped to do. Masson, who already knew Morris, invited him to come up for a luncheon the day he picked up the wines. Martin joined them, so the three men had a most enjoyable repast, in which a series of elegant wines were served from Masson's personal "library."

In the meantime, Paul's cellarmaster at the winery was drawing off two sample bottles of wine from each cask. One set was to be carefully tasted and assessed by Morris as well as given a chemical analysis; the other was for Martin Ray. Each pair of bottles was numbered, in case they wished to discuss any particular wine.

Morris promised to give Martin his report in a few days. After some days passed, Martin became impatient, as the delay was holding up the sale. He phoned Morris, who apologized and said he hadn't realized Martin was awaiting his word before making the decision to buy. "You're a lucky young man to be able to acquire such wines; they're all excellent!" he told him. "You need not hesitate. You couldn't find finer ones anywhere—certainly not here in California." Greatly relieved, Martin went ahead and promptly closed the deal.

From the day Martin took over, he made it his habit to check the cask cellars daily. Gradually he tasted through them, acquainting himself thoroughly with each variety, each vintage, and each individual cask of that vintage, which sometimes varied considerably. Masson had been making red and white still wines throughout Prohibition, declared for his personal use; he could not sell them. Like other bonded wineries, as Repeal drew near he had increased the quantity of wine made, anticipating the time ahead when he could resume bottling and marketing it.

Over the years Martin had known Paul Masson wines intimately, and of course loved them. He was still drinking sparingly, as his doctor ordered. To taste accurately, he would simply roll a mouthful of wine around in his palate, allowing his tongue to sample the composite flavors while pushing the aroma into the nasal passages. Then, having subjected the mouthful of wine to various internal sensory tests, he spat it out into a bucket.

Now he was worried. Many of these wines in cask didn't please him entirely. In fact—how he hated to admit it!—some seemed downright bad. Perhaps his palate hadn't yet regained its earlier sensitivity. Yet as he continued to taste through these cask wines, the more he fretted. Morris had pronounced them sound, in fact superb. But Martin no longer felt confident of this expert opinion. So finally one day he decided to double-check the evaluation. He sent off all the duplicate sample bottles for chemical analysis to a firm other than Morris's. The report came back swiftly: every wine was high in volatile acidity, exceeding the legal limit. Some of Masson's wines, in fact, were very close to being vinegar.

Martin Ray was badly stricken at the news. He was scarcely prepared to take the loss of the large amount of money he'd paid for the bulk wines alone. He depended on a profitable sale of these liquid assets. When bottled, they'd substantially recover the sizable investment he'd made.

Frantically he sped into San Francisco to confront Morris. He asked how could he have made such a mistake, and showed him the lab report.

"Impossible!" said Morris. Finally, though, he admitted under Martin's sharp questioning that he hadn't even opened the wines he'd gotten from Masson to sample, as he was saving them for important tastings. "After all, didn't Paul serve us some of these very wines at the luncheon? And they were superb!" There was some mistake; he would have another test done on the premises right now, while Martin waited.

But these new tests confirmed the others. Martin Ray was totally shaken. How in God's name could he weather the loss of his entire bulk wine inventory?

Morris expressed surprise over Martin's disturbance. "You needn't take a loss at all, Martin. Just handle it this way: You have a new vintage coming. Buy two huge blending tanks, and blend this old wine with the new. You'll be able to get rid of it nicely. It may even be advantageous, since you can sell the new wine sooner after blending it with the old."

Aghast, Martin stared at him. "You mean . . . this is what *you* would do? To avoid taking a loss, you'd ruin good wine by blending it with the bad?"

"Why, of course," Morris said blandly. "It's the only sensible thing to do under the circumstances. I'm surprised you don't realize that most vintners do this."

They looked into each other's eyes, and Martin felt his very spine curl. Such an act to him was unthinkable, criminal. It violated every principle in his nature. He was suddenly seized with a violent nausea.

(No wonder, during all the years that followed, Martin Ray stormed so furiously and endlessly against the prevalent practice of indiscriminately blending wines, which so devastated California prestige and prices on the world wine market. He despised the very word "blending.")

Immediately after the shocking reports and the confrontation with Morris, Martin sold off his entire inventory of wine in cask to another winery for six cents a gallon, either to be made into vinegar or distilled for making brandy. A year later, not yet paid because of the continued depression in both wine prices and the national economy, he accepted but three cents per gallon, simply to close out the account. So he took altogether a loss of $60,000— an enormous sum in those days.

It was a bitter lesson. Yet Martin did manage to survive the experience, impossible though it initially seemed. Very gradually he actually came to regard the loss almost as a future asset. For he determined never again to depend upon anyone else to judge a wine in which he was financially concerned. He would so sensitize his palate as to be absolutely positive about his every judgment. And he did. (He always said that *anyone* could learn to taste to a high degree of accuracy if he had enough money on the line!)

One alarm persisted, though. Martin couldn't help but wonder whether some collusion had taken place between Masson and Morris. They *were* friends. And the very thought was devastating, for he'd almost worshipped Masson over all the years—as his boyhood hero, role model, mentor. And now his dear friend. He simply did not want to think that Paul would deliberately have foisted upon him wines he knew were defective. But of course Paul *had* fought furiously against selling to him! On the other hand, Paul might have lost his own acuity for judging wines—which often happens with advancing age to connoisseurs' palates.

But what of Morris's part in it, then? Overconfidence could explain his not bothering to run a chemical analysis of the wines. Yet why hadn't he even tasted them? Eventually Rudy, his longtime assistant, divulged to Martin a well-kept secret: the "expert" actually lacked tasting ability, so relied entirely on him for judgments. And being so confident of their quality, he had not asked Rudy to taste the Masson wine samples.

Martin also talked with Paul's old foreman, and from him learned about cellar procedures followed through Prohibition years and to some extent even afterward, when Masson's financial condition was still impaired. Always a single 60-gallon cask each of the still wines—one red, one white—from each vintage was bottled, for Masson's personal use. The only bottles Masson stocked were the heavy, dark green ones used for the champagne he could legally make and sell through the Prohibition years, so the still wines went into the same heavy champagne bottles. All remaining wines were left in cask indefinitely. Masson intended to bottle them for marketing when (and if) Prohibition was repealed.

Martin now felt certain that Paul never realized that all his wines had deteriorated. Paul had been unable to check the casks himself since his doctor forbade him, with his heart condition, to climb up and down the flights of steps at the cellars, as he had done as winemaker. Probably a number of the old casks that Masson still used, dating back to Charles Lefranc's time, were infected by bacteria and thus tainted any wines kept in them.

Martin was vastly relieved to gain a final conviction of Masson's integrity. For he so loved and admired Paul. He needed to believe that his hero would never knowingly dupe him.

In any case, Martin never mentioned to Masson this great loss in assets acquired from him. Convinced that Masson was a man of firm principles like himself, he wanted to shield him from the hurt and shock he had experienced when finding all those wines unsound.

However, I myself question Masson's unawareness of his wines' condition. In his situation, Martin would have realized that most wines held so long in cask and neglected were certain to be ruined. A winemaker doesn't have to go down into the cellars to know that. Nor would Masson, with his long years of winemaking experience. This might explain why Paul stormed and fought so vehemently against Martin's buying the business. He probably wouldn't care if it happened to someone else, a stranger. And hadn't he told Martin that he couldn't let him be a damn fool?

Yet when Martin persisted, Paul finally gave way—doubtless lured by the prospect of those great dinners he'd have with Martin when he took over. And when the chips were down, Paul, always short of money, knew he could use the hefty sum Martin Ray would pay for that wine inventory.

It's also interesting that Masson admitted to Martin some while after he'd sold to him that he had been seeking a suitable buyer for years. So his vehemence at the very suggestion that he might consider selling out was duplicitous. Various incidents in Masson's life revealed that he could be selfish, even ruthless, whenever money was involved. For instance, in business relations with his family in Burgundy, as divulged in correspondence preserved by Nelty Lefranc. He owed considerable sums to them, which apparently were never repaid.

Martin's boyhood hero was probably not so pure and wonderful as Martin wanted to regard him. Fierce loyalty in friendship was one of Martin's virtues. But it also proved a defect, sometimes making him blind to others' character failings and self-serving machinations. Which would recur all too often in the years ahead.

18

La Cresta Changes

DURING THE TRYING EARLY months at Masson, it was well that Martin had some pleasant distractions. Elsie provided many of them, giving Paul's old chateau new life and color, creating special delights for him at every turn. A tiny bouquet of freshly picked wildflowers at his place at the breakfast table; a warm bath drawn for him as he came in, wet and chilled from a late-spring deluge, after inspecting sumps and drainage ditches in the vineyards; a huge bowl of piping-hot bouillabaisse served by the fireside.

And as an extra diversion Martin enjoyed watching Paul Masson's new house going up on that fourteen-acre hillside he'd so adroitly withheld from the property transfer, directly across the road from the mountain winery's entrance.

Earlier, Paul had told Martin he'd like to invite an architect friend to join him for dinner up at his former chateau, to discuss plans. Elsie and Martin were agreeable to this, and so it came about. Since the architect and his wife had known Masson from earlier days, the dinner made a pleasant reunion, a time for reminiscing.

Paul had brought a photograph of a favorite house of his in Burgundy to show the architect. "Could you duplicate its appearance," he asked—immediately adding, "for less than $10,000?" That was his budget. "I want my house to look impressive but at minimum cost," he explained. "After all, it will have very limited usage, serving merely for occasional midday dinners here ... and for the small amount of time remaining to me at my age."

The architect himself liked the idea well enough of trying to replicate the building's overall look. But for a mere $10,000? Impossible. However, he agreed at last, as a favor to Paul, to attempt this miracle. He could only do it by stinting a great deal on construction costs, including quality materials. Which seemed to suit Paul fine.

The plans were quickly completed, and construction began. As Martin dropped by to watch the rapid progress in house-building, he often found Paul there. "This will make a handsome new chateau for you," Martin told Paul, knowing that he regretted having to give up his old one above.

"This will serve me nicely for a short while," Paul agreed, but then corrected him. "Never call this my *château.* For my chateau will be up there on the mountain—always."

And true this was. Paul's heart would remain permanently high on the mountain, where the great events of his career had taken place. Here below, he wouldn't even bother to pull out the old prune orchard and plant a vineyard, knowing he probably wouldn't live long enough to enjoy wine made from its harvests.

Almost every day Paul had his chauffeur take him out to the site so he could watch its progress. There he would pace about, inspecting everything, making suggestions, often criticizing workmanship or changing past directions, generally getting in the way. Usually then he couldn't resist a drive up through his former domain, stopping by his old place to talk with Martin. He seemingly timed his arrival so as to be invited to lunch—or to impending dinners, if Martin was entertaining at midday as had become his own custom. (Sometimes I happened to be there, so witnessed a few such occasions.)

If in the right mood, Paul Masson served as an asset to Martin Ray's entertaining in those early days, his very presence adding considerable charm and interest for any guests. He might recount tall tales of early California events so often connected with the mountain. Even Prohibition now could be recalled in the safe perspective of time, and with great verve Paul would describe apprehending some skullduggery on the premises, when he risked his very life in defending his vines and wines. His rugged face would tremble with excitement as he recalled for others these dramas of the past. His eyes first blazed with intensity but then began watering, so that he had to wipe them with his handkerchief, after removing his pince-nez suspended by a thin ribbon at one side of his neck.

At other times, though, Masson was less affable and charming, or caused problems when he simply "took over," acting as if he were still the host at La Cresta. He might even order Martin and Elsie around as if they were his attendants.

Certainly Masson, as co-host, served anew as a role model for Martin, whose style at the head of the table came more and more to resemble Masson's—particularly when his elderly mentor was absent. Martin swiftly assumed and maintained complete control of all proceedings at the long dinner table. He too would spellbind guests with both true histories and outrageous stories, so that it might be hard to distinguish between them. As his blue-gray eyes seemed to pitch sparks of excitement, he kept an audience spellbound, hanging upon his every word. Sometimes he'd run a hand up through his reddish-brown, now slightly thinning hair—as if to release pent-up steam from this pot-boiling, tale-telling intensity.

During those years, when Paul Masson spent so much time in Martin Ray's company up at his old chateau, a fascinating rumor inevitably got started. It told how Martin was actually Paul's bastard son—for hadn't Martin known him from boyhood on? This genetic connection explained their close and fond association, in which the aging vintner shared winemaking secrets and marketing know-how with his ambitious young successor. Martin, hearing the gossip, had some hearty laughs over it, imagining his mother ever falling for a French imbiber and roué. His own minister father lay beneath grass and trees at Saratoga's peaceful Madronia Cemetery. But might his youngest son's new profession be disturbing that adamant teetotaler's eternal rest?

Though Masson belittled the house he was putting up, the very act of building it actually underscored his feeling that he still owned the whole domain above—and could do anything he liked there. Martin was inclined to smile at Paul's seeming inability to realize he'd relinquished ownership, for it fitted with the king-of-the-mountain stance he'd held for so long. And to be sure, Martin was compulsively collecting a treasure-house assortment of amusing and insightful tales about this man he'd emulated since boyhood.

But Paul's house-building created incidents that snapped even Martin's indulgence and forbearance. Old John continued his job as general caretaker at La Cresta, now working for Martin Ray, since Masson had no need for his services at his San Jose home. However, as Paul's new house began going up at the base of the mountain, Masson borrowed John much of the time to help with construction and finishing work. Though still on Martin's payroll, he was expected to be on hand whenever Paul was there, to carry out incessant "errands" for him.

And such errands! One day, for instance, when Martin entered his chateau he found all the chandeliers had been ripped out of the ceilings, as well as bracket lights from the walls. Apparently Paul figured he could use these fixtures in his new place. Then he noticed another outrage: the marble mantelpiece had been yanked from above the fireplace. Martin was thunderstruck at such rapacity. He hadn't remonstrated about various similar incidents in the past, but of a more minor nature. After this episode, he told

old John in no uncertain terms to cease and desist. No more!

Martin noticed, though, that Masson had neglected to remove the large framed photograph of Anna Held and her troupe of girls situated there on the wall since time immemorial. Paul would surely want to hang it in a prominent place at his new house. But when Martin asked Masson about it, he dismissed the invitation to take it away. "You keep it there, MAR-tan. It means nothing at all to me anymore!" If Paul had ever provided this glamorous turn-of-the-century showgirl with the champagne bath publicists claimed for her, Martin speculated, wouldn't he want to keep this memento of their association?

Another incident revealed Paul's quirky attitude toward La Cresta's new owner. On moving from the chateau months before, he'd left his trio of dogs behind, and Martin accepted them as an inherited responsibility. But one of them, an old dog named Pedro, became vicious and constantly attacked the other dogs—even visitors. So Martin, having decided he'd have to go, took him to the Humane Society.

Just at that time Paul's house was nearing completion, and he wanted to keep a dog on the premises. So off he went to the Humane Society, where he'd usually obtained his dogs in the past. He was invited to view the dogs in various pens. Suddenly one dog leapt up and yelped. Paul leaned down and shouted, "Why, Pedro! That's my old dog Pedro! Pedro, what are *you* doing here? Pedro, you dear old fellow ..."

The dog now went berserk with joy, barking frenziedly. Masson became alarmingly excited. The attendant, trying to calm him, explained that Mr. Ray had brought in the dog the previous day, hoping he'd get a good new home. "How lucky for you, Mr. Masson. You can have your very own dog back!"

"Oh no no, he's no good," Masson said quickly and turned away, selecting instead a young terrier. But as Paul went off with him, he muttered, "Oh, that Martin Ray—he has no heart. Such an awful thing to do to my old dog Pedro!"

Aside from leaving his dogs with Martin on departing, Paul also left his great flock of pigeons. Squab was a favorite food of his, and his men had always provided him with whatever squab he wished, already prepared, for his table. He also doted on robins that they shot for him. He'd roast the birds in front of fireplace logs in a special "robin rack" specially constructed for him; then serve them up in Italian-style polenta feasts.

Masson now figured that John could continue to bring pigeons down to him from his former ranch.

Well, up at La Cresta those pigeons were now flying all over, messing the whole place with their droppings and annoying guests with their fluttering and begging. Of course Martin did not intend to endure that. But he was stoically holding out until Paul's house was near completion. Then he told old John to construct pigeon quarters down there so that he could move the pigeons to their new home. Which he did. But he couldn't catch the entire flock, so of course they all flew right back to the mountaintop.

By now Martin had had enough. After all, the pigeons had been an intolerable nuisance for some time. So he took his gun and began to pop them off. In short order they got the message. The whole flock took off, to descend on Paul's new pigeon quarters.

What relief on the mountaintop! But Masson was irked. He'd planned on their being out of his way, up above with all their mess, yet always available whenever he wanted squab. "Martin Ray has no heart, driving those pigeons out of their home!" he sputtered.

On the day after he assumed ownership, Martin Ray began the work of refurbishing the complete mountain property that had been Paul Masson's. The long-neglected vineyards and wine cellars in particular needed complete overhauling.

In the vineyards Martin made sure that the land was plowed deeply in both directions. He took measures to halt the erosion of the slopes, which had carried off topsoil and created deep gullies. He had the men give special attention to each individual vine (and there were thousands) by removing suckers from the rootstock, extracting ailing ones and replanting, replacing broken stakes, and cutting canes back to just two buds to stimulate healthy new growth. Finally the old vineyards were resuscitated.

But the cellars presented a colossal problem. To Martin's orderly mind and tidy habits, the winery had become a disaster area. Unable for years to do much work there himself, Masson hadn't provided necessary attention to maintaining order and cleanliness. Moreover, because of financial hardship, he could not repair or replace some basic winery equipment, let alone add efficient new equipment coming out of the European wine industry, which had not experienced the setback of Prohibition.

Feeling financially secure and with his new country home nearing completion, Paul Masson left for a trip to Europe. Martin decided to make the cellars absolutely shipshape during his absence, and in preparation for the first vintage to come. The bottom cellar was the worst offense and eyesore. He now concreted its dirt floor that Paul had tolerated all those years. The winery interior was thoroughly cleaned, and then carpenters were called in to start renovations. He bought new winery equipment, so badly needed. He also removed Masson's deteriorated outsize oak casks and replaced them with smaller new ones.

By the time Masson returned several months later, all four cellar areas looked wonderful and were spotlessly clean. Even the wood floors had been sanded smooth and varnished to a mirror shine.

Martin, mighty proud of his handiwork, looked forward to showing it all off to Paul. He'd be amazed and delighted, of course, to see how Martin had painstakingly made the venerable premises resplendent, to demonstrate his dedication to carrying on Masson's own great contributions to American winemaking.

Paul phoned Martin as soon as he got back, and was invited up to luncheon the next day.

When he arrived, Martin saw he had trouble walking, even with his stick. It was a result of some leg injury he'd experienced on his trip, Paul said, and because of his diabetes it wasn't healing well. So they started their winery tour at the hillside entrance at the top, since it would be much easier for Paul to descend stairs rather than ascend.

Slowly they traveled along together, and Paul was silent during the tour. Martin expected that. Both impressed and moved when seeing all the improvements, Masson might well be speechless for a while. When they reached the lowest cellar, much activity was going on. Some cellar boys were bottling wine. Paul Masson looked around, noting the immaculate new concrete floor, modernized equipment, new French casks, the whole spick-and-span achievement. But still he offered no comment.

Then, as they turned and were going out the main door, Paul turned angrily toward Martin. "So you think that because you have spent all this money and have everything so fine and orderly . . . you think you are going to make better wine than I made!" he bellowed.

Martin was horrified. "Paul, I didn't say anything about that. I thought you'd be so pleased to see how we've fixed things up here."

"Well, I'm not!" he snapped. "I am very disappointed in you. I can tell you right now, you are going to fail at winemaking."

Martin was stunned that his dear Paul could insult him like this. In front of his employees, moreover. Unforgivable. But he knew it was best to say nothing at the time. He just hustled Paul out the door and escorted him away.

As they approached Paul's car, Martin finally said, "Paul, I'm going to ask you not to return anymore. I just can't have that sort of behavior here." Paul looked baffled and hurt. As the chauffeur helped him into the car before driving off, Martin noticed how feeble Paul had become.

The next day Martin sent a close friend of his to see Paul

Masson. "I want you to tell him," he said, "that I've cancelled that big welcome-home dinner up here for him this weekend. And make this very clear: he can never return, as I told him yesterday. His outburst has ended our relations."

Martin's friend returned a few hours later, badly shaken. "Oh, it was dreadful!" he said. "The old man just broke down and sobbed and shook all over. He said, 'Yah yah, I know it was awful—saying what I said. But I couldn't help myself. Martin has done everything I would have liked to do!'"

Hearing that, Martin went to the phone and called Paul—rescinding the banishment and restoring the weekend dinner party. Once he realized that Paul's jealous outburst had been a very human reaction, Martin forgave him. This was a classic response of an aging man fearing that his authority and power may in time be superseded by a competent and ambitious younger one, whose accomplishments are then interpreted as a challenge.

(As a matter of fact, many years later I saw Martin himself react with wounded pride and inner fury to a similarly imagined threat. At a festive wine dinner with many guests we were drinking the superb Martin Ray Cabernet Sauvignon 1952. One of Martin's best-loved young friends, who had recently planted a "cab" vineyard of his own nearby, leapt to his feet to make a toast. "We're toasting with this greatest of all cabernet sauvignons," he said—then added laughingly, "greatest, that is, until my own first vintage comes in two years from now!" Martin failed to laugh with the rest of us. He turned pale and expressionless, and left the table soon afterward. I could see that he had been deeply hurt. Going in to our bedroom to talk with him, I told him he shouldn't overreact like this. Again and again I tried to assure him that it had been just a typically male, "one-upmanship" jest. "No," he insisted. "He *meant* it." Thus a highly treasured friendship disintegrated. Vintners can be extraordinarily touchy. Especially, perhaps, when sensitive to competition from the next generation.)

After the near break between Paul Masson and Martin Ray, the two men were closer than ever before. Both knew they needed each other—the one ending his years as a great winemaker, and the other just beginning.

19

Starting with Varietals

Now THAT HE WAS the proud possessor of Paul Masson's kingdom, with its vineyards and winery, what was Martin Ray going to do with it all? He had chosen not only an inspiring way of life far removed from urban stress, but also undertaken a business that must pay off its initial investment.

After taking over the Paul Masson Champagne Company, Martin Ray steadily met and solved one crisis after another. As he did so, he focused on handling just one problem at a time, as Dr. Francis had taught him.

He had the inventory under firm control, having stopped the massive thefts of the wines. He'd replaced the deceased merchandiser of Masson wines as well as his discount-gouging successor by assuming the marketing management himself for the time being. To prepare for his first vintage, he had completely refurbished the winery building.

Yet he'd sustained a disastrous financial loss by selling off all those defective wines held too long in cask. And he must surmount it speedily. But how could he—given the wine industry's current depression?

Finding an effective way to reverse the downtrend in both public interest in wine and price became Martin's great challenge. Paul Masson's two years of post-Repeal experience had scarcely been encouraging. At first Martin had expected to turn prospects around quickly. After all, he was younger by almost a half-century, having the prime energy of a man in his early thirties. He also brought an infusion of new capital to devote to urgent improvements. But he hadn't realized how the continuing depressed wine market would militate against success. Surveying the dismal wine scene, he—the eternal optimist—sometimes felt doomed to fail.

Orders for champagne did not cover Martin Ray's operating overhead. During the Dry years, when the public could only buy wine on prescription, Masson—with the sole license to make and sell champagne—had enjoyed a clear advantage. But by now plenty of both still and sparkling wines were available. Other vintners were making what they called champagne—carbonated white wines, which of course could be sold at prices much lower than his.

But how about the Masson table wines? It was tragic that most wines Masson had managed to make, both through Prohibition and since Repeal, had spoiled through neglect, due to lack of funds and proper attention. Certainly in the future Martin could produce fine still wines from La Cresta's vineyards. Yet he soon realized that dry table wines, available since Repeal, had no market. Most wholesalers refused to carry them. Only a handful of customers across the nation seemed to want them.

The only wines selling reasonably well during the mid-'30s were the sweet, brandy-fortified ones. These quickly had reentered the wine market upon Repeal. Martin Ray knew that this dominance wasn't new. He remembered Masson blaming the tremendous increase in these wines—the result of the 1890 McKinley "sweet wine law"—for the oncoming temperance movement.

Martin also became keenly aware of the fierce competition among literally hundreds of wineries. Some were old, having survived through Prohibition by legally producing sacramental wines and vinegar. A few others had survived to Repeal, having held onto facilities and vineyards. But many were upstarts, often begun by families mostly from southern Europe—some using new wealth and property gained from their bootlegging Prohibition days.

In the slim market existing for dry wines, reds dominated. Just as they had done during Prohibition, wine drinkers often continued to buy directly from local winegrowers, frequently Italian, whose small operations largely produced the wines preferred by their compatriots. Their unpretentious yet wholesome wines at least provided a drinkable *vin ordinaire*. Martin Ray did not regard them as competition.

His real threat came from a more ambitious group of vintners. Mostly large-scale bootleggers in the past, they had built up close contacts with criminals in alcohol-distributing networks. Repeal simply legitimated their business. With profitability as their only motive in business, now they aspired to control the American wine industry—and do so ruthlessly, if need be. Having shrewdly turned earlier profits into extensive landholding and secure investments, they were poised at the start of Repeal to go into winemaking on a massive scale. They could readily invest in huge winery facilities with state-of-the-art equipment and in research aimed at large-scale production. Quality was the least of their concerns.

No wonder Martin found it impossible to deal with many winery owners and the wine distributors. Paul had been so right in warning him that this was no time to go into the fine wine business. And so right too about former bootleggers ruining the wine market, flooding it with their cheap, shoddy wines. Nameless and shameless, most of these wines had high residual sugar, which people with bootlegger-produced palates expected when they drank wine. More discerning consumers would not buy wine at all. Or, if they did, European wines only.

During his first half-year at Masson, Martin became increasingly worried about his situation. He was anxious to get Paul's suggestions about how to deal best with competition from the sweet-wine promoters in the industry who had pushed dry table wines out of the running. Actually, so little wine was being consumed nationwide that Californians drank the largest share of wines on the market—of imports as well as American-made wines.

So Martin at last corralled Paul, back from his trip to France, for a serious business talk—during a lunch with just the two of them. "How in God's name can I get table wine sales moving?" he asked Paul almost desperately. He had hired wine salesmen in vain.

Old Paul shook his head. "It will take time," he said. "The only way, really, is to do as we have always done in Europe. You must find those important people who know and love fine wine, and entertain them with elegant dinners here at the chateau—as I used to do, before Prohibition. If they are really impressed with your wines, they will spread the word. And slowly your sales will grow."

But just how was Martin to go about finding those rare "important people"? Paul admitted it wouldn't be easy, for the current generation was ignorant about wines, and uninterested. To find those who did know and appreciate fine wines, Martin simply had to persevere. As well as *make* the best American wines available.

"You must remember always," Paul reminded him, "we are fighting our way out of a terrible situation brought on by Prohibition. A taste for wine, along with the habit of drinking it, has been lost. So it will take years to regain the prestige of my name on a bottle of wine. You must practice patience while cultivating influential people. And gradually they will persuade the better retail outlets to carry your wines."

Paul was silent for a few moments. His next words came warily, wearily. "But this will happen only after better dealers and distributors come into the wine trade . . . for the bootlegger types have taken over there, too."

Martin was thoroughly shaken by this protracted prospect of ultimate success. "But just how long will it take, for the love of God?" he asked later, when discussing the predicament with Elsie. Then he recalled his grandfather's oft-repeated saying: "A quitter never wins, and a winner never quits." Growing into manhood, Martin had adopted that as a motto, and it had sustained him during many trying times.

"Well, Papa, we're both young and determined," Elsie said, hugging him with encouragement. "You're full of energy and dedication—along with big dreams. We can do it, even if it *does* take years!"

At this Martin smiled, infused again with the vitality that taking on some impossible-seeming challenge always gave him.

Martin now asked himself several questions. First: Just where could he locate those rare "important people who know and love fine wine," whom Paul said he should cultivate? And second: Even if he did find them, could he offer them wines so marvelous that they'd spread the word to others? Definitely he must make wines comparable to the finest French—starting this year, with the vintage of 1936!

In the past, though Paul Masson wines had ranked among the very best that California offered, unlike great French wines they were motley mixtures of various grapes, following American winemakers' long-practiced custom. And Masson had also gone along with other top vintners of his day, marketing blends as burgundy, sauterne, chablis, and claret, using generic names to indicate a type of wine. In fact, even these types were often interchangeable with each other within the general classification of red or white wine. And why not? Few Americans who bought and drank such wines realized this, or cared.

At least Masson's wines, Martin knew, had included some of the greatest European wine-grape varieties, such as the pinot noir and chardonnay, which gave extraordinary character, depth, and complexity to them. This was because he had grown such varieties in his vineyards.

The typical California growers prided themselves on their huge acreages, comprising mostly mongrelized mixes of inferior varieties of unknown identities and origins. A few knew they had some alicante bouschet and burger suitable for making red and white wines. But these weren't premier varieties. Most vintners didn't recognize that knowledge of grape varieties is crucial in fine wine production. Not that this concerned them, for the long years of Prohibition had dulled any interest in quality among themselves or their customers.

Another enduring effect of Prohibition compounded the problem for that uncommon vintner possibly interested in using higher-quality varietals. Where would he find such grapes? Most vineyards harboring fine-wine varieties had long since been grafted over or replanted to vines that were prolific producers of good boxcar-traveling grapes. Or else had been ripped out and planted to orchards: to apples, peaches, walnuts. If a vintner actually contemplated growing superior varieties himself, he knew it would take years of effort and expense before any payoff came, if any. Given the current deep wine depression, a winegrower would be mad to do so.

Martin Ray knew that the old Masson mountain vineyards still contained many top varieties, some of which no other wineries had. Having studied the seemingly hopeless situation within the wine trade, he recognized that it was up to *him* to create a demand for truly fine wines—by making them himself and then marketing them in a special way. He must ... if he hoped to survive in this double depression. And if he could make wines superb enough to merit connoisseurs' attention, *they* would surely locate those "important people" for him!

Martin therefore decided to take French wines as his precept, leave all blends behind, and concentrate on capturing the special identity, bouquet, and flavor of each grape variety—kept separate and distinct. This was the Burgundian way of keeping fine varietals distinct from each other, as opposed to the Bordeaux style of blending them in a manner pleasing to each individual estate.

Having made this momentous decision to focus on producing and featuring pure varietal wines, Martin Ray now needed to know exactly which grape varieties grew in the Masson vineyards, and in what amounts. Paul himself could not help much. Not only had his record-keeping been imperfect, but his memory of details was fading fast with age. All the Prohibition-period plantings and regraftings of vines added further to the confusion.

So in the early summer of 1936 Martin walked up and down the slopes of his mountain vineyards, to identify and map all varieties. He carried with him an invaluable French wine-grape *ampelographie,* which pictured grape varieties on full-color plates and gave detailed descriptions. It was fascinating work, and what he learned through direct observation and careful comparison—of grape forms and leaf structure and special growing habits of each variety—would be good for a lifetime.

Finally, with his charts completed, he considered what he had: some large, separate blocks of splendid varietal plantings. Included were most of Europe's greatest and most distinctive wine grape varieties, cuttings of which Paul had gotten on his frequent visits abroad and then brought back to graft onto rootstock growing on his own land.

Martin saw he occupied a unique position in California. For by now, in his study of the grape-variety situation, he'd traveled through the other major California vineyards—encountering mostly miscellanies of common varieties.

He had one huge block of pinot noir vines—expectably, since this was the premier red wine grape of Masson's native Burgundy. For many years this pinot noir clone represented America's sole authentic planting. He also had a sizable block of the French province's great white grape, chardonnay. It was practically the only planting of it in the mid-'30s. (In America, for years this grape and the wine made from it was erroneously known as "pinot chardonnay." When the variety became highly popular in the '70s, cuttings originating from Masson's original vines, or else propagated through Martin Ray and his unique Mt. Eden plantings, eventually engendered the starts of many other vineyards. Still another clone, distinctively different, got its start in the Wente vineyards in Livermore Valley, started earlier by wine pioneer Theodore Gier.)

Martin also noted a massive block of Burgundy's secondary red, gamay beaujolais. (This was later identified by UC Davis as the only authentic Burgundian-derived variety in California; a clone of the pinot noir, it was unrelated to the inferior, so-called gamays grown elsewhere.) There were two blocks of folle blanche, a tart and fruity white wine grape often used in making cognac in France and champagne in California; a block of aramon; three blocks of pinot blanc *vrai* (again the sole authentic American planting of the variety, a pale-grape clone of the pinot noir that Masson himself had brought over from France); and blocks of burger, verdal, duriff (petite sirah), and mondeuse.

There was even a small block of cabernet sauvignon—though Masson discounted its value, as it was the primary Bordeaux wine grape of Burgundy's rival province of Médoc. Inclined already to be a "claret man," Martin decided to plant more of it at once. In the meantime, he could buy grapes from Almaden, the Lefranc family's old winery property.

Aside from these segregated blocks of special varieties, the remainder of Masson's extensive holdings—sixty planted acres in all—resembled vineyards elsewhere. Of course there was ample salvador, the bootleggers' friend. Many grapevines defying anyone's identification no doubt were descendents of the mixed lots of European vines imported by nurserymen and early vintners, or brought over and distributed by the Hungarian-born wine-promoting enthusiast, Agoston Haraszthy, in the 1860s. They had started the craze to collect as many types as possible and therefore claim to have more varieties than anyone else. Wines made through the years from this hodgepodge of sources had been, expectably, mongrels.

Martin humorously posted a sign on this wildly mixed area of vines: HARASZTHY WAS HERE! Yet he acknowledged that some experimental planting, using trial and error, had been—and still was—helpful. For it was the most practical way to determine which varieties or distinctive clones did best in particular localities, taking into consideration numerous variables: soil factors like texture and mineral content; climatic conditions—such as temperature range, fog and wind patterns, and amount of annual rainfall; differing exposure to sun; elevation, degree of hillside slope, and other important elements. He believed, though, that once the experiment was run and the results studied, the inferior subjects themselves should be removed, yielding vineyard space for the acknowledged superior varieties certain to prosper there.

Martin would replant all those mixed-vine areas next winter. Now every minute he could spare away from vineyard care he spent in two intensive pursuits. First, to better educate his palate, he was accumulating an imposing collection of the greatest French and German wines—emphatically spending $1,000 every month for their purchase. Thus he could carefully taste each celebrated pure varietal wine or fine-wine blend against another equally prized. As had become his custom, he was recording every observation in his cellar book, preserving these specifics for future reference, correlated with his growing knowledge of French winemaking techniques.

Secondly, to aid these analytic strivings he spent many nighttime hours poring over French winegrowing treatises involving distinguished *châteaux* and *domaine* operations in Bordeaux and Bourgogne, gathered over the years from official French sources. Martin was impressed by this evidence of the intensive care going into every minute operation at vintage time. Whenever he needed detailed translations, he asked his secretary, Daisy Haig, to provide them, or hired a professional translator.

But Martin's absorbing study of French winemaking procedures did not interfere with his equally close watch over his vineyards. After identifying the various blocks of supreme varieties, he checked daily their progress toward vintage. For those grapes simply had to be sumptuous, so as to ultimately dazzle the wine virtuosos and bring immense success to his first wines ... from this, the vintage year of 1936.

20

A Vintage All His Own

FOR MONTHS MARTIN RAY had been readying the cellars for his first, crucial vintage. He also carefully planned his quota for making still and sparkling wines, as now required by the government in attempting to regulate supply and demand aspects in the depressed wine industry.

From reading the French winemaking texts Martin knew that oak barrels were a necessity. Fortunately, he had inherited from Paul Masson plenty of these, many removed earlier from Almaden's cellars. From his study he also knew they would require extensive treatment before being suitable for receiving newly fermented wines. So for many days prior to vintage he conducted various operations to make them usable.

First, the wine casks must be made absolutely clean and free from bacterial growth inside—which they weren't, judging from a bunghole smell of each. So each cask was given a thorough interior cleansing, involving vigorous "rock-and-roll" maneuvers, activities both necessary and intriguing. Boiling water was poured into a cask set upon a shallow base, and then for some minutes several men rolled it back and forth, producing enormous sloshing within. The procedure might be done a second time. For all its seeming absurdity, it proved most effective, cleaning out the inside of a cask completely so it smelled sweet when drained. Each renovated cask was then rolled back across its cellar supports with the bunghole placed at the bottom, so that the cask could drain and air. Later it would be plugged with a wad of sterile cotton to absorb any remaining moisture and also prevent flies from entering.

That was but the beginning in readying the casks. Martin planned to start the fermentation in large open oak puncheons rather than the huge fermenting vats, of redwood or steel or even concrete, usually used by American vintners, including Masson for his commercial winemaking. It would allow better control over the fermentation process. This meant that one end must be removed from each cask to be converted into a fermenter. Since the job had to be done by an expert, Martin had to truck six large empty casks down to San Jose to a skilled cooper. The ends could be usable later as tight-fitting lids.

Since Masson was already renowned for its champagnes, Martin chose not to change them in any way, for now. Instead, he would follow Paul's customary practices—as he did in mid-August, picking the grapes when they were sweetening yet still had the requisite high acid for champagne.

The still wines, however, Martin would make mostly as pure varietals. And he was intent upon getting them as close to perfection as possible. As vintage time approached, daily he gathered a selection of grapes from different vines and exposures, squeezed out their juice, and tested them for both sugar and acid levels. Martin hoped to pick his top grape varieties at precisely the 23.5° of sugar on the Brix scale that he deemed ideal, based on his study of French vintage practices.

Luck seemed with him. The late summer and early fall weather was glorious for ripening grapes: warm and mellow days, the sun never too intense, maturing the grapes steadily; afternoon ocean breezes coming through gaps in the mountains, cooling the vines and the ground below them. The pinot noir leaves began turning a gorgeous flame color, while the chardonnay's became a brilliant yellow that reflected back the golden harvest-time's sun.

From the Viticulture Department at University of California at Davis Martin already had obtained a premium starter yeast to quicken the fermentation. He prepared it for future action by dissolving the granules in a five-gallon glass jug containing sterilized juice of freshly picked grapes, crushed and pressed in a miniature basket press.

As expected, the pinot noir ripened ahead of the others. Then when Martin's first actual vintage day dawned, Martin really turned zealot, determined that the basic ingredients for the crush would be in perfect condition. He roamed the vineyards to make sure that only the pinot noir was picked from the irregular patches, and showing every picker how to snip the grape bunches carefully with clippers, removing any defective berries, and then lay each neatly in an immaculate box, avoiding the least bruise. And let no leaf fall into the picking box. . . .

So the great pinot noir first crush was on! To Elsie went the honor of ceremoniously pouring the first box of grapes into the new crusher—with joyful acclaim from everyone around. And then, under Martin's watchful eye, workers carefully tipped box after box into the fantastic stainless steel contraption that Martin designed and then had metal craftsmen construct for him. A long rectangular shape, it had a roller inside with whirling blades, propelled at breakneck speed by electric current, that caught and smashed the grapes, sending juice and skins down a chute into the waiting fermenter, while shooting the unwanted stems out one end, discarded.

As the crusher-stemmer rapidly churned the grapes, a cloud of aromatic pinot fragrance wafted through the air—an aroma like no other. Pleased with the success of this compact, beautifully engineered device, Martin inevitably thought back to that first vintage he'd participated in, as a boy at Masson's—at this very place, now his own—when he was so appalled by the primitive method of crushing grapes and removing stems.

Now each fermenter when but half-filled was covered with a clean white cloth to safeguard it from fruitflies. Soon it needed to be replaced by others, for when fermentation really got rolling, the future red wine would turn into a bubbling brew. Every four hours, day and night, using a simple tool—that flat piece of wood screwed onto a long pole, favored by Masson—Martin or an assistant would punch down the thick "cap" of solids in each open vat. Each time Martin thrust the implement through the top layer, volcanic explosions resounded in the lower depths of the liquid, sending up geysers of burgundy ink and a heady blast of carbon dioxide, which carried the delicious and potent scent of fermenting wine grapes.

As he performed this task, he vividly remembered the first time of doing this, as a boy. Paul had told him how this work was crucial: not just in assuring constant contact between the crushed grape skins and the fermenting must to obtain maximum color and flavor, but also in keeping the ever-rising skins and pips from forming a hard crust that would attract contaminants like fruitflies and aerobic bacteria.

This punching-down procedure continued for a few days. Several times each day, using a hydrometer, Martin tested the declining sugar content. He first dipped a tall, narrow glass vial deep into the fermenter and filled it with the warm liquid. Carrying it over to the laboratory table, he now carefully inserted the slender hydrometer—reading the gauge as the tube bobbed around in the liquid, floating ever lower as alcohol replaced the heavier sugar in the fermenting grape juice.

At last the reading approached zero Brix, signaling the minimal sugar content that Martin desired. Then the must was transferred, skins and seeds along with juice, into the press basket. Afterwards, all hands took turns pushing and pulling the ratchet handle back and forth. Slowly, steadily, heavy wooden half-disks were lowered, pressuring the must to yield all its fluids. Thin red rivulets trickled down through the slats to collect at the base, then gush in a small waterfall from a spout, falling into pails quickly carried to waiting casks.

By the time the long metal press handle became hard to budge, the flow of wine had slowed to a trickle. When the wooden halves of the press basket were removed, a solid cake of pomace remained, made of spent skins, seeds, and bits of stem. Removed chunk by chunk with a flat shovel and set on a tarpaulin, it would be distributed later among the vines as a fertilizing mulch.

Martin's first pinot noir vintage was set down now for a long rest in the refurbished casks. They were filled almost to the top, with the bungholes at the high center merely stoppered with cotton swabs, as a milder fermentation would persist for some days. Finally the yeast activity lessened to the point where the wine could safely be "put to bed"—its casks filled almost to the brim, then stoppered with heavy oak bungs banged down firmly with a mallet.

Martin used the same thoughtful and meticulous care in vintaging the chardonnay grapes, which attained the desired 23.5° Brix only a few days after the pinot noir. The grapes were a glorious sight as they came in, with ripe-to-bursting golden berries. Quickly crushed and poured into the press basket, they remained there for several hours, for skin softening before being pressed.

Martin even experimented by pressing these white grapes several times—as the French sources advised, to bring out every nuance of flavor and bouquet. Between each pressing, the mass of grapes was removed with stainless steel shovels, churned about, then returned to the press, thereby extracting maximum juice. The last press juice was a deep gold almost butterscotch in tone, and with tremendous flavor. Martin distributed this precious pressing among the various oak casks, where the fermenting white wine would stay for several months before its first racking.

The casks to hold the chardonnay—Burgundy's superb white wine—were absolutely new ones of French oak he'd had shipped to him well in advance of vintage time. The supreme vintners there had learned that not only must casks be new for chardonnay, but also should be made from their special Burgundian oak, to contribute the right character and flavor to the developing chardonnay. The casks must not be "treated" in any way, merely rinsed in boiling water and drained overnight before use.

Martin was hoping almost desperately to get that same specific nose and taste, which he called "ripe chardonnay," which characterized the truly great white burgundies. He soon discovered that the new casks had some esoteric quality which did contribute this very special flavor in abundance. It was a fabulous discovery! More than with the red wines, Martin had to make sure that the fermenting white wine would have minimal contact with air, which would oxidize it.

Sometimes Paul Masson came to observe the cellar procedures, no doubt hoping that Martin would faithfully adhere to all processes learned from him. He seemed taken aback, even offended, whenever he noticed that Martin had methods varying from his own. He was overjoyed, though, to note that Martin had retained and encouraged the malolactic fermentation period for his wines, learned from helping handle Paul's wines years before. The process, occurring as a second-stage, lighter fermentation, converts the appley, slightly astringent malic acid in the new wine into lactic acid, giving chardonnay a faint but pleasing butterscotch nose and flavor—rarely known to or achieved by American winemakers of that day.

But Masson was often puzzled, sometimes even horrified, at all Martin's new methods he'd adopted from his French sources. Most of all he couldn't understand why Martin felt he had to have new casks for his whites. "I've left you more good, sound French casks than you'll ever need!" he objected. "They served Lefranc and they've served me too all these years—and are still in perfect condition. I've never had to buy even one new cask!"

Martin knew it would be pointless to explain to Masson that French wine authorities had discovered how to improve miraculously their chardonnay wines this way. And so as Martin worked, he simply smiled. He recalled what Masson had emphasized often enough with him. "MAR-tan," he'd say, "when procedures have been established that bring the results you want, for the love of God don't *change* anything!"

In principle, Martin agreed with Paul's conservatism, his traditionalism. But now it was vital for him to try out modern and perfected French methods, to get the excellent results he sought. And whenever he, like Masson, found the results he wanted, he rarely veered from the means of achieving them. After all, in time, as superior innovations have proven their worth, they become the "classical" methods. (Later on, Martin himself would be inclined to scoff at the avid technocrat chemists who notably began in the '60s to tinker with proven success and to dictate changes in equipment and methodology—usually, he noted, for purpose of producing more wine, more quickly and cheaply than before.)

And so Martin Ray's first vintage proceeded, with the cabernet sauvignon ripening last, in mid-October. Each wine in the making had enjoyed in turn Martin's same fastidious attention in harvesting and vintaging as he concentrated his attention completely, one after another, on the succeeding grape varieties. Then each deliciously fragrant crush was cellared, using the precision and cleanliness stressed by both Masson and the French treatises. But Martin had given the greatest attention of all to the pinot noir. Instinctively he knew that the table wine made from it would be his best chance for acclaim, his *pièce de résistance.*

How enraptured Martin became when a marvelously distinctive character emerged in each varietal wine kept separate and unblended! As the wines matured, suspense grew. What reception would they meet, these first *pure varietal* wines of California, when finally they were ready for release, each one bearing a proud French name all its own on the label? The first wines to be bottled were, of course, the whites and the gamay beaujolais—to be released and enjoyed when young and fresh.

Paul Masson himself was skeptical of Martin Ray's intention to market these pure varietals. The notion was so radical to him. "Can't possibly pay," he'd say to him. "Probably not for fifty years at least. It will take the American public that long after Prohibition just to begin to regain its taste for wine—and probably another fifty to become knowledgeable enough to appreciate fine varietals. You won't live that long . . . and *I* certainly won't! All you will do is make enemies of the other winegrowers, who will accuse you of putting on airs. And of wholesalers and retailers too, because you're going to challenge their assertion that California can only make *vin ordinaire.*"

Martin knew he would have to wait at least several years before knowing whether that first vintage would bring him the acclaim he needed for the new Masson wines, and thus begin to alter the future direction of winemaking in America. In the meantime, there were the wines to tend in the cellar, vineyards to expand or replant ... the champagne to bottle and age, to riddle, disgorge, label and dress, and finally ship out. And yes, the next vintages to come.

The champagnes, at first created with the still-wine cuvées Masson had made in the two previous years, often occupied much of Martin's attention. He was learning how to do the precise and sometimes chancy work of starting the secondary fermentation, of riddling, disgorging, adding the *dosage,* and then the final corking and labeling—activities he'd only watched occasionally as a boy.

The disgorging process was especially difficult yet fascinating. After fast-freezing the sediment-containing "plug" within the upside-down bottles' necks, he'd pick up a bottle firmly in his left hand and turn its temporary cork carefully until suddenly— WHOOSH! the champanized wine would shoot out. Whereupon, quick as a flash, Martin's right thumb covered the opening as his hand swung the bottle upright, to stop the entire contents from spilling out. Always there would be a small loss of the liquid, to be replaced from a ready supply of the dosage syrup, prepared for brut or demi-sec. Then the bottle was inserted into the large cast-iron hand-corking machine with its heavy pull-down lever—the same one that Paul Masson had brought from France and had used for fifty years.

Only now was the bottle ready for its final dressing before being sped off to market. A metal agrafe (coming, like the corks, from Portugal) was spread over the cork and clamped over the lip of the bottle to secure the cork tightly. The bottle top was then covered with foil, tightened, and finished with a special paper band around its lower edge, held in place by a Paul Masson medallion that Martin had designed. At last the handsome Paul Masson label was glued onto the bottle, tissue paper was wrapped around it, and then it was packed into a sturdy wooden case with eleven identical companions, all stenciled with the Masson name, year, and wine variety.

Martin took great pleasure in these champagne-finishing tasks. The riddling and disgorging particularly required special skills. Unable to successfully train others to do them as well as he did, throughout the years he often undertook them himself.

It was the spring of 1937 when I encountered Martin Ray so unexpectedly in San Francisco. Thus he told me during our lunch together about his purchase of Paul Masson's corporation, his current relations with Paul, first vintage, and his future plans for marketing pure varietal wines.

I was greatly heartened to see that he showed the same "Rusty" exuberance dating back to our college years together—that dashing and dauntless vitality. I could see no trace of that devastating collapse and invalidism of a few years earlier.

"Now tell me again," I asked of him, "what you said years ago, when I first knew you, about your theory that few people ever experience life the way a winegrower does. I was so impressed! Do you remember it?"

He laughed delightedly. "Remember it? ... I *live* it now. So it's not just a theory!" Pouring more champagne into our glasses, he finished off the bottle. Then he began to summarize his current life.

"Almost no one ever experiences the real joy of living, the *joie de vivre,* that a winegrower has constantly. It's that thrill of being intensely alive, rushing happily into each day. Those years when I was a boy, and so much with Paul on his mountain, that thrill seemed always with me, from morning to night."

As if a dark cloud just swept over Martin's spirit, the luster in his eyes dimmed and his voice lost its verve. He was remembering the life that came later. "When I was out in the business world—the publications, the brokerage work, all the mundane money stuff—I lost it. After some years, I came to believe I'd never know again that happiness in just being alive. Thought of it merely as something to be experienced only in youth. That this was what happened when 'growing up'—you put away the magic of childhood."

"Yes, I know what you mean," I said. "That's why I get such delight in being able to relive childhood through my children."

"And it wasn't as if my marriage was at fault in any way," Martin went on, "for it is absolutely *wonderful*. No, there was just something elemental missing from my life that not even Elsie could supply.... It took a long while before I understood why the joy had gone. It wasn't just that I'd become a man. In that period of my illness I began to realize that I'd become too involved in matters far removed from 'the Good Life' I once had known directly as a boy, especially in Paul Masson's world. I recalled so clearly that he too had seemed infused with happiness, with his work and his life up there on the mountain. And he was a *man,* not a child.

"That's why I really determined to buy La Cresta when I did—if I could. And Elsie of course encouraged me. For most of all, I hoped that when I took up life on Paul's mountain myself, that thrill in just being alive would come back to me."

"And obviously it did!" I remarked.

"No," he said, "not right away. And I was disappointed. Elsie told me to be patient; said maybe it would take some time to return." He paused, looked pensive, and smiled suddenly as if a stray ray of sunlight had struck a cold, shadowy place in his heart. "Then, one morning, unaccountably, I felt it again! I'd leapt out of bed at daybreak, and in the cool of early morning went out and picked a luscious bunch of bluish-purple pinot grapes. Suddenly a thrill surged through me. Simply agog with joy, I had to rush forth and do so many things! In a few minutes the exultation passed, though. Would I never experience it again? But at least I knew that because it had happened once, it *could* come again."

Expectant, I waited for what would come next. "And it did return one day," he continued. "Then more and more often—always in the vineyard or the cellar. Often I felt it just as evening came on, after working hard all day somewhere on the mountain. Now this remarkable feeling comes to me almost daily in my life up there. Elsie tells me that mystics have various words for this feeling of exhilaration or ecstasy within a simple existence. 'And the Christians you are so suspicious of,' she says, 'call it an epiphany. When God comes down and pays you a little visit.'"

How wonderful that this transcendent thrill of Martin's youth had returned, to become a vital ingredient of his new life! I was overjoyed for him. And of course a bit envious too. After our lunch together, I hastened back to my job at the Emporium, feeling as if I were floating along on a silver cloud. What turnabouts our lives had made in the several years since we'd seen each other. . . .

Now that Martin and Elsie knew where I was, they often invited me down from San Francisco to their mountaintop retreat for a delightful and restful weekend stay—away from my "Why Not Worry Farm" in The City. And there I witnessed the happiness and fullness that life held for them both.

Paul Masson's magnificent hilltop property in the Santa Cruz Mountains above
Saratoga, with its 60 acres of vineyards, was acquired by Martin Ray in 1936.

After selling La Cresta to Martin Ray, in the late 1930s Paul
Masson often visited his old chateau, winery, and vineyards.

Old Queen plows the vineyard in front of the Masson winery.

The beautiful old façade of the Masson winery is now used as the
backdrop for outdoor summer concerts at the Mountain Winery.

Paul Masson's traditional wooden basket wine press.

One part of the large Paul Masson wine cellar.

An ornately hand-carved wine cask, which was later destroyed
in the devastating fire at the Paul Masson winery in 1941.

A stock certificate issued when Martin Ray
owned the Paul Masson Champagne Co.

Martin and Elsie Ray in the 1930s.

The Rays entertain guests—in this case, some of them Russian nobility—at one of their many elegant dinner parties.

21

Making Connections

A S THE TIME APPROACHED for releasing his new Paul Masson varietal wines, Martin Ray surveyed the current wine market. There was still no demand at all for American table wines. Imports from Europe were increasingly abundant—certainly enough to satisfy the fractionally few connoisseurs who bought premium wines.

As for the "better" table wines that a few California winegrowers furnished the market, hardly anyone wanted them, Martin knew. Though superior to those made earlier, they had still been produced from the usual mongrel grapes. Experiencing dismal sales, the vintners inevitably blamed imports for the continuing wine depression. They demanded that European wines be either banned or taxed prohibitively so that few people could buy them. And why should Americans drink French and German wines, anyway? Martin knew that their chauvinistic and parochial attitudes struck wine connoisseurs everywhere as absurd.

Nowadays, decades later, it is hard for wine drinkers in younger generations to comprehend how unacceptable California wines simply were to epicures accustomed to France's classic, fine-varietal wines. American wines were still almost entirely characterless generics—wine blends, mostly without a vintage year.

Europeans were scarcely dismayed by the utter lack of competition from the New World's vineyards. As for wine lovers in America, they reluctantly had to admit, often after innumerable tastings, that they simply must abandon all hope of ever getting truly fine wines out of California. They assumed that this impossibility must be endemic—perhaps a faulty climate or the wrong soil types, or both. They rarely considered the real cause: cheap wine blends including non-wine grapes, winegrowing habits and winemaking techniques geared toward the lowest common denominator in the marketplace, and dismissing the importance of establishing and maintaining standards for excellence.

California was no place now for quality interest, Martin realized, let alone control. Prohibition had wiped out the few traces of past achievements in California wine production that at least had demonstrated a certain potential for greatness. California wines occasionally had even won medals in international wine-judging events. But not until Martin Ray arrived on the scene in the mid-'30s was anyone courageous—or foolhardy—enough to devote a lifetime effort to regaining that lost high ground, then superseding it.

So as Martin began readying his first varietal table wines for release, he gave great attention to strategy. They should be packaged in ways guaranteed to compel attention wherever they appeared. And they had to look entirely different from the run-of-the-mill offerings from California wineries sitting on retailers' shelves. Martin had prepared himself well for this challenge. For months he had closely studied French labels and wrappings, deciding just how his bottled wines must look when proclaiming their supremacy.

He ordered the finest finishing corks from Portugal and the richest lead foil capsules from England. He fussed over the design and printing of impressive labels for each varietal wine as well as for his champagnes. Perhaps most important of all was his special treatment of the new still wines. Each bottle was decanted before being prepared for shipping, to remove the heavy deposit laid down after the wines in cask were finally racked and then bottle-aged. He was determined not to artificially "process" any of these wines, as ordinary shippers did, to clarify them.

Like Paul Masson, Martin loved the thick-glass, dark-green champagne bottles, with their deeply concave punts at the base. Right after Repeal Masson still had on hand a large supply of them, dating from the years when he could sell only champagne. Paul then used these bottles too for his still wines, thinking that a wine served from such bottles looked marvelous and *felt* impressive. Martin agreed, so decided to use them for all his new varietals as well.

When Martin's supreme wines were ready to be shipped, he prepared heavy wooden cases on which the Paul Masson name, the varietal name, and the vintage year of 1936 were engraved. He knew that wines so presented would make a stir among wine retailers and their customers. How could they not?

Imagine the astonishment when in 1938 and 1939 these first 100-percent varietals began appearing from Paul Masson—as created by Martin Ray. Each bottle's label, signed by him personally, bore the name of the grape variety used exclusively for the wine. First came the whites and light reds: chardonnay, pinot blanc, folle blanche, gamay beaujolais. Then the heavier reds: pinot noir and cabernet sauvignon. They little resembled the usual California blends with generic names and bearing no vintage dates.

Discovering the new Masson line of wines gradually—often by happenstance or word of mouth—wine epicures went into raptures. How incredible to get those distinctive, unmistakable varietal flavors out of California! Martin Ray-made wines indisputably proved to them that the United States *could* someday produce many great wines—no doubt by changing its winegrowers' ways. Vintners would have to plant the finest grape varieties, and then vintage them pure and unblended, as these astounding wines of Martin Ray's proclaimed. (Years later, after the American winegrowers had learned considerably from experience with different varietals, they might choose sometimes to deftly combine them, as with the "Meritage" wines, balancing characteristics in forms attractive to the expert palate.)

Rumors of Martin Ray's wondrous varietal wines reached the wine-promoting writers new on the scene since Repeal. They lost no time in investigating the tantalizing place of origin. The youthful Robert Balzer came racing up to Saratoga. "We wound our way up a mountainside to a winery where a young winemaker is at work producing the finest wines in America," he recounted of a visit to Paul Masson's cellars.

Retailers and their customers were also astonished by the new Paul Masson offerings—and their prices. Not in the accustomed one dollar to two dollar price range, but bottles at four dollars and up! (Correcting for inflation, the equivalent price at the present time would be about $30.)

These comparatively high prices did not come about because Martin Ray was greedy for profit. The prices automatically classed his wines with top European imports, where they belonged in quality. They also reflected the cost of making such time-consuming, labor-intensive wines. For Martin Ray did not run then, or ever, the factory-style assembly line that had become America's trademark, providing low-cost, mass-produced products for the world marketplace. His style of handling his wines harked back appropriately to preindustrial artisans, who had given loving consideration to shaping each product. Such hand-crafted commodities could no longer be made, or sold, cheaply.

Publicity about Masson's new, handsomely packaged, pure varietal wines aroused curiosity among knowing wine consumers around the country. They bought, and after drinking rapturously, told friends. News of Masson's suddenly booming table-wine sales, and at prices four times higher than the norm, electrified California's wine industry. Other vintners wondered whether Martin Ray might share his secret formula.

A small delegation of established winegrowers came to visit the Paul Masson winery, to see for themselves what magical tricks Martin Ray was performing there. As their host graciously conducted them through the winery, he offered sample tastings from various casks. All the while Martin explained the crucial importance of vintaging the fine varietals separately, rather than blending everything together in one vat. That way, he said, a distinctive wine could be made to reflect fully a fine wine grape's merits. Later, up at the chateau, Martin opened bottles of finished wines for his guests to try. Sadly, he observed that none of them possessed sensitive palates. To them one varietal clearly tasted the same as another.

Obviously they concluded that Martin Ray had cleverly devised a gimmick as a new marketing trick when putting varietal names on his labels, such as pinot noir and pinot blanc. Word spread like wildfire, fanned by the enthusiasm of super winesalesman Frank Schoonmaker. Having quickly latched onto the idea, he began using varietal labeling as a dramatic new sales pitch with the California wines he represented as a broker, encouraging wineries to follow the Masson lead: print varietal names on all their wine labels, and raise their prices accordingly.

Soon almost every winery leaped on the varietal bandwagon, eager to strike the same bonanza by giving their blends varietal names—even though few had any of the varietals so labeled. They could also retroactively label blended wines of older vintages with varietal names. No law against it! Even the volume producers with jug wines discovered they could greatly expand sales of red wines by calling them cabernet sauvignon and pinot noir instead of the plain old generics, claret and burgundy. Varietal names obviously had come to stay.

Martin was horrified at this deceptively favorable turn for varietals. Why wasn't something being done about this situation? How could California allow its winemaking reputation to be further degraded on the world market by such fraudulent labeling? No wonder the state's wines couldn't get a respectful reception and decent prices! Federal and state authorities were wrongheaded not to impose quality controls *now,* to ensure the same excellence in America's premium wines as the French did—which would also allow them to command the same high prices.

Weren't there other vintners who would support a change toward quality in varietal wines? Martin asked. Creating prestige wines would enable them not only to take great pride in their products, but also to earn respectable incomes. Because of overall abysmally low prices, Martin's own superb varietals had to sell for far less than comparable French ones. It was maddeningly inexcusable!

Martin Ray now tried to rally the few better winegrowers to his new cause: initiating quality standards within the wine industry that would raise the prestige of California wines. He found, to his great shock, that not a single winery or individual vintner would join him. So he then realized he must simply bide his time. Even the French, he reminded himself, had met with extreme difficulty some years back in setting up quality regulations. They had passed their first "delimitary" laws in 1911 after the Champagne War's ensuing riots and interminable conflicts over varietals. But it required many years to regulate quality still wines under the special provision of its *Appellation Contrôlée*. In the complex 1933 ruling the French government guaranteed not only authenticity of origin, but quality to a certain extent as well. Martin regarded this *A.C.* as a touchstone and model for future legislation in California and the entire U.S. regarding wine quality standards.

Despite his contemporaries' deceptions in mislabeling blended wines as varietals, and then continuing to do so in all too many years ahead, Martin Ray's own authentic varietals triumphed prodigiously in the late '30s and the dawning '40s. To his delight, they were proving exactly what he had intended for them: if he created wines exceptional enough, the wine world would beat a path—albeit a narrow one—right to his cellar door. So he didn't have to seek out "those important people who know and love fine wines," which old Paul Masson had advised was essential for his wines' ultimate triumph out in the marketplace. His wines themselves were finding them.

Martin ran into problems with eager wine promoters. Most notably, with New York wine salesman Frank Schoonmaker, who in the late 1930s took on California wines to supplement the European ones he hawked. It was a shrewd move—a hedge against business collapse in case hostilities generated by Hitler's Germany assumed larger proportions, to decrease production and even cut off European wine exports.

Schoonmaker was thrilled at the prospect of selling these amazing Masson wines—true varietals and so labeled, resembling French wines as no other California offerings did. However, Martin's own chosen representative customarily handled all sales. But due to Frank's special brand of persuasion, Martin did agree to let him have part of an already scheduled shipment ... if he'd promise not to release it in California. Promised. Then marketing problems exploded: Schoonmaker *had* released it in the state! When an infuriated Martin berated him, Schoonmaker imperturbably passed the violation off simply as an unfortunate slipup somewhere. But Martin was left with an enduring wariness.

Martin later learned that Schoonmaker had started his career in the early '30s by aiding America's first outstanding wine authority, Julian Street, in research and writing. Such an industrious young fellow this Frank was! Julian reported to friends that at night he could see his office lights still burning—which meant his employee was still plugging away at some project in his behalf. What Frank was actually doing, it turned out, was copying Julian Street's extensive list of wine customers. Shortly thereafter, Frank launched his own business himself with these priceless contacts already provided him. In no time this entrepreneur with dubious beginnings became known nationwide as a wine expert. He flew back and forth from coast to coast, straining to keep up with the results of his great success.

Now Schoonmaker was adding to his sales fame by authoring a book on American wines. He would devote an entire chapter, he said, to the fabulous 100 percent varietal wines Martin Ray was creating at Paul Masson. On a subsequent visit he showed Martin galley proofs of this chapter, ready for printing. Supreme acclaim he accorded them!

At that time Frank greatly needed, he said, a shipment of pinot noir. Martin agreed to send it, but because of an unhappy earlier experience with Frank, he insisted on payment in advance. No problem: Frank would mail it on his return to New York. When no check arrived, Martin held up shipment and waited. Then Schoonmaker phoned to say he had to have the shipment at once. Payment? Why, he'd send it immediately on the wine's arrival.

"So you say now," Martin said. "But once you get the wine—which you've doubtless presold already—you'll have some bigger project pending and use up the money you've taken for my wine. I've come to know you, Frank. No shipment till I'm paid!"

"But those wines of yours already have my strip label on them," Frank reminded him triumphantly.

"Oh no, I've been waiting for the cash, before I label them," Martin said.

At that, Frank blew his top. "If you don't ship, I'll yank that whole chapter about you out of my book!"

"Then yank the goddamn thing!" Martin exploded.

So that laudatory chapter was removed. When the first edition of *American Wines* appeared in 1941, Martin Ray's name wasn't mentioned in the book, despite the fact that his first authentic varietals made at Masson were the most dramatic news in wine circles across the nation. But no doubt by oversight, one remark was not excised: "Probably the best wines of California ... are those of the Paul Masson Champagne Co., which, paradoxically, produces even finer still wines than Champagnes and is no longer owned by Paul Masson."

Certainly Schoonmaker stressed varietal labeling as the key future trend for American wines. His book became a landmark publication, accepted as the quintessential guide to American wines and winemakers, and consulted repeatedly as a basic reference in historical research. Writers delving into wine history often pick up and perpetuate others' earlier ideas, errors, and false claims. Five decades later, incredibly, Frank Schoonmaker is sometimes credited with actually *inventing* the whole concept of varietal labeling. But in 1936 it was Martin Ray, in his first vintage at Paul Masson, who in fact *proved* that using fine wine-grape varieties exclusively should be the high road for premium California winegrowers to take in the years ahead.

Relations between Martin Ray and Schoonmaker eventually were patched up, as it was Frank's way to keep all lucrative channels open to him. Certainly Martin enjoyed Frank's keen appreciation and knowledge of fine wines. So ensuing contacts with him continued, with Martin garnering a new set of intriguing tales from each new experience with the flamboyant fellow.

Martin Ray's launching those early varietal wines with such acclaim took the two men in widely different directions. Wily promoter that he was, Frank Schoonmaker continued encouraging other California winemakers whom he represented nationwide to keep labeling their wines as varietals—no matter what they actually were ... to bring both them and Schoonmaker much higher prices. And Martin Ray meanwhile remained the adamant purist.

Here and there in America, Martin Ray was discovering, epicures did exist who harbored a special passion for fine table wines. One of them was former President Herbert Hoover, who lived close to the new institute founded in his name at Stanford. In 1939 Hoover made an epochal discovery: Paul Masson's new varietal wines. Enthusiastically he relayed news of it to an East Coast friend, Julian Street—the gourmet and writer (and Francophile) who was America's supreme international food and wine authority.

Martin Ray's first inkling of this fortuitous association came one morning when a messenger sped into the courtyard with the telltale yellow envelope that always held arriving telegrams.

Quickly Martin pulled out the sheet of paper with its unpunctuated message strips. He scanned it, then raced into the chateau to show it to Elsie. "Look at this!" a breathless Martin exclaimed.

YOUR PINOT NOIR 1936 TASTED TONIGHT IS FIRST AMERICAN RED WINE I EVER DRANK WITH ENTIRE PLEASURE COLOR SUPERB BOUQUET BEAUTIFUL FLAVOR UNMISTAKABLY PINOT NOIR BIG AND FULL WINE STILL SOMEWHAT HARD WITH SLIGHTLY BITTER AFTERTASTE NEVERTHELESS REMARKABLY FINE I AM ASTOUNDED WARMEST CONGRATULATIONS

JULIAN STREET

Stunned, they read the words over and over, at first unable to contain their exultation enough to speak. Finally, a tear trickled down Elsie's cheek. "That does it!" she exclaimed, her voice breaking.

"Darling . . . this is what we've worked so hard for," Martin said, kissing her cheek. "And just think: it's always been said that Julian Street never, never would approve *any* California wine."

And from the day that telegram arrived, events moved at a fast pace for Martin and Elsie Ray. Julian Street carried on a vast correspondence with wine devotees, and he began alerting them all to the remarkable wines now being made at Paul Masson. Among them was noted New York publisher Alfred Knopf, who in turn got the word out to an ever-widening circle of connoisseurs. They raved at dinner parties, wrote letters, made long-distance phone calls—telling each other of this new marvel. Masson's sales zoomed within the small orbit of fine wine fanciers and sold to the limit of supply, at prices that quadrupled those asked for other California wines.

Soon those influential "important people" from everywhere clamored to visit, whether or not they were wine experts. Before they quite realized what was happening, the Rays found themselves putting on elegant dinners several times a week—just as Paul had advised. This socializing came on top of Martin's strenuous work in the winery and vineyards. But he well knew from Masson's example that such entertainment was a vital part of the great life on the mountain that he'd envisaged and set his heart on so long ago.

Among the first who asked to come up was writer John Steinbeck, who then lived close by in the green hills of Los Gatos. Hearing about the wines, he called to say that he and his wife, Carol, wished to look around and see for themselves what was rumored to be so "fascinating" up there. John discovered ideal ingredients in this vintner's lifestyle. "God almighty, here it is—the perfect life I've always imagined might exist somewhere!" he proclaimed. And of course the amazing wines were a revelation too.

Immediately attracted to Martin Ray and his premises, Steinbeck returned so often that La Cresta became almost his second home. He and Carol spent many fabulous weekends on Martin Ray's mountain, drinking wines and swapping stories. The writer's early Monterey- and Salinas-set novels and stories weren't yet famous—though of course Elsie had already read and loved them. She and Martin were delighted when Steinbeck would read aloud to them parts from his current book in the making, *The Grapes of Wrath,* that portrayed the harsh life of the state's migratory workers during these Depression years.

Through Steinbeck came Charlie Chaplin. The brilliant, already legendary film comedian and director had been hounding his friend John to get him in on a vintage with Martin Ray. No dilettante, he was seriously interested in the art of winemaking. He had already visited famous vineyards in Europe. Since he was keen to learn more about how great wines were made, he hankered to see the Paul Masson operation.

So Chaplin took part in the vintage of 1938. Early one autumn morning he arrived on the mountain with Steinbeck. He quickly donned overalls and pitched in, pouring box after box of chardonnay into the crusher. (With his touchy back, Steinbeck had to avoid wrenching work, but still managed to be in on everything.) For Martin it was an astounding sight: seeing the celebrated Chaplin hoisting heavy timbers atop the grapes in the basket press, then swinging on the press handle vigorously with the rest of the vintage crew. At some outrageous hour, after the day's work finally was finished, Charlie insisted on taking full command of the turkey roasting in the fireplace *rotissoire*—which the Rays had inherited from Masson. Then in the wee hours, he pulled out his accordion and played furiously while everyone sang. Yet he was up early to recommence the work.

Chaplin even took an enthusiastic hand at various cellar tasks, such as punching down the cap of the pinot noir must, picked earlier and already lustily fermenting in open puncheons covered with white cloths. As Martin was distributing his special Montrachet yeast to fermenters that had just received the latest crush, Charlie asked how much sulfur he added. Abruptly Martin stopped his work. "None!" he exploded. *"Anyone* can make wine with sulfur dioxide—even the sloppiest vintner."

"Good Lord, you mean to say—" Charlie spluttered, astonished—"that you use no sulfur at *all?*"

Sulfur was so offensive, Martin now told him, that the slightest tinge of it ruined a wine for him. He had found that sulfur wasn't necessary as a disinfectant if he maintained the utmost cleanliness in every minute winemaking procedure. Martin explained, though, that by eliminating sulfur he knew he was also eliminating the customary preservative used in wines. He therefore was taking a big risk in shipping his bottled wines out into the unknown. For without the sulfite protection, they might deteriorate if exposed to any heat en route or later. Then he'd have to refund the purchase price or replace the order—along with risking a reputation for making defective wines. But in his near-fanatical desire to attain the highest possible degree of perfection, he was willing to take that risk.

No wonder, Chaplin remarked now, that he so loved these wines of Martin's: their pure varietal aroma and flavor were untainted by sulfur. After "tasting through" the casks in the cellars, he asked Martin to reserve certain ones whose contents he favored most, to be bottled later and shipped to him as needed. This arrangement earned extra publicity for the Paul Masson winery whenever visitors' eyes fell upon signs on various casks: RESERVED FOR CHARLIE CHAPLIN.

After this first visit, Chaplin frequently dropped by, usually arriving in his odd limousine. The self-proclaimed proletarian insisted upon owning a Ford ... a custom-built one! He also kept his chauffeur waiting outside for many hours as he quaffed wines and reveled in his usual skylarking time with Martin Ray.

In making his wines, Martin Ray achieved a rare degree of consistent excellence, maintaining it from his very first vintage. Risk-taker though he was, he firmly believed that the best wines can almost "make themselves" from the best grapes. He was proud of being a classical winemaker, not a modern-day technical chemist. Thus he interfered as little as possible in a natural process that had been known and performed with success in the Old World for several millennia. Once he found a particular procedure that achieved what he wanted, Martin usually stopped there. He never tinkered as did inveterate experimenters elsewhere; their vintaged products constantly changed, not always for the better.

No bottle ever left Martin's cellars that was less than excellent, in his appraisal. (Through the years he sold off wine lots that did not meet his own exacting standards.) That did not mean, however, that a wine of his—transported and stored elsewhere, and possibly exposed to detrimental conditions—would remain unequivocally in good condition. Nor did it guarantee that anyone opening a bottle would *like* it. For his wines were classically bone-dry, in extreme opposition to the sweet-wine trend of the time when he first began making them. Thus for decades their immense body and varietal richness—the very qualities that so astounded and delighted Julian Street—put them far outside the typical palate's range of appreciation. But to those few who did "know and love fine wines," Martin Ray's provided an incredible experience.

And what were his best early wines, at Masson? Most notable were all those he made from one varietal wine grape, the authentic pinot noir—significantly planted nowhere in California except his vineyards. Even if any other California vintners had appreciated this variety, they wouldn't have bothered to grow it. First of all, because most winemakers threw all their grapes into one enormous blend, using mostly bland-tasting, big producers, whether unaware or else uncaring that superior varieties existed. Moreover, pinot noir posed many difficulties to a grower; special climate and soil demands made this finicky "shy yielder" too costly and risky to try. How could pinot noir possibly appeal to growers who wanted a grape crop to produce at least five tons per acre, not two or three (if lucky)?

Paul Masson had been the first winegrower to import and plant pinot noir, then use it successfully through the years as the main ingredient in both his red table wines and champagnes. But after all, he *was* a Burgundian, and for him this difficult and demanding grape had ancestral appeal. He was also strong-willed. No other grape would ever please him as much or present such annually daunting challenges. So his spiritual heir, Martin Ray, in his first years of winemaking, took the pinot noir produced magnificently on the slopes of those vineyards in the sky and made it perform many wonders to eye, nose, and palate.

It was symbolic too that Elsie Ray especially loved the wines made from that grape. Martin awarded her an appropriately honorary title, "Madame Pinot." He then gave this name to one of his most famous champagnes made from the grape, a *blanc de noir* fermented from the free-run juice coming from the press before crushing. The delicately golden champagne was a rarity on the market, first created by Masson after he'd seen it made in Reims when on a visit to France.

Martin naturally continued producing a great Masson favorite, *Oeil de Perdrix,* so prized on the wine market. This pink champagne of rare color and flavor was made from a first light pressing of pinot noir grapes. Martin also made the delightful pinot noir rosé, aglow with the same glorious partridge-eye pink as the champagne, but a still wine—America's first varietal rosé table wine. It was so adored by Mrs. Harrison Williams, an East Coast moneyed socialite, that she sometimes took Martin Ray's entire yearly output! Another special favorite was Martin Ray's blanc de noir table wine, yet another pinot noir-derived product—so versatile in complementing a variety of foods.

And of course, climactically, there was the superbly elegant pinot noir still wine itself. Big, richly fruity, ruby-toned, it had all the bold, long-lived but early-drinkable features that for years many an ambitious vintner in the future frantically strove vainly to achieve. These wine dreamers were defeated because they either lacked the authentic pinot noir grape, or proved unsuccessful in raising this temperamental grape from cuttings Martin Ray had generously given them—ever hoping to encourage its use among other vintners and thus raise California's winegrowing prestige.

Martin Ray also made a splendid and authentic gamay beaujolais, whose grapes were produced by vines grown from selections brought from Burgundy by Masson. It was completely different from and superior to any out of Napa from the same claimed variety. Lacking its character, the Napa variety later proved to be an inferior gamay cousin.

Through ingenious methods he achieved notable results with various little-known varieties such as pinot blanc, folle blanche, traminer, and sylvaner. He marketed a sensational *blanc de blancs,* a rare *mélange* of white grapes few other vintners grew at the time. And he produced "limited editions" of white wine varieties produced in odd lots in his vineyards, such as semillon, sauvignon blanc, and burger.

All his fine still wines Martin sent out to the world within the heavy green champagne-style bottles and sealed with mushroom-headed champagne corks and metal agrafe clamps. (This was almost a trademark for Martin Ray-made wines, and such bottles are now cherished collectors' items. He did this for many years. But in the early 1960s, the Bureau of Alcohol, Tobacco, and Firearms [BATF], the primary government agency regulating wine production and marketing, put a stop to the practice. It maintained that customers might confuse the still wine therein with champagne.)

Most notably, however, during those first years at Paul Masson, the elusive pinot noir grape had revealed its secrets in splendid array to Martin Ray. The wine he made from it would live on for many years as a vivid, tantalizing memory. Decades later, when California's famed enologist Dr. Maynard Amerine was asked by one of his students to name the greatest pinot noir he'd ever tasted, after several moments' thought he responded, "A 1936 made by Martin Ray." Wine lovers stunned by its extraordinary debut in the tepid California wine scene might never match that experience again.

22

Celebrities and Celebrations

B Y THE LATE 1930s and early '40s Martin Ray's tenure on Paul
Masson's mountaintop had achieved a soaring splendor. Successive waves of those "important people who know and love fine
wines" created an exalted atmosphere. These were epoch-making
days and nights of celebrating the Good Life with rare people of
tremendous spirit. Their visits highlighted great dinners replete
with wonderful wines—not just Martin's but also the acknowledged best from French and German vineyard estates.

And at the center of all the activity and merriment was the *real*
Martin Ray his vitriolic critics never knew—the exuberant host
loved and even idolized by wine devotees who sought him out. Not
feeling he had to defend or attack, Martin was at his magnetic
best. Over copious champagne, he laughed exuberantly and told
his fantastic stories, making the very atmosphere vibrate.

Guests, mesmerized, likened him to a sorcerer or prophet. And
certainly his charismatic presence cast a spell of enchantment,
just as his wines delivered some magical potion. (I'm not exagger-
ating. I was around often enough then and afterwards, taking part
in some magnificent events of those early Masson years. Though
I didn't bring my three children, who weren't ready for such a
stratospheric experience!)

Dinners were simply glorious at "high noon" on spring days
upon the mountain, with brilliant sun on the panorama of vines
bursting into fresh green leaf, and the aromatic scent from millions of prune and apricot blossoms wafting up from Santa Clara
Valley below. Equally fantastic were dinners on autumn days, the
vines then all flame and gold, with their lush, juice-filled grapes—
the deep blue-violet pinot noir and golden chardonnay—coming
now into vintage. No wonder everyone visiting there fell madly in
love with the Masson mountain!

Many of these visitors returned again and again, usually becoming devoted friends. Alfred and Blanche Knopf came when they were out West, separately or together, often bringing luminaries of the publishing world. They were wonderful private customers, since they found the wines Martin Ray was making superior to some French favorites. And due to their formidable influence on wine lovers across the nation, through social contacts as well as wine books they published, the Knopfs greatly amplified Martin's wine sales.

Herbert Hoover came regularly with wine-loving guests in his entourage. Most were in academic circles, but on one occasion he was accompanied by a Supreme Court justice. Prince Vasili Romanoff—nephew of the ill-fated Czar Nicholas II of pre-Revolutionary Russia—and his lovely wife, Natasha, spent many weekends on the mountain. Often these distinguished guests brought others of European royalty, including the charming Grand Duchess Marie, cousin of the czar.

(Recalling here the hundreds of visitors to the mountain reminds me to remark about an unfortunate hazard in entertaining throngs of people through the years. Some proved to be incredibly light-fingered. An early theft was of several irreplaceable albums that Grand Duchess Marie had presented to Elsie and Martin. They were filled with stunning photographs she had taken of the Masson vineyards and winery, and of the Rays and their guests, when she was working with Eastman Kodak. Another lift of a priceless memento was of a laudatory verse John Steinbeck had composed to the Rays. Framed and hanging on a wall, it was deftly removed by some guest, no doubt to add to some prized private collection. Other human magpies—doubtless rationalizing that they would appreciate better these souvenirs—similarly went off with precious books, paintings, silver, dishware, stamp collections, and sundries.)

British stage star Gertrude Lawrence was a most exciting visitor, gorgeous in her lynx jacket worn over slacks (long before other women dared to wear pants). Authors Charles and Kathleen Norris came frequently, for they lived on a nearby mountain. Then there was Irvin S. Cobb, who always held everyone breathless when telling his stories. He could tell them almost more dramatically than he wrote them, which few authors can do. A highly cherished dinner visit was made by the Marquis de Lur Saluces of famed Chateau d'Yquem. Another memorable visitor was the Waldorf-Astoria Hotel's ebullient president, Lucius Boomer. (More later about both these men.)

But it was John and Carol Steinbeck who contributed the ultimate delight to those early days, spending long, enchanted hours on the mountain. John's writing was beginning to hit the big time, and he was working hard to raise it to even greater heights. A marvel of a storyteller himself, John greatly admired Martin's narrative abilities. Martin's photographic mind supplied richly detailed pictures, and he replicated whole scenes in dialogue, voicing all parts. Steinbeck would lean forward and listen intently, gleaning gems for possible future use.

Sometimes John brought a special friend to the mountain. One was the prototype for "Doc," the marine biologist who was a Martin Ray favorite among Steinbeck-tale characters. Martin found Ed Ricketts every bit as lovable as in John's stories about him. The times they had together on the mountain became legendary. Doc particularly loved the gigantic old bell that Martin had bought to ring in Repeal for Paul Masson. These days it took on an important new role: to "ring in" and "ring out," like a flourish of trumpets, a succession of illustrious and fascinating visitors.

When their own activities permitted, the Rays sometimes lunched with the Steinbecks at their place, after John finished writing in the early afternoon. He'd read them the morning's work, so they'd follow along with the progress of his stories.

Martin shared with the Steinbecks his own intensifying campaign to promote pure varietal wines as *the* solution to California vintners' bad "press" nationally and internationally. One day at the Steinbecks' house, as he was holding forth on this favored topic, John told him for God's sake to hold off. "Want to kill yourself, keeping up this fight on top of all your cellar and vineyards work ... *and* your colossal entertaining?" he exclaimed. "Why should you care what wines are being ridiculously labeled? The worse they are, the finer yours will be in comparison. Just let it drop, Rusty!"

Certainly John had a point: Martin's fixation was not simplifying his life any—as the doctor had ordered him to do.

Just at that moment, by odd coincidence, John got a phone call from Harry Hopkins at the White House. President Roosevelt's close advisor had discovered in Steinbeck inexhaustible material for his various social causes. Martin hung around while they talked, for over an hour, watching Steinbeck waving an arm excitedly to emphasize some point, and repeating "Now what we want is ..." and generally carrying on.

"Who the hell is WE?" Martin asked when the conversation finally ended. "You kept saying, 'What *we* want.'"

"Why, We the People!" John exploded, his fist in the air challengingly. Whereupon Martin laughed uproariously, and shook his own fist in the air. "We the Varietal Wines!" he came back at him. After that, John gave up trying to take the fire out of Martin's cause, and expected reciprocal consideration.

Actually, Carol Steinbeck was probably responsible for much of her husband's social-cause leanings. She remains the unsung heroine of John's best writing years. (And her father's monthly $25 check had actually supported them in the early *Tortilla Flat* days.) Inquisitive, she had registered in the Communist Party and also joined the John Reed Club, an elite group of radicals. She brought to John's attention societal wrongs and economic problems that won his writing its greatest acclaim.

Carol not only typed up John's handwritten manuscripts; she usually thought up the titles for his new books, as well as their basic themes. Though she wasn't a "literary" type, she possessed remarkably sound judgment about Steinbeck's writing. Often she'd speak up, tell him he'd branched off too far here or there, or advise him to cut something. She even persuaded him to discard an entire book he'd finished, a diatribe against a Salinas lettuce-grower he disliked, since it demeaned his art by reducing it to political assault. (Years later, some of that early, impassioned anger apparently found a better outlet in his *East of Eden.)*

John adored Elsie, as did everyone who knew her. Upon finding his first novel *Cup of Gold* on the Rays' bookshelf, he specially inscribed it to Elsie—who was, he said, truly his *copa de oro.* And after receiving his first copies of *The Grapes of Wrath,* he gave one to the Rays, writing, "My vintage for yours." (These Steinbeck-autographed first editions and others sit proudly—and protect-edly—on a bookshelf in my bedroom today.)

The Steinbecks' companionable marriage suddenly changed when *Grapes of Wrath* became a tremendous literary and commercial success. At parties John was the big celebrity, while Carol received little or no recognition. Feeling rudely dismissed, she acted out her anger, sometimes raising her voice to compel attention. Increasingly she was sharply criticized and socially ostracized. The once-amicable pair no longer visited the Rays' mountaintop together.

Steinbeck publisher, Viking, gave a big party for him in New York. He flew back there, leaving Carol behind. Immediately snatched aboard the East Coast celebrity circuit, he never really came back. It was a great loss. To Carol. To the Rays. To everyone who had loved him as a friend. But most of all, perhaps, to himself and his writing. Those romantic, anti-Establishment Steinbeck years in California were over.

In a brief interlude between 1939 and 1941, as Europe became engulfed by war and before the U.S. entered it, California wines experienced their first golden dawn. During this fleeting spell, genuine interest suddenly flared in California's better wines. An avid curiosity about wines now stirred among several generations who had barely if ever known wine. The high-powered promotion of California wines by Frank Schoonmaker, that phenomenal wine virtuoso, certainly helped stir up public enthusiasm.

The great influx of visiting enthusiasts to Martin Ray's first vineyards in the sky at Paul Masson's reflected this high point of allure. Martin Ray was becoming a celebrity of sorts, particularly from Julian Street's extensive publicizing of the Paul Masson wines. Street's influence radiated far and wide, and his imprimatur on a wine was the ultimate encomium. Preparing feature stories for their readers, various newspapers and national magazines, notably *Life,* sent up writers, accompanied by photographers to record the gorgeous vistas of vineyards in their mountain setting. When *Vogue* ran a lead story, its cover depicted Queen, Paul Masson's magnificent old white horse, plowing the vineyards with the picturesque winery in the background.

This rapt fascination was not sheer illusion. It was now demonstrated that California winegrowers, when encouraged by wine writers and consumers, *could* reach toward greatness, as in Europe. And at rare times they might approach or even attain it. Left behind in the dust were the Prohibition-stunted era and its dismal aftermath in the Repeal years. Not yet had the looming Second World War severed imports, to halt the California vintners' spirit of competition with European wines which had caused them to aspire toward quality.

Martin Ray read reports of Beaulieu and Inglenook operations and sampled their new releases. If improvement came about in overall California winemaking, those were the wineries where he would first notice it. And sure enough, California's vintners during the three years between 1939 and 1941 did upgrade their wines here and there, hoping to outdo each other. Having enviously witnessed the acclaim Martin Ray was getting for his pure varietals, they noted that he had no trouble selling at prices much higher than theirs. So a definite but erratic trend started toward producing better wines: not just the *vin ordinaire* in jugs, but also the indistinctive bottled generics that Great Depression economics had seemingly dictated.

Encouraged by the new consumer interest in prestige wines, many winemakers actually improved their standard blends. They were rewarded. Their better-quality wines—far superior to those formerly released—did sell well. And, for the first time, at higher prices. However, they remained largely blends because their makers couldn't risk planting, at best, more than a few low-yielding premium varieties. So, lacking those fine varietal grapes that could have made a significant contribution, even the top-rated wineries continued to market mongrel blends—while brazenly printing varietal names on their labels instead of appropriate generic titles.

Actually, a few established winegrowers, thinking that quality might someday pay off, by now were planting some vineyard blocks with fine varieties. A rarer few, lucky or astute, already had small acreages of desirable varieties that somehow had survived Prohibition's destruction.

But not everyone wanted to take that investment risk. One day at a chance meeting, a premium Napa winemaker boasted to Martin, "I've discovered that I can make a superb pinot noir by combining three varieties!" Martin of course asked what they were. He was told—and shuddered. Pinot noir itself wasn't among them. Martin had already noted, in grim irony, that the vintner's label even proclaimed "PURE Pinot Noir"—seemingly assuring consumers of 100 percent of that varietal!

Martin now asked the man how he could release such a fraud. Martin reminded him that he'd offered to give him all the genuine pinot noir cuttings he might want for a planting, and thus be able to produce a truly prestigious wine. But the winemaker said no. Since his pinot already was highly successful, why get into an unnecessary planting project that would be both expensive and time-consuming?

During this period Martin Ray introduced a new concept in wine merchandising. He announced that for the coming vintage season of 1940 he would give customers, between Thanksgiving Day and Christmas, the opportunity to reserve wines in advance of bottling, at a price set in late November. At a later date the wines might cost much more—if indeed they were obtainable at all, with his Paul Masson wines now much in demand by connoisseurs around the country. For a 50 percent down-payment in advance, the young wines would be held first in cask, then bottled and cellared securely until ready for release to their owners several years hence, when final payment was due. Martin Ray's idea, so novel at the time, was widely publicized. (Now, of course, "wine futures" are offered by a number of premium wineries.)

Most interestingly, foreigners had begun to play a big part in whetting American curiosity about wines. Like many people of culture and means in Central and Western Europe, Jewish or not, wine merchants in vast numbers fled from Hitler's takeover of their lands. They poured into America, joining the ranks of wine promoters here.

"Why, they're like locusts descending on our wine industry!"

an amazed Martin Ray exclaimed to Elsie after lunching at a San Francisco restaurant. There Europeans obviously in the wine trade, seated at several tables next to his, had volubly discussed wine with prospective customers. And to his astonishment, he heard *California* wines praised to the skies! Heretofore, these wine merchants from abroad were past masters at deprecating all but the products of France and Germany. Now in 1939 they'd about-faced and were running down everything they'd formerly praised. Sometimes a mere gesture would suffice, a shrug of the shoulders, or a raised eyebrow at the very mention of Château This or Domaine That—tactics they'd formerly used against California wines.

Over the next several years a number of these refugees came to the mountain seeking employment, whether as representatives or as cellar men. "Too bad about European wines," they'd say to Martin Ray. "They've lost the art of making wine over there."

One immigrant who knew a great deal already about the art of winemaking arrived in Napa Valley in the late '30s, becoming the principal winemaker at Beaulieu Vineyard—and remaining there for many years. The winery started by Georges de Latour in 1900 was now directed by his widow, Madame de Latour. (Its initials, BV, on bottles have long been familiar to serious drinkers of California wine.)

André Tchelistcheff was a young Russian emigré who had studied winemaking, first in Czechoslovakia and then in France. Acquainted with the various Russian aristocratic exiles who were frequently entertained by the Rays and interested to see what went on at Paul Masson, he got himself invited to visit the wine cellars on his own. Martin had heard from their mutual friends that André was eager to be involved in the making of truly great California wines. So he might even contemplate taking charge of the technical operations at Masson.

Tchelistcheff brought with him some wine he thought might be of special interest to Martin. A recent bottling of his pinot blanc, he was obviously happy with it. Trouble flared the moment Martin smelled and tasted the wine. "André, what gives you the idea that this is pinot blanc?" he asked. "Because it isn't. There's not a trace of it." Having thoroughly familiarized himself with identifying the fine points of varietals in the Masson collection of vines and wines, Martin *knew* what was pinot blanc *"vrai"* . . . and what was not.

As for Tchelistcheff, not only had he studied enology intensively, but he knew intimately the vines in the Beaulieu vineyards. He was proud of his knowledge and didn't expect to be challenged—in effect, called either ignorant or a liar. And his temper in those days could be just as volatile as Martin Ray's at maximum. He leapt to his feet in fury. "It's from our pinot blanc vineyard!" he roared. "And the cuttings came from your very own pinot blanc vineyard here on this mountain: as you well know, the sole source of it in this country."

From then on, hot words flew back and forth. Neither would yield to the other's authority. Martin declared that he'd lay his life on the line that this wine didn't come from pinot blanc grapes. And Tchelistcheff, just as fiercely, insisted it did. Very shortly the Russian stormed off down the mountain, after exchanging final insults with the proprietor host.

The very next day, Martin's analytical nature impelled him to solve the mystery of Tchelistcheff's wine. Impressed with the Russian vintner's knowledge and integrity, he knew there had to be a mistake somewhere. So off he drove to Napa Valley to see Beaulieu's supposed pinot blanc vineyard. Just as he suspected: not a single pinot blanc vine in the entire area so designated! All vines in fact were aligoté, the secondary Burgundian vine with similarities to the pinot blanc but far more vigorous and productive, and not exactly desirable.

Now how in the devil did Beaulieu get those cuttings, said to be pinot blanc, from Paul Masson's vineyard? True, in Masson's block of pinot blanc a few aligoté vines had gotten in by some oversight in the original planting, and then had been allowed to remain there through the years. That was how Martin had learned to identify them—by the pinkish stems that Burgundians called "rouge," and by their larger size. But surely nobody would have knowingly given cuttings from them! Since Martin never had tasted a wine labeled aligoté, he had no idea what it would taste like. Otherwise he could have identified right away that wine Tchelistcheff had brought.

On returning home, Martin hastened to find old John Bussone and probe his memory. Did he remember Mr. Masson ever giving pinot blanc cuttings to his friends Monsieur and Madame de Latour of Beaulieu?

"Oh yah!" said old John—that he clearly recalled. The de Latours had come for dinner, and afterwards Mr. Masson called him and asked if he would make some pinot blanc cuttings for his guests to take back to their Napa winery. Martin pushed John further for more details. Finally John revealed this: Just as he started off toward the vineyard, Mr. Masson called him back. "John," he said, "be sure to take the cuttings just from the *big* vines." And it had been obvious to John which grape variety Masson meant. So here was the revelation that Martin had sought.

Paul Masson, that wily old Burgundian, fond though he might be of his winemaking friends the de Latours, had been unwilling to share his pinot blanc with them. Having brought over the stock from France and kept it exclusively in his vineyard, his pride would not permit him to relinquish his advantageous position as sole possessor.

Martin knew that Masson had assumed an attitude of superiority whenever he dined with the de Latours at Beaulieu. Invariably he brought his own wines. "When you make wines as good as mine," he would blithely tell them, "I will drink them. In the meantime I will drink my own!" They allowed him his quirky humor. His half-jesting boast not only bolstered his ego, but underscored his pattern of guarding against all professional competition—even from friends dear to him.

This instance of Masson's crusty idiosyncrasies spilled over into the next generation of winemakers. Two wine perfectionists, in some ways kindred spirits, severed their budding relationship. The breach was never healed. Tchelistcheff said later of the incident that he definitely was made to understand that he shouldn't darken Martin Ray's door again. And he never did, in all the ensuing years. Which is too bad. Once their brash young years were over, they might have become great friends. For basically they admired each other's single-minded dedication to the art of making fine wines.

In later years, despite his run-in with Martin Ray, Tchelistcheff—"the dean of American winemakers," as he was often called—sometimes privately acknowledged that Martin Ray served usefully as an oracle of future trends. He might not agree with his tactics. But from the sidelines he watched Martin's energetic individualism propelling him into zealotry as he fought to elevate wine industry standards, which included proposing an appellation of origin system for wine grapes. Martin fixated upon issues that other vintners dared not discuss publicly, for to do so would have made them pariahs within the trade. Inevitably he earned the reputation of a crank.

Already by the late '30s and early '40s Martin Ray uniquely served as a lightning rod, a catalyst for change—a pioneer who set off alone on the pathway toward imposing strict varietal and quality criteria upon an unreceptive, even hostile wine industry. Martin would become ever more notorious as a solitary, uncompromising purist, whereas other respected winemakers of his time—such as his Russian counterpart, André Tchelistcheff, who never owned a winery of his own—chose to fit into the camaraderie of the trade.

Even when California winegrowers tried to apply higher standards, their aspirations were compromised. For the all-important wine marketplace did not encourage them to replant their vineyards wholly to the fine, shy-bearing varietals. There was no apparent profitability in it. And would not be for many years yet.

Julian Street would soon be coming West for a visit! Or actually, to make a stay of indeterminate length, as far as the Rays could learn. Now a problem of epochal proportions loomed: how to prepare perfect gourmet fare befitting a world-renowned epicure. And not just preparations for one great dinner, which the Rays had already handled many a time. But for three meals a day, on and on, without let-up.

In a flurry, to glean outstanding menu ideas Martin and Elsie consulted Julian's published gastronomic writings. They also combed through his copious correspondence, for in letters to them he'd discussed favored delicacies along with occasional rare specialties. But once they began delving into his delightful letters, it was impossible to let go. They reread all the accounts of his daily epicurean life.

Through reviewing these letters the Rays relived the excitement of their first contact with Julian: the telegram giving his reactions to the Pinot Noir 1936. And then the long letter following it that detailed the many surprises and glories and comparisons in the newly discovered wine. "I'd love to try it on a good Burgundian," he wrote. "It would greatly astonish him to get that unmistakable, unforgettable flavor out of California. It knocked me silly."

Then too, through these letters Martin recalled that mounting suspense as he had shipped wine after wine to Julian, his heart beating fast awaiting reactions to those the oenophile had not yet tasted. The bond he felt with Julian grew even closer as he viewed anew those enthused, perceptive responses. In one letter was his almost explosive clarion over the case of chardonnay, finding it incredible to taste that same buttery-rich special flavor akin to a great Corton-Charlemagne—but actually out of California! Julian especially loved the champagnes. Martin became so engrossed in the letters that he almost forgot his original purpose in rereading them: the better to plan suitable gourmet foods for Julian's visit.

When Julian Street's arrival was imminent, a telegram came—so typical of Julian—punctiliously wishing to set the perfect number of days to visit in a friend's home. What was perfection? Perhaps seven days? Would twelve be overstaying the ideal? Martin and Elsie, highly amused, wired back: THE LONGER THE BETTER.

Nevertheless, taking on as a house-guest such a perfectionist as Julian Street was no small responsibility. For the first time in all their entertaining, Elsie's cool at first deserted her. "He's simply the utmost," she told Martin. "I keep thinking, every time I look at him ... Well, he looks just like Jesus Christ!"

Elsie got so excited preparing Julian's first breakfast that twice she threw it out the door to the dogs. Finally she calmed herself enough to settle for her third attempt. Trembling like a leaf as she set it before him. From then on, it was easier. For in spite of his fearsome reputation as a gourmet, he proved such an accommodating companion that all hours were relaxed, through day and night.

Julian Street's long stay was one of the most enjoyable interludes of all time for the Rays. As for Julian, he simply basked deliciously in the ambience of their congenial household, intriguing winery activities, fascinating visitors, and the inspirational mountaintop setting.

23

California Wines to the Fore

SHORTLY AFTER JULIAN STREET returned home from his visit to the Rays, he sent a wire asking Martin to ship two cases of the 1936 Pinot Noir to a New York friend of his. This man of high social rank was soon giving a dinner to honor a distinguished French guest, and Julian was sure the wine would greatly impress him. Frequently he made requests like this for wines to be shipped here or there. So Martin rushed off the shipment by his usual fastidious carrier, then eagerly awaited Julian's response.

The aftermath to this particular shipment would reveal some dramatically changing conditions in the international wine world.

Because of another engagement Julian himself was unable to attend the dinner. So he too was especially anxious to get his friend's reaction along with that of his illustrious French visitor. The first news Martin received was a dismayed wire from Julian. Could Martin positively identify the wine sent as exactly the one he himself had so enjoyed—from the same year, same cask? Martin wired back that it was identical. What could have happened?

Then an anguished letter came from Julian. His friend had suffered the worst humiliation possible. After the wine was served, everyone's eyes naturally turned toward the Frenchman for his reaction. And he, after bringing the wine dubiously to his nose, quietly set it back on the table. Not once did he touch it again. Of course everyone else followed suit, treating the wine with open aversion.

At length the host inquired delicately if his guest found something wrong with the wine. With an air of embarrassed restraint, he replied that, to speak honestly, he could bring the wine only to his nose; could not permit it to cross his palate. The host was mortified. He apologized for the unfortunate error in serving it and substituted a renowned French burgundy in its stead. And called Julian the next day for an explanation.

Martin studied Julian's letter for some time. He was sure nothing was wrong with his fine Pinot Noir 1936. But who was this French guest? He wired Julian for information. Julian knew only that he was a famous French wine authority. He promised to inquire further. Shortly thereafter he reported that man's name was Etienne Jouveau; he was vice president of a foremost wine firm.

Martin knew that a number of French wine representatives had been appearing of late. Usually they arrived first in New York and were entertained there by distributors and well-to-do customers. Then they came out to California and made the rounds of the prominent vineyards, presumably to size up any possible competition from America. (However, Martin speculated, since the French were nervous about Hitler's accelerating land grabs, perhaps they were also quietly investigating possible business relocations.)

So a few days later, Martin was not at all surprised to get a phone call from San Francisco—from none other than this Frenchman. Jouveau, now on the customary winery circuit tour, asked to visit the Paul Masson premises.

"What!" Elsie exclaimed. "He has the nerve?"

"I'm sure he never even noticed *which* California wine he had snubbed." Martin said. "To him they'd all be the same—beneath his contempt. But if he can come here after what he's done, I'd like to get a look at him." His voice held a hard, steely challenge.

"But Papa, we can't really entertain him ..."

"Sure we can!" An enigmatic smile crept onto Martin's face. "Don't worry. It may even be good fun."

With bated breath, Elsie arranged a delightful luncheon for Monsieur Jouveau—which Martin naturally planned around the Pinot Noir 1936. When their French guest arrived, Martin showed him first through the cellars, where they tasted various wines. The visiting "wine authority" expressed great interest in and even liking for them, particularly the pinot noirs. The grapevines of course had originated in his native Burgundy, and he knew they were difficult to grow successfully elsewhere.

Watching the Frenchman closely, Martin became convinced that at that New York dinner he had not noticed the name of the California wine he was insulting. All the while, with each successive vintage tasted, Jouveau's enthusiasm mounted. Finally, as he raved over the Pinot Noir 1936, Martin asked him: "If you were tasting blind in your cellar in Beaune, would you be able to distinguish this wine from one of your own vintage?"

"To be perfectly honest," Jouveau replied, "no. I could not tell. Except that this 1936 would stand out as a very great year."

At the luncheon later, their guest proved a most attractive companion—handsome, witty, most appreciative. And a great drinker. Elsie and Martin were astounded to see him drink, in addition to other wines served, more than a bottle of the pinot himself, commenting ecstatically on its merits. He showed no effects of having partaken excessively, only a relaxed pleasure.

When the luncheon drew to a happy close and it was time for the visitor to depart, Martin accompanied him only to the door. "Monsieur Jouveau," he said, "you have praised at length our wines, and at the table showed most of all your true love of the Pinot Noir 1936 by drinking it with great relish. Now I want to tell you something: This wine is identical to the wine you were served in New York—the one you could bring only to your nose and would not permit to cross your palate! . . . Good day, sir."

There was a split-second of incredulity on the Frenchman's face. His jaunty demeanor collapsed into shock and horror as Martin calmly closed the door between them.

Martin telegraphed Julian the whole drama, which both appalled and delighted him. Soon intimate wine circles around the country were buzzing with the hilarious story of how a California vintner disposed of a French wine snob. For American connoisseurs were beginning to take new interest and pride in their nation's potential for winemaking . . . thanks in good part to those Martin Ray varietal wines from the Paul Masson winery.

In commercial wine channels, salesmen were dumbfounded that a Frenchman would try to pull such outdated tactics against California wines nowadays, when the scene was changing so fast to favor America. Jouveau's firm, they knew, was in a financial bind, like so many others. War threatened France from Hitler's direction, exports had fallen off sharply, and he'd journeyed to the U.S. to repair the marketing damage. But after this incident he found himself with even fewer customers.

Times were changing. One simply couldn't get away with insulting all California wines any longer.

Not only French vintners and wine merchants were noticing that California wines were encroaching on their American sales. The government of France took alarm at this situation too. So it decided to send some knowledgeable person overseas to learn what actual threat the wines of California might pose, now and in the future.

Martin Ray wasn't aware of this when he received a cordial note from the renowned Marquis de Lur Saluces, proprietor of the magnificent Château d'Yquem. This man whose wines and reputation he greatly admired was asking to visit during his coming trip to California.

After pondering the daunting prospect of suitably receiving the Marquis, Martin decided to simplify the visitation as much as possible. He could converse with him better on a wide range of wine topics without the distraction of other guests. "We'll have a plain yet elegant dinner, just the three of us," Martin told Elsie. "Let other wineries provide all the lavish entertaining! And I think you should do the cooking yourself—with maybe chicken roasted on the rotissoire. You see, if he's the great winegrower I know him to be, he will like simplicity—with perfection."

And so it was. The Marquis came, was most delightful. As to the dinner, he enjoyed the chicken so much he had three servings of it, said he never had tasted the like of it in France. (Perhaps he was playing the appreciative guest, since they have some mighty fine *poulet* in France!) And he seemed to relish the entire unostentatious meal, accompanied by some of his and Martin's finest wines as well as other French ones. For the first time since arriving in America, he said, he was able to relax completely. Big dinners had greeted him everywhere, with foods imitating French cuisine. Whereas he keenly had wished to taste American cooking—which he was now doing.

After dinner, asked if he would care to see the cellars, the Marquis endeared himself to the Rays for all time. In their years on the mountain, entertaining many hundreds of people, Lur Saluces alone made this request, and in his gentle way: "If you don't mind, I would like to walk in your vineyards." What tremendous joy in those words!

It was late afternoon of an early June day as they approached the vineyards. The setting sun was flashing its rays straight across the mountaintop in a burst of glory, catching each vine in luminous light. The Marquis stopped and drank in the enthralling sight. "A most remarkable light effect," he said, his face radiant with pleasure. Then a familiar scent wafted into his nostrils, and nostalgically he lifted his head, inhaling deeply. "Ah, the vines in blossom! I love that fragrance above all things."

"Tell me, how many days do you count here from blossom to vintage?" he then asked, turning toward his American host. A hundred days, Martin told him. "Ah, it is the same with us," he said with satisfaction. "One hundred days."

The Marquis took keen interest in the Rays' "basket method" of pruning. Martin explained how all canes but two or three (depending on a vine's vigor) were clipped off above two buds to make spurs, potentially next year's canes. The remaining canes were then bent into loops and fastened with metal straps to the stake, creating a basketlike area for enclosing grape clusters, with the framework of branches hiding them from marauding birds. Martin said he had slightly revised Paul Masson's pruning method to foster greater production.

The Marquis also asked about cultivation techniques, scrutinized and compared the leaf color and vigor of the various varieties. The mountain soil particularly intrigued him. Time and time again he reached down and picked up a handful, letting it run through his fingers, observing it closely, even smelling and actually seeming to *taste* it! And he was fascinated with its rough Franciscan shale content. "You know," he commented, "we French winegrowers believe that soil is supreme in determining the great wines."

Martin and Elsie could not imagine anything in the wide world that could please them more than the Marquis' visit. Evidently Lur Saluces greatly enjoyed it too, for he wrote them most appreciatively, and continued correspondence with them over all the years to come. (At his Château d'Yquem he also entertained my son Peter Martin Ray several times.)

Not long after his return to France, the Marquis de Lur Saluces sent Martin Ray a copy of the report he had made to the French government, confiding to Martin only then the real purpose of his recent California visit. He thought it proper for Martin to know what he had concluded from his extensive inquiry: he found no competition for fine French wines. He did note, however, that he had discovered *one* American vintner who was creating superb varietal wines that met the highest French standards ... but on such a small scale that he posed no threat to France.

Not long afterwards, a compatriot of the Marquis came for a visit. Dr. Dutrait (I may not have recalled his name precisely) was a brilliant, elderly biochemist given the great responsibility of making Dubonnet in this country for the American market, since the ever-widening war in Europe threatened to cut off exports of the elegant *apéritif.*

Replicating this famous fortified sweet wine, long produced in France from a precise, secret formula of wines blended with certain herbs and flavorings, had been a real challenge to Dr. Dutrait. Could he match Dubonnet's unique character when using American wines as the primary base? By the time he visited the Rays' mountain, he could take pride in having met this emergency. His American-made Dubonnet was already a great success. He could now relax a bit and travel around with his charming wife.

Martin wanted to find something special to serve the distinguished French visitor, something appropriate for him. Searching through his private cellar, he came across a thirty-year-old bottle of Dubonnet—surely a rarity by now even in France. Dr. Dutrait with his knowledge of this wine would be, above all, the one to appreciate it. So Martin brought it forth, with the label masked with a cloth, and as he poured the wine he told his guest that he had a special treat for him.

The wine's color was a clear tawny flame. "Now what can this be!" Dr. Dutrait exclaimed. He raised his glass to his nose, obviously puzzled. "What a lovely bouquet ... I have never encountered anything quite like it."

Martin assured him, however, that he had. "You'll catch up with it," he laughed as Dr. Dutrait continued lifting it to his nose. At last he tasted it. Then he set the glass before him on the table as he considered, professionally eyeing it, trying his best to place it. After tasting it several times, he was positive. "This is something entirely new to me. It is delicious. What is it?"

Then Martin teased him. "Why, my dear doctor, you're a fine one not to recognize it. It's a venerable, thirty-year-old Dubonnet!"

The elderly Frenchman stiffened, quickly snatched up his glass, smelled and tasted the wine again. "This is *not* Dubonnet," he said decisively. "There is some mistake. Look at the color. And Dubonnet neither smells nor tastes like this. Surely you are joking!"

No indeed, said Martin. "But I *make* Dubonnet, you understand," his visitor insisted. "I know it thoroughly. So this is absurd. Let me examine the bottle and cork." Although bottle and cork appeared authentic in every way, Dr. Dutrait proclaimed that obviously some hoax had been perpetrated.

Martin let the matter rest for the time being. As they resumed their pleasant conversation, the French guest kept picking up the glass, raising it to his nose, and with focused attention tasting the wine again and again. "It *is* most delightful," he admitted while accepting a second glassful. "As a matter of fact, it is quite extraordinary. Quite possibly it is even finer than Dubonnet. But it is not Dubonnet. That I know."

As he continued to sip it, sometimes closing his eyes to concentrate the better, sensory impressions came flooding back to him out of some distant, near-forgotten past. "I remember having a wine distantly like this when I was young," he reminisced. "Something with the same unique bouquet and flavor ..."

With the third glass Dr. Dutrait suddenly recalled the memory complete—like the face of a dear friend from childhood not seen in almost a lifetime. "Monsieur Ray, I am sorry. This *is* Dubonnet," he then said, and hung his head in chagrin. "I have forgotten. I've been making Dubonnet for so long without having the old-time wines on which to draw and compare. It doesn't seem possible. To think that I, who *make* Dubonnet, could forget entirely what the magnificent original Dubonnet years were like!"

Dear Dr. Dutrait—so utterly ingenuous and apologetic about his slowly dawning revelation! He left with the Rays an unforgettable example of what can happen to one's tasting ability without constant comparisons. "Remember Dubonnet!" became thereafter a merry motto for Martin and Elsie in many a crisis. And at times it served as a rousing battlecry too, whenever traditional winemaking values came up for a challenge.

Martin Ray's incessant round of entertaining, combined with hands-on cellar and vineyard work, left him no time at all to spare for other activities. Nevertheless, he was growing so concerned over the wine industry's sham varietals that he decided to do something really effective about the deplorable situation. To other wineries, varietal names just seemed "classier" than the old, interchangeable generic ones like burgundy and claret, chablis and sauterne. And they could sell at better prices, too—hopefully like the Paul Masson wines Martin Ray was making.

Martin began dedicating late-night hours to launching a campaign to declare it illegal to falsely label blends under varietal names. He wrote personal letters about his efforts to many friends of fine wine throughout the country and to the press. And he wrote especially to California's better vintners, urging them for their own sake to take a stand with him against fraudulent varietals—thus ultimately to raise California's desperately needed prestige on the world wine market, so crucial to them. "Look at the French," he'd write. "Because their fine wines are truly elegant, their prestige permits France to market not only those finest wines at fabulous prices in this country, but a vast volume of shippers' mediocre blended wines at prices far higher than for *our* volume wines. So *prestige* is the key. California never can compete with French wines until we protect truly fine varietals as they do."

In the long run, Martin argued, it would make good economic sense for the American wine industry to impose strict controls on itself—as France had done for more than a century, culminating in the government's *Appellation contrôllée*, which dealt intricately with the entire spectrum of wine production, from growing and vintaging to bottling and marketing.

Martin Ray had started his fight for true varietals as far back as 1936, when invited to become a member of the newly created Wine Institute. Its primary work of promoting California wines would be mainly supported by a portion of fees paid by all wineries to the state. Martin agreed to join the Institute if it merely went on record as sponsoring the making of true varietals. He did not expect it to launch any drive against false varietal claims—as yet, anyway. Since his request was turned down, Martin never joined.

Martin early recognized that the Institute would be largely supported and governed by the industry's big-scale producers. These firms' profits depended on selling vast amounts of cheap wine, and by the late 1930s they were increasingly using varietal names. The wine-promoting organization would not want to offend these producers by demanding truth in labeling and other essential reforms he might propose, then and thereafter.

Through the years, the Wine Institute carried on a subterranean campaign against Martin Ray within the wine trade and through their many media contacts and outlets. Their strategy involved ignoring him in their own articles, while exerting pressure to prevent any mention of him in the publications in which they and high-budget clients advertised.

For years, not a single vintner would stand publicly with Martin Ray on the varietal issue. Actually, none could afford to, since they grew few of the grape varieties claimed, or else had insufficient quantity to make a 100 percent pure varietal wine. Nor was there any incentive or necessity to plant such low-yielders. For not yet did enough expert palates exist for the public to demand that a wine bottle contain primarily the varietal named on the label. And who was to prove it didn't? So why change?

For a long while, Martin's lonely, one-man crusade for quality controls certainly did seem a fruitless effort. But he always said that at some point a person must take a stand against an injustice or untruth that gravely offended—and fight, no matter how hopeless the prospect. Otherwise, how could you live with your conscience or retain your integrity?

Martin Ray had the satisfaction at least of knowing that he was the first winegrower to prove conclusively that pure varietal wines from California could stand as equals beside their French counterparts sharing the same noble ancestry.

24

End of an Era

Paul Masson puzzled over Martin Ray's purist approach to winemaking and merchandising. What on earth was his successor doing—vintaging each grape variety separately? Like all other growers, he himself had made and marketed all his wines as blends. It was customary practice. And now Martin had come on the scene, altering the entire procedure and sales tactics. Somewhat grudgingly, though, Paul acknowledged that Martin seemed at last to be making a profit by doing it this way. And certainly he was getting plenty of new attention for the name—Paul Masson Champagne Company.

In the first years Paul Masson often came up to the winery and also joined Martin when he entertained guests at the chateau, but less as time went on.

When he was up there, it was clear he had not relinquished his role as king of the mountain. He gave orders—totally oblivious to the fact that he'd sold to Martin Ray, who reigned here now. This didn't amaze Martin. He would have been amazed had Paul surrendered his dominating personality upon retirement. It simply would have demeaned him, Martin felt. And so, both awestruck and touched, he'd watch Masson hold forth with guests, at the dinner table or out on the terrace. "Good God, look at Paul carry on!" he'd say to himself. From nobody else would Martin have tolerated being upstaged like this.

Old and infirm though he was, there was still something marvelously rugged about Paul Masson. His appearance reminded Martin of an old grapevine in wintertime—stout-trunked, gnarled, weathered, bare of leaves . . . but staunch and deep-rooted as it withstood icy blasts. And Paul's character remained as sound and majestic as a fine old wine. From the vintage of his living he'd pressed a juice that had long since passed its prime, but still it retained traces of its potency.

As time went by he came up to La Cresta far less often to take part in social events. Though he still enjoyed the foods and wines served to him, the strain of meeting and talking with people exhausted him. It was more than he could handle, he told Martin. And sometimes when he did attend some dinner up at his former chateau, the outcome proved disturbing to everyone. On one occasion, for instance, he verbally scorched a famed guest who had the effrontery to light a cigarette during dinner.

Another sorry instance when Paul's crusty behavior got out of hand was when *Life* magazine was doing a big feature story on America's costliest wines, and its editors asked to take pictures at the renowned vineyard estate. Old Paul Masson condescended to be there that day. He was seated regally on the sunny terrace of his former domain, his ever-present stick in hand like a scepter, when the magazine's celebrated photographer rushed up to greet him. "What a great honor to meet you, Mr. Masson!" he exclaimed, eagerly grasping the vintner's big hand.

Instantly Paul yelled out in pain, and quick as a flash struck the man over the head with his stick. "You goddamn drummer!" he cried. "How dare you crush my hand like that . . . can't you *see* I've got arthritis? Just go down the mountain and never return!"

This was scarcely the first time Masson had banished someone from "his" mountain. Hastily Martin escorted the photographer elsewhere, making amends to salvage the invaluable publicity story. And then he hurried back to smooth matters with Paul Masson—still massaging the painful joints of his right hand.

After such experiences Paul Masson was inclined to withdraw all the more from his former domain.

As he became more debilitated with age and infirmities, he considered returning to France to live among his relatives there. But actually he couldn't, what with the looming threat of a war with Germany. He also could not be sure where his deepest loyalties lay: in his beloved birthplace, or here where he had formed close human ties and created a magnificent winegrowing estate. When Martin told him of the retribution he'd exacted on the French wine shipper who'd insulted his wine, Paul, like Julian Street, was both appalled and delighted. Yet deeply mortified, too, because the story damaged French prestige.

Nor did Masson appreciate how French wines—which had long set the highest international standards—were now being belittled by wine merchants and promoters in America, who increasingly had fewer imports to sell to the nation's enophiles. "That growing mess in Europe those goddamn Nazis are making strengthens the California winegrowers' hands," he observed. "But the *wrong* hands—the worst possible. And just when our wines were beginning to improve. Now comes the real catastrophe, MAR-tan. You'll see what will happen when all imports are cut off completely!" Masson based his prediction on his experience of World War I as a vintner.

Paul became openly despondent after the morning of April 9, 1940, when news came that the German war machine had struck at dawn, with savage ferocity, against neutral Denmark and Norway. All day long he sat by his radio—an instrument he'd never permitted in his San Jose home until recently—and listened to the march of disaster. By mid-afternoon Denmark was occupied. "This means they will attack France in a month or so," he predicted, anguishing over his family in Burgundy.

He was right. The Nazi troops invaded France on May 10, and by June 14 had occupied Paris. Paul paced back and forth, utterly beside himself, picturing the horrors suffered by the people of France. The Germans pushed southward, down through his beloved Burgundy, and when the French government capitulated, Masson's village close to Beaune was included in Occupied France.

Paul's blood pressure soared with all the stress. He was tormented with worry over what was happening to relatives and friends. Suddenly one day he clutched his chest in acute agony. He was rushed to the hospital by the live-in nurse. Already he'd survived several serious heart attacks, but this one was more severe.

"All that terrible news should somehow have been kept from him," Martin told Elsie as they hastened to the hospital. There they saw Paul lying still, lifeless. The doctor gave them little encouragement. Mr. Masson might not live through the night, he said.

Martin and Elsie hovered at Paul's bedside for a long time. It seemed inconceivable to Martin that this inert figure, whose spirit might already be departing, was all that remained of that vigorous, all-powerful character he remembered so vividly from his childhood. A giant of a man, with a thundering stride, rushing about his winery operations with such decisiveness, giving sharp orders, taking part in strenuous field work . . .

How could time have so reduced Masson to the same pitiful state that is the lot of ordinary mortals who hang on to the very end of the lifeline? Some special fate should have been reserved for a man like Paul. Martin just couldn't accept this.

Finally, before going home, each of them laid a hand gently on Paul's forehead, then gave a last farewell pat to his own gnarled hand that lay so still on the white coverlet. Always they'd known Paul eventually would die—but that was some far-off time in the future. Now, suddenly, the time was here. And they couldn't imagine life without him, for even the shadow of his former self was still dynamic.

Martin and Elsie drove back to their mountain, Paul's mountain, in silence, too sorrowful to speak.

In the morning the ringing telephone awakened them. They were afraid to answer, but knew they'd have to hear the message.

"MAR-tan?" an animated voice began—elderly, male, French accented. Why, it sounded like Paul himself! Yet *couldn't* be Paul. But . . . "Will you please bring me some champagne?"

Martin was struck dumb with bewilderment. He doubted his own ears. "But Paul—" he stammered. "I thought . . . you were so ill last night. . . . How *are* you, Paul?" His clumsy words sounded absurd, fantastic. If this was Paul he was speaking to, it must be his disembodied spirit. Elsie's amazed expression mirrored his own.

"Oh yes," Paul said, "I *was* sick. Very sick. But that was last night. Now I'm fine. But MAR-tan, this hospital—" There was a pause. "It's dreadful. I want to go home. I simply can't bear it here. And then the nurses . . . you know, MAR-tan, they're either too old or too young!" Martin laughed at that last comment, reassured. Incredibly, it really *was* Paul Masson! He promised to bring him champagne and thought he heard a sigh of relief. "But they say I can't have champagne before lunch," he exploded. "Can you imagine that? Such dismal people here!"

Martin did take the iced champagne to Paul, with two glasses, and sat by his bedside to share it with him—before his lunch. Nurses came and went, darting shocked glances. Paul looked reassuringly himself again. And the champagne braced his spirits considerably, to the point where he demanded to go home that very afternoon. Martin later learned that he even managed to get his way.

So again Paul Masson had triumphed over the Grim Reaper. Now, though, that specter was ever dogging Paul's heels. Paul declined all dinners at his old chateau. His appetite was as good as ever, he told Martin, but contact with most people had become wholly unbearable. His doctor now forbade him to listen to the French war news. He distracted himself by reading his favorite French classics. He rarely even came out to his country place anymore.

Then came the morning Martin got a phone call from a nurse at Paul's home. Paul had suffered another heart attack the day before. He seemed to have recovered, but over the phone his doctor had ordered him into the hospital—and was arranging for an ambulance to transport him there. But Mr. Masson refused. He would not go! She'd just talked again with the doctor, who said he *must* go, to be on the safe side.

And that's why she was calling. She knew Mr. Ray had some influence. So would he speak with Mr. Masson right now and persuade him to go peaceably? For if her patient resisted the attendants, he'd risk another attack—maybe a worse one. A phone was by his bedside . . .

When Paul heard Martin's voice, he grabbed the conversation at once. "MAR-tan, can you come over? I really *need* you—to keep them from pushing me around. And you understand. You know how I hate those confounded hospitals!"

Martin cut in, promised to rush right over. "But Paul, stay very quiet. Don't talk. Lie right there and relax, see?"

"Maybe—maybe some champagne to fix me up?" Paul asked. His voice held an unfamiliar quaver.

"Righto!" said Martin.

"He really should do what the doctor says," Elsie said. "A hospital can handle any emergency that might develop."

Maybe so, Martin admitted. "But if Paul Masson wants nothing to do with a hospital, nobody is going to get him there without a terrific struggle. So the best hope is to keep him calm and quiet for now. When we get there, we'll try to talk him into it. The champagne should help."

"Well, he must be already on the mend if he's asking for champagne," she commented as they rushed into the cellar.

Martin agreed. "Yes, I think this is a happy mission, as before." He reached for a very special bottle he knew Paul would appreciate, "Ah, my splendid wines ... I come for one of you, as eventually I will come for *all* of you," he said playfully, as he often did when selecting a bottle here. Quickly they set the champagne in ice, and were off.

"What a man he is, Paul Masson!" Elsie exclaimed as they got into the car. "Can't you just picture him lying there, with his doctor on the phone trying to talk him into the waiting ambulance ... and all he's thinking about is how soon we'll get there with the champagne!"

"Yes, and thinks about what he'll have to eat *after* the champagne!" Martin chuckled. The very thought cheered them, for they felt apprehensive despite their mutual reassurance.

As they drove up to the house, no ambulance was parked outside. Had the doctor managed to persuade Paul to go after all, or had the stubborn Frenchman won out and remained at home?

Neither. Their spirits plummeted when the nurse somberly greeted them at the door. Paul had suffered a massive heart attack. The ambulance had taken his body away.

Paul Masson was dead. Martin and Elsie were too shocked to say a word. It happened shortly after Mr. Masson had talked with Mr. Ray over the phone, the nurse said. The doctor came, and after the examination insisted on crisis care in the hospital at once. But when he called in the two ambulance attendants with their stretcher, Paul got so furious he struck out at them. That must have brought on the attack, for he cried out with pain and fell back, unconscious. "It was a mistake to force him, as I feared," she commented.

On seeing the Rays' great distress, the nurse made an effort to relate something cheerful. Her gaze fell on the bucket of iced champagne that Martin was still holding. "After talking with you, Mr. Masson was so happy—looking forward to the champagne," she recalled with a painful little smile. Then, with a puzzled expression, she added: "Just before the doctor came, he was asking to have some pears baked for his lunch. Pears from a special tree he'd brought from France. 'The *little* pears,' he kept repeating. It seemed terribly important to him."

"It *was* important," Martin said solemnly as tears began to trickle down his cheeks.

Paul Masson departed on October 23, 1940.

The memorial service was held in the intimate setting of Paul Masson's country house across from the mountain winery entrance. The formal rites were already under way when Adele Masson entered, causing unnecessary disturbance over seating herself. However, once seated, she bowed her head reverentially as all those around her were doing. Martin and Elsie then breathed easier, hopeful that she'd now show more respect than her manner of entrance had indicated. Adele's relationship with her father had always been stormy and unpredictable.

But as the ceremony was coming to an end, Adele suddenly leaped to her feet and burst forth in a torrent of abuse against her father. She charged him with ruthless selfishness, debauchery, neglect of home and family—and the total ruination of her life. Then abruptly she turned and left, almost running out, as if expecting reprisal from the assembled mourners.

Everyone was stunned. Gentle music soothed the shattered mood. Martin and Elsie remained with heads bowed and eyes closed, trying to push out the memory of what had occurred . . . wanting only to remember Paul Masson's dynamic presence and how, incomprehensibly, he could actually be gone.

Adele's theatrics weren't yet finished. The Rays heard later that on the day Paul's will was read, she created another hysterical scene after learning that her father had left most of his money for her in a trust. Obviously he'd hoped it would prevent her from spending it all. She was to receive a set amount, $500 per month. Then, as a further insult—so far as she was concerned—he had left instructions that forbade her from inheriting his country house, since it was not built for permanence. His statement ordered it placed on auction.

Explicitly denying her this house was the final affront. Adele determined to get that house in spite of him—even though she admittedly loathed it. She was as strong-willed and hot-tempered as her father, though without his attributes, including a counterbalancing shrewd practicality. So when the house came up for auction, she used every cent she had to make the highest bid—and won it. Then came the aftershock. What could she *do* with that odious house? She never wanted to see it again!

So "Adele's house," as it was now known, quickly became a derelict. She never went there, and let the gardens die and the house go to ruin. Whenever Martin and Elsie drove to or from their mountain, they saw the place there beyond the road—abandoned, haunted.

Adele revealed the same bitter and perverse fury over her Aunt Marie's will, knowing that her father had a hand in composing it. All the money left to her was in a trust. Anyone contesting the will would be cut off with one dollar, with the allotted portion to go instead to Nelty Lefranc. Working herself up into another rage, Adele of course determined to break the will. She hired a costly San Francisco lawyer—mortgaging her house at Pebble Beach to pay him. She lost the suit, so the inheritance went to her cousin.

From then on, Adele became increasingly peculiar, notorious for eccentric and antisocial behavior. People often told Martin that she seemed deranged. He consoled himself that at least Paul was now spared Adele's tirades and painful reports of her mad capers.

It took months for Martin to adjust to the fact that his lifelong mentor Paul Masson was really gone forever. But ever since his own illness, he had learned to value and tend to the day-to-day life around him. The many issues to focus on distracted him from prolonged grieving.

As French wines were becoming cut off by the accelerating European conflict, California wines enjoyed a great flurry of activity, keeping all the wine promoters busy and happy. Then, at the end of 1941, as America entered a world war taking place across the two wide oceans, the wine market inexplicably went wild. Grain-derived alcoholic spirits like whiskey and gin became unobtainable. No need for promoters now! Customers around the nation clamored to buy any and all wines, at whatever prices.

Thus the splendid period that promised truly better overall quality in California wines was eclipsed almost before it began—dealt the disastrous blow to wine quality that Paul Masson had predicted of another world war. Alas, the wine-elevating season had only been a false spring. The heady mood would not return again in full force for another three decades.

The boom part of the perennial supply-and-demand cycle was in full swing, on a tremendous scale, with ever-mounting pressure to provide wines in vast quantities—any kind at all. The prevailing attitude: when wines could be sold quite profitably whether good or bad, why bother to improve them?

A limited number of premium growers in California had been turning out about 2,000 cases of still wines annually, as had Martin Ray at Masson (in addition to 3,000 cases of champagne). He persisted in holding to those figures, which represented the maximum amount of wine from quality grapes grown in his own vineyards.

Martin heard, to his horror, that his champagne-producing friend Tony Korbel suddenly upped his production astronomically, then raised it further. So likewise did most others. "But what will happen to you when the war's over and imported champagnes flood our market?" Martin asked Tony. "Can you survive then?" Tony shrugged and said he saw no reason to worry about the unknown when the present was so gratifyingly profitable.

(It worked out as Martin had anticipated for some who thus greatly expanded their operations—sacrificing quality now for the lure of quantity, and later unable to compete with imports. Korbel was among those who sold out in the postwar era.)

When pressured by suppliers to increase his production, Martin would ask "Why?" And then tell them: "I wanted the finest life in the world and found it—in winegrowing on this mountain. More production would ruin the peace I've found." So he held his course exactly as before.

If pushed into further argument over the matter, he would point out that throughout history men have turned to winegrowing for the same reason. That is, to small-scale, quality winemaking, often when they'd found no lasting satisfaction in worldly success and pleasure. "There's also the challenge of trying to make a truly great wine. It lights a fire within you that time can't put out. Time merely fans the flame, intensifies your determination. And remember, a winemaker has relatively few chances for achieving that noblest wine. Vintage comes only once a year, and even if he starts young and continues well into old age, he might have at the most only forty to fifty shots at greatness—but usually far less than that."

What other profession, after all, could offer this daunting challenge? Or give the satisfaction of meeting such a challenge over the years? No, Martin was taking no chances of ruining his way of life by increasing production just to meet the demands of the time and thereby secure profits.

But here we're getting ahead of the story. For shortly before the United States entered the war, Martin and Elsie Ray were thrust into a prolonged battle that would affect them far more personally, since it involved the continuance or death of this dream of the ideal winegrowing life.

PART IV

THE OTHER SIDE
OF THE MOUNTAIN

1941-1951

25

Some Dream of Wine

THROUGH THE YEARS, WHENEVER Martin Ray pondered the many people who had been strongly attracted to his way of life on the mountain, he'd invariably think of "The Man Who Came to Dinner."

Alexander Woollcott, that irascible Renaissance man of the '30s, was currently appearing in San Francisco in the hit Broadway play of that name, which George S. Kaufmann and Moss Hart had actually based on Woollcott's character. Offstage, his theatrical performances continued on ... one day to put him on a collision course with Martin Ray.

Elsie and Martin were giving a dinner honoring a famed European champagne producer from Épernay. Various prominent San Franciscans and New Yorkers were on the guest list. Harold Price, head of the Bay Area's prestigious Wine and Food Society, arranged for Woollcott to be invited too, since he was an epicure and had expressed a keen desire to attend.

Following Masson's custom, Martin served champagne at high noon out in the sun. Dinner was set at one. All strolled about enjoying the panoramic view while drinking their champagne—all but Woollcott, that is (and Price, who was to bring him).

Martin already had heard the Bay Area gossip: that Woollcott came late to every dinner he'd been invited to. And that when he finally arrived, he insulted everyone. Supposedly he'd picked up that quirk from membership in the Algonquin Hotel's famed "Roundtable" group of wits. (Another denizen, the *New Yorker's* Harold Ross, had characterized Woollcott as a "goddamn butterfly in heat.") The writer-actor, an aesthete and self-styled genius, came to regard savage wisecracking as the essence of sophistication. Having taken it up, he established his own ferocious reputation. But it was rumored that the celebrity's nasty communication style, perfected in Manhattan, wasn't going over so well in the cultural outback of San Francisco.

Dinner was due to be served, and Martin proceeded as scheduled. He guided the group toward the long, white linen-covered dining table, which faced the picture windows overlooking the vast valley. The guests leisurely ate their salads and enjoyed the chardonnay that Martin had opened. The cook, Louisa, came in frequently to open quietly the door of the French peasant rotissoire sitting on the hearth and baste the chickens revolving on the mechanized spit. A tantalizing aroma came forth when she did this.

When the chickens reached their golden state of perfection, Louisa removed them to an outsize platter that was placed on the table. And Woollcott still had not arrived.

A wine cradle was now set before Martin holding a Louis Latour Chambertin 1921. After serving it, he proposed a toast to their distinguished French visitor, to his champagne, and to all fine French wines. Everyone lingered over the Chambertin's incredible bouquet. "Magnificent!" they declared it, one and all.

Suddenly, while all were savoring their main course, the dogs set up a furious barking. So Woollcott finally was coming! Presently a car was heard pulling up in the parking area. All eyes looked anxiously at Martin. What would he do? Everyone knew Woollcott's predilection for staging a scene. And he would be greatly affronted that the dinner had not been held up for him. Martin appeared unconcerned, conversing with the guests at the table.

Now came the unmistakable sound of car doors being slammed. Woollcott, looking squat and rumpled in a tweed suit, was approaching with Price. Obviously he expected Martin Ray to rush out and greet him. But Martin continued conversation as if nothing was about to interrupt. Only when a hand touched the door did he arise. He strode over, opened the door, and gave the men a hearty welcome. He really had given them up, he said.

Woollcott, when introduced, dispatched Martin's handshake abruptly, clearly furious at having his arrival utterly ignored. But when he made his grand entrance and saw everyone actually at the table, and eating, he was speechless with rage.

Before he could whip out a fearful enough insult, however, Martin beat him to the punch. "Now don't apologize," he said. "You've only missed a few wines and several courses. . . . Latecomers can't be choosers, you know! However—" he added brightly— "good wines have a way of compensating." He smiled on the new arrivals benignly as he escorted them to the table and introduced them. There was no response from the stony-faced Woollcott. Martin seated the actor to the right of Elsie. Without comment, Martin served them the course then in progress.

With skin flushed and eyes bulging, Woollcott looked apoplectic—beyond fury. He sat bolt upright, as if poised ready to spring forth either into some outrageous act or to rush from the room. He touched neither food nor wine.

Martin figured that if conversation just continued to flow, with nobody paying the slightest attention to Woollcott, quite as if he didn't exist, this complete disregard might possibly subdue him. The others picked up the tactic. They exclaimed over the remarkable juiciness and superb flavor of the rotissoire-roasted chicken, unlike anything ever tasted before. Martin then told how Paul Masson, on his last trip to France, had tried to buy a peasant rotisserie like this for a friend.

"Think of it!" Martin said. "Paul told me that only a few years earlier, every household still centered about its rotissoire on the hearth. But he looked in vain all over Paris and the provinces. Couldn't find one anywhere!"

The French champagne producer said he'd never seen one like this himself. "Could it perhaps be a Burgundian specialty?"

Out of the corner of his eye Martin glanced at Woollcott and noted that the extreme agitation on his face had somewhat abated, icing over into a frozen mask. Martin now told his guests about Paul's singular veneration for the art of roasting. "He said it's an old French adage that cooking might be learned, but roasting— never. One has to be *born* knowing how to roast."

Then he described how Paul as a boy never had seen an oven, because all roasting was done entirely before large open fireplaces. "Paul always thought it was the only way to roast."

Martin noticed that Woollcott's rigid expression was relaxing a mite. He actually seemed to be listening to him! So he decided to go on talking to see if he could lure Woollcott's attention further, melt the ice a bit more.

"If this chicken seems unusual," he continued, "it's probably because few people today know what chicken actually tastes like. It shouldn't be cooked till it loses all character—smothered with herbs, wine, God knows what all. It should be still plump and fresh when done, springy to the touch, a delicate golden brown, lush with its own juices—and its flavor brought out only by pure butter, salt, and freshly ground pepper. Nothing else. Then only is it a dish worthy to be served with Louis Latour's Chambertin 1921."

At this, Martin to his amazement saw he'd captured his disgruntled guest's attention despite himself. Obviously food exercised an interest Woollcott couldn't resist. But he was not admitting it, certainly not joining into the conversation. In a loud supposed whisper to his friend Price he pronounced, "They're all bores here but the host!" Then, assured that all had heard his message of supreme contempt, he felt better; even started to converse in whispers with Price. And began, tentatively, to drink and eat.

Gradually, as Woollcott enjoyed his dinner, the gourmet in him won out. Finally he entered into the talk around the table. With vast relief, everyone relaxed. By now he was even talking with Elsie at his left, who'd been previously ignored. Setting his glass down, he said to her, "You know, wine is a miraculous thing. Here I was, just a mass of jangling nerves. And now . . . everything is delightful. Fine wines gently rein in one's galloping nerves. Leisurely you pick up a glass, let the rich, spicy aroma and taste envelop you completely." He continued spinning his wine fancies for her, carried away by the sound of his own words.

Meanwhile, all others around the table were listening to Martin as he told some dramatic story. Like Paul Masson, he usually dominated most talk at his table, possibly out of a sense of responsibility for keeping guests entertained. And he definitely resented it if someone cut in and tried to take over to any extent. (The only one ever to challenge him on this was Burgess Meredith, many years later. As an actor he expected to occupy center stage and perpetually hold forth. After Martin had been talking for just too long, Burgess leaped to his feet and shouted, "Shut up! *I* want to talk!" Martin was stunned silly. But he thought it very funny, and let Burgess carry on. When this happened I glanced at Alfred Knopf, seated opposite Meredith, and he was so astonished that his eyeballs actually quivered!)

After their final dessert course of glistening fresh wild strawberries with Château d'Yquem 1928, everyone was relaxing with coffee and cognac when Elsie, glancing toward the window, noticed that their "magic hour" was at hand. Martin would like to share it with their guests, she knew, so when she caught his eye she pointed toward the window. He got her message.

"Come take your cognac along to see this," he said. Outdoors, there were cries of wonder at the sight before them. The last rays of the sun drenched the world in luminous gold. Suddenly the sun dipped behind a peak, and the gold turned to a delicate mauve that suffused vineyards and sky in pearly iridescence,

"What magnificence . . . what peace!" Woollcott sighed, his hand resting on Martin's shoulder. "How I envy you—because this is a life that must satisfy deeply, completely. I have only my temporary satisfactions," he added, biting down on his underlip. "As every year ends, I plan what I'll do next. Always something different. One year I write a play; again a book of sketches. Sometimes I turn critic; another season I create a radio show. Or even turn actor, as now. I'm searching for some lasting satisfaction. But it always eludes me. You have this precious thing that I never can find. *This is it!* How can I have this life of yours?"

Price appeared. "We've got to leave," he announced. "I'm not fond of driving that mountain road at night." So Martin didn't get to answer Woollcott's question.

After all the guests had departed, Martin and Elsie Ray returned to the deserted table and shared a final bottle of champagne as they discussed the highlights of the dinner, laughed over the Woollcott challenge, and caught each other up on various incidents they hadn't shared. They always said this replay of each dinner over champagne was much the most enjoyable part.

The "Woollcott" event turned out to be a "twenty-one bottle dinner," as categorized by Martin Ray. Martin had his own way of assessing in retrospect the success of any dinner. He'd reappraise all the wines, foods, conversation . . . and finally total up the number of bottles drunk of the various wines. Merely counting the bottles consumed of each wine made it quite apparent which were preferred, and to what extent, without any conversation about them. Over the years he found that at a successful dinner an average of one and a half bottles were consumed by each person. Of course some guests drank less, others more. And the usual party stretched out for many hours.

That day it worked out to almost two bottles per person. But the bottle count dwarfed in significance to this achievement: not only had Martin subdued the cantankerous Woollcott, but he actually won him over!

Afterwards, reflecting upon the dinner, Martin couldn't help but marvel at how differently a man could appear to the world from what he actually was. Woollcott was not at base the insolent swaggerer known to most people. Behind the façade was a sensitive, lovable human being. And an insecure one. For a few moments, standing there with Martin, he had looked longingly through the bars of his self-imposed cage at the perfect life eluding him.

Of course Woollcott and other visitors only *thought* they'd like a winegrower's life. They viewed it as far removed from dull, frenetic, or painful realities in the outside world below. They had no idea of the enormous hard work involved. Or, up in a remote mountain location, the problems posed by such occurrences as winter storms that cause week-long power outages, freeze water-pumps and waterlines, wash out roads and mire vehicles in mud; malfunctioning machinery, including tractors and stranded cars; canyon brushfires; migrating rattlesnakes and grape-marauding deer, foxes, jackrabbits, birds, and raccoons. Life for a winegrower is no perpetually sunny picnic!

And putting on these wine dinners several times a week was no small undertaking. Certainly Elsie knew well that casting this spell of enchantment over visitors required more than magicians' skills. The scrumptious feast should seem leisurely, effortless— not showing the careful planning and time-consuming preparation behind it.

Over the decades, a veritable parade of people passed through Martin Ray's life. Usually their experience with him reached the pinnacle of sheer elation at the dinner table. Ending their visit, almost inevitably they announced their intention to become wine-growers too! There were rare ones who actually did so, in time . . . and rarer ones still who actually made a success of the endeavor.

Sometimes Martin mused about how nearly everyone who spent a few hours with him on the mountain had a sudden urge to cast aside all personal and professional encumbrances and become a vintner. Even in the early years, in an era not yet tuned to fine wine, many visitors got carried away with enthusiasm, were suddenly inflamed with this notion, and seemed to think they were the very first to think of doing such a daringly romantic thing. In most cases, of course, it was but a passing fantasy, wildly unrealistic, but surely a tribute to the dual magnetism of Martin Ray's personality and way of life. Something about Martin's spirit was undeniably contagious.

Over champagne as the sun set Martin and Elsie Ray (later on, I was his companion) would talk over the day's latest visionary. Martin had a way of summing it all up. "Well," he'd say, and Elsie knew how he'd conclude: "Some dream of wine." His voice lingered dreamily over the words, and even though intending humor, he was identifying with the very glow of the reverie. And Elsie would smile, sensing the same fantasy wreathed in his own lifetime romance with wine.

But of all visitors in the early days who came and "dreamed of wine," only one commanded credence and respectful awe. Here was no impractical or sometime dreamer. The eminent Lucius Boomer definitely seemed created to become one of the world's great wine-growers. At the time he visited Martin Ray at the Masson winery he was at the zenith of his fame and success as president of the Waldorf-Astoria Corporation.

Boomer fell instantly in love with Martin Ray's way of life. But as he drank of his wines—amazingly big of body and flavor and bouquet—he also realized with startling impact that on this mountain Martin Ray grew some of the greatest wines he'd ever tasted from anywhere. And Boomer had tasted the best of Europe's offerings.

So at once, without any buildup, Lucius Boomer got caught up in his own fantastic dream of wine. It came to him full-blown, combined the ideal life with the most satisfying and elusive aesthetic achievement. "I will join you," he told Martin decisively. "Think what we can achieve together, in making this the greatest vineyard estate in the world! And whatever money is needed I can supply."

This economic factor was significant in itself. Top-quality winegrowing was (and still is) a costly pursuit; one continually faced limitations for lack of money. To think now of having unlimited capital for development and equipment and improved technology! Then too they could do the educational publicizing of fine wine to create a sufficient responsive clientele for necessarily higher-priced products.

Boomer's entry assured perfection in perpetuity. Martin was simply overwhelmed at the magnificent prospect. Together he and Lucius Boomer made astounding but sound plans for the future.

As his visit neared its end, Lucius was finding it almost impossible to leave. He had an overpowering urge to go into action immediately. However, he first had to make a quick European trip already scheduled. He would rush it so as to get back at the earliest possible moment. He sent Martin a joyous note when he sailed homeward from Liverpool: "And now for the greatest adventure of my life! Can't contain my impatience to get there, to launch our exciting plans...."

But a dark fate intervened before Martin received the note. Lucius Boomer, in mid-Atlantic on his return voyage, suffered a heart attack. He died before he could achieve his greatest dream. Martin Ray mourned his death through all the years—the shocking personal loss of his delightful friend, as well as the distressing loss of their anticipated great venture together.

Beyond this, there was the incalculably enormous loss to quality winegrowing in California. Not only did Lucius Boomer have the dream, combining enthusiasm, intelligence, and soundness, but he had the worldly cultural background for appreciating the finest in wines as well as pursuing the finest way of life that alone could produce such wines. And he had the unlimited wealth necessary to fulfill this high-caliber dream. Perfection he would have pursued, with no expense spared to achieve it.

Often in later years when Martin Ray was straining to the utmost to handle some difficult strategy, he'd think of Lucius Boomer—of how, together, they could have solved the problem so easily, without the great effort it cost him alone. By himself, it took a lifetime to accomplish but a fraction of what the two as partners might have achieved synergistically, in a minimum of time.

Wealth in Boomer's case would have furthered Martin Ray's quality ideal. Ironically, however, most wealthy people who "dreamed of wine" and then actually pursued the fantasy into reality, veered in the opposite direction—toward enormous acreage and huge production, with a consequent loss to quality.

Studying California wine history, Martin was confounded that moneyed notables such as Leland Stanford, "Lucky" Baldwin, and Henry Huntington followed a megalomaniacal pattern when they moved to realize their winegrowing dreams. They might have created moderate-sized estates of jewel-like perfection as in Europe, of priceless value and unexcelled prestige. "For the love of God, why didn't they see it!" Martin would exclaim, utterly frustrated. "They could have founded a wine aristocracy here that would have ennobled them, instead of making their ventures absurd failures."

Martin was most infuriated about what Leland Stanford did. He always admired him otherwise; and sympathized besides, because he felt that Huntington had browbeaten him. "Just imagine—" Martin would say whenever the subject of huge vineyard projects came up—"in the 1880s Stanford paid out a million dollars for 55,000 acres in the hot climate of the upper Sacramento Valley, where you couldn't possibly grow acceptable fine wine grapes. He planted in a single 2,500-acre block the staggering number of some three million vines! He even boasted that Vina was the world's largest vineyard, yet planned to extend it even further, so if you started walking through the vineyard at dawn you still couldn't reach the end of a single row by sundown...."

Despite the vineyard's stupendous size and its impossible location, Stanford insisted his wines were going to be far superior to those of France. Of course the wines proved hopeless, so he tried desperately to convert them to brandy. But that required acidity, so even his brandy was frightful. "Think of it, he wasted a vast fortune on this mad venture," Martin would say, "when with his money he could have created a superlative reputation for winegrowing, to reflect prestige on *all* California wines!"

It wasn't only Stanford and others of wealth in *his* era whose dreams of wine were always on a grandiose scale, Martin would point out. Americans invariably dreamed of winegrowing on an outsize scale, even much earlier. "Remember the early Los Angeles Vineyard Society started at Anaheim way back in 1857? That was their fatal mistake too—aimed to be the largest of all vineyards while at the same time achieve highest quality."

Martin always mentioned then how Haraszthy's Buena Vista Vinicultural Society fell victim to the same unwieldy ambition, getting sidetracked from its original objective of growing fine wines. "And as its financial troubles multiplied, what did they do?" Martin would ask indignantly. "Desperately try to grow even larger! Claimed to have 'The World's Largest Grape Ranch.' Well, it soon proved to be the world's costliest and most unprofitable, so it shortly was gone."

Martin Ray would always battle against this chronic American penchant for making everything colossal. One day in 1950 he got a frantic phone call from a young man named Martin Stelling— whose dream was also of wine. Martin hadn't met him. Stelling already had plunged into winegrowing on a big scale in Napa Valley, was in the act of planting hundreds of acres. Evidently he realized he was heading for financial disaster, so at this point desperately sought Martin's advice.

It was a rushed period for Martin, but he took time out to drive up to Napa to see Stelling's situation and give him whatever guidance he could. He found that Stelling had acquired an enormous old brick mansion on the first rise of hills to the west of Oakville, distantly overlooking his first planted vineyards.

The moment Martin stepped in the door and looked about him, the solution was obvious. Instantly he saw how this mansion could be transformed into a vintner's magnificent chateau, the very heart of a splendid vineyard estate. The wild slopes intervening between chateau and vineyards must be planted, bringing the entire vineyard up to the chateau and becoming an invaluable atmospheric part of it. A great balustraded veranda, of dramatic dimensions, should front the chateau, and from it visitors would look directly down on the rolling slopes of vineyards and at the panoramic view of the valley, as they did from his own terrace at Saratoga.

Here, indeed, was the perfect setting for a supreme quality operation. Martin tried his best to transfer to Stelling his own inspired vision; told him he had overlooked his greatest asset, in this potentially glorious chateau. He should create splendid concrete cellars beneath it, ample for all the needs of a reasonably sized, top-prestige winery. All activities would center here in this one majestic building that already existed. And this chateau that symbolized his aspirations and achievements would, as with many European wines, be artfully depicted on his labels.

As Martin talked, Stelling paced nervously up and down the room, a man obviously under unbearable pressures. Martin began to describe the wonderful life that would be lived here at the chateau, with the interesting people who would come to him from all over the world, and how through entertaining them his wines would be publicized and attain the prestige necessary to command high prices. In a while, Stelling paused in his pacing, and for the first time his eyes lit up with enthusiasm.

"But you must give up the idea of many hundreds of acres of vines," Martin warned. "You must keep no more than one hundred acres for a prestige operation at this time." From Stelling's alarmed expression Martin knew he had to be firm. "With more than that, you won't be able to make the finest of wines. And to succeed in the prestige market, you must of course actually *achieve* quality."

Stelling was absolutely horrified at such an acreage limitation—exclaimed that he must have his thousand acres as a minimum. Actually, he really wanted *two* thousand! Martin patiently tried to explain to him the basic economics of growing and marketing fine wines in that era, when but a fractional demand existed for fine wines at high prices. For hours he pleaded with Stelling to change the focus on his dream, confine his operation to one that would fit into the fine wine category, and be manageable and successful. But size alone seemed to be the only criterion Stelling understood for success.

When Martin declared that it would take a million dollars to bring in a thousand acres of vineyard, and still another million to sustain the enterprise during the waiting period before wines could be marketed, Stelling looked aghast.

"Do you have that kind of money?" Martin asked. Stelling didn't answer, seemed to have gone into shock. Evidently he'd never included such staggering costs in pursuing his dream of fantastic proportions.

Martin Ray finally left, deeply discouraged that he'd failed to inspire Stelling with his own vision of the perfect chateau-based operation he could have there. Marvelously successful and rewarding, it would have set a remarkable style and tone in Napa Valley winemaking. (This, of course, was long years before Napa became the mecca of American wine operations and a vast tourism, when grand old Victorian-era residences like this one of Stelling's were spruced up into estate centerpieces.)

A week later Martin Stelling died, when at 100 miles an hour he crashed head-on into a giant oak tree growing right next to his vineyard. What a tragic, unnecessary denouement . . . and, again, what a loss to California winegrowing! Stelling might have worked out his glorious dream of wine to his immense gratification, if only he could have held it to practical dimensions. (At least the vineyard already planted at Stelling's To Kalon remains today. Through the years it has supplied fine varietal grapes to premium wineries in Napa.)

Fortunately, with each generation a new set of vintners, full of a glorious idealism sometimes tempered by realism and practical plans, emerges to renew that age-old dream of wine.

26

Fire on the Mountain

In THE SPRING OF 1941 two men came up to see Martin Ray and present a proposition for his consideration. He already knew them both. Louis Benoist and Wilbur Brayton wanted him to combine his Paul Masson Champagne Company with the Almaden Winery, which they had just acquired. To them such a pairing seemed historically fitting because of the two firms' interwoven background with the Thée–Lefranc–Masson families.

For various reasons Martin turned them down on the spot. He wanted to remain in sole charge of any operations at Masson. Any advantage in a partnership would be Almaden's, he saw, since it never had any of the glamour or appeal that Paul Masson's name, personality, and wines perennially held for the public. And since Almaden had been inactive most of the time during and since Prohibition, its name meant little if anything to wine purchasers.

Moreover, Benoist had no financial inducement to offer. Instead, he offered Martin stock options in the proposed merger. Impossible! Martin well knew Benoist's reputation as a prodigious spender whenever he had the money—which he did from time to time. Wilbur had helped him acquire Almaden, as not much investment was involved in its moribund state. Now they hoped that by merging with Paul Masson, they'd have a valuable enterprise.

"Almaden will go broke with Benoist heading the company," Martin predicted afterwards to Elsie. "It can't be otherwise. Time is the only unknown." (And eventually it did. By the time it was sold to National Distillers, in 1967, Benoist had been living it up with seven houses, a couple of airplanes, and a luxury yacht.)

This thwarted attempt to inveigle Martin Ray into fusing the two companies, however, may have triggered a sequence of drastic events that affected the course of his life. The story that I tell here is basically Martin's version and interpretation of what happened.

To backtrack a bit: In October of 1940 the San Francisco Wine and Food Society would be giving a splendid dinner to honor Martin Ray and his wines. Hearing of it, Julian Street expressed delight that Martin was receiving this well-deserved homage. Rarely was a single winegrower so honored.

Julian took it for granted that his friend Martin would attend the dinner. But Martin declined to go, promising to send a winery representative in his stead. It would be better, he said, if he himself were not present, so that they could freely discuss his wines in his absence. (Actually, a main factor in this decision was doubtless that he abhorred association banquets—and never attended one in all his winegrowing years.)

The only problem now was that there was no executive to send in his place. He directed everything himself. He had no winemaker: *he* was the winemaker. He didn't even have a worker entitled to be called cellarmaster, for he himself assumed all major cellar responsibilities.

But Martin simply had to come up with someone to sit in for him at the ceremonial dinner. Finally he decided on a cellar worker named Orry, who had formerly worked at the nearby Novitiate Winery. He was personable and could converse well enough about wines to pass as the Paul Masson winemaker.

From all reports, Orry's presence at the party had worked out well enough. But it created a lasting problem for Martin Ray in the cellars. For that fleeting honor encouraged Orry's most vexing foible: overconfidence. Although not educated about winemaking (or seemingly anything else), he learned quickly. Yet just as quickly assumed he knew all he needed to know about wines and cellar techniques. Then too, he brought ideas and practices with him from Novitiate that did not conform with Martin's, which were based on his knowledge of French winemaking, historically and currently, as well as his own experience and Masson's.

So Martin had to supervise Orry closely to prevent his rushing headlong into faulty action. Also to catch errors, especially in any projects requiring arithmetic, such as calculations as to the number of bottles needed for bottling several casks of wine or estimated grape-tonnage yield from x number of vines. Figuring simply befuddled Orry:whether to add or subtract, multiply or divide; how to compute with fractions or translate them into decimals.

Now, having been Martin Ray's stand-in winemaker for that ceremonial evening, Orry began to cause new friction. His magnified ego made him openly resent being directed or corrected in any of his actions. Martin considered letting Orry go, as apparently Novitiate had done for some reason. But the man was an exemplary worker if kept under firm control.

Actually, Martin thought Orry might have a screw or two loose somewhere. His trouble wasn't simply due to a lack of education and a hyperactive ego. Things he did sometimes seemed damnably odd. As when he'd drive into town on some errand and pin a note to his shirt pocket giving his name and address. Did he anticipate some accident that would put him in a coma? Was he fearful of losing his memory—or mind?

Despite Martin's firm patience, Orry was more of a problem every day in the cellar. Increasingly he ignored orders—sneaking in his own pet ideas about making wine. When Martin rebuked him, Orry became stealthily defiant.

For one thing, Orry liked his wines sweet. After all, sweet sacramental wines were all he had known in his past employment at Novitiate. And the public's wine consumption—even of so-called table wines—still favored high residual sugar. So Orry felt justified in aiming at wines that would have a wide commercial appeal. Which he knew Martin Ray's varietals would not, since in them most sugar had been converted into alcohol. From his warped perspective, Martin Ray's dry-wine bent was wholly wrongheaded.

Champagne was where Orry began his surreptitious campaign. With no knowledge or experience whatsoever in making it, he was always trying to get Martin Ray to add more of the syrup that precipitated the secondary fermentation. Martin explained to him repeatedly that the French had perfected the formula for champagne over a century ago, and Paul Masson had continued *la méthode champenoise* successfully in the U.S. This methodology was not to be flouted at Orry's whim, under the guise of an "experiment."

"Moreover, get this through your head, Orry: too much sugar explodes the bottles when fermentation gets going."

But Orry couldn't grasp the possibility. "Those heavy bottles?" he asked, obviously incredulous. Orry certainly believed Martin Ray was saying this just to justify the dry champagnes he himself heartily disliked. And *he* was becoming a wine expert!

One day Martin had to go off to San Francisco, but before leaving he had a champagne cuvée all ready to bottle, with the fermentation begun. He forgot something, came back, and at that moment caught Orry pouring more sugar solution into the cuvée. Great God, it meant absolute ruin to some seventy-two cases of superb champagne!

"So you finally got your way!" Martin bellowed, so angered that he had to hold himself from knocking Orry flat. "How many bottles have to explode before you'll admit your mistake?"

Orry, though shaken, said sullenly that he didn't think any would explode. "You'll see," Martin promised.

Soon, of course, bottles were exploding all over the place, making the cellar a shambles, and so dangerous to work in that protective gear had to be worn. But Orry stubbornly held that it was no result of what *he* had done!

Martin wanted to fire him. But it was now the height of their bottling season, preparatory to releasing new wines. A multitude of casks could then be emptied and readied for holding the new wines to be vintaged shortly, in late summer. He needed every trained worker he had. And Orry was handily efficient in performing specific tasks. So he'd try to put up with him until the bottling was done and shipments were made.

Now, on the day of Benoist and Brayton's visit to him, Martin had shown them through the Masson cellars. Young Orry stepped right up and entered into the conversation with the same jaunty air he'd assumed ever since his banquet appearance as the Paul Masson "winemaker." Benoist had attended the event, so assumed the title was legitimate. Now he chatted with Orry, and on leaving invited him to come and look over the refurbished Almaden cellars.

Orry quickly took Benoist up on his invitation. Over at Almaden he also met Frank Schoonmaker, who recently had become associated with Almaden and was by chance visiting that day. Orry ingratiated himself by showing keen interest in their plans for starting a big operation there. (Martin heard later that Benoist was seeking a winemaker; so Orry must already have known of this.) Though Benoist might regret being unable to combine the Paul Masson business with theirs, what they failed to acquire in immense prestige they could compensate for in sheer volume.

Martin wasn't bothered by Orry's openly pursuing the Almaden contact. When Elsie brought it to his attention, he said it might be the best possible way to rid himself of Orry, avoiding the unpleasantness of firing him.

But then a more serious concern began nagging at Martin after he visited the Novitiate's vineyard to see how their new pinot noir planting was progressing. The Brothers on the winery staff there always had been sociable. In the previous spring, when they asked Martin for cuttings, he happily agreed to supply them at no cost, since he always tried to encourage the planting of that noble grape. The Brothers would field-graft them onto rootstock already growing in the vineyard. After preparing the cuttings, Martin asked Orry to deliver them. But he made strange excuses as to why he couldn't. His flustered manner didn't totally surprise Martin, because he knew that Orry had left the Order under questionable circumstances. Which he'd sometimes wondered about.

So when he was looking over their new vineyard in company with the Novitiate Brother in charge, he asked about the Order's past experience with Orry.

"Hasn't he worked out all right for you?" the Brother queried noncommittally by way of an answer.

Yes and no, Martin told him. He caused trouble in the cellar—doing things his way, contrary to orders. And he certainly had some odd quirks.

"But how was he here?" Martin pursued.

The Brother obviously wished to avoid discussion, since the man was now an employee of Martin Ray's. But he could see that Martin's persistence meant some cause for concern. So finally he dealt with the matter as best he could. Hadn't Martin ever heard the rumors—that this lay Brother had somehow been involved in the burning of Novitiate's winery? He himself couldn't say much, as he hadn't been there at the time, around Repeal in 1933. Orry had stayed for a while but then abruptly left, perhaps sensing growing suspicion.

Now, heading toward home, Martin had a troublesome new worry. He couldn't have a fire-setter in his employ, for God's sake. . . . even if only just *suspected* of arson! Fire had been the ruination of many a California winery. And the risk of fire was a far more serious consideration high on his remote mountaintop than if the winery were located in a more accessible spot in the valley.

He talked it over with Elsie. She too was perturbed. Both agreed, though, that it was highly unlikely that fire would ever endanger their great concrete winery. The sole vulnerability was the shingle roof; but it was high above four floors, with no surrounding trees or anything else near that could transfer a fire. Always mindful of the extreme fire hazard in mountain areas, Martin never allowed any outdoor burning of vineyard prunings or anything else after the rainy season ended; no bonfires of any kind or size, not even barbecues. Of course no smoking had ever been allowed in the winery, endangering the wines with its fumes; but now smoking was forbidden anywhere on the premises.

In fact, the Rays felt so secure from fire outbreak that only recently they'd reduced insurance coverage to a mere $50,000, thereby cutting the overhead cost of unneeded higher coverage.

Of course if Orry's very presence made them worry, they'd certainly have to let him go. But after vintage, less than two months away now. In this rush period every worker was needed.

As for Orry, he acted as though he knew his days there were numbered. He well knew that Martin Ray had never forgiven him about the ruined champagne. Maybe he also suspected that Martin had heard that old Novitiate rumor. However it was, by now

Orry felt assured of a definite understanding with Almaden. He'd work for them as soon as their expansion plans reached the stage where he'd be useful to them. So he didn't much care what Martin thought of him now.

Martin became ever vigilant. He felt sure someone was sabotaging his winemaking in unlikely and devious ways. One day, for instance, he came across a diminutive evil with horrific potential. A tack had been inserted in the bottom of a bung. If undetected and left in contact with the wine, the iron in it would ruin the contents of the cask. On checking further, he found the tack duplicated in every bung, in every cask in the cellars!

As a vital security measure, Martin now made sure that Orry was never left alone in the cellars. He himself opened up every morning and was the last one to leave at night, locking the cellar after him.

Meanwhile, Martin wondered if he should risk waiting until vintage was over to rid himself of Orry. If what he concluded later from all the evidence was correct, he shouldn't have risked one more day, one more minute . . . one more second.

It was mid-evening on July 7, 1941. Martin Ray was talking on the phone with his Los Angeles agent. Through the window he could see the great dark bulk of the winery silhouetted against the sky. Suddenly a great burst of fire appeared at the winery's top corner, high above the portal—followed several seconds later by an enormous flash of flames that shot across the entire length of the winery's roofline. For a few brief moments, he was stunned, incredulous.

How could this be?

Martin immediately knew, of course, that the firehad been deliberately set. How could it be otherwise? Frantically he dialed the local fire department while calling out to Elsie. Then he rushed outside to see if anything at all could be done with the winery hoses. Obviously nothing was possible: they'd have to wait for the professionals.

But before fire fighters coming from the valley got to the mountaintop, the whole flaming roof had collapsed onto the top floor. And soon within its concrete walls the entire winery was a vast inferno, with fire spreading down through all four floors. A half-million dollars' worth of bottled still wines and champagnes exploded like hundreds of machine guns firing all at once. Another half-million dollars' worth of fine wines in casks—some rare, hand-carved casks brought from France by Charles Lefranc in the 1860s—detonated everywhere, the sound like deafening roars from heavy artillery.

Great blasts shook the very earth. The fire lighted the entire sky above the premises for hours through the night. When the flaming holocaust concentrated on the lowest floor—concrete but with a mountain spring flowing under it—the heat became so intense that steam blew up the whole huge slab with the mightiest blast of all. Streams of hot burning wine roared down slopes and canyons. Blazing timbers were crashing everywhere at once, and the great concrete shell was being completely gutted. Nothing could be saved inside the winery's great cauldron of fire.

For a time, the nearby chateau was endangered. Though it too had concrete walls, the roof had flammable shingles. Firemen kept a continuous spray of water upon it, holding the swirling flames at bay.

Standing there helplessly, Martin and Elsie were unable to talk, numbed to the horror of the spectacle they witnessed—the thing they'd been sure could never happen. They felt as irretrievably ruined as the great winery itself. All their dreams had gone swirling into the heavens with the skyrocketing flames and dense smoke.

Now, everything they'd worked so long and hard for was gone. It was futile even to think of rebuilding the winery, the large inventory of wines, and the business itself. An unimaginable amount of strenuous labor would be required, along with a fortune in recapitalization. And where would the money come from? Their minimal insurance would not begin to help.

By morning, tired workers began digging beneath the charred ruins to determine whether a small fortune in rare bottled wines might still be intact. But the intense heat persisting in the wreckage drove them back. Like their finest wines buried deeply and no doubt reduced to molten shards, Martin's and Elsie's spirits lay beneath the debris themselves.

It was grotesquely ironic that this tragedy struck just at the pinnacle of their success. When their fine wines had no real competition. When illustrious people from all walks of life were coming to the mountain in numbers as never before. When the winery was filled with an enormous backlog of their greatest wines—for it was always Martin Ray's policy to limit the sales of the very finest, and to save vintage specimens for further aging and future comparisons.

Once the grim reality sank in, Martin pondered how the fire had gotten started. He remembered his first reaction on seeing it: how obviously it had been set. Right under the eaves of roof, which overhung the fourth floor of the winery at the level area used for grape-crushing and other work, cut into the steep hillside against which the winery had been built. Or else started among flammable winery supplies stored in the top-floor corner close to the roof. Since Martin believed he knew exactly who the culprit was, he considered any evidence of the heinous deed.

He recalled how Orry's car, parked against the winery, could have been saved at the outset of the fire, but he'd warned everyone off, claiming it too risky. At the time, Martin had thought it strange that Orry actually had chained the car's front bumper to a heavy post, ostensibly to prevent anyone's stealing it—though Orry always had complained constantly about what a "lemon" it was. If burned in a fire, of course he'd collect insurance on it while getting even with Martin over his petty resentments.

On the morning after the fire, Schoonmaker phoned Martin. First, saying he'd just heard about the great loss, he offered condolences. Then he made an offer on behalf of Almaden: $25,000 for the Paul Masson Champagne Co.'s remaining assets: the name, business, the 185 acres (with 60 of them in productive vineyards), chateau and other buildings, cars, trucks, winery and field equipment.

"For Christ's sake, are you trying to joke?" Martin snapped. "Get this, Frank. I'm not selling. Ever. At *any* price!" Bang.

A question now plagued Martin. If Orry actually had set the fire, did either Benoist or Schoonmaker know of his intention to do so? He couldn't believe that either man would take part in a plot to burn the winery. But they certainly would delight in taking advantage of his situation, once an arsonist had set up the ideal takeover for them.

Martin naturally reported his suspicions of Orry to the local sheriff, who was already investigating the possibility of arson. Following up various leads, the sheriff found hidden in the brush some empty gasoline cans whose contents had clearly had been used as fuel in firing the roofline. He then traced the date and location of their purchase to Orry.

Naturally the sheriff expected Martin to prosecute. But Martin, like the Brothers at Novitiate Winery, decided "What gain?" Orry had no money to reimburse the company for the horrendous damages. And Martin had a second concern. "He'd be jailed but for a short time anyway, and then be on the loose again," he told the sheriff. "He's unstable and could become a murdering maniac. There'd be no safety on this remote mountain ever after. No, let him go. But tell him never to set foot on this property again. For if he does, I'll take the law into my own hands!"

If Orry was indeed the arsonist, he had contributed the greatest possible aid to his future employer. Through Masson office workers he could have found out that the Rays, feeling secure with their concrete winery, had greatly reduced the amount of insurance a few months back. He'd know a mere $50,000 policy couldn't begin to rebuild the winery if destroyed. So Almaden's new proprietors might then acquire from a ruined Martin Ray the entire Paul Masson "package" that they coveted, at a fire-sale price.

Several weeks after the fire, Orry, long since terminated by Martin, was already working for Almaden. Martin, receiving the recent phone bill, noted that in the early morning of July 8 a call had been made from Masson's to Schoonmaker's number in New York, well before Frank's call to Martin. Obviously it was Orry's doing.

(Martin Ray, who always studied other people's behavior patterns, was fascinated to note some months later that a fire had occurred at Almaden—the third major one associated with Orry's tenure at a winery. Apparently he had stored a quantity of defective wine he'd made in a building, then set the place on fire, afterwards collecting insurance.)

But any Almaden-connected corporate raiders miscalculated about Martin Ray. As has been said of him many times during his lifetime and afterwards, he was definitely a Hemingway-brand of hero—forceful, romantic, stubborn, driven, opinionated, incredibly strong, drinking deeply of life . . . and fate-bedeviled.

Martin's approach to any disaster was to leave it behind fast, and get on with the good fight against any and all odds. To endure and then prevail. He had no idea how in hell he could survive the latest disaster, this catastrophic fire. But he damn well *would.* Somehow.

27

Rising from Ashes

ON THE SECOND DAY after the fire, Martin Ray realized the thing he had to do first, before even thinking of how he could go forward again, was to clean up the towering heaps of blackened debris everywhere. At once he had a crew of men carting it away in wheelbarrows. With pickaxes they then attacked the exposed molten glass that covered the entire surface of what once had been his bottle cellars, on the winery's lowest level.

One happy discovery came of all this work: here and there were bottles of wine still intact—on the lowest quarter of the once ten-foot high stacks of bottles. The melted glass from the bottles above had managed to insulate a few bottles sufficiently to preserve them. The only other salvage from the fire was a newly arrived French corking machine that had been snatched from the main cellar entrance. This Martin used and prized all his days, its blackened gash a poignant memento of the Paul Masson fire of 1941.

Also many tons of fine wine grapes were developing under the hot July sun. So they could have a vintage that year ... if there *were* a winery. Otherwise, the grapes would be sold off to another winery.

The Romanesque façade and the great concrete shell of the winery behind it still stood, though blackened and damaged in places. Martin had loved that old building since he was a boy. Somehow he must resurrect it. To survive personally in the business, he not only would have to rebuild it, but also completely reequip it—with all the expensive machines, casks and bottles, tools and utensils indispensable for operating.

Impossible as the job appeared, Martin determined to do it. Elsie supported his unwillingness to submit to defeat. However, the lowest contractor's bid he could get for rebuilding the winery was $100,000—which he simply could not afford. The $50,000 insurance benefit wouldn't even pay for re-equipping the winery if it *did* get rebuilt.

Martin had one hope for financial assistance: getting aid from the few shareholders he had in the business at the time. But none was willing to invest a single cent toward rebuilding, even though Martin would shoulder the major part of the cost. All considered it hopeless. In fact, they wanted him to buy them out at any price.

At this point he was tempted to reconsider. Mightn't it be wiser just to accept his losses and go down the mountain forever; to put the whole experience behind him . . . and try to forget all about this winegrowing business? He could easily reactivate his Ray & Co. brokerage firm—a cinch compared to what he faced here. But that wouldn't regain the life he'd always wanted, and actually *had* achieved here.

Martin Ray's own "dream of wine" persisted. He felt it was well worth fighting for. After talking it over, he and Elsie decided to meet the shareholders' offers to sell at ten cents on the dollar, even though it would take much of their precious cash. They would fight it through somehow, all by themselves. They knew it would be tough. But they had no idea, then, how fearfully tough the fight would be.

At night Martin paced nervously about, wondering how he'd rebuild when he couldn't even afford to hire a contractor. Yet still he refused to give up. Then one night, several weeks after the fire, he suddenly stopped short in his tracks. "By God, I'll rebuild it myself!" he told Elsie. She didn't think he really meant it; it was just talk, trying to overcome despair.

But he did mean it, and once he'd made the decision he figured out exactly how to do it. Instead of pacing the floor, he threw his tremendous energy, revitalized now, into intricate plans and calculations.

And without any knowledge at all of engineering or architecture, he would indeed rebuild the winery. Just by using his common sense. (Never underestimate common sense! That's the one thing the most advanced computer simply can't do: duplicate the human brain's common sense. Experts say it's because the computer can't conceive of an idea, think about it, and act—all at the same time. Martin Ray could do all three things, and fast.)

To duplicate the winery he had first known and loved as a boy, Martin above all had to preserve its handsome sandstone façade that Masson had brought up from St. Patrick's Cathedral after it was destroyed in the earthquake. Out of sentiment too he wanted to save the old winery shell if possible, thereby retaining the beautiful old walls whose concrete had been hand-mixed by Paul

Masson in 1900. But all contractors said that the old walls should be torn down completely.

So to make his own decision, Martin began chipping away at the walls of the gutted building. Masson had built them three feet thick at the bottom, but tapering as they went upward, so that at the top, on the fourth floor, the walls were but one foot wide. Testing them at various heights, Martin saw that at the topmost level the concrete walls *were* no good, as he'd been told. Soft and crumbly, they had been too thin to retain any solidity through the fire's intense heat. But lower down, after peeling away the "dead" outer skin, he encountered solid concrete. He now believed the three lower levels of wall, though badly damaged, could be preserved—but only if treated really as a veneer and consolidated with massive new inner walls of reinforced concrete. Since the top floor certainly had to go, the rebuilt winery he now envisaged would be no higher than three stories.

Martin needed to be fast with this project, for the winery *had* to be rebuilt within thirty days to be ready for the oncoming 1941 vintage. And equally important, the ingenious plan he now devised to finance it would require him to finish the work completely within a month.

The next day he rushed out to find workers for the rebuilding. By great good luck, a group of a hundred Swedes was just ending a construction job at Kaiser Permanente nearby. He hired them all, including their working boss, Ole Olsen, with his son as "straw boss." They weren't skilled workers—just laborers, young and strong. Exactly what Martin Ray needed!

Martin figured that to build the winery in thirty days they must work around the clock, with thirty men and a boss on the job all the time. With the help of giant floodlights the work could be carried on at night. Having the boss and his son work separate twelve-hour shifts, with three separate crews, would do it. He himself would sleep just an hour or two whenever he could, for he had to be on hand at all hours, overseeing and directing every aspect of construction.

For four days, while awaiting delivery of materials and equipment ordered, Martin hurriedly studied construction work going on in various places in the valley. He learned that an "eight-sack" concrete mixture—primarily used, he was told, for gun emplacements—was the strongest. Therefore, he concluded, the safest: so that's what he would use. For the whole structure was to be of solid concrete: poured walls, beams, pilasters, floors.

By watching and asking questions of others, he now learned how steel was used to strengthen the concrete, so he could teach that to his men. Learned all about various-sized stirrups and steel reinforcing rods and their uses. (Looking back later, when the winery was completed, he was amazed at how he had actually based all decisions on a layman's personal observations and his own and others' experience, nothing more!)

By the time all materials arrived at the site and the crew was ready to start, there were just twenty-six days left till vintage time. So the terrific construction job was undertaken at once.

Very early in the job Ole Olsen came to Martin to ask what width the big square pillars would be on the first floor—those that must support the enormous weight of the concrete floors and other weight above, including hundreds of casks filled with wines. Martin thought for a moment, then extended his arms, asked Ole to measure the distance between his hands.

Ole measured: "About thirty-six inches."

"Then three feet will be the width for every pillar's base," Martin decided.

Later, Ole returned. He'd been wondering how Martin had arrived at that dimension just by spreading out his arms. "Well," Martin said, "when I had my brokerage office in the Russ Building in San Francisco, for years I parked my car daily in their basement garage right alongside one of its big concrete pillars. And I remember exactly the size of that pillar. So when you asked what size pillars we'd have, I told myself that if I make pillars of a size to hold up the Russ Building, they'll certainly hold up a mere winery." (And yes, Martin Ray's "common sense" pillars are still holding up the historic old Paul Masson Mountain Winery to this day!)

Martin saved those thin old outer walls by having reinforcing rods driven through the massive new inner walls into the thin shell of the old winery, combining them solidly in one. Olsen, all the while, kept asking Martin how in the devil they could eliminate the top ten feet of outer walls above the third floor, as planned, and make a clean line of it. Martin counted on the success of the plan in his head. But would it actually work? The day when they tried it out provided the most suspenseful drama of the reconstruction effort.

First Martin had the men make a great batch of eight-inch-long wooden wedges tapering to four-inch sharp blades. Then they drilled holes deep into the cleaned-up old concrete along the horizontal line where Martin wanted the break to come. Next they smeared the wedges with axle grease, put three of them together, and jammed them into each of the holes where the top was to be felled. High platforms had been built all along the inside of the lengthy perimeter of the old walls, and on them the men now took their places, in pairs ten feet apart. They stood there tense, poised for action.

When Martin gave the word, boss Ole Olsen began to yell out ONE, TWO! ONE, TWO! and all the men high on their platforms began to swing their long-handled heavy sledgehammers, banging in unison at the wedges penetrating the walls. A most spectacular sight it was, and beautiful to hear—those powerful young Swedes stripped to the waist with their muscles shining, swinging simultaneously ONE, TWO, ONE, TWO, all down the lines high on those platforms inside the walls of the huge enclosure!

And suddenly, before their very eyes, a long straight crack opened on the inside line marked by the wedges. And then CRASH! With one mighty blast hundreds of tons of concrete broke off and toppled to the ground outside the walls, forty feet below. A clean horizontal line was left around the top of the entire building—just as Martin hoped. The hazardous job that everyone said couldn't be done was finished, just like that, in but half a day's time. What powerful common sense!

Then they were ready to pour the new bond beam at the top, and roof the winery—with just a few days to go now before vintage. To save money, Martin had the heavy boards used in framework for the concrete pours cut to make the interior rafters and trusses for the sloping roof's structure. (You can still see them up there, some cement-covered.) And for the best security from fire, for roofing he put on the heaviest concrete-and-asbestos shingles. The roof was finished on the thirtieth day after Martin had decided to rebuild.

Martin now collided smack into the vintage period, exactly as foretold. Trucks were coming and going, bringing in all vintage needs: a newly made stainless steel crusher of Martin's design; the old basket press rebuilt; fermenters and casks and all else—just in the nick of time.

Martin's greatest luck in refurbishing the winery had come in securing several hundred French oak casks. By mid-1941, with Europe in a death struggle, imported casks like these were impossible to obtain. They were a virtual gift from sherry importer Munson G. Shaw in New York. Reading of Martin Ray's fire disaster, he'd phoned him to offer all these fine old casks just received, after the wine from them was bottled in New York—glass bottles being unavailable from Spain because of the war. Martin was eternally grateful to Shaw for this generosity.

Droves of young Swedes now moved in the huge timbers to support these casks, which had been washed and aired thoroughly. Others rolled in the casks themselves, ready to receive the wines, in splendid row upon row.

The pinot noir had reached the 23.5° Brix sugar Martin wanted, so all up and down the vineyard slopes his Piedmontese field hands were picking the grapes. And in the delicious cool of evening Martin Ray's pinot noir crush commenced outside in the courtyard, flowed through wine hoses into the handsome fermenters, which were then rolled on dollies into the glorious new cellars.

The epochal vintage of 1941 was on! It was the happiest of occasions. The greatest of triumphs. And at the center of it all stood the proud and venerable winery, its external walls looking exactly as they did in Paul Masson's prime, its internal structure totally created by Martin Ray. It was now as solid as a fortress. And Martin couldn't help but hope that from somewhere on high Paul Masson himself looked down upon it ... and beamed his gratitude.

Not only the oncoming vintage had compelled Martin Ray to rebuild the winery in thirty days. His entire financial strategy depended on this schedule. The plan demanded as much skill as his rebuilding the winery.

Martin knew he didn't have cash assets to cover the winery reconstruction costs. But no one should know that. When he purchased the initial construction materials, he'd paid a portion of the total amount on the spot or by return mail. Thus his credit was immediately confirmed A-1, as it had been before the fire. He paid all laborers every week. Then, when the great avalanche of bills poured in at month's end, he went immediately to each of his creditors, explained his situation, and promised to pay something each month—whatever amount he could. He and Elsie listed all bills; the amount to be paid monthly on each was its percentage of the total owed. It was vital that their creditors go along with them.

Now Almaden again revealed its acquisitive interest in Masson. Well aware of Martin Ray's financial predicament in rebuilding the winery, its managers sent a lawyer to contact all creditors and scare them into closing on him. In the end all but two creditors stayed loyal to Martin Ray, and these he paid off and never dealt with again. So Almaden's takeover plot was foiled.

So confident, in fact, had the Almaden executives been of capturing Masson through forcing Martin Ray into bankruptcy that they hadn't even waited for legalities to start usurping Paul Masson's glamorized image. Two former Masson cellar boys, now working at Almaden but maintaining a friendly association with Martin, reported delivery there of an old bathtub. They had then been asked to clean it up, carry it into the house, and install it. Tub fixtures were gold-plated and affixed, and a sign was posted proclaiming this the very tub in which Paul Masson gave Anna Held her "famous" bath in champagne! This absurdity brought many a laugh from those who knew that Masson never had entertained at Almaden in all the years. (And in any case, nobody was sure this much-ballyhooed event ever took place anyway.)

For Martin, triumphing with his creditors at this crucial time, and against Almaden's fierce determination to acquire Masson, was almost as monumental a feat as rebuilding the huge concrete winery himself.

But where was the money to come from now to pay the creditors each month? The Rays cut expenses drastically—cellar, vineyard, office, and sales help were all minimized. But that couldn't start their business rolling again. For what *wines* were there, to be sold to bring in cash?

They'd lost all wines in cask. They'd managed to save but a tiny fraction of their bottled wines. But if they sold those wines they'd end up immediately with no inventory at all. For the wines of their recent '41 vintage couldn't be marketed until matured in cask, racked, bottled, and allowed to age further.

In this emergency Martin Ray did make an effort to buy wines in cask from other wineries, but few had the quality he required. True, some top winegrowers had phoned right after the fire, offering to sell him whatever wines were needed to tide him over this period. Later all but one reneged, making various excuses. (Was this too perhaps the work of Almaden's lawyer, still engaged in trying to bankrupt him?)

Only Madame de Latour of Beaulieu kept her word. Great lady that she was, she not only provided a fine light cabernet sauvignon—made by André Tchelistcheff—but graciously billed Martin Ray at a very minimum price. He never forgot this generous kindness at a crucial time.

It soon became obvious to Martin Ray that he had to cut expenses to the bone. By letting all employees go, they'd avoid having the high payroll overhead. He and Elsie must do the work themselves, somehow. Whenever some assistance was absolutely needed, they could pay hourly wages. And they must make all the wine possible to build up the wine inventory again, selling only what was absolutely required to meet their reduced expenses and pay their creditors monthly, as promised.

To do all this work, they'd both have to labor seven days a week, on an eighteen-hours-per-day basis. Could they really do it, just the two of them? They did—though when they recalled, at a later time, the enormity of their work for two long years, they found it hard to believe.

Together they assumed complete care of all the sixty acres of vineyards. In the winter months they pruned from dawn till dusk, even into the evening if the moon was bright. They pruned in drizzling rain, wearing oilskins and tall black rubber boots, sliding and sinking into the muddy slopes. They pruned in bitter winds strong enough to knock them over, and cold enough to freeze their fingers right through the leather gloves they wore. They pruned in fog so dense that they could scarcely see the row of vines next to them. And they pruned on days when the sun shone so sharply through crystal-clear air that it burned their bare arms and faces. Ah, if those wine dreamers with their romanticized notions of the winegrower's life, if those effete wine fanciers in their elegant milieus, could only see them now ... for *this* was how each vintage year really began!

Then, after the vines leafed out in the spring, Martin sulfurdusted each one by hand, mostly by himself—some 36,000 of them! In those days it meant carrying the equipment on his back up and down the steep slopes, pumping hard to spray the yellow powder. This most wearing of tasks had to be repeated again and again during the growing season to prevent mildew; for he couldn't risk the future crop.

Martin planted thousands of new vines, replacing those whose yields were depleted by disease or old age, or of questionable identity. First he started the rootstock vines, and in the following year budded and field-grafted thousands of fine varietal cuttings onto them.

He also had to plow all the vineyards thoroughly, as early as possible in spring so as to retain moisture. Vine rows had been planted too close together for a tractor with a disking attachment to pass, so Martin plowed with a horse, just as Paul Masson had done.

But to plow sixty acres of hillside vineyards using horses required a massive amount of time. And time was precious to Martin Ray. Moreover, he repeated the plowing a second time after the turned-over grass cover had had time to rot, fertilizing and leavening the soil. For one man it was a never-ending, herculean effort.

Sometimes when Martin was plowing those steep slopes, and he and his horse would stop for a rest, he would look northwestward, across the canyon—at that other half of Table Mountain, still wild and untamed. This was the land that Paul had urged him to buy and develop instead of taking over his own vineyards, so neglected and eroded during the Prohibition years. Over there it did look enchantingly peaceful—and a pensive longing would come over him for a moment as he gazed at its oak-covered summit, still untouched by human occupation, with none of man's perennial conflicts, tragedies, or burdens.

The magnificent old white horse Queen was growing old, so he'd let her stop and rest longer than the other horses required, whenever she felt like it. Because she seemed to enjoy her job and still felt needed, she was allotted enough work to keep her contented. Then came the night when Martin awoke to hear Queen trudging restlessly around the chateau, pawing and snorting, as though looking for him. Somehow she had broken out of her stall. Well, he'd find her in the morning. And so he did—stretched out on the ground. He wept as he tenderly touched her lifeless flank, knowing how attached she had become to him, and realizing that their partnership was now over.

In the midst of all the vineyard work, Martin did a stupendous amount of cellar work all by himself too. When tasks required two people—which was almost every day—Elsie, his much-beloved Madame Pinot, helped him. (How I wished I could be nearby to aid them! But I'd moved down to Southern California to take on an advertising job.)

The next vintage rolled around almost before they knew it, they'd been so busy. To catch up, they tripled their production by buying all the cabernet sauvignon grapes available, the only top variety much grown then. And Madame Pinot helped Martin crush all the grapes, and punch down the cap on a hundred fermenters every four hours day and night—and punching down is strenuous work. Then she helped him press all the wines, pushing back and forth on the handle of the old basket press, with each swing encountering increasing resistance. And later she helped him rack all the wines, filter, bottle, and label.

Through all those strenuous months Madame Pinot worked tirelessly at Martin's side, uncomplainingly and with great spirit. She was tiny and inherently elegant—certainly not created for the hard work she was doing. But it had to be done, and she did it.

Whenever they bottled, they worked always as a team. Martin filled the bottles, still using the handsome, heavy champagne bottles for table wines too, following Paul's custom. He put on the agrafe and stacked the bottles for tirage—arranging them in wide rows on supporting wires from floor to near the ceiling. And when readying them later for shipment, he laid them carefully in the wooden shipping cases, each elegantly wrapped in tissue, and then firmly nailed down the lids.

But it was Elsie who always ran the corking machine. Over the next years she corked thousands upon thousands of bottles, always using the special champagne corker—which meant lifting high the heavy weight twice and dropping it to drive in the corks. "Look at the muscle I've developed in my right arm from bottling!" she'd say, showing off the unbelievably firm bulge in her small arm. Once when some top generals were allowed to visit, one of them laughingly twitted her about her powerful muscle, then teased her to prove her power. She gave a little flex of her arm and the hefty general fell flat on the floor. What pandemonium of laughter!

As if all those winery and vineyard activities weren't enough for Madame Pinot, she managed to do all office work formerly performed by a full staff. She answered letters, prepared publicity, acknowledged orders, handled shipping details, sent bills, paid bills, maintained the accounting books and all records, figured the taxes, and kept up with all the endless, complicated reports of various kinds constantly due the federal, state, and county governments. Her sole assistance came from part-time bookkeeper Rose Caglia.

Of course all these arduous tasks were being done under a grave financial strain. But by working eighteen hours a day, with never a day off, they could accomplish a lot. They knew they must hold to this schedule for two years. After that, they hoped, they'd be caught up, and return to the wonderful life they'd had before the fire.

Thus they had no time for play. Now, most company had to be turned away. The chain across their entrance road remained locked. For these two years Martin never had time to go down the mountain—not even once. Any such trip would take two hours minimum, time he couldn't spare. So every two weeks his barber came up at night to cut his hair!

Shopping was done by their housekeeper—who was their only luxury. A dear family friend named Etta, a superb cook, came to them in this time of urgent need. She had magnificent lunches ready for them when they came in dog-tired from working since dawn; served them glorious dinners every night—and always with such a radiant air of happiness and contentment herself as to rebuild their spirits for another day of unending labor.

Some of their happiest hours were spent enjoying to the utmost the large upstairs room that they had added to Paul's chateau when the winery was being rebuilt. It was a delightfully sunny room, with great windows for viewing the magnificent panorama of the valley below. Most appreciated of all its features during this trying period was the corner fireplace. The two bone-chilled and weary workers ate many a late supper there by its comforting blaze.

Because of their invaluable Etta, Elsie and Martin occasionally could stop work long enough to enjoy one of her beautiful dinners with favored, vitally interested wine devotees, who loved the Rays and continued to keep in touch. But there were none of those great affairs as of old, starting with champagne at high noon and going on sometimes through the wee hours, after the custom of Paul Masson. Now they usually ate in the kitchen. Irvin S. Cobb told the Rays some of his great stories seated at the table there.

It was in this period that Mary Frost Mabon, a wine writer for *Town & Country* magazine, visited the Masson property. Her fresh portrayal of Martin Ray, published by Knopf in book form the next year in *The ABC of American Wines,* provides enduring insight into his abiding character:

> To say that Ray has put his whole heart and soul into this spur of the Santa Cruz Mountains is stating the case mildly; he might be described as a fighting idealist who never hesitates to speak his mind and sometimes becomes unpopular in consequence. About forty years old, "Rusty," as his wife calls him, looks younger, bearing a startling resemblance to Lindbergh. He almost never leaves his eagle's aerie, and works in his vineyard or winery from dawn to dusk. A mesmeric talker, with qualities that would have made him a religious leader in another age, his great theme is his hand-groomed vineyard, planted more and more with the finest varieties, and his wines.
>
> His are the highest-priced, most expensively made (by true French methods), most carefully bottle-aged native vintages in the country.

By the close of their first labor-intensive year, the Rays were able to see in their cellars two vintages of the finest wines they'd ever made. They couldn't sell at their former volume and keep any inventory, so they'd raised their prices to cut down the number of sales. They had filled all of their wine orders: from the whites that could be marketed early, and from the reds—the bottled ones salvaged from the fire as well as the cabernet so considerately supplied by Madame de Latour. Their future business looked remarkably good, with the red wines they'd been making in casks or aging in bottles, though not yet ready for release.

At the outset, had they despaired over their precarious financial situation or foreseen the overwhelming amount of work they themselves would have to do for two years to solve it, Martin and Elsie might not have done what they did. But their hearts still beat with a young and gay pace, beneath the daily toil. They were brimming with health and enthusiasm. And they were still deeply in love—which of course supplied the magic element that made it all so much worth while.

Finally the big effort to recover from the fire was over. Their debts were paid off. At this point Martin and Elsie, reveling in this final victory, gave a great party on the mountain for all their loyal creditors. By then they had become devoted friends.

28

Exit to Adventure

THEY COULD TAKE it easier, Martin Ray promised Elsie. Think of it: With their debts now erased, they'd be able to hire a staff to handle the office and sales, cellar men to care for the wines, field workers to prune and sulfur-dust the vines, plant, graft, and plow the vineyards!

But the colossal effort had been overwhelming. Though they finally had triumphed over grim adversity, they felt very tired. Perilously exhausted, really. Martin often found himself gazing almost wistfully to the northwest, at the peaceful wooded summit on the other side of Table Mountain. Would he ever regain his idyllic life on this mountain as it once was before the fire? Elsie assured him that they'd get it back. But only after they first had a good long rest from all the work.

The time for taking a break from their labors hadn't yet arrived. When it did, maybe they'd manage to take a long, well-deserved vacation somewhere. Though certainly not in France and Germany, as they would have loved to do in the past. For it was 1943. Much of France was occupied by the Nazi forces, and the United States was now in the midst of World War II. The ocean liners crossing the Atlantic carried troops, not tourists.

The war naturally had affected the wine industry, as it affected everything and everybody. Following Pearl Harbor, in December of 1941—a half-year after the Masson winery burned—the government began regulating and limiting the production of all alcoholic products, to conserve grains and also reserve alcohol for various industrial uses in the war effort. Eager to stay in business by diversifying their holdings, the large distilling corporations moved swiftly and determinedly to buy up all the wineries they could. Wines could also be distilled into brandy. They weren't subjected to the same stringent measures as hard liquor, so people bought them eagerly and indiscriminately as an easily available intoxicating beverage.

At first Martin Ray had been perplexed when distillery executives began calling him, intent on buying him out. He was too busy rebuilding the Masson business to pay much attention to them, and certainly had no time to accept their invitations to dine and talk.

Elsewhere, he saw, the distillers were fast taking over California wineries. Cresta Blanca in Livermore Valley sold to Schenley. Valiant to Hiram Walker. And to the same firm went William Hoelscher, famed in pre-Prohibition days for its old Isaac de Turk brand. Then the world-famous Italian Swiss Colony with its vast vineyard acreage at Asti was purchased by National Distillers. Larkmead sold. Then Roma, a huge bulk wine producer in the Central Valley, was absorbed by Schenley.

Martin noted all these buyouts with deep dismay. To him they revealed a distiller pattern emerging: dual purchase of a top name and a bulk plant. Schenley would be able to sell the vast output from Roma under the prestigious Cresta Blanca label they'd already acquired.

He told himself he'd certainly keep his wines, along with his life, exactly as they were—perfection, in his view. But then corrected himself: or rather as they *had* been, before the fire, which had drained so much of his and Elsie's energies.

In the meantime, some distillery execs persisted, in spite of his telling them never to entertain the notion he might sell. Week after week, these men continued to besiege him by telephone and telegraph. Now they were even coming up the mountain, uninvited, to see him. He managed to be gracious to them as visitors but their assiduous courtship strained his civility. He now realized they wanted *his* business for one all-important reason: Masson had the highest "ceiling prices" in the entire wine industry. As a war measure, the government had instituted a price control that allowed no wine to be priced higher than it had been earlier. So if a distillery could acquire Paul Masson with its high established prices, it could make a fortune by selling vast quantities of ordinary wines at Masson's established high prices—before the quality change would be perceived by consumers and then affect their sales.

The question was, could he, in his spent condition, keep holding out against the distillers' increasingly attractive financial blandishments? Martin began noticing that, oddly, the distillers' pursuit of him no longer annoyed him as much as before. No doubt the tremendous overstrain of the past two years had altered his attitude toward selling out.

Maybe, he proposed one day to Elsie, they should reconsider

Paul's advice of way back. What if they sold the Masson enterprise to some well-financed pursuer—even though a distiller? They could take a long rest. Then plant a vineyard over there, as Paul had urged, on the summit across the canyon. If they could buy the land. And there carry on a small-scale, top-quality wine operation that could be handled easily, without such effort as this. Thus they could get back to enjoying to the full the greatest of all lives—the winegrower's.

To their surprise, they even managed to talk over this far-out idea. They examined all the reasons why and why not. True, they both were ready for a revitalizing rest. But a new life? It would be so difficult actually to make such a break. And of course by now they had everything at perfection again on the mountain: Paul's old winery rebuilt, replenished with superb wines; the vineyards in the best shape they'd been in for years; all work just about caught up for others to handle.

Well, the notion of selling was just preposterous, of course. But Elsie then reminded Martin how Paul always said you must learn how to bend to your advantage. They laughed over that. Dear Paul! So they agreed to try to bend, just a little. And once they did, their long antagonism toward the distillers so eager to buy them out actually began to recede a bit.

A few days later, two Seagram executives dropped by. These were the ones who'd been most assiduous in their courtship, though without being given any encouragement. This time, they were treated rather cordially. And when they said they had a new proposition to make, Martin now didn't cut them short, but allowed them to present it.

They very much wanted to preserve the supreme quality of the wines Martin Ray had been making, they said. So would he possibly consider selling to them, yet remaining on at a high salary to direct all operations?

Such a thought never would have occurred to Martin. Although initially it seemed preposterous, he quickly realized it offered a new approach to his situation here. This way, he would not have to leave his wines and vines that he so loved but would stay with them, living at the chateau and continuing the life on the mountain as they had lived it for seven years, but without the extreme labor of the past two.

Martin told the Seagram men that their proposal did have some merit, so he'd think it over further in the next several days. Which he and Elsie did, involving deep discussions. They liked the Seagram executives, liked the whole plan for their future. And they had a great desire to take a long rest from the heavy work they'd been doing. Right away.

They decided to say yes to the deal. The Seagram men expressed delight over the news. A deal was drawn up in which Martin Ray agreed to sell Paul Masson assets to Seagram for a mere $200,000. That was the sum Martin had paid Masson for it all, in installments. Martin felt a certain sentiment in releasing it at that same figure, although by now the property and the business were worth far more. But when relinquishing the ownership responsibilities, he'd still retain the life he loved and be in total charge, plus receive an excellent salary.

While the papers were being drawn up for Martin to sign, the Seagram people then phoned to say that only one thing held up the transfer of ownership: They must have a $25,000 cut in the price. By that time Martin, having made the decision to sell to them, agreed to the cut without giving it much thought, not considering it an all-important factor.

But by not objecting to the cut, Martin surely appeared easygoing. So when the executives brought the final papers for him to sign on a Saturday morning, they figured they could make an even better deal. For they declared that the deed of sale must include a further price reduction of $25,000.

At this Martin Ray ceased being the affable person he'd seemed to be. He leaped to his feet, his face flushing with explosive anger. Banging his fist on the table, he blew his top. "Goddammit, I already gave you a $25,000 cut—and now you want still another!" he exclaimed. "Now, if you still want to make a deal with me, I'll tell you what you'll have to do: Pay the original $200,000 price . . . and have the money in cash, in my hands, this afternoon. And hereafter I want nothing whatsoever to do with you and Seagram—ever!"

"But it's Saturday, the banks are closed!" they protested. "We can't get the money till Monday."

"That's just too goddamn bad, then!" Martin said, exiting the room—figuring that ended the entire matter.

The Seagram men, however, were determined. They managed to contact someone with the right bank connection and got a cashier's check drawn for the full amount, made out to Martin Ray. They rushed it over to him. Martin was surprised when the men returned, for he'd expected never to see them again.

Not only did they have the money, but they had one question to ask him now, before their relations were severed. Because Seagram was acquiring the Paul Masson firm, they felt entitled to get a vital secret of his operations. They knew, they said, that to stay in business he had to turn over his inventory once a year—just as distillers did. "So give us the truth now," they said. "All this talk of the need to age wines is just a publicity gimmick, right?"

Martin was appalled at such ignorance. "*All* wines must be

aged—some more, some less. No use discussing it!" he snapped, and left the room.

But the men obviously didn't believe him. And remained convinced that Martin Ray refused to reveal his big secret about timing his wine releases so as only to make it *look* as if aging actually had taken place. Today such an opinion seems inconceivable. Yet to distillers taking over wine and wine production—operations totally unfamiliar to them in the post-Repeal era of the '30s and '40s—it seemed entirely logical.

For sentimental reasons Martin Ray had not sold to Seagram Paul's old corporation, the Paul Masson Champagne Company. This he retained, merely changing its name to Martin Ray, Inc. through its Articles of Incorporation, thus retaining the early founding date of 1852 (derived from Charles Lefranc's company, which took over Etienne Thée's original company) for his own future winemaking business; and selling to Seagram the corporate assets, the Paul Masson name, property, business, equipment, etc. Seagram then established its own corporation in 1943: Paul Masson, Inc.

It meant something very special to Martin Ray to retain legally Masson's original business title, recalling those early years of association with the man he'd so revered. As well as with all those years afterwards, both glorious and tragic.

As for Seagram, from the time it took over, not one mention was probably ever made of Martin Ray's name over the years in any publicity story about the Paul Masson Company. Always it was implied that Seagram acquired the property and business directly from Paul Masson himself, or through some very temporary, often unnamed, and interim ownership. For Martin Ray this was just as well, since Seagram's mass-produced Masson products plunged from the previous nationwide top quality to an abysmal low.

Still, it's both sad and ironic that Martin's seven-year tenure at Masson, which brought the winery its highest social fame along with supreme acclaim for its superb wines selling at America's highest prices, today is so little known or remembered. If a rare mention is ever made of Martin's ownership of Masson, usually it's cut off just after the disastrous fire, utterly ignoring his heroic personal rebuilding of the winery. This was done, for instance, in Robert Balzer's Seagram-subsidized "corporate biography" of the Paul Masson Company. And of course subsequent wine writers and wine historians repeat these and similar omissions and errors.

Seagram's apparent veto of any acknowledgment of Martin Ray's ownership of Masson, in interviews or publications, evidently extended to its staff. Until recently, they and their successors either ignored or remained ignorant of the Martin Ray period of glorious prestige in the firm's history, and how important it was in the difficult post-Repeal era.

(At a social gathering at the Masson Mountain Winery some years back, I encountered a corporate executive who at one time had visited our mountain. Whereupon he introduced me to an East Coast visitor thusly: "Her husband used to work here." Shocked and deeply offended, I simply said, "He *owned* the place!" and turned away. In more recent years, Paul Masson, Inc. was purchased from Seagram by another corporation. Paul Masson's original winegrowing property in Saratoga, La Cresta, over the years has experienced a succession of owners, and is now well known simply as The Mountain Winery.)

Despite their annoyance over the sale-negotiation outcome, the Rays in their worn-out condition were relieved when the colossal burden of operating the Paul Masson company was lifted from them. They badly needed to recuperate from their two years of enormous and incessant labor. As they drove down the mountain for the last time together, to take a beatific vacation from all cares, they felt unbelievably happy and carefree.

Fantastic at it seems, for Martin this was the first time off the mountain in several years. As he looked around him now, everything seemed strangely unfamiliar. Like old Rip van Winkle, he was astounded. Even cars looked entirely different to him, as did the clothes people wore out in the streets or were displayed in department store windows.

Ahead finally would come their longed-for rest. Evidently, though, Martin Ray was never geared to relax, at least for more than brief intervals. For with his eighteen-hour workdays now behind him, and the Masson sale now completed, his buoyant spirit quickly rebounded. Daily he grew more impatient to get on with the project that had been at the back of his mind for a longer time than he realized: creating a superb vineyard estate of his own on the northern half of Table Mountain, across the canyon from the Masson property.

But upon inquiring about the wild, untenanted land, he received a bad jolt. It was not for sale—at *any* price! He now recalled Paul Masson saying that someone was "holding onto it." This he'd overlooked in his dream of ownership. Well ... his determined spirit had just received a new challenge.

He began to pursue the matter. He learned that the upper and lower portions of the mountain had two different owners, neither willing to sell. The lofty summit property Martin coveted most was a quarter-section of land once owned by a man named Gano. Rising to a 2,000 foot elevation, with broad southeastern exposures of flat areas and slopes, the oak-studded summit was ideal for vineyards, as Paul Masson had pointed out. The 160-acre property was now owned by a speculator who'd purchased it from Gano's estate. But he intended to hold onto it for years, while its value escalated.

Yet even if Martin could get hold of Gano's mountaintop, he would have no access to the property, for the lower quarter-section was held by a wealthy, retired old gentleman named Claflin. The man refused even to discuss its sale, he was told. Martin investigated various ways of contacting him but failed. Claflin's address as well as telephone number were not listed anywhere. Claflin obviously wanted no one to be able to locate him.

In the meantime Martin had no better luck with acquiring the upper property. But though fulfilling his dream was temporarily halted, he had become single-minded about ultimately realizing it. While pursuing these two properties, he was intrigued to learn of their histories. These had to suffice him for the time being.

Gano had homesteaded the mountaintop land in the 1870s, at the same time that a man named Lathwiesen was homesteading the lower quarter-section. Both built cabins and lived up there, making charcoal from manzanita roots, prolific on the mountain, for a living. They sledded the charcoal down over mountain trails and thence somehow to San Jose, where they sold it to early-day French restaurants. From the restaurants they brought back oysters.

Some seventy years later, when Martin climbed the zigzagging trail up the mountain he so desired, scouting the land, he came across the remains of Lathwiesen's cabin overlooking a picturesque canyon, and then Gano's on the heights above. At both sites he found great piles of oyster shells. Martin delighted in this proof that even in early days this mountain was a true epicure's paradise!

Martin also found Gano's drinking cup still hanging on the branch of a small tree by a mountain spring. By this time nothing was left of its intricate enameled decor but the thinnest lacy metal shell. Martin later had this fragile metal cylinder gold-plated—now preserved in true heirloom glory as the "Gano cup."

Both cabins were long since gone, but here and there among decayed redwood boards sturdy weeds and grass blades poked up. When Martin touched the boards with his toe they fell into dust. Near Lathwiesen's cabin site he came across a big square nail. Through all the years he treasured it as a symbolic relic of the mountain's history.

"Just think—" Martin would say, showing the previous relic, which by then was impressively framed against a colorful fabric—"this nail is the sole remaining evidence of Lathwiesen's entire life on this mountain. I hope I leave more than a nail to show for mine!"

Apparently this Lathwiesen was a spirited fellow. For when he finally had "proven up" on his land and acquired the property deed, he went into San Jose to celebrate the occasion. And what with one thing and another he ended the night in a barroom well into his cups, buying drinks for everyone with vast gusto.

Finally, though, he ran out of funds, but was in no mood to stop celebrating. He whipped out his deed, held it up, and shouted, "What am I bid for this deed?—160 acres of the greatest land in the western foothills!" One of the barroom celebrants offered him $25 for it—and thus became the sudden owner of Lathwiesen's acreage, which he had worked so hard to acquire.

Nothing was ever heard of Lathwiesen since. But one day, many years later, Martin unearthed a small, strange-shaped bottle near the cabin site, and took it to his druggist, trying to trace what it might have contained. An ancient apothecary identified it as very similar to an old-time container of lethal powder. Martin doubted that. He liked to think of good old Lathwiesen continuing on his merry way, perhaps on some other resplendent mountain. His name lives on, for Martin named the great hogback on the old pioneer's property "Lathwiesen Ridge." (It's where Peter Martin Ray and Mount Eden Vineyards now have extensive vineyards.)

But what happened to Lathwiesen's deed bought by the barfly for a mere $25? Next morning, that chap, not bright enough to realize his luck, went around to the courthouse. He asked if anyone knew of a possible buyer for the quarter-section. Sure enough, a certain young man named Claflin had left a standing order to buy any large block of land in the western foothills. So the 160 acres passed to Claflin for only $100!

And now Claflin, some sixty-five years later, was still hanging onto it with a vengeance. Why?

Martin didn't uncover Claflin's secret until almost too late. By then, he'd already tackled again the problem of buying the Gano summit land from the speculator who wouldn't sell. He'd gone to see him three times, argued, cajoled, wheedled. He'd offered him a substantial profit on what he'd paid for the property, too. Nothing worked.

Give up, then? No, not Martin Ray. That mountaintop he *had* to have. He'd persist until he got it. He'd wear the fellow down. But just as he was going out the door—this was his final bid, he said—the speculator called him back. Evidently he'd got to thinking that a bird in the hand was worth two in the bush, so decided to accept Martin Ray's last offer after all.

So Martin now at least owned the cherished summit of the mountain. But it wouldn't do him much good without any access to it. He began concentrating his efforts on finding Claflin's whereabouts. It took some wily maneuvering among the man's safeguards, but finally Martin got the address. It was in Monterey. Martin intended to see him, by fair means or foul. But see him he would—and with a deed in his pocket ready for signing. For Claflin *must* sign!

Martin roared down to Monterey early in the morning. Arriving at the Claflin hideout, he rang the doorbell. Fortunately he didn't initially encounter the formidable Mr. Claflin himself. From an upper window a little old lady looked down and inquired about his errand. When Martin said he needed only a five-minute interview with Mr. Claflin on a very important matter, she said she'd arrange it, and told him to return in one hour, as Mr. Claflin had not yet breakfasted. Little did she realize she had gotten her husband into a stormy session lasting for hours!

When Martin returned in an hour, Mrs. Claflin admitted him for the interview. Martin quickly explained to Mr. Claflin that he wished to buy the 160 acres he held on a mountainside in Saratoga; the land was most important to him. Mr. Claflin said no, he would not sell. End of interview intended. But Martin went right on talking, with all the charm and persuasiveness he could muster, acquired over the years he'd been a masterful stocks-and-bonds broker.

All to no avail. Old Mr. Claflin turned angry, cut him off. Martin deftly diverted the subject to recapture a more pleasant mood. After easing the situation somewhat, he then plunged again into trying to alter Mr. Claflin's decision. But Martin held back in revealing his purpose in wanting the land. For if Mr. Claflin knew how greatly he valued it for a vineyard estate, he no doubt would raise his price prohibitively, even if he could be persuaded to sell.

Now and then Mrs. Claflin, a dear little old lady, would look up from the needlepoint on which she was working and interrupt pleadingly, "Mr. Ray, you can see he will never sell. Won't you please go?" But Martin would weather that crisis by another charming change of subject, later to launch anew into his drive.

By this time he had been arguing with the old gentleman for hours, preventing any lunch from being served him. By supreme maneuvering, interweaving more agreeable topics, he'd at least managed not to be thrown out of the house. Yet by now it was late in the day. And he'd made no headway whatsoever. The two old people were obviously exhausted. And he himself felt frantic. He simply could not give up and leave—despite Mrs. Claflin's entreaties. Yet there was nothing left to say he hadn't said before, it seemed.

Finally the Claflins, with trembling determination, had risen to

their feet and shakily moved toward the door, forcing Martin to follow. Martin was beside himself. At the very door, as Claflin grasped
the doorknob, Martin in sheer desperation turned on him angrily
and said he'd found him to be exactly as he'd always heard he
was—extremely selfish, the kind of man who'd deliberately stand
in the way of a younger man with a wonderful plan to develop this
beautiful, wild land.

"What do you mean? How dare you say this to me!" Claflin exploded. "And what would you do anyway with the land if you had
it?"

By now it all looked hopeless, at any rate, so Martin threw caution to the winds. "Why, I would plant a vineyard!" he tossed back
defiantly.

"Ha, what do *you* know about vineyards?" Claflin's scorn was
venomous, but a note of curiosity had crept into his voice. "And
what varieties would you plant there?"

"Pinot noir," Martin started off by saying as levelly as he could.
"Cabernet sauvignon, chardonnay ..."

Mr. Claflin interrupted. "Well, do you know anything about pinot noir?" he scoffingly asked, his old jaw working violently. "There
is only one authentic planting of it in all of California!"

"Exactly," Martin said calmly now. "In my old vineyard adjoining your property. Paul Masson's, which I recently sold to Seagram."

"*You* owned Paul Masson's vineyards? Why didn't you tell
me so from the start?" Claflin cried—and collapsed in the closest
chair.

Martin explained that he had feared Claflin would then triple
the price for the land. "But this is quite a different matter," Mr.
Claflin said, "now that I know you want to plant a vineyard there."
His voice trembled. "All my life I've dreamed of having a vineyard
on those mountain slopes—the finest vineyard in the world."

Martin was stunned. Old Claflin too had dreamed of wine?
Good God, how could that possibly be?

Then Claflin went on to tell Martin how he'd bought the land
for that very purpose when he was young. But his mother, holder
of the family purse strings, was against the idea, so he had to
postpone the plan. For years he had worked for British mining
syndicates in faraway places all over the globe. "Every night I went
to bed vividly remembering the one night I'd spent on those slopes
right after I bought the property. That was the way I always went to
sleep and then to dream . . . planning my wine estate there."

He sighed. "I spent all my vacations visiting the great vineyard
estates of Europe, learning all I could. But my mother remained
adamantly opposed to my plan. And I depended on her to help

finance the development. She lived on and on. And, well, finally it just got too late for me ..." His voice trailed off, then abruptly returned with a tone of vicarious excitement: "So now you plan to do this same thing!"

Claflin's old eyes were scrutinizing Martin in a different way. A gleam came into them, strangely reminiscent of youth. "Young man, you should have told me of your intention much earlier in the day, and spared us all. You can *have* the property!"

The sudden turnabout was astounding. In no time at all Claflin set a moderate price on the land. A notary was called in to witness their signatures on the document. And then Martin left, his energy utterly spent. He knew both of the old people were worn out too—though happy now to be deeding to him Claflin's own dream of wine.

With the rest of the mountain now in his pocket, Martin Ray staggered into the nearest telephone booth to call Elsie: "Darling, I've got it!"

29

Virgin Vineyards

S O FINALLY THE WILD, untamed mountain was his—"the other half across the canyon," as Paul Masson had called it. Martin Ray immediately launched a titanic effort to transform the rank wilderness into a winegrower's paradise. There was no road on the mountain. Never had been. To decide where best to build the necessary road, Martin first got a local contractor, "Slim" Kennett, to cut through solid brush and trees with his bulldozer, blazing a westward trail up to the 2,000-foot summit where his vineyards would be. The growth was so thick and towering Martin couldn't tell when Slim reached the very top, until the bulldozer began to nose downhill.

Having gained a foothold on his unruly mountain, Martin now planned the road to the crest. It should go along the sunny southern flank so as to dry out fast after winter rains, and have huge drain-pipes buried at all turns to drain the road in winter. To maintain no more than a ten percent grade, the road must zigzag with numerous switchbacks. Then, after the road was bulldozed up to the top, the herculean work of clearing the whole summit would begin, for the initial acreage of vineyards and building site. Great rocks posed one of the most challenging problems. The massive boulders, some weighing tons, would have to be removed somehow.

Then there were the trees. When Martin had viewed the towering oaks up there from afar, he considered them among the largest he'd ever seen—which augured well for good topsoil to nurture his vines. It seemed criminal now to cut down the great oaks, so noble and venerable. But as Martin said to Elsie as they wistfully admired the giants soon to be felled: "Well, we have to decide if we're going to grow oaks or vineyards up here. We can't have both!"

With the road finished, colossal-sized bulldozers began clearing the mountaintop, removing the gigantic oaks, groves of madrone and bay laurel, and thick chaparral. They attacked the huge rocks, and those that the heavy blades could not push along were chained and dragged to the vineyard's lower edge for depositing there. Then tractors worked the earth back and forth both ways many times with a scarifier, its long curved teeth reaching deep into the ground, ripping out huge roots, which the men following in their wake tossed into piles that were burned daily.

Poison oak was a rampant grower, and Martin knew its subterranean tangle of roots would persist. So he let the land rest until fall, now well over a year since he'd acquired it. By then some poison oak had come back, so again he dug into the earth to maximum depth. During this interval he put in a six-foot-high fence around the entire area, to protect the future vines from deer damage.

Early in the spring, before planting, he went over the ground thoroughly a final time—and yanked out some last roots, and occasional rocks. Then he disked the soil until it whipped up fluffy as cocoa. But before planting, he had to dig drainage ditches and install a complete underground system of sumps and culverts to carry off excess rainfall in winter, thus preserving topsoil.

He also designed the precise layout of the vineyard. No trellises here! he decreed. He followed Paul Masson's footsteps and knew that vines were healthier, more productive, if planted singly. But he would set them farther apart, leaving plenty of room for a tractor. He marked out rows ten feet apart along the slopes, then determined the exact placement of each vine by moving a ten-foot-long string tied to two short stakes, which he moved along each cordway, driving in a stick at the desired place. With a gas-powered augur he then drilled hundreds of holes into the ground.

Finally Martin Ray was ready for planting. He had decided to limit his production to just these three great French wine-grape varieties: pinot noir, chardonnay, and cabernet sauvignon. All had well proven their ability to yield excellent quality wine grapes in this region and soil, and microclimate of altitude and exposure. The first two would probably come from cuttings taken from the Masson vineyard and bench-grafted onto rootstock at a local nursery. The latter variety would be put in later—from precisely which clone he had yet to determine.

For each vine an ample, deep hole was dug two feet in diameter, giving roots encouragement to expand and go deep where moisture held. A six-foot redwood stake was driven down straight, until it was firmly held. Then he lovingly set each tiny vine down into its proper spot in the earth. Rich leaf mold was thrown in about the roots, along with topsoil, for a vigorous start. He secured the vine loosely to its stake, and firmed the dirt around it with his heel. As with all else he devoted himself to, he aimed for nothing short of perfection.

Yet despite his complete involvement in creating his own vineyard estate, Martin Ray could not turn his back on chivalrous causes. He now commenced a noble but taxing extra job: rescuing Paul Masson's hillside country house from utter oblivion.

Commuting daily between his valley residence and his mountaintop, Martin had to drive past "Adele's house," the French Provincial-style place Paul Masson had built in 1936 across from the Masson entrance gate after selling his winery and vineyard property to Martin. Through his will, Paul had tried in vain to prevent his daughter from owning it, since he had skimped on its building costs, figuring on only a short-span use of it. And though Adele had mulishly sacrificed her assets to acquire it, she now deliberately abandoned it.

Always as he drove by Martin turned his eyes away from the house and surrounding property, for he couldn't endure the sight of Paul's place now gone to rack and ruin. It was an affront to Masson's memory—which surely was what Adele perversely intended. For Martin to accept this circumstance meant condoning a permanent insult to Paul—and that he was unable to do.

Martin felt impelled to do something about restoring the house and its dilapidated surroundings. But what—and how? He had no right to meddle, albeit well intentioned. And what spare time did he have, anyway, even to consider doing such a thing? Besides, saving the place might well be impossible by now; it appeared too far gone. The years of complete abandonment had taken a harsh toll on the house that had been quickly and cheaply constructed for Paul's limited, temporary use.

Yet each time he drove past Adele's house, the urge seized him again: to save it somehow, for Paul's sake, before it got condemned and had to be torn down.

Then one day en route to his new domain, a sudden idea came to him: the house was so much closer to his mountaintop than the place he and Elsie had bought in the valley. Adele might consider renting it to them—during this period before their own home was built at the summit, above his newly planted vineyard. Living there would save him driving time and gasoline, the latter a vital factor because it was rationed in the wartime. While living there, he could repair much of the damage to the house—and hopefully its surroundings too.

Then why not do it? ... But when he told Elsie, she disapproved, knowing he'd get involved in far more work than he realized. However, when she saw how much it meant to him as a tribute to Paul's memory, she gave in.

So Martin went off to see Adele Masson in San Francisco, where she now lived. As he stepped into her apartment, he was startled to see, right there at the center of the room, suspended from the chandelier, her years-old satin wedding gown, yellowed with age. Naturally he wondered whether this never-worn white dress had become the centerpiece of her odd life.

Martin tried to avert his eyes from the dress as he talked with Adele. This was difficult, for it dominated the room. Then his eyes caught sight of a framed photograph of Adele seated beside some young man—surely it was Lloyd—on a huge rock. Rock? The old photo revived a memory now, of something ... Ah yes: when the deed of sale of the Masson property was drawn up for him and ready for signing, Paul's lawyer had mentioned Adele's wanting the right to come and sit upon a certain rock on the premises. Which everyone had dismissed as absurd. So this photograph combined with Martin's recollection solved the weird puzzle of years ago. Martin recognized the rock, too. And he couldn't help but believe that if Adele had married the man who'd won Paul's strong approval, the stormy relationship between autocratic father and willful daughter would have been permanently healed.

It took Martin a few moments to rally his wits enough to ask Adele about renting the house on Pierce Road in Saratoga. Adele obviously wished but minimal discussion of a subject unpleasant to her, so quickly agreed to let him lease the place. But she was very firm on one point: she would not spend one cent on repairs. It would be entirely his responsibility to pay for any work done on the property. (And she clearly didn't welcome any improvements.) He agreed to her terms.

Although prepared to face difficulties at Adele's house, nevertheless when Martin first saw it at close range, he was shocked. All was catastrophic. Outside, the once-attractive garden was completely dead. And mud lay a foot deep inside the house—for the roof had disintegrated and let in the elements.

Well ... he had really gotten himself into something now! But once committed, he had to proceed. After a new roof was put on, he had Slim and his men shovel out all the caked mud, hose down the rooms repeatedly, and scrub them clean. When wall-to-wall carpeting was laid down and the furniture moved in from the Rays' valley house, the place got back much of its old charm from the time that Paul Masson owned it. And that pleased Martin greatly.

Just after moving in, Martin and Elsie became alarmed by the wild noises battering the house, especially at night. There was a constant, furious pounding like hooves of galloping horses racing across the ceiling, making it almost impossible to sleep. Martin soon discovered the source. Literally thousands of rats had lodged in the attic for years, due to openings left where corner joints of the house failed to fit properly. Moreover, wasps and bees long had occupied the abandoned premises too and by the millions swarmed everywhere, even invading the living quarters.

Martin addressed this new challenge with a vengeance. He bought crates of rat traps, caught rats daily by the hundreds, and finally cleaned them out. In the meantime carpenters sealed all corner joints. The bees and wasps were eliminated as well. So peace and quiet now reigned.

Once all was refurbished and the garden replanted, Martin and Elsie actually enjoyed their stay for a year or two, while working on their mountain vineyards and building a first modest home on the heights, eventually to be their guesthouse.

Then one day Adele contacted Martin. She must have driven by her house and seen its thriving condition, with even the dying prune orchard revived. She sounded annoyed. Martin Ray had turned it into a place that reflected well on her father, whereas she clearly wished it to remain a slap at his memory. Apparently unable to bear this improvement, she asked Martin to take the place off her hands. She offered the house with its fourteen acres to him for only $10,000—an offer she didn't think he could refuse.

But Martin and Elsie shortly would be moving to their new home atop the mountain. However, Martin did interest a friend of his, Dr. Ray Wayland, in buying it. Martin always had been vexed to see that inappropriate prune orchard there instead of a vineyard, on a place once owned by Paul Masson. So he now suggested the change to Dr. Wayland, who was delighted with the idea. As soon as he could, Martin tore out the old fruit trees and replanted the land to pinot blanc and cabernet sauvignon.

(The house is still there, now beautifully cared for. Whenever Martin drove by the place, he had the deep satisfaction of seeing it continue on because of his own enormous efforts to rescue it. The broad, picturesque vineyards over the slopes now mostly are gone, having succumbed to an upscale suburban housing development. But they did flourish there all through Martin's lifetime, as a fitting and sentimental memorial to Paul Masson.)

At about the same time Martin Ray was developing his land for planting a vineyard, Seagram decided to expand its vineyards. Workers began to clear and plant their top acreage, directly across the canyon from Martin Ray's summit and at the same elevation. This highest point of Masson's property never had been cleared before. The development work proceeded much faster than Martin's— almost as if the endeavor were a race. Giant bulldozers roared along, shoving all growth and accompanying dirt ahead of them, and then dumping all of it over into the ravine.

"Great God, look at that!" Martin Ray exclaimed, amazed and

disgusted. "Are they nuts? They're pushing all their precious top-soil right over the cliff!"

After a light surface disking, the Masson workers planted their extensive vineyard rapidly—drilling small holes in the rock-hard soil, inserting the vine roots, covering them with soil, then swiftly moving on, as in an assembly line. Their vines were up before Martin's were even planted.

By the time Martin's vines were growing luxuriantly in their trim, clean rows over the mountaintop, not a vine could be seen in the tangle of wild growth that had taken over completely across the canyon. By fall Masson's entire new vineyard acreage flamed red with poison oak. Tractors worked back and forth cutting up the surface growth. By the next spring the poison oak had multiplied into a solid mass.

Finally they bulldozed the entire area clean and started all over—again planted. But the wild growth was even worse than before. The young vines fought for existence, and those that did survive were fast chewed by the deer roaming freely over the un-fenced acres.

By this time Seagram executives concluded that monumental project had been a terrible waste of time, money, and effort. They simply abandoned the area permanently. As the Mexican workers were removing the vine stakes—the sole vestige of the misguided plan—Martin shouted across the narrow canyon his commiserating farewell to them. *"Qué lástima, señor!"* they called back. What a shame!

Moreover, the same fellow who made such a disaster of the new Masson planting practically destroyed the old established vineyards that Martin Ray had left in splendid condition. He decided it wasn't necessary to disk, so didn't. He was dead wrong, for if Franciscan shale isn't broken up every year by disking, it congeals almost to solid rock. In the first year production dropped to one-quarter of the tonnage Martin Ray had gotten; and shortly worsened to zero.

By the third year all the vines were dying. So the fellow fertilized them, frantically throwing on three times the amount prescribed. Forced into vegetative growth, the vines went crazy with bilious-looking blue-green leaves . . . but bore no fruit. Then they withered, canes drying up to gangling sticks. Dr. Winkler of UC Davis, summoned in this emergency, said the vines had contracted a virus because of the mistreatment they'd experienced; they must be pulled out and the vineyards replanted. So at this point Seagram forsook the vineyards on this difficult mountain and moved their operations increasingly to a major new locality in Monterey County far to the south. The old Mountain Winery became a ceremonial center, where at its impressive front portal summer concerts and other entertainments were provided for the public. Tourists were directed to the champagne-making cellars in the flatland of Saratoga. (The Champagne Cellars were torn down in 1990. And before the Paul Masson firm made its final exit from its mountain premises, it used the historic old winery for storing and aging ports and sherries.)

Tragedies like this vineyard ruination typified the post-Repeal era, when few trained and skilled viticulturists were available. A generation of young experts was yet to be developed in specialized university programs and practical field work.

Consider, for instance, the Almaden-Madrone vineyards, Almaden's attempt to increase its prestige with better varietal wines. They wanted to plant a hundred acres of pinot noir, and Martin helped by furnishing them cuttings, hoping as always to promote the popularity of this superb variety grown for so long exclusively in the Masson vineyards.

Later he went down to see the vineyard. The young vines were coming along wonderfully. But a chap was watering them from a truck, going down each row squirting water directly into the ground with a long nozzle with a tapered end. "For Christ's sake, you're also shooting air into the vine roots. You'll kill them!" Martin cried out.

"Oh, no," the fellow said nonchalantly; he'd devised this fast method of watering and it was working fine. In a month, *all* of those beautiful young pinot noir vines were dead—one hundred acres of them!

The stupidity, slovenly laziness, and arrogant presumption characterizing the work in the Masson vineyards after Martin Ray sold to Seagram were paralleled in the wine cellars. There, inevitably, total calamity occurred. This one hit Martin Ray even more cruelly.

One day Martin dropped by his old cellars at Masson to pick up a treasured silver funnel that Julian Street had given him, which he'd inadvertently left behind when he moved out.

When he entered the upper cask cellar, a solid dark mass of vinegar flies engulfed him. The air was so thick with them that he choked. Then he saw, to his utter horror, that all bungs had been removed from the casks! The air reeked of acetic acid. Black clouds of tiny, fast-breeding vinegar flies were billowing from each cask. Billions multiplying every second—from his own fine wines he'd cared for so lovingly! Now they were ruined ... all of them.

A man came toward him through the swirling black fog. "For God's sake, get those bungs in!" Martin shouted at him. "Look at the vinegar flies you're breeding!" Just in saying those few words, his mouth filled with flies.

"You don't know nothing!" the fellow shouted back. "Wines have to breathe!"

Martin couldn't believe it. Trying to calm down and be patient with this ignoramus, he explained that he was the former owner of the winery. "Who's in charge here?" he now demanded to know.

"I am," the man said. "Seagram sent me out from Kentucky." Trying to look menacing, instead he seemed terrified.

"I don't give a damn where you came from!" Martin exploded. "Those are wines that *I* made and you're ruining them. Get those bungs back in those casks and do it goddamned fast!" Obediently, the fellow started putting the bungs back, though muttering all the time that wines had to "breathe." Paul Masson would have said that he obeyed the command impelled by the power of blasphemy—something Martin had taken over from Paul along the way, instinctively using it in his own authoritative way.

"Well, they're already ruined anyway," Martin said, holding himself with difficulty from throttling the cellar man. "The flies and the air have already turned the wine to vinegar."

He staggered outside, forgetting completely about the silver funnel he'd come to retrieve. "Great God, all those splendid wines lost!" he groaned to himself. He almost broke down and sobbed right then over the tremendous and utter loss of these superlative wines he and Elsie had worked so hard to produce. Such gross mismanagement as had taken place in the Masson cellars was simply unendurable to the man who had made and then nurtured so fastidiously those great wines stored here for aging.

And that wasn't the complete horror of the wanton destruction. Later on, Martin learned that the same fellow, looking over the huge inventory of the finest wines Martin Ray had ever made, now safely in bottle, couldn't understand what the deposit was at the bottom of each bottle. He shook them, and the wine clouded. Didn't look right to him. So he poured the entire inventory of Martin Ray's superb wines of the past years back into casks—the same casks of wine already turned to vinegar!

Martin was told later that all the casks of wine were emptied into huge tank trucks and sent down to Fresno, for whatever use possible, such as distilling for brandy or vinegar; or else to be dumped.

It seemed as if Seagram had destroyed, whether through sheer ignorance or malicious intent, all evidence that Martin Ray had ever been head of the company once owned by Paul Masson. Wine connoisseurs who had already safely laid down Paul Masson vintages made by Martin Ray in their cellars now possessed veritable treasures.

30

New Wines from Old Vines

THE TERRIBLE LOSS TO wine lovers of those precious wines that Martin Ray had left in bottle and cask in the Paul Masson winery hit Martin Ray badly, too—for his own drinking purposes. He hadn't taken many wines with him when he left, assuming he always could buy cases of his favorites from Seagram at any time. Now after this senseless calamity there were none!

It would take at least several years before his own grapevines planted on the north side of Table Mountain would bear enough grapes just to make wine for himself and Elsie to drink. And perhaps five years after the planting before he'd have sufficient yield for commercial purposes. And further years for the resultant wines to age sufficiently.

Becoming desperate as his own supply dwindled, Martin wondered if he could find any chardonnay grapes to make a little white wine for the two of them to drink without waiting long. He asked his friend Dr. Maynard Amerine if he knew of such a planting.

At first Maynard said there just wasn't any; but then recalled a few vines along the fence at Garatti's old vineyard in Pleasanton. They might yield fifty gallons or so and would be of no value to Garatti—who made a couple of million gallons a year for other wineries from his huge acreage. To Martin, the prospect of making fifty gallons of chardonnay was pure gold. So he quickly approached Garatti about buying the grapes. Garatti, however, said he couldn't possibly part with them.

"Why can't you?" Martin asked, amazed and greatly disappointed. "Here you make two million gallons a year . . . what the hell do fifty gallons mean to you?"

"But Martin, that's the basis of my whole chardonnay blend!" Garatti exclaimed. And how large was the blend? Martin wanted to know. "Why, it's 10,000 gallons," said Garatti.

"Do you mean to tell me that fifty gallons in 10,000 has any significance?" Martin asked, thunderstruck.

"God, yes, Martin," Garatti said. "Otherwise, I couldn't truthfully call the wine that I sell those other wineries chardonnay."

Martin filed the experience away as one more example of the absence of any quality controls. Winemakers could make whatever claims they wished on wines they marketed. That's how it was in the first decades after Repeal, when fine varietal names were given to vast blends of nondescript grape juices that rarely contained even a tiny fraction of the claimed wine variety.

But it wasn't time quite yet for Martin to resume, and even more strenuously, his battle for better wine standards. For a while longer he'd work patiently at developing his new vineyards in the sky . . . and making some wine to sell from other growers' grapes.

Martin Ray wanted, and needed, to keep his hand in commercial winemaking, if only on a very small scale. He figured that during the period before his own vines matured, he could locate and buy premium grapes grown locally, whether by wineries or individuals. From them he would then produce varietal wines to be marketed within several years, to tide him over until his own mountain vineyards yielded sufficient wine grapes.

He knew of excellent sources for modest amounts of pinot noir and chardonnay within the Saratoga area, in small vineyards he'd actually planted earlier for friends. But he still lacked a place to obtain fine quality cabernet sauvignon grapes.

Then he thought of Dr. Emmett Rixford's old La Questa Vineyard in Woodside, about thirty miles to the north. Its cabernet, the finest on the market in pre-Prohibition days, had been perfected by Dr. Rixford, who attempted to replicate in California the special Bordeaux-blend formula of the great Château Margaux. Martin, who had been fond of Emmett, hadn't heard of any wines coming recently from his vineyards. After Rixford's death in 1928, the winery was supposedly being managed by his sons, Halsey and Allen.

How wonderful it would be to get some of La Questa's wine grapes! Martin decided to investigate, and next day drove up the peninsula to the old Rixford place. He was horrified to see the vineyards hadn't been pruned. It was now July. The vines, running wild everywhere, were overloaded with grape bunches. What was going on here?

As Martin neared the house, he met the younger brother, Allen, who was an artist. Halsey had been ill, he said, so they'd just let everything slide. Allen didn't look all that well himself, Martin thought.

Martin told Allen that if they'd let him have the grapes, he'd try to get the vineyard back to normal. Allen liked that proposition. But Martin would really have to talk to Halsey about it ... and Halsey wouldn't see anyone at all. He was really in bad shape. Martin, finding this all decidedly odd, gradually wheedled Allen into allowing him to see Halsey, against his mandate.

Martin found Halsey Rixford lying on an old cot, wearing a disreputable-looking, tattered robe. He hadn't shaved for weeks, his hair was uncut and straggly, and he looked haggard, even emaciated. But, surprisingly, he acted glad to see Martin. They always had been on friendly terms.

Martin eased into the situation with newsy talk about his own new vineyards on the mountain, the new house and cellar he was building. And when he casually asked Halsey how he and Allen were getting along, Halsey said, "Just fine!" And then amplified. They'd worked out an ideal way of living—subsisting on just soy milk. Actually, Halsey said, it had all the food value they needed. Martin realized that accounted for the stacks of empty soy cans tossed in the corner of the room.

"Yes," Halsey continued. "Soy three times a day. Eliminates all the trouble of planning meals and cooking. It sure simplifies our life. We still have our martinis before dinner, though, just as before . . ."

Martin of course was appalled at such a strange shift in their lives. What in the devil could be wrong with Halsey? Mentally he seemed alert enough, but he had let himself deteriorate physically to an alarming degree. The environment around him too. Martin figured that for some reason he'd lost his grip.

Then he spoke of caring for the Rixford vineyard in exchange for this year's crop. Halsey seemed greatly relieved at the idea that Martin would take over responsibility for the neglected vineyard.

Finally Martin wormed the story of the vineyard's decline out of Halsey, by bits and snatches. It seemed that neither Halsey nor Allen—Harvard graduates both—were good at business details, making government reports, keeping account books. So over a period of time they'd put things off, until by now everything, including the winery, was in a hopeless mess—and they simply couldn't deal with it.

All manner of problems were closing in on them, and they could see no way of extricating themselves. For instance, their sister, who had an equal interest in the Rixford estate, lived in South America. Her husband had been pressing them for long overdue financial reports, and by now threatened legal action.

"Meanwhile, those Bureau of Alcohol, Tobacco and Firearms inspectors are hounding the daylights out of us," Halsey went on.

"And of course various state and county agents, because I haven't returned any of their wretched forms for a long time. By now I'm so far behind I couldn't possibly make out any. Everything's in such a muddle, I wouldn't know where to begin—"

Lying there wanly on his cot, Halsey spread his bony hands in a despairing gesture. "So I figure I'm heading for the last roundup." He closed his eyes. How utterly gaunt and despondent! Martin realized in a flash it was a lucky thing he'd come that very day—for, from Halsey's frail look and depressed manner, he might well be approaching his end.

"Say, Halsey, don't you have a cousin who's some sort of power in the local Democratic party around here?" Martin asked. "And isn't he a lawyer?"

Yes, Halsey did have such a cousin, though he wasn't very close to him. But how could *he* help?

"He could help plenty," Martin said. "Here's the idea: call him at once and put everything in his hands. Have him right off contact the BATF, tell them you're ill and he's handling things for you. If he contacts them before their inspectors move in on you, there's no problem at all. But if you delay until they move against you first, then you're in real trouble. See?"

Martin got Halsey to phone the cousin immediately, in his presence, as he wouldn't trust a prostrate Halsey to do anything at all on his own, without actual prodding. The cousin said sure, no problem, he'd contact BATF immediately. And told Halsey not to worry about a thing: he'd have all the records fixed up for him pronto.

Halsey got up from his cot and wrapped his ragged robe bravado-fashion round his gaunt frame as he carefully prepared a frosty martini mix in a cut-glass pitcher—the only sign of elegance on the premises. Meanwhile, he thanked Martin for rescuing them, when all had seemed so completely hopeless.

By the time Martin left—after having a martini with them, despite his aversion to spirits!—both Allen and Halsey were changed men. Thinking that one more helpful comment was definitely in order, Martin saved his final words for when he went out the door: "And boys, drop that damn soy stuff from your diet. For God's sake, that can't possibly be a very interesting way to eat! A man could starve to death from the sheer boredom of it."

Martin went to work immediately to save those Rixford grapevines and the 1946 crop. He had a big problem, for the unpruned vines had madly sent out runners in all directions, and the canes were loaded down with bunches of tiny grapes. It was the heaviest overcropping he'd ever seen. It was too late to attempt any regular pruning. So he cut all the canes short, thereby eliminating a great number of grapes. Those that were left would thus prosper better.

Once relieved of responsibility for managing his father's old place, Halsey Rixford was amazingly restored to normalcy. Before long he even secured a well-paying job as a Port Commission official. He decided to close the winery. For several years, until the land was sold and subdivided, Martin continued to farm La Questa vineyards for its grapes. (Some of the original planting was resurrected, much later, by Bob and Polly Mullen of Woodside Winery.)

When giving up the winery business, Halsey offered Martin Ray some dozen puncheons of cabernet sauvignon he'd made a few years back. Though they'd been kept overlong in cask, Martin was surprised to find them excellent. This was the wine he labeled "La Montaña." It made a big hit on the market, helped tide him over, and kept his winemaking reputation viable until his own vineyards produced wine ready for release.

When that 1946 crop was picked at La Questa, the grape berries resulting from the extreme overcropping were so small that in the coming vintage they produced no doubt the most intense cabernet sauvignon in all history—due to the enormously high proportion of skins to pulp and juice. Martin Ray's 1946 Cabernet Sauvignon actually took twenty years to tame down; but when it eventually mellowed, it was superb.

Incidentally, when Martin Ray planned his own cabernet sauvignon vineyard on his mountain, he delayed the major planting. He needed time to try out the stock from three different sources to see which was best—which meant waiting not only for a first vintage, but also some maturing of the wines, then comparing the products of the three clones. He'd gotten cuttings from Rixford's La Questa, from the Jackling estate (also in Woodside), and Lefranc's old vineyard at Almaden. He found the Rixford supreme, so carried out all further plantings from La Questa budwood. In fact, he thought it produced an even finer wine when grown on his mountain—with more flavor and complexity—than from the original planting in Woodside, with its lower altitude, different soil and microclimate.

Martin grew these clones in the small section of his vineyard land fronting his original house built on the mountain. It remained his experimental plot, and he always kept there, conveniently close, various varieties and varietal clones he wanted to track and compare.

Another valuable comparison Martin made was of the four Médoc-type wine grapes from La Questa. Dr. Rixford long ago had planted these varieties in precise proportion to their use in the

Château Margaux claret: cabernet sauvignon, merlot, verdot, and malbec. First, he evaluated the grapes themselves growing in the vineyard, for taste, productivity, and other qualities. The cabernet sauvignon grape was much more pungent, spicy, and richly flavorful than the others. But it did not produce as large a crop as its companion vines.

Then he vintaged and aged them separately so that he could determine the qualities of wine made from each. Just as he'd suspected, the cabernet sauvignon alone was great. "It has *everything*." he concluded. Wines from the lesser varieties were faint echoes of the great one. His conclusion: the French grew the other three varieties as lighter, blending materials, to be added to cabernet sauvignon to stretch its quantity and also be able to market the wine earlier, since the lesser varieties didn't require the same long aging period.

He recognized, however, that few winemakers or wine drinkers would have the patience to accord the "enormous respect due the cabernet sauvignon entity." Because of cabernet sauvignon's high tannin content (if not blended out), he recommended aging it for at least ten years. And before serving it, he said, it should be decanted and warmed to around 80 degrees.

Later, Martin Ray also tried another experiment with some of the cabernet sauvignon vintaged from Rixford grapes. In 1949 he blended part of it with cabernet grapes from the Stelling vineyard in Napa. But the resulting wine, though fine, was not robust enough to be a Martin Ray red wine. So he got the idea of combining it 50/50 with the intense 1946 Rixford. It was glorious! He invented a special name for this partnership of two vintaged wines of the same varietal: the French word *Mariage*.

The public loved this wine. And loved to say the name (MAH-REE-AHJ), which had a romantic roll to it compared with its equivalent English word "marriage." In fact, Martin Ray's Mariage became so popular—was a White House favorite too—that from time to time Martin would release another Mariage from another 50/50 combination of two later vintaged wines when they complemented each other in a similar way. Martin's Mariage name proved attractive; Beaulieu later used it for a 50/50 wine of its own.

Experiments inspired by the Rixford experience went on, in their unique way, with Martin Ray over many years. So the Rixfords and their historic vineyard always occupied a very special place in his heart.

Finally Martin and Elsie could enjoy their new redwood home on the mountaintop, surrounded by young vineyards. Its huge plate glass windows provided a panoramic view of the valley and

of south San Francisco Bay, 2,000 feet below. The house was sheltered by giant oaks that filtered sunlight into the one huge room
with its mellow redwood walls. Centered on one long wall was the
perfect brick fireplace, flanked by open shelves of colorful books
from ceiling to floor, running the entire length of the room.

They planned this first home on the mount to become a spacious guesthouse someday, once the extensive vineyard development was completed and there was time to build an impressive
chateau above, on the very crest of the mountain. The chateau
would surmount a wine cellar much larger than the one beneath
this first house—which was just the right size to hold Martin Ray's
first vintages.

(However, this redwood house was such an endearing retreat
from the world and all its cares that it remained Martin's favorite
place on the mountain. Sometimes on a hot summer day in later
years he'd say, "Let's go down to the guest house." He'd revel in the
wonderful peace abiding in the redwood refuge shaded by great
oak trees.)

Ironically, Martin Ray, now involved in the herculean work
of clearing and developing his new mountain estate as well as
undertaking assorted rescue missions, actually was working as
strenuously as during those last two Masson years that nearly
annihilated him.

He was ever in the midst of urgent new projects of all kinds up
on the mountain. Yet when enthusiastic wine devotees of former
days came as of old, or interesting-sounding new ones wrote or
called and asked to meet him, it was refreshing to drop any and
all work temporarily to enjoy them. So life for Martin and Elsie
picked up much as before, with winegrowing endeavors and delights combined with entertaining. But the latter was now on a
simpler, streamlined scale entailing fewer demands on their time
and energy.

Of course guests often were treated to a Martin Ray diatribe
about the varietal frauds in California's wine marketing. Peacetime
had come to America toward the end of 1945. But in the perpetual
varietal war he'd taken on, Martin never found enough encouragement to lay down his weapons.

31

The Sad Farewell

FINALLY THE TREMENDOUS EFFORT was behind him. By the late 1940s Martin Ray had created out of that untamed mountain a beautiful vineyard estate. Not only was he growing three of the finest varietal grapes anywhere in the world, but he and Elsie had their small but enchanting home among the vines. Again he had attained a mountain paradise—the sky-high realm of his dreams that he'd wanted since boyhood, inspired by the one ruled over by Paul Masson.

There would be time now to enjoy it too, after the enormity of the work that had pressured him and dear Elsie, from those final years at Masson through the development of this new mountaintop. Martin was determined to live at a more leisurely pace in the future by having a small, top-quality wine business that could be easily handled mainly by the two of them. They'd be able to relax often—to enjoy champagne out on the sunny veranda at day's end, by themselves or with a few choice guests, with nothing at all to disturb their complete peace and happiness.

It seemed too wonderful to be true. And it was. For unmerciful disaster struck. As it had before. And would again and again. This turn of events proved the most distressing by far to Martin. For his dear little Madame Pinot's life was threatened.

It had started with some minor surgery in a local doctor's office. The MD had removed a cyst in her breast. He assured them that it had been a routine, trivial procedure. There was no cause for worry. So Elsie and Martin went about their normal life and assumed all was well.

But soon a second operation became necessary—this one in the hospital. This time, it revealed a fast-growing malignant breast tumor. The doctor claimed that Elsie's chances for full recovery were good. But she was not convinced: Martin could read it in her eyes. Her whole life seemed held in abeyance. A grave watchful-ness undermined Martin's usual optimism. A tautness lurked at the corners of his eyes and mouth. And though he always spoke confidently, Elsie could sense his apprehension.

From then on, perhaps weakened by the very doubt in her own mind, Elsie seemed to tire easily. Martin insisted that she stay in bed every day till noon. Given that extra rest, she managed bet-ter.

Meanwhile, Martin performed only the essential tasks in the vineyard, and confined his winery work mainly to keeping the casks filled so air wouldn't harm the wines inside. He devoted most of his time to Elsie's well-being and comfort. He kept her hours happy with little surprises: each day a new record or delightful book, some tantalizing new perfume or lotion, an amazing new gadget, or a few wild scarlet delphiniums picked along the moun-tain road.

And almost every other night they went out to dinner. Actu-ally this was to save her strain, but Martin made of each dinner a veritable party, finding romantic, out-of-the-way restaurants and taking along champagne and several of their finest wines. They felt like young lovers again, stealing off together, drinking the wines they loved, laughing and talking, whispering sweet endearments. And as they drove homeward, Martin put his arm about her and they sang favorite songs.

But these long drives up and down their rough, curving moun-tain road came to be a trial for Elsie, Martin could see. So one day he found a charming house for them in the valley and surprised her with it, as a "temporary convenience" until she was strong again. Elsie was excited over it, loved the house.

Elsie's doctor still insisted that she was doing well. She looked as pretty as ever, and relaxed, with all the rest she was getting and the good times with Martin. Not for many years had the two of them been able to enjoy such long, unbroken hours together in just having fun.

"Papa, this really has been the happiest year of my whole life," she told Martin one day. "Because we've been so close and unpres-sured. Every minute is crammed with joy."

Martin, however, was finding it difficult to maintain his bright-ly confident manner. Night after night he lay awake—wondering, torturing, as he listened to Elsie's breathing, because it seemed to have changed somehow. "Could I be losing my mind from worry?" he'd ask himself.

Martin would never have believed, had someone told him, that a time would come when he'd no longer care about his mountain. But so it was, now. Some days he would drive up there, of a morning while Elsie slept late, and he'd look over the vineyards that he'd once thought of as the very center of his being.

One mid-spring morning when he was up there, he realized sharply how much work needed to be done. The vines were reaching out, making fountains of fresh green leaves. Fortunately, he had managed to get them pruned in time, likewise disked around the young vines.

And now the vines must be sulfur-dusted regularly to protect them from mildew. But he felt no urge to do anything. He couldn't even bear to think about it. Looking off over his vineyards now, the spell of their beauty simply emphasized the vast loneliness that closed over him—so terrible an agony that he never wanted to see the place again, if he had to come here without Elsie. Tears streamed down his face as he stood there looking about the resplendent mountaintop, once so passionately loved and tended. Then he turned and drove down the long winding road to the valley.

A man he knew had expressed great interest in buying his mountaintop: a wealthy wine and liquor merchant whose son was recently graduated from UC Davis's Department of Viticulture and Enology. So the next day Martin arranged to sell it—the vineyards, the house, the whole mountain. But he still kept the keys to his wine cellar, where he'd continue to hold his wines and care for them, at least for the present.

It consoled Martin to think what a great boon the place would be for a viticultural graduate. With his family now owning this splendid winegrowing estate, he could put all his recent learning to immediate practical application.

The father brought his son up to see this wonderful gift. After an introductory tour was conducted by Martin, the estate's creator, the son seemed a bit perturbed. "It must be a terrible job to take care of a big spread like this," he commented. Then the lad's mother spoke up, saying he should look upon it as a nice retreat; he could bring his friends up to have drinks and enjoy the view. It needn't be a heavy responsibility, she assured him. Workers could do whatever needed to be done. "Why feel you must *do* something, dear?" she asked. "We can afford to maintain your life so you needn't feel pressured to do anything at all except enjoy yourself."

When Martin next came up to his cellar he found the young viticulturist standing out on the porch, looking off into space and actually appearing disconsolate. Perhaps he didn't know how to get into action. For surely, as a man, he would want to escape his mother's coddling!

So to get him started, Martin grabbed a hoe and asked the fellow to accompany him over to the edge of the vineyard. There, as he vigorously applied the hoe to the soil at the base of a vine, he explained that all the vines needed such hoeing to aerate the heavy clay soil around their roots and remove weeds. Then he placed the hoe into the young man's hands. "You're the master here now!" he said as he walked away. But when he looked back, he was staggered to see the lad merely tapping the top of the soil around the vine, not actually *hoeing*.

Martin was mightily puzzled. The fellow had graduated in viticulture. Didn't he intend to work in his own vineyard? Days went by. To Martin, visiting his cellar there, it was apparent that the new owner only came to the mountain occasionally, with a friend or two. And then he sat in the house drinking wine and looking out over the view of the valley below. Martin realized that the beautiful mountain vineyards he had planted certainly would not survive without someone who really cared for them. This young man was not even interested enough to hire skilled workers to tend them properly. So Martin became greatly discouraged.

But he had a worse worry now.

Always Elsie had loved champagne. As they drank it now at the sunset hour, she seemed to delight in it more than ever before. But this posed a problem: they'd taken just a limited amount of champagne with them when they sold Masson, thinking it would last until they produced their own again. As the supply dwindled, Martin laughingly put it on a quota basis. They could drink only so much a month, he said.

Whenever she could, Elsie wheedled him out of an extra bottle. It became a playful game between them. Martin wished to let his dear Madame Pinot have all the champagne she wanted. But he couldn't. For if he did, she'd know he had lost faith in her recovery. So he thought of a solution. Much as he disliked working much up at the wine cellar right now, he did. He added rock candy syrup and yeast to a cask of chardonnay and then bottled it for a secondary fermentation. Then he went home and announced to Elsie that they now could drink all the sparkling wine they wished—for that day he'd begun to make more. Before long they'd be rich again in champagne!

When Martin imparted the joyous news, for a split-second Elsie was stunned. Then, recovering quickly, she said, "Oh, how heavenly!" Because now she was facing a new problem. For the past few days she'd lost all pleasure in drink and food. How long could she keep up pretending to enjoy her champagne, without Martin's noticing? When that day came, he would know what she knew already. She wanted to fend off for as long as she could the sorrow that would come to him then.

And in the early spring of 1951 that day did come, in a different way. Suddenly a pain shot through her side, and she winced in agony. Martin saw her stiffen against the hurt and clutch her side. They looked at each other, congealed with fear. When they phoned her doctor, he said it was no doubt a neuralgic reaction to the change of weather. But they weren't convinced. Nothing the local doctor had done or said had proven worth much.

It was time to check with some outstanding specialist, Martin declared. Initially Elsie's older sister Marie, a registered nurse, had arranged with the local doctor, a friend of hers, to perform the "trivial operation" on Elsie. Martin blamed Marie for placing Elsie in the hands of a doctor he now believed incompetent, for never even sending a tissue specimen from the original lesion for laboratory analysis.

He rushed Elsie up to the Palo Alto Clinic. There he was able to obtain, with some difficulty, an emergency consultation with the eminent physician Dr. Albert Snell. After giving Elsie a thorough examination and x-rays, the great doctor paused. Gently he asked in what manner they'd like her condition presented. Some, he explained, insisted on details; others preferred him just to outline his recommended treatment.

Elsie looked up at him, her brown eyes never calmer or more searching. "Doctor, I want to know everything ... all there is."

The x-rays, Dr. Snell then had to admit, showed the worst lung involvement he had ever seen. Cells from the cancerous tumor in her breast had spread there—and elsewhere too. Nothing could remedy the condition.

There was not the quiver of an eyelash as Elsie heard the fatal verdict. Nor did her hand tremble as she wrote something on a bit of paper she'd taken from her purse and slipped to the doctor, who was talking now with a shattered Martin. On the slip she had written but two words: "How long?" And the doctor scratched his answer in one word, and dropped the paper into her hand: "Weeks." That meant less than months, she realized. But more than one week.

Now was the true test of how much she loved Martin, Elsie thought, as they walk toward the car, holding hands and speaking not a word. She must use all her knowledge of him, gained over the years, to spare him pain in every way she could. She must plan the difficult days ahead. Arrange everything. For he'd be in no condition to decide anything; that she knew. But she must hurry. There might be even less time than the doctor thought.

But that wasn't enough. How could she help him survive beyond her going? For Martin was not one who could live alone. He'd shown so clearly, in the past year especially, his utter dependence on their love, as the vitalizing element of his life—of his tremendous drive and his intensely creative spirit. To others Martin might appear a pillar of strength and she a delicate, protected creature. But she had long realized that not only was she capable of prodigious labor in helping him in his work, but she also supplied the central core and purpose of his existence.

All these thoughts she had as Martin drove toward Saratoga. She knew he strained every nerve just to hold himself together like this in order to get them home safely. Each word she spoke would be anguish, yet it had to be said. "Martin, you must promise me one thing," Elsie finally said. "No matter what you may feel now, you must marry again. You *must.* That is my greatest worry now."

"Not that," Martin said, turning even more pallid, and trying to keep a steady hold on the steering wheel. "You know I'll promise you anything else, my darling. But don't ask me that."

"I understand. But it's so important—that's why I must say it quickly. I can't risk any chance of its going unsaid."

"Don't!" he cut her off. "I just can't talk about it." He looked straight ahead, his lips tightly compressed.

She squeezed his hand. "I know. Just remember always what I said. We won't speak of it again."

When they reached home, she stepped from the car into his arms. Quite unbelievably, her eyes were shining with anticipation. "Papa, do you know what I want now? ... A bottle of champagne!"

Martin was trying to be equally gallant and emotionally steady, but his hand fumbled as he turned the cork of the bottle. "To the Good Life!" he said. This had always been their favorite toast, especially when luck went against them.

"And it *is* good, to the very last drop, like our champagne!" Elsie murmured.

They drank deeply of the wine, looking into each other's eyes all the while. And the terrible tension of their knowledge began to ease. Soon they were able to speak almost normally again, of everyday things. And as they went on drinking the champagne—Elsie drinking despite her recent aversion—they found themselves almost gay again, for a little while.

"How many times do you suppose we've had another bottle of champagne, after a party?" Elsie asked. "Just the two of us, when all the others have gone?"

"Maybe hundreds," Martin said wistfully. "We've always had such a wonderful time together, haven't we?"

"That's it," Elsie said. "I figure we've had at least twice as much fun as any other couple. I don't know any husband half as loved as you. Nor any wife so happy as I. And I had a happy girlhood too. So all in all I'm ready to settle for what I've already had in life. It's been so good, I hate to give it up. Still, I've lived twice as much as anyone else my age, by my standards ... so in a sense I'm very lucky."

"I guess everyone's luck runs out sooner or later," Martin said. "You and I couldn't hope to live on forever. Still ..." His voice grew hoarse and he tried to hold back the tears.

"You know how we should look at it?" Elsie proposed. "It's bad luck, and we can't change that. But we *can* decide how we're going to accept it. We needn't let it spoil any of our days at all. We'll go right on living as we've always done. Don't you think that's the best way?"

Martin could see it was. And he marveled at her—at how she was now taking life's most terrible moment in her hands, and handling it quite as beautifully as she had life's very best.

Elsie felt fortunate that she at least could set the procedure that would make the difficult days ahead more normal. She asked Martin to promise her just a few things. The household should be run as usual, with no tiptoeing, whispering, or sickroom atmosphere. She would never be taken to a hospital, but would be allowed to run her own home to the end. No strangers would attend her—only her sister Marie, trained as a nurse.

And lastly, looking gravely at Martin, she said, "Then I want a bottle of sleeping pills always on the night-table where I can reach them. I won't take them unless things get unbearable. But having them there will give me confidence and control—over whatever comes. . . . You understand?"

Martin certainly did. That's the way *he* would want it too.

All went well for a few days. But Martin's nerves couldn't handle the awful emotional strain. Suddenly one night he broke down and cried hysterically. Elsie, devastated by his sorrow and her helplessness to remedy it, sobbed with him, uncontrollably, until she began to cough. The coughing seemed to tear her apart.

Martin, realizing the damage done to her lungs, was stricken with such remorse that he held his emotions in an iron grip ever afterwards. There were no more outbursts. But from then on, Elsie failed rapidly. She often found it difficult to speak. Then she'd write Martin notes, in rapidly deteriorating handwriting, on many matters, including planning the meals, which she insisted on doing for the woman now cooking for them.

It was this woman who mailed Elsie's letter to me. It was but a few lines, scrawled in a handwriting I didn't recognize: "Don't mention this note when writing us. I have only weeks to live ... this pesky cancer! I'm so worried about Martin. His nerves are shattered. You're the only one who can help him. Don't come now, but later. I count on you. With all my love, Elsie."

What a terrible shock! When I'd visited them several months earlier, with my son Peter along with me, Elsie had seemed in normal good health. Through the years, she and Martin had been "family" to me. Always there when I asked for their advice or emotional support. Or just needed to get away from things. Visiting them on their mountaintop, invariably I'd get a fresh perspective on my life.

It was well that Elsie hadn't asked her sister Marie, now attending her, to mail the letter. She might have destroyed it, as she was showing extreme jealousy and resented Elsie's showing affection for anyone but herself. Even Martin. She hovered over her younger sister constantly, guarding her last days like a veritable lioness.

And it was Marie who prevented Martin from keeping his most solemn and sacred promise to Elsie. The hour came when Elsie could bear no more, and reached for her sleeping pills. They were gone! She asked Martin for them, her eyes wide with terror and pleading. (The last few days she'd begun to speak again, since increased morphine helped her endure the effort and pain involved.)

He looked for the pills. It was true: the bottle had disappeared. He knew instantly that Marie had taken it. When he found her, he demanded the pills.

Marie turned on him with fury. "I removed them! God is taking my little sister soon enough, without tempting her with sleeping pills right within her reach!"

"But I promised her!" Martin entreated. "She said she'd take them only if her pain grew unbearable. The time has come, and she wants them! Where are they?" He was frantic.

Marie folded her arms across her chest. With set lips and eyes blazing, she said, "You'll get those pills over my dead body! I'm keeping my baby sister with me as long as possible. If she dies from taking sleeping pills, so help me God I'll charge you with murder!"

The two looked at each other with a hatred beyond all enmity. Martin finally went back to Elsie. And choking back his emotion, he told her why he couldn't keep his promise to her.

"My own sister could say that?" Elsie asked, disbelieving. And closed her eyes. Martin gripped her hand in silence. For a long time he sat there. If she had to suffer long, he never would forgive himself. He'd just have to keep his word to her despite the consequences. As he sat there, she lapsed into a tortured unconscious state, evidently of the kind she'd tried to tell him about lately—which made it too frightening to go on, together with the pain.

The doctor again stepped up her morphine injections, instructing Martin so he could give them in between his calls. Marie was right there, every time Martin injected the morphine. Each time she counted the tiny glass vials to be sure he'd given no more than the exact amount prescribed.

Martin's tension grew explosive as Elsie's condition worsened. Now she was fighting for every breath. He frequently had to endure watching the doctor plunge a long needle into her lungs to draw off accumulated fluid to relieve her breathing.

Finally he could stand it no longer. The next morphine injection he gave ahead of schedule, before Marie got there. Deliberately he added several extra tiny vials, to inject a lethal dose. Then he collapsed on his knees, his arms reaching out to cradle Elsie as he broke into wild sobs.

Marie came rushing in, quickly counted the vials, and flew into a rage. "It's done!" Martin cried. "What can you do about it now? You can't undo it, thank God. Report me to the police if you want. Sue me. I don't give a goddamn! For she'll finally be at peace."

By now Elsie was gone. With a groan Martin fled from the room. He went out into the night, taking a bottle of champagne and a goblet. Leaning weakly against a tree, he drank of the wine, looking around at the foggy night, waiting and hoping for the champagne to make his grief a little less overwhelming. Gradually it did seem to help detach him slightly from the nightmare of reality.

After a long time he was roused from his exhausted state by noise and movement from the house. Figures were emerging through the fog, bearing a stretcher. "Great God, they're taking Elsie away!" he suddenly realized. He called for them to stop. And with what seemed enormous effort, as in a dream, he made his way toward them, holding his champagne glass steadily in his hand.

He drew the sheet from Elsie's face and looked down upon her, in desperate despair. Lovingly, he leaned over and kissed her for the last time—lingeringly and full on the lips. Then dipping his fingers in his glass of champagne, he sprinkled a few drops on her forehead as a final blessing ... the champagne she so loved.

"Sleep, my dear little Madame Pinot," he whispered, covering her again with the sheet, as tears streamed down his face.

"Are you mad?" Marie cried as she tore off the sheet and dabbed at Elsie's forehead, where the champagne drops glistened in the light from the house. "What will people think ... if you carry on like this?"

"People! What people?" Martin was shocked into reality. "Nobody is to see her again."

"You mean to say her casket will be covered at the funeral?"

"There will be no funeral, no memorial service," Martin said, looking at Marie in final retaliation. "She'll be cremated. Elsie and I arranged it long ago. Our ashes are to be scattered together in the vineyard someday. When we're both gone."

No minister's eulogy would have been adequate for Elsie Ray. But there was John Steinbeck's durable handwritten inscription in his book *Cup of Gold*, when she was very much alive: *"Á Elsie qui es (espero) mi copa de oro—y qué oro!"* Ah yes, she was (hopefully) his, Martin's, and everyone's cup of gold. And what gold!—as Steinbeck had said, tempering his awe in Spanish.

Now Martin had to live his life without her. Somehow.

PART V

DOMAIN IN THE MAKING

1951-1976

32

Renascent Winegrower

During the weeks following Elsie's departure, Martin frantically tried to adjust to her permanent absence from his life. Not so much adjust—for that's too positive a term for any goal then possible to him—but merely to try to keep on living without caring. He was almost belligerently set against caring for *anything*.

He did make an effort, though, mostly to gratify the pleadings of friends. They'd assured him it would help to travel, get away from familiar surroundings. So he tried short sojourns with them—couldn't face anything more extensive. But that only plunged him into deeper depths of despondency. He also made visits to city friends, seeing urban places he hadn't seen in years. Yet nothing stirred him, to rouse him from his gloom.

Coping with his loss somehow seemed more bearable when he didn't seek distractions, but just drove up the mountain to tend his wines still cellared there: to fill and to rack; to wash casks, drain, and sulfur them. His wines still needed him—which struck a responsive chord in him somewhere, even if the old joy in his work was gone.

I'd received several rather incoherent notes from Martin. One said something about the river finally reaching the sea, but I couldn't figure out exactly what he meant. If and when Elsie died, wouldn't he say so? Each week or so I wrote brief letters to them both, not knowing what was really happening. I was shocked early one morning to receive a telegram from Martin. No ordinary wire, this—a long and scary one, clearly a love-and-farewell message. My seventeen-year-daughter, Bobo, thought so too. Could the ever-indomitable Martin Ray possibly come to suicide?

Right away I got on the phone. No response from his end. So quickly I called Elsie's sister Marie in San Francisco and read her the frightening wire; asked her to lose no time, try to locate Martin at once. Had I learned of their bitter enmity, never to be eased, I wouldn't of course have appealed to her. She evidently didn't wish to disclose that, but instead promised to drive down to Saratoga right away and check on him.

That was early morning. I heard nothing from her all day. By that time I was sure something dreadful had happened. But it turned out she didn't go till evening, though the San Jose area was only a forty-minute drive from her home. No doubt she hoped he'd killed himself by then, by whatever means—which to her mind would be what he deserved. Instead, Martin returned home almost simultaneously with Marie's arrival. She told him of my distressed phone call, then immediately left, having fulfilled her promise to me.

He phoned me at once. What relief, to hear his voice! "Rusty darling, you're really all right?" I cried. "I've been so terribly worried!"

He couldn't understand my alarm at first. He'd been up on the mountain all day with his wines. Well, yes, he *had* sent that wire—which by now he'd forgotten about, for it seemed so long ago. And it was true, he *had* meant it as farewell, he then remembered. Around midnight he'd gone to the San Francisco airport: he intended to fly to Burgundy, live there among the vines and try to forget. He'd wired me goodbye from the airport. But in his emotional state he'd forgotten completely that he needed a passport! So he came back—drove up to the mountain instead.

"Do come up tomorrow, you and Bobo. I need you!" he entreated. Great God, this was the first time in my life that the vibrant Martin Ray ever *needed* me! It must be a good sign. Now he intended to live. I knew we could cheer him up—help revive that great spirit of his. So off we headed for Saratoga in the morning.

When we arrived, he was out on the veranda of his valley home, a lonely figure. Then I was in his arms. "Rusty!" The old nick in my heart from college days went ping—burst wide open. I loved him madly. Always had, always would. I felt somehow that I'd come home at last—to all that I ever really wanted.

Martin did look much too thin. Evidently he'd blanked out on food as on all else. I rushed to make him something good to eat. But in the kitchen I could find no cooking equipment. "Oh, I just threw them out after I'd used them," he said. "I figured I wouldn't be around to need them anymore." Sure enough, I went out and found all his pots, pans, dishes, glassware, and tableware tossed in the garbage. So he'd been planning on leaving for Burgundy (though not giving a thought to the passport!). But in the end he came back to his wines. Prophetic.

We wanted Peter and Barclay to join us too, and finally managed to get them on the phone. The worst had been trying to reach

Peter in rural Cuba, where he'd been all summer on some Harvard field biology project. The search for Barclay was almost as bad; he was spending the summer out in the Mojave Desert working on some Caltech-connected outer-space probe. They were both about to leave anyway, they said, as it was summer's end. So they'd come at once!

Next day at the airport, after Peter had zoomed in from Cuba, at first we didn't recognize him. He was tanned a deep bronze, garbed like a native Cuban, and bent forward under the weight of a huge bag with all his possessions slung over his shoulder. Also clutching a wicked-looking machete in one hand, with only its tip sheathed in a leather holster.

Peter went a little berserk with pleasure at seeing Rusty again. Both boys had always doted on him. Peter kept bursting into Spanish, making it a bit confusing to follow; but as he said, he'd been speaking Spanish all summer. Martin had a special love for Peter. (And Elsie always had said that if she could have chosen a son, he would be exactly like Peter Martin.)

Then Barclay came roaring up from the desert, and leaped out of his Jeep to give Martin a mighty bear hug. I never saw Barc's face so lighted up, his eyes agleam with such quicksilver radiance.

So we had the most wonderful get-together imaginable on this glorious late summer day. And of course we all had to drive up the mountain—deserted in these days—and have a picnic supper there.

First, of course, Martin had to show us through his wine cellar, for the boys long had been intrigued with his winegrowing. And young as they were—nineteen—they already had developed quite an appreciation for his wines, as over the years we'd been sent many a case of them by Martin and Elsie.

Martin had timed it perfectly, for champagne at the sunset hour. We all took readily to his ritual of having champagne to give a happy salute to the end of each marvelous day. And this special day surpassed any day we could imagine. As we drank our champagne, the gold-struck vines gradually were caught in a pink alpine glow all about us. We proffered enthusiastic toasts to everyone and everything dearest to our hearts, including a lovely toast to Elsie.

In a flash, it seemed Martin had recovered his dash and spirit—really found himself, and a purpose for living, again. And as we finished our champagne, he asked for a vote. How about a permanent Martin Ray Family Fivesome? . . . Unanimous!

"Glorious idea!" I murmured. "Just like my college dream when I was so daffy about you!"

"What?" Martin was shocked. "Walter always told me you disliked me—were only nice to me because I was his friend! So of course I kept a careful distance . . ."

We looked at each other dumbfounded. Now, for the first time, we understood. Incredible to think we'd let Walter so bamboozle us way back then. And by now, what could we do but just laugh over our youthful credulity.

My three children missed our wedding by the ocean in mid-September of 1951, at the Santa Barbara Biltmore Hotel, as they all had returned to college.

Having his loneliness amply filled now by a rousing "instant" family's warm embrace, Martin regained his terrific spirit. With a renewed reason for living, he found he even could play again. We did have a fantastic, dreamlike honeymoon by the Pacific. One night under the full moon, we raced up and down the beach. How vividly I still recall Martin in sudden exuberance tossing his fine Borsalino hat far out into the Pacific waves! And when we finally returned late to the hotel, we found the lobby evidently just deserted by some big party. Nobody was around, but all manner of fine wine bottles had been left, both opened and unopened, which we had fun exploring. And one morning we were served breasts of pheasant in our room for breakfast, with freshly baked croissants.

Only one element intruded into our quiet hideout in Santa Barbara. Someone had tipped publicists off to our wedding, and the news was noted nationwide in Walter Winchell's column, with a mention of my memoir *We Kept Mother Single,* recently published and already a hit. A rollicking account of the great life that the children and I had created on our own, it was the first humorous book on the "broken home," taking an upbeat attitude toward single parenting.

Apparently it tickled the press to make a tie-up of bestseller author with the maker of top wines. So a flood of wires and phone calls came in, contributing a flurry of attention that we'd thought to avoid on our honeymoon. Still, we felt gratified that others were pleased with our happiness.

We were having such a wonderful time together we felt we could stay there forever. But one morning Martin phoned a friend in Saratoga whom he'd asked to keep track of the grapes ripening in his old vineyards—for he doubted that the new owners were even watching them. He learned that the sugar in the pinot noir grapes was nearing the desirable 23.5° Brix, and that nobody was around up there to pick them. All very odd. Martin promptly announced that we had to rush back and have a vintage. He had decided that we should save the crop on the mountain though it no longer belonged to him.

Most fortunately at this point, Martin arranged to buy back the property. It had been held unchanged, as if fate was watching over it. Great good luck this time for Martin Ray—to have been able first to sell it instantly when he needed to devote all his time to Elsie, and then to get it back when again it was vitally important to his life.

We moved at once from the valley house up to the little redwood home on the mountain, where we belonged now. Martin Ray right away picked up where he'd left off, as winegrower par excellence. And just in time, for the pinot noir vintage rushed up to meet us!

"Couldn't be a more appropriate initiation for you," said Martin, "since you are the new Madame Pinot now." He reminded me that the female head of our family must always be called Madame Pinot. "We've named our *blanc de noir* sparkling wine in her honor, you know—Madame Pinot champagne." I loved that. I was fast discovering that marrying Martin Ray meant coming into all manner of fascinating traditions of his own creation—which made it all such marvelous fun.

Of course I hadn't gotten into all the vintage *work* yet. But I soon learned this: it's only through the terrific work that you catch the real spirit of creating wine. Once you've gone through this enthralling experience, you're hooked forever. There's nothing else in the world like it. No wonder Charlie Chaplin went berserk on the subject!

Martin and Peter and I carried on the vintage mostly by ourselves, with several friends joining us for picking grapes far and wide over the mountain slopes. Luckily Peter wasn't due at Harvard yet, was still at UC Berkeley finishing some experiments, so was able to come, as well as Martin's dear friend Dr. Maynard Amerine from UC Davis.

We were about to start crushing when Martin said to me, "Oh, Madame Pinot always pours the first box of grapes into the crusher. It's our tradition. So hop up there by the crusher and let's go!"

I leapt up on the crusher platform and Peter handed me the first big wooden box of tight-clustered indigo-blue grapes, from a huge stack behind him. Martin had rolled a puncheon-fermenter out from the cellar on a dolly, and now switched on the crusher's motor. The blades inside the stainless steel crusher began to spin. Now, my big moment. I tipped the box, and with a churning roar the blades caught the grapes. What a tremendous fragrance exploded into the air as the blades whirred! Stems were torn off and shot out one end, as the crushed grapes and juice cascaded down into the puncheon below.

"Ah, that's pinot noir!" Martin exclaimed with pleasure, breathing in the rich fruity smell. Dipping a glass in to taste the juice, his face lighted up. "The acid held!" he proclaimed happily. "I was afraid we'd delayed too long. But we've got both high acidity and sugar!" We all then had to taste it.

"I never smelled such fragrance as when I poured those grapes into the crusher!" I said. I would notice a different aroma during fermentation, Martin pointed out—like fresh, spicy mincemeat. "It seems to expand—till it fills the whole cellar," he said. "If you know this smell, nobody can fool you about pinot noir."

He switched on the motor for another round of crushing. This went on and on, filling many puncheon-fermenters to levels safe for fermenting. Then some of the pinot noir grapes were put in the press basket and lightly pressed, yielding bright pink juice for creating the brilliant sang de pinot champagne. (At 23.5° sugar, the juice was already too sweet to make the more tart Madame Pinot champagne from the free-run juice.) And the leftover crush was then added to the fermenters. I saw how these separate crushings and fermentings complicated the pinot noir operation greatly, adding many hours of extra work.

Then, to extend that round of vintage for many days more, right on pinot noir's heels a week or so later came the chardonnay, so golden and gorgeous. So it went, every day, often through the night, until the cabernet sauvignon grapes from the young vines were vintaged in mid-October.

The very word "vintage" still brings back to me the tremendous excitement of my first vintage on the mountain: especially pouring in that first box of grapes into the crusher as it roared, enveloping me in a cloud of rich pinot noir perfume. Also, later, seeming to swing back and forth endlessly the handle of that charming old basket-press—on our final chardonnay night blessed with a harvest moon, full and golden, overhead! Somehow such experiences are the very essence of a winegrower's life.

(Today, of course, it's quite different in most winery operations. Grapes are often picked by machines, systematically conveyed and then dumped into the crusher, which may even be located out in the field. Automated pumps douse the cap of pips and skins above the fermenting reds: no more punching down! The modern wine press performs its labors at the touch of a button. In some, inflated air bags steadily squash the grapes down. All this and more saves an enormous amount of work. Great, I suppose, for many winemakers. They no longer need to be involved in "hands-on" vintaging. Just let the machines do it all, with fancy electronic gadgets measuring and testing and calculating. Even substitute for tasting and smelling too. But where's the joy and fun in that? What vital role can you *feel*, just in pressing a switch?)

What great times Martin and I were enjoying together, at every turn! Yet I was also becoming aware that beneath his joyfulness and zest bubbled a cauldron of confused emotions. Often, right in the midst of our happiest moments, he would suddenly go to pieces, break into tears. "It's just the confusion," he'd explain.

I thought I understood how it could be—the jumbled images of the two women he loved and depended on, in past and present, as well as his hesitation to fully accept this unexpected new happiness, after all the pain of watching Elsie slowly die.

But initially I didn't realize how dangerous *any* confusion could be to his central nervous system, permanently damaged by that stroke of long ago. Then I asked him one day what had been the most valuable advice given to him years ago by the Stanford psychiatrist during his treatment regimen.

"To simplify," he answered. "If I had two problems, I *must* put one aside. Maybe for five minutes, or five months. Maybe forever. It wasn't as easy as you might think. I had to be tough with myself. But it worked. It saved me. Gradually the confusion subsided. At first it took tremendous willpower. Then it became my set approach: handle just one issue at a time, no more."

Now I understood him better. Even as to why he couldn't bear controversy. Argument meant tossing a second opinion at him, when he had geared himself to consider but one at a time . . . which of course had to be his own!

I must have been hard on Martin at first, in contrast to Elsie. As were my children. But for a long time I wasn't aware that during Martin's recovery period, Elsie had had that year of psychiatric counseling—just to learn how to keep everything around Martin as tranquil as possible. Martin could have benefited greatly had I too learned how to smooth his path. For as a dynamic, energetic man, Martin often got himself into high-tension conflicts in spite of the instructions given him long before, which he tried to follow religiously. Elsie was skilled at spotting potential disasters and could step in, ward off his taking on too much. Many times I regretted not having had that ability—especially toward the end of Martin's life.

I never was "sent down the mountain," as Martin liked to tell of Paul Masson's precipitous ostracisms. But only by the grace of God I wasn't! For I'd grown up in a family devoted to arguing—about politics, art, food, you name it—especially around the dinner table. And the family life I'd created with my own three children continued this rowdy habit. To us debating was sheer diversion.

So when first married to Martin, I was always flubbing. He'd say something and I'd pipe up, "But on the other hand ..." and start expounding an alternative point of view, with fervor. Just as a matter of interest, not that I necessarily cared pro or con. His face would cloud up, so I had sense enough to stop. Though I was puzzled over why the least tilt toward controversy upset him so. He certainly wasn't that way in college days! We'd often argue like mad then, about anything and everything, and he seemed to delight in it, the rougher it got.

What puzzled me was that he still *looked* as easygoing as ever. So I could understand how people would misread him. Somehow, the neurological damage done by that early stroke must have re-wired his brain. Like a powder-keg, it should have carried an exter-nal warning tag in red: "BEWARE! DON'T ARGUE!"

I found it rather fascinating to study the tautly strung indi-vidual he had become, seen now close up—so opposite to the man I thought I'd known so well. I learned to watch his face for signals, noting what kinds of talk and actions disturbed him. I caught on fast, and came to certain intriguing conclusions. All making me more prudent.

Accustomed as I was, before marrying Martin, to have people around me freely and noisily expressing their ideas and readily challenging others', it was difficult at first for me to keep disagree-ments under wrap. But I knew that Martin's well-being, even survival, depended on maintaining a calm, controversy-avoiding household. I regarded this as gracefully accommodating myself to a beloved spouse's chronic disability. Others not as close to him, unaware of this vulnerability, naturally misunderstood his dis-concerting reactions that could come whenever his opinions were challenged or when he was in the company of someone who loved to argue just for the sheer sake of argument. And my own three children—all quite unaccustomed to paternalism and still teen-agers, at that time of life notoriously inclined toward questioning authority of any kind imposed upon them—were inadvertently apt to stir things up in the new family nest. Most of the time, at least, they were away in college, with their periodic visits noisily punctu-ating our usually tranquil household while adding youthful high spirits.

Fortunately, on marrying Martin I saw my role ideally as pro-viding for him the feeling that no break in marital bonding had ever really taken place—that he could carry on his life quite as usual. And I think I successfully created that illusion. Years later, Martin confided that our two images—Elsie's and mine—somehow had gradually blended, so he came to think of her and me almost as one person. He proposed then that we might combine the years of the two marriages. Someday, when they were added up, we'd be able to celebrate our golden wedding anniversary! I thought that a colossal idea, and we toasted it in champagne. Alas, we wouldn't quite reach that fifty-year mark.

33

A Wind in the Night

By THE SPRINGTIME OF 1952 Martin was up to entertaining visitors again, including many who'd kept in touch from earlier years. Our expanding social life naturally called for quarters greater than our house with its one large room. We'd also need accommodations for my children. When they came home from college for holidays and vacations, Martin often spoke of the future, when they—and before long their chosen mates and offspring—could take an active and perpetual part in sharing "the Good Life" that winegrowing offered to us here.

Martin found he'd fallen in love not just with me but with the challenging potential of having a whole family to help him develop and maintain this winemaking estate and to cherish and perpetuate its traditions. The whole enterprise of winemaking took on a new meaning and importance for him. It was no longer just an avid dedication of his own, but something that could involve and inspire three young lives, reshaping them in special ways. Having had no offspring, Martin took very seriously this unaccustomed role of paterfamilias. (Elsie once told me she realized after his stroke that Martin's nervous system never would be able to endure all the commotion attending babies and young children—which meant they must have no children.)

With quite a family around him now, Martin decided it was time to build the splendid big house he'd visualized at the very top of the mountain. He also needed a larger underground cellar for holding more wine, now that his young vineyards were coming into full production. So this was built first: a big concrete cellar, ample enough for all future needs. Rising above it would be the new house, made of redwood like the little house below that we loved, but on a more imposing scale.

This time Martin decided to take it easier with the construction. Rather than direct it all himself, he turned it over to a reputable contractor. We were entranced with the picturesque house as it was abuilding—its rich, warm redwood color, and how it stretched across the very crest of the mountain in such a relaxed, natural way. Its wide brick veranda, surrounding the entire structure, was roofed over so that even on rainy days we could stroll around, wine glass in hand, enjoying the glorious view in every direction.

So accustomed to directing past building projects, Martin now found it hard to keep from involving himself in every detail of this house, too. Apart from wanting precise workmanship, he insisted that the structure should be absolutely secure and solid. Perhaps this came from his working largely with the solidity of concrete in the past. He insisted on using again, as when rebuilding Masson's old winery, that "eight-sack" mixture so hard it was used mainly for gun emplacements. He'd always meet with grinning disbelief from contractors and architects when they heard of it. But that way he was confident of having maximum protection from the elemental hazards of fire, earthquake, and storm.

The contractor, however, resisted being bossed about by Martin. In a notable and ultimately fatal example, as the covered walkway around the house was being finished, Martin wanted all the staunch uprights supporting the veranda roof to be bolted into the concrete base under the bricked porch, to be sure they'd hold absolutely securely.

"Not *hold*, with all the weight of this roof on them?" the contractor scoffed indignantly. This was the heaviest roof imaginable for a porch, he declared. The posts were solid, sturdy, certainly secure, without going to a lot of unnecessary fussing with them, as Martin demanded. So for the sake of accord, Martin finally gave the man his way. He'd just finish the job himself later, he decided, by drilling and bolting the posts into the concrete below, to get absolute security.

Finally our dream house was finished. You drove up the mountain, rounded the last turn, and behold! There it was, reclining so enchantingly across the very summit. Its four-sided veranda commanded a panoramic view. You could look eastward clear across the whole Santa Clara Valley and northward toward the southern end of San Francisco Bay. To the west and south, you saw fold after fold of forested slopes ascend into the cool reaches of the Santa Cruz Mountains. All vistas were visible even from within the house, through huge plate-glass windows.

Martin brought up all the beautiful furnishings he and Elsie had collected over the years, but held in storage for some time. How I loved those gorgeous deep-pile white rugs that gave the place an aura of exotic luxury! I brought my own treasured furnishings too. My curved coral sofa never before looked so beautiful as here in the big livingroom. Our commingled contributions added up to a splendor even beyond our maddest envisioning.

Our expansive master bedroom was the loveliest I'd ever seen, with its sky-blue Chinese rugs and a great antique mirror on the wall behind the king-size bed. A second, smaller bedroom could be used by our children and by guests.

The kitchen was the last room to be completed. After the walls were painted, the most up-to-date appliances moved in. Best of all was the cozy dining area with a raised-hearth fireplace, where already Martin kept great oak logs burning, so we could sit and toast ourselves whenever we came in from the cold. For autumn was racing into winter.

We moved in officially on the first of December, spending all day transferring all our clothing and valuables from the little house below. We finished the work and decorating just in time for the first big party to be given in the new house. Barclay and twenty of his Caltech male friends were coming, along with Stanford gals invited to add to the merriment.

Such a wonderful house—and such a happy young crowd, dining and dancing in the big room! At a late hour, as we saw them off—Barc going with them—we noticed sudden strong winds blowing. We collapsed happily in our beautiful new bedroom.

But the gods must have looked down on us and become angrily envious. For later that night we were roused from sleep by the damndest noise imaginable. It sounded like pile-drivers pounding at our house: BANG BANG BOOM!

We sprang out of bed. A wind of almost cyclonic fury had hit, carrying driving rain from a wholly unaccustomed direction, the southeast. Martin switched on the porch floodlights. We were thunderstruck! The ferocious wind had picked up at its base the corner upright supporting the porch roof, blasting it upward and hurling the roof high, in great waves. Shortly, one by one, it lifted *all* supports, banging them fiercely against the veranda tiles. Soon the entire porch roof was shaking like a blanket, in ever wilder waves, in savage downswings smashing and hurling supports.

Damnation, if that fool contractor only had bolted those posts into the concrete base as he'd asked him to do! Martin cursed. He hurriedly dressed in his ranch clothes and rushed out to get ropes, hoping to tie down the uprights. But the wind, surely over 100 miles per hour, hurled him the entire length of the porch—sixty-five feet—and over the end! He landed below on the porch furniture, all of which had already been pitched off. I ran to the phone to call someone—anyone!—for help. But of course the phone was dead, with all lines down in such a blast.

From a window I then watched Martin laboring under the flood-lights, trying to swing a rope from off and below the porch—an impossible feat, it seemed, in this wind. In a while Martin came in to tape his hands, which were bleeding badly. Just then the post on the south side facing the full storm came crashing down inward, smashing the big window there. The brutal wind now howled in, hurling torrents of rain, flooding our gorgeous big room.

Great God! It was horrifying, this utter hopelessness in fighting such savage forces. Both feeling totally desperate, we tried to move the big Steinway grand piano away from the window area, but couldn't budge it. I stacked rugs on top of it, but Martin then shouted at me to stop. Why do that? For if we couldn't stop the wind from howling in, all windows would go shortly. The roof of the house would blow off and we couldn't save anything.

Though panic was upon us, Martin somehow kept a cool head. He rushed out, brought in timbers and a tarp, pegged the tarp to a board he nailed above the vast gap where the window had been; nailed vertical boards from top to bottom, nailed the tarp all around. It never would have held on its own, but the south porch roof had fallen by now, sheltering the window gap from the storm's worst blasts.

Then the collapsing east roof began scraping the three huge windows there, nails digging at the glass. As crisis followed crisis, I lost all sense of time. The porch roof fronting our lovely big bed-room still held, miraculously, but the posts on the far south side seemed ready to go at any time.

With each moment our terror increased. Martin made a frantic effort to save the corner upright on the west end. He said if he couldn't anchor that one somehow, the whole house was lost. I watched him out the window, though he warned me to stay clear of all windows. He had a great mallet, was trying to straighten the upright that was leaning badly, and seemed to be making some headway. Then suddenly the roof leapt high above him, and he sprang clear just in time as it smashed down.

Finally he came in, gray with fatigue and despair. "I guess it's time we begin to take things down to the little house," he said gently, "since there's nothing further we can do now." It didn't mean giving up; just a desperate need for two worn-out people to forget the struggle long enough to get a bit of respite.

At this point we were far too tired to think logically or realistically about our predicament. Or really to think at all. What to take? I picked up breakfast needs, that's all: coffee pot, cream, bacon, eggs, bread, jam. I should have put on a warm coat; it was so cold, and I was just wearing a sweater. I must take these things now.... But what if the worst happened, and the house simply blew to pieces? I couldn't even ponder such a possibility. Not once in my sorry state did I think of the many valued, irreplaceable things I should take with me, just in case.

Martin, in his soaked and soiled old ranch clothes, came out lugging two big electric heaters and put them in the car. Then I drove off, to unload what I had into the little house and then come back for anything else we might need to get for now.

The storm had made the road down over the crest of the hill very muddy. After unloading, when I tried to turn the car around it mired deeply in the mud. I was panicky! For suddenly I realized how many vital things we'd need, which hadn't occurred to me earlier in my benumbed condition. Clothes—we had none at all down here!

I was frenetically trying to get the car out of the mud when Martin came running down through the storm. "Get this car out fast, there's fire blowing this way!" he cried. Fire? He yelled about the latest fatal disaster in a staccato message: the kitchen's windows blew out; wind blasted the fireplace embers all over, so fires caught on everywhere at once!

Now I saw a huge cloud of fire roaring down the slope toward us. Above, against the dark sky, the whole house was one gigantic blaze. For a few seconds I stood there paralyzed, in utter awe.

Martin quickly saw I'd never get the car out of the mud, so jumped in and wildly maneuvered it about until it cleared. Then he said, "Wait right here till you see I've gotten the other car out of the garage and safely to the gate. Then shoot up the hill as fast as you can, right through the flames, and follow me out. As he rushed away, he called back, "Don't dare move till you see I've made it toward the gate!"

I was terrified that he'd never make it out. Though the garage was offside from the house's roaring blast of flames, he'd have to back the car out right into the fire before heading toward the driveway. I couldn't see what was happening to him. Then my heart leapt with relief to see the car zooming out like a shot into the driveway, escaping through the fiery onslaught. So I gunned the engine in my car and practically flew up over the hill and straight through the blazing path of flames, following Martin out to safety.

Great God in Heaven, what an experience! We parked both cars safely way down below the gate. For all we knew, everything on the mountaintop would soon be incinerated.

"For Christsake, the wines!" Martin suddenly exploded. Of course the wine cellar under the house was solid concrete, including its slab ceiling. But could he possibly have left ajar the small iron door on the interior concrete wall? He wasn't sure, because sometimes he did, for extra ventilation. When building, he had this small opening left in the wall to make it easier for electricians and plumbers to get under the house. Now he realized that if that iron door to the gap wasn't closed now, the wine cellar would be exposed to the fire above. Fiery debris could pour down through that opening—and explode the casks. At the very least, the cask wines could be ruined by the smoke.

Martin hoped that via the east slope—comparatively safe because the wind came from that direction—he might approach the house close enough to slip down into the cellar entrance, go inside and make sure that the little door was closed. We ran together up the road. But when we saw the awful ferocity of the fire roaring across the cellar entrance, we knew he never could make it. Great fiery timbers and flaming objects sailed through the air. Just then we beheld a heartbreaking sight: our treasured Steinway grand burning, then toppling over onto the brick veranda, blowing up the bricks tumultuously with its intense heat.

We stood there, transfixed by the spectacle of that wild night. Weird sights were etched into my memory. Like the incredible moon, which the furious winds seemed to blow straight across the sky as they brushed all the clouds this way and that with angry thrusts. And the mammoth oak directly in the fire's path, at first blazing into a gigantic torch, now brutally flattened to the very ground by the fierce winds.

Massive waves of fire engulfed everything, sweeping over the mountaintop. The sky turned red with flames and bursting natural fireworks. Then the wild winds caught the fire up into one mighty holocaust. The roof blew off with a tremendous explosion— sent aluminum roofing strips far and wide, their sharp shrapnel edges shearing off everything in their northerly path, even limbs of staunch oak trees. Such hellish horror seemed to obliterate our personal fear of being hit. (For years thereafter, we'd keep finding these metal strips, some many miles away.)

From the start of the fire, we kept hoping that firefighters with trucks would arrive to help us. But no engines appeared. Afterwards we learned that the various fire departments in the valley, having received reports of a spectacular fire up in the mountains above them, squabbled over which one was responsible for our remote area—so *none* dispatched a single fire truck!

Certainly no one would choose to venture forth to fight a fire in such a storm. Firemen of course could never have saved the house, but they could have saved the massive garage and storage building, initially offside from the fire. The basket-press was standing in front of it, and eventually stray sparks fired its wood basket; that soon fired the garage door behind it. So helplessly we stood by and watched that burn too. Thus we lost that building with its invaluable farm machinery, winery equipment, and precious supplies.

For a while we even gave up hope for the little house nestled below the mountaintop, especially when the big oaks above it caught fire. By now we were too exhausted to move. But miracle of miracles! A lone man—and a stranger, at that—arrived just in time to climb atop the little house and, with the aid of rain starting to drizzle, put out the fire that had begun to burn the roof. This good Samaritan saved our sole remaining structure on the mountain.

So we did have our dear little house left to us after all, to collapse in—when all else was gone. And collapse we did, after what we'd been through: fighting the elemental forces like characters in a Greek tragedy.

34

Building Anew

Morning came belatedly to the little house on the mountaintop, to which we retreated after the wind and then fire had destroyed our beautiful new home. It was deadly still. The vicious storm had passed. When we first awakened, the awful conflagration seemed at first like a terrible nightmare.

We huddled close to the cheery log fire in the fireplace. With us was our little terrier dog, Joseph, brought indoors to give us consoling company; usually he stayed outside in his own house.

Each of us thought the other looked dreadfully pale and listless. And no doubt we were—like shell-shocked patients who'd barely survived some frightful bombardment. We were thankful that at least I'd managed to bring those few things last night for our breakfast.

As we drank coffee, our talk meandered vaguely. I said something to Martin about Hemingway's saying "to endure is to triumph, and perhaps triumph enough." But Martin was in no mood to accept those fine words now. "All right when you're on top of the world," he said, "but hollow comfort at a time like this." We both agreed with one conclusion of Hemingway's, anyway: that the price of enduring is very high, and must be paid again and again. Surely by now Martin Ray had paid his quota for enduring—many times over!

Martin was far from alert, except for the one immediate worry on his mind. First thing after breakfast, he'd have to face it: go into the cellar and find out if he'd left that small wall-door open as he'd feared. If so, were all his wines lost?

I went with him. It seemed something we should brave together. It was a beautiful sunny day on the mountain—so still, it didn't seem the same world as only a few hours ago. Incredible.

As we walked up the hill we tried not to look at the sight, but couldn't avoid it. The wild winds had blown debris far from the top, so the blackened summit looked barren, but for the two great fireplace chimneys left standing there, gaunt and lonely against the sky.

Martin's hand trembled as he singled out the cellar key on his key ring, then fumblingly opened the lock. He swung wide the heavy iron cellar door to a blast of acrid smoke. "Jesus!" he gasped. I squeezed his hand. There was nothing one could say.

All was black smudge. The concrete cellar walls, ceiling, floors were smoked black, as were the rows of casks. So obviously the small wall-door *had* been left ajar, and through that narrow opening had poured burning debris as well as smoke. One puncheon near it bore charred streaks and burned fragments, and the floor below was littered with blackened rubbish. The fire, however, had been unable to make further headway.

Seeing all this, Martin held little hope for any of the wines in cask. After all, even a cigarette smoked in a cellar could affect casked wines. Without a doubt they would taste smoky, he said. And if so, he'd lost his wines too. He didn't dare open a cask to check for sure until the cellar was completely washed down—everything wholly scrubbed, to remove all the smoky coating.

The cellar tragedy at least did give us something to *do* immediately; otherwise we'd be left to brooding and despair. We set to work at once, and friends came to join us. We washed down the complete cellar: ceiling, walls, floors were all scoured furiously with scrub brushes. And Martin gave a special washing to the cask exteriors.

This work took days. But when it was finished, the acrid smell was gone from the cellar. Then Martin could taste the wine? Not yet. The cellar must be completely dried out first, with the door left wide open for many days to air it thoroughly.

He was increasingly tense about this crucial test, for on it so very much depended. But one morning he faced it; went alone to the cellar, to have absolute quiet, no distractions. He tasted first from the cask just inside the door. If any cask was free of smoke, surely this would be the one. Carefully he drew off a sample with the glass wine thief. Just as he feared. He could identify, clearly and unmistakably, a smokiness both in smell and taste.

He returned to the little house, completely disheartened. All the wines were lost, he told me. The beautiful new house and the storage garage with its valuable belongings both gone . . . and now all his wines ruined as well.

Following the fire, we had also pondered the disturbing matter of insurance. Because Martin hadn't used the storage garage until recently, he had allowed the insurance on it to lapse and hadn't gotten around to insuring it again. So that proved a very bad, and needless, financial loss.

As to possible insurance on the big house, we held our breath. Did we have any or not? Up to the last few days it was insured only for building supplies used in construction. Martin now thought he remembered writing his agent a few days back, reporting the house now about finished, so thought it should be covered at least minimally until he had time to appraise things and insure it properly; and asked him to cover for $50,000. But he wasn't positive he'd mailed the letter. Or if he did, had the agent done anything about it right away? And if so, had he mailed the confirmation back? For if he hadn't, we had no insurance.

We had luck in a small way. When we got our mail, we were elated to find the agent's confirmation, mailed the very day before the fire! So that insurance, minimal though it was, came as a godsend—even if near meaningless when measured against our staggering losses. A mere drop in the bucket when adding up rebuilding costs and figuring the loss of all our uninsured furnishings, personal possessions, equipment, supplies. Perhaps worst of all was the ruination of all wines in cask. Except for the little house and the very minimum left in it when we moved out, we had lost everything.

And of course we had the children too, all three of them arriving for the Christmas holidays. Their exuberant youth couldn't have burst upon us at a more wonderful moment. We all walked together, on that first morning of their arrival, around the survived brick veranda rimming the charred summit, with only the two stark chimneys left of all that had been. The weather was sunny and mild for mid-December, and they found it impossible to visualize any such great storm as we described.

And something was said that led the way out of disaster to eventual mastery over our misfortune. As we were standing there looking over the barren site of all we had created there on the summit, Barclay said, with tremendous spirit, "I think this can be a good thing for us. It's a *challenge*. Our coming achievements will mean so much more to us, having to work harder for them than if they'd come easy, without all this trouble."

Dear Barc! How very wonderful, those words, just at that abysmally low point. Somehow his spirit carried us away. We never again found it quite so difficult to put our disaster behind us. Martin even began to talk with Barclay and Peter about plans for rebuilding the house. He would build it himself, by God, this time! And of course in indestructible poured concrete. Then he began planning exactly how he'd protect the roof, support posts, and windows from being blown out by violent winter storms.

Peter was very touchy about any mention of the big house, now gone. For he'd worked all summer helping the contractor build it. We often forgot, now, that he'd experienced only its beginnings. And when we mentioned to him something about the house in our conversation, he'd interrupt with indignation: "You must remember I never got to *see* the house!" Barclay was the sole family member who held wholly beatific memories of the house—the Shangri-la dream palace built for his one glorious party, then vanished!

Peter and Barc were concerned that we had no clothing. They persuaded Martin to cable Burberry's in London to airmail him a warm plaid topcoat—and phone Magnin's to send a natural vicuna coat for me. So it was great to be cozily warm again in the chill wintry weather.

But the loss of all our fine clothes deterred us from ever trying to build up wardrobes again. We simply ignored the situation. From then on through all the years, Martin never owned a suit. Spurned all but rugged ranch clothes, or jackets worn with sturdy Klondike whipcord pants he ordered from Texas. This denial of conventional fashion perhaps provided some sort of counterbalance for his losses, in a refusal to acknowledge damage done.

I myself from then on began to design and make my own clothes, creating fabulous knitted outfits with delicate wool yarns—skirts, sweaters, dresses, jackets, tunics—using ethnic motifs in wondrous color and texture combinations, in what I called "needlepoint knitting." So we both got even with our terrific wardrobe losses by simplifying, and by creating our own styles. Increasingly liking our own self-made fashions, we spent practically nothing on clothes. Which was an immense help.

Finally, one morning Martin went again into the cellar. He decided to retaste the wines in his now more relaxed state. He started with that same puncheon near the door. To his amazement, he found no hint of smokiness in either the nose or the taste of the wine! He moved on to other casks; found no smokiness in any of them, either, to his great surprise—and relief.

How could it be? It seemed a miracle had happened. At length he realized that his very tenseness that first time had triggered his misjudgment. Fearing and *expecting* smokiness made him smell and taste what he so feared, though no smokiness actually was there.

Martin then recalled a past tasting incident. He was asked to taste some wine in a cask that previously had held wine from native American grapes. Could he catch any lingering labrusca flavor? Looking for it, he caught it immediately. Then he asked Maynard Amerine to give his opinion of the wine, without mentioning the suspected labrusca taste. Dr. Amerine, with one of the keenest palates in America, pronounced it a good cabernet and asked what was being questioned about it. When told, of course he caught a faint "foxy" taste immediately. As he then pointed out, if you're looking for any particular taste or smell, it's easy to catch it, even if very faint; or even *imagine* it though it doesn't exist at all.

So all of our wines in cask were fine! They had prevailed, despite the calamitous fire. After the joyful revelation about our wines, we knew that we too would prevail. We were ready now for the spirited challenge Barc had proclaimed. We would start re-building the big house in the spring.

In the meantime, Martin picked up his wine sales again, which he had neglected for so long, too preoccupied to handle them. After all, cellared under the little house was quite a volume of bottled wines ready for market. We could commence the preparatory work for the cask wines preserved in the big cellar above, for bottling in the springtime. And we also could ready ourselves to handle the coming vintage in the fall of 1953.

Our life once again was good, and the future seemed glorious.

Now Martin's activities went into high gear. On top of all his vineyard and cellar care, wine sales, and occasional social or business entertaining, he was rebuilding the big house; and after that, replacing the garage-storage structure—both made of concrete this time, of course.

We took great joy in beholding our new home rising atop the mountain. It had the same floor plan as before, with the exception of the large master bedroom, which Martin eliminated. "I never want to sleep on the storm side again, ever!" he declared.

And, as planned, the new huge picture windows had heavy redwood shutters affixed to the concrete above them, ready at a moment's notice to be lowered by winches and locked below into the concrete walls. (They did prove marvelously assuring when big storms hit; down they came, locked tight!) There was the same roofed brick veranda surrounding the house, but this time, you can be sure, every upright supporting the roof was bolted firmly into the concrete at the base, with the roof's heavy cross-beams also bolted into the concrete house.

The house was even more impressive than the first, we thought. It had a weathered chateau look, especially after the concrete walls became graced with Boston ivy. But we had no beautiful family heirlooms for this house; no rich furnishings accumulated over our two lifetimes, as before. We now had to buy everything that went into it. No wonder I felt prompted to generate reams of publicity, to promote the sales of Martin Ray wines as never before, so that they'd help to pay such formidable expenses!

Finally our household was all organized and ready for entertaining, in this perfect setting. Favored clients and wine writers and renowned connoisseurs increasingly clamored to come up for a visit to our mountaintop. Just as in the Paul Masson days, Martin recognized—as did I—that a continued success would ultimately depend upon cultivating invaluable relationships within the special ambience of our homeplace and winery.

We had no Louisa, Martin and Elsie's wonderful cook who had created such delicious *gougeres* to serve with champagne, and such fabulous dinners. That era was long past. So it was up to me now to be the resident gourmet chef. Martin took for granted that I could cook anything, and his great expectations no doubt induced me to make good.

From the time we were ready to welcome guests to the new house, any cookery skills I had were propelled into high gear! It was fun creating culinary masterpieces that amazed Martin. Of course he was quite a master cook himself, from years of practice. He even enjoyed marketing, so could be of immense help.

Sometimes, though, I ran into problems. Martin had certain dishes traditional with him over the years, which he hoped I'd perfect, something neither he nor Elsie had found time to do. Such as Paul Masson's *gâteau*. Old Paul had a decided Burgundian winegrower's aversion to fancy desserts. His favorite was fresh fruit in season combined with a wonderfully simple but elegant Old-World "cake biscuit" (as he translated it). It had a light, marvelously complex spongelike texture, and a subtle fragrance—absolutely divine.

The Masson gateau was made with only three ingredients and in these proportions: 4 egg yolks, 3 egg whites, 3/4 cup sugar, 1/2 cup cake flour. That was all. Martin told me the amounts—which was all he knew. I was so determined to perfect that cake that I tried making it again and again—even three separate times in one day!

All attempts were failures. I handled the ingredients by the best recommended methods. But these confounded cakes wouldn't rise to the height Martin said they should. In desperation, I wrote food editors. Each said a liquid ingredient was lacking; that some liquid, perhaps in the form of butter or oil, was essential. Martin was annoyed. Paul Masson had made that cake with no liquid other than eggs, and it was perfection—nothing like it at all.

After innumerable tries—more than fifty million, it seemed to me then—I finally struck gold. Martin was happy as a clam in a tidepool when I finally mastered Paul's dear cake. Know what the secret was? Just two seemingly trivial differences in handling separated failure from success. The eggs had to be room temperature, not refrigerator-cold; and the whites should be beaten by hand with a French whisk to preserve more moisture, before being folded into the well-blended sugar, egg yolk, and thrice-sifted flour mixture.

The successful cake was baked in a 350-degree oven for 50 minutes, in an aluminum tube cake pan with a removable bottom, and cooled upside down on a rack for an hour before removing. Once I got the knack of it, I usually doubled the ingredients to make a cake twice as big.

And so it went with other favorite specialties. But this one had presented the most devilish problem I ever faced in all cookery. And so, dear reader, if you're curious about sampling the result, try making Paul Masson's endeared "cake biscuit" yourself!

When Martin Ray gave dinners, quite as important to him as the food was the timing. Before every dinner he never failed to say to me, "Now, I want this to be very leisurely. Remember—don't start to prepare any course until the previous one is finished."

"Yes, yes," I'd say. But if I'd followed his request literally, I could have had plenty of trouble, as some foods required much time to prepare. But far be it from me to start any controversy with him! I knew what he wanted as host: a relaxed pause between all courses, while people could continue enjoying the wine and conversation without being hustled into the next offering. So I timed everything to give that result. Of course the easiest trick was to pre-prepare certain courses so as to be readied with minimum effort and delay.

It worked out splendidly. All went so leisurely that dinners starting at one in the afternoon, after Paul's tradition, might go on until two or three in the morning. And Martin no doubt thought this happy outcome was due entirely to his standing order to start no course until the prior one was finished. Don't think I ever hinted otherwise to him. For he prided himself in this unique procedure!

Actually, it wasn't difficult for me to make life absolutely blissful for Martin Ray. He always had been a top-of-the-world person by nature, from the first time I met him. Such fun we now had, round the clock! He had a way of keeping his flair for romance shining-bright through everyday life. Little love notes pinned to my pillow when I'd awaken tardily in the morning. Praise for little things I'd do. And greatest of all, I realized that he really appreciated me, admired me deeply, far more than any other human being ever did before. What sweeter balm to a woman's heart, in all the world!

However, I had to have sense enough to avoid annoying the dear fellow, with that touchy nervous system of his following his nerve-center damage in the distant past. I realize now, of course, that my protective "coddling" of Martin will strike many contemporary readers as overindulging the male ego. That demanding but needy ego, usually hiding well below a tough, strong-man surface, can be highly fragile—vulnerable to breakage when emotionally engaged in a loving relationship.

So I did what many sensitized women have done centuries before me, and will do long after me. Unconsciously I measured the net worth of the man against whatever forbearances, pretenses, or sacrifices might be required of me within the marriage. Not just to keep peace and equilibrium but, more importantly, to support and even sustain him in the important, committed work he must do out in the larger world. My own three children were virtually grown now, ready to launch themselves into lives and careers of their own choosing. They might not want to remain involved in this new life of mine. I saw my primary place now as right at Martin's side, come what may.

This decade at the start of our marriage, the '50s, provided the happiest and most fulfilling years for Martin and me. There weren't too many visitors as yet to occupy our attention and energy, and we had time to enjoy to the fullest the life we loved, often with Peter and Barclay. Barc flew up almost every weekend from Caltech to help Martin with the wines and the vineyards, and we had rollicking good times together. And Peter usually managed to fly out from Harvard for the spring disking of the vineyards, summer vacation, and vintage. And of course Christmas. Bobo, who had gone off to faraway New York City to work as an editor in the book publishing industry, rarely got home.

Family members and friends gravitated to the mountaintop at vintage time, which provided the climactic excitement for each year. To Martin Ray, of course, vintage season was far more than that—and far more than anyone else could imagine. For here was his once-a-year chance to make a great table wine from each of the three grape varieties we grew ... as well as superb champagnes. In any other pursuit he might have chances every day or every week throughout the year to achieve his goal. But a vintner has comparatively few vintages in his entire lifetime. So during our harvest festivities that eternal challenge flamed high within Martin: to bring forth truly great wines.

I'd always liked Martin Ray's conception of the perfect life for a winegrower. It wasn't making money. From the start at Masson's, it had been his policy to profit from his wines only enough to cover expenses and sustain the enchanting life a winegrower had—and no more. When earnings in any years began to exceed that, he'd cut sales to the end of the year. He preferred keeping his wines rather than pay more taxes.

Many assumed, from the way Martin Ray wines sold out at such high prices, that he was making a fortune. Not so. Only just enough to support what to him was the best possible way of life—what he always called "the Good Life." With the cellars filled with great wines, his and other winemakers' (mostly European, of course), it was ideal!

After our marriage, as Martin began to fill orders for his wines, some long overdue, I spotted a role for myself. With my public relations and advertising background, I became a publicist for Martin Ray wines. My news releases and other materials, both educational and promotional, sometimes stirred up more sales than Martin wanted! He'd have to double his prices to prevent depleting his inventory.

Publicity-wise, one thing really bothered me. Our mountain should have its own name. Absurd to refer to it as the north half of Table Mountain (its southern half of course being Masson's), as shown on topographical maps! What appeal in that?

One day as we were driving home to our mountain along Mt. Eden Road, where our mailbox was, I asked, "Just where *is* Mount Eden, anyway?" Martin had never known of any such mountain, though he'd lived here most of his life. But why the name Mt. Eden Road, then?

On researching the history, I found that in the 1880s a group of Englishmen founded the Mt. Eden Orchard and Vineyard Company on land at the base of our mountain. So that's how the road came to be called what it was. "Ha!" said I to Martin. "Ours is the high mountain above that road. So it *has* to be Mount Eden." I loved the name's paradisiacal implications.

From then on, all our publicity heralded Mt. Eden, so it became an established fact. That's how we writers from the advertising world operate—free-lancers with words and ideas. We revel in seeing our created names take hold in the real world and go on forever. Like the Masson-attributed phrase *Chaîne d'Or* for our chain of coastal mountains supreme for wine grapes; and similar inventions. (This French-phrased "chain of gold" has become the accepted, classy name for the entire winemaking region within the Santa Cruz Mountains stretching between Woodside in the north and the Lexington Reservoir area to the south, above Los Gatos.)

Incidentally, all my Martin Ray publicity sent out over the years was somehow assumed to be written by Martin Ray himself. Why, I don't know. Promotional literature is rarely if ever written by a firm's CEO. Thus it's amusing to consider how wine writers sometimes referred to Martin Ray as being "bombastic" (whether high-flown, pretentious, bragging, or posturing). For I, not Martin Ray, did all the writing about our wines—except when some informative article was partly dictated and then signed by him. And I did this of course as his chosen "alter ego": with his full knowledge, and in accordance with his own ideas, experience, observations, and strongly expressed opinions.

Naturally those of us serving in the ranks of advertising want steaks to sizzle, champagne to bubble. So, yes, I was the one who wrote all those high-flying wine newsletters, articles, brochures, and what-not. Critics by nature must carp: for isn't that how they justify their name? But our customers loved these mimeographed publications. They'd write us ecstatically, ordered cases of wine like mad. Many even photocopied my newsletters, sent them to friends all over the country. So they did most of our publicity for us.

Martin was always much too busy to get involved in writing anything. But how he loved to *talk*! His talk was keen-edged, direct. He was a legendary storyteller. And though he waxed eloquent on the subject of wine, he wasn't inclined to discuss *his* wines. He just loved to make them and drink them . . . and let others do any talking or writing about them.

Martin loved getting letters but rarely had time to respond to them personally, even if dictating them to me. So I'd answer them in his name (except with our friends), which naturally gave recipients maximum joy. When some letter arrived from an all-important personage, he might say, "I'll answer this one myself," and set it aside. Stacks of such one-way correspondence accumulated, got lost. Once you got on his A-1 Preferred list, you might never hear from him at all!

The only notable exceptions over all the years to Martin Ray's non-writing were his legendary blasts on paper against all the fraudulently labeled varietals that so damaged California's prestige on the world wine market. And this activity merits a chapter all to itself.

35

Crusading for Quality

W HEN MARTIN RAY AND I married, he took on my three children. I acquired, I soon discovered, partnership in a great cause. Sometimes it assumed a dominant dimension in our lives.

Through the years, in the midst of all his activities—mountain clearing, vineyard planting, winery and house building, wine-selling trips, and business-connected entertaining—Martin Ray somehow always managed to find time, or really make time, to keep up his single-minded, solitary campaign for authentic varietal wines. It rankled him that years were passing by with no improvements in California's claimed varietals. Instead, the volume of fraudulently labeled wine blends just kept on increasing.

In the mid-'40s, as Martin pored over the state's annually published agricultural statistics, he noted with irony that few varietal vineyards existed, whereas the volume of wine produced claiming varietal content continued to mount. At first he exercised patience, reasoning that now peacetime had come, new prosperity and leisure-time interests would inspire fascination with gourmet cuisine and fine wines. And surely then the folks who ran the wine industry would have to change their ways.

In 1948 Martin Ray thought that finally there was real cause for celebration. The first move to protect California's varietals came when the Food and Drug Administration decreed that a varietal wine must contain at least 51 percent of the grape variety labeled on the bottle. He certainly welcomed the ruling, coming twelve years after he'd begun his campaign in behalf of varietal wines.

But this FDA measure was an empty gesture. There were no "teeth" in it, since no inspection was mandated. So the wine industry of course paid no heed at all to the 51 percent ruling. Blends continued as before. And consumers continued to be deceived. A bottle labeled chardonnay still might not contain a single drop of chardonnay. Yet since the law was publicized extensively, naive wine drinkers of the time assumed that the wine *must* have 51 percent or more chardonnay content. (Not that chardonnay was in demand as yet by retailers. Martin Ray, however, managed to get his chardonnay vintages placed on retailers' shelves by accepting no large order unless at least a few cases of this superb dry white wine were included. It worked! Gradually this great Burgundian varietal found devotees, long before it became sensationally popular.)

By the late '40s, Martin saw with mounting alarm that the predominant tonnage of the state's yearly wine crush was not in wine grapes at all, but in Thompson seedless grapes! Thompson was now being grown on a vast scale in the hot, irrigated, interior valleys of the state. Its vines yielded twenty-four tons or more to the acre compared to but one to four tons for fine varieties from the coastal climates favorable to winegrowing. Initially developed for use as table grapes and for drying as raisins, Thompsons were easy to grow. Costing wineries little to buy, they provided a copious tasteless juice—the main ingredient in wine blends passing themselves off as varietals.

Since there still was no regulation of varietal content in blends bearing varietal labels, and the more Thompson in them the higher the profit, as demand for wines grew, producers simply demanded more Thompson grapes. To Martin Ray it was preposterous that three-quarters of the wine crush of the state was coming from non-wine grapes, mostly Thompson seedless!

How could both quality wineries and state officials permit this fraud not only to continue, but proliferate? If the trend wasn't stopped, what would happen to California's claimed varietal wines in another decade or so? It could destroy any credibility the wine industry hoped to create, even economically. Certainly it would make California permanently the great international laughingstock among wine connoisseurs.

Martin felt that FDA's ignored 51 percent ruling in 1948 at least had made an invaluable *statement* in favor of more authentic varietals, though it failed to improve actual quality. It also provided an early warning signal to the better commercial wineries to start planting varietals. And it presaged the appearance in the '50s of a few small new wineries whose vintners were almost as fanatically devoted to the pure-varietal approach as Martin Ray long had been.

Most importantly, the ruling had a psychological impact on the American public. Many wine consumers began to taste more alertly, to note if they were getting the 51 percent flavor they'd paid for. From that time on, it became increasingly obvious that inspection should be imposed.

Watching the sales figures, Martin wondered when the phony-varietal balloon would burst. Much to his perennial frustration and irritation, further progress in quality regulations would take many more years. It was scarcely surprising that the status quo was successfully sustained. For wine lobbyists, wine promoters, and wine association representatives were mostly minions of the large wineries that dominated industry decision-making and continued to make high profits from inexpensive blends bearing varietal labels.

Only when quality winegrowers and the buying public itself raised their own standards and asserted themselves strongly would the situation improve dramatically. (And it finally did, with official rules and regulations—although three decades later!)

Martin Ray viewed Americans' current lack of interest in producing truly fine wines essentially as a dismal legacy from the long Prohibition years, which had interrupted any progress toward the quality achieved earlier among a few wineries. But he noted other significant factors, such as the emergence of high profit-oriented wine entrepreneurs. Industrialists, not vintners—some of them ex-bootleggers—operated vineyards, wineries, and marketing outlets like assembly-line factories. When the distilleries had been closed down in World War II, their personnel moving over into the wine scene added further disregard of or even contempt for quality

The horrors that Martin Ray had witnessed in the mid-'40s, after Seagram had bought from him Paul Masson's former winery and vineyard premises, typified the problems that the big distillers faced, and perpetrated, in taking over wineries in the two decades following Repeal. In that wine-ignorant era Seagram's executives newly in charge at Masson simply had no idea of what special care was demanded by wines any more than they understood anything about vineyards. And their executives, unlearned and inexperienced in both viniculture and viticulture, were entirely ignorant of what abilities were necessary for those they hired to operate vineyards and cellars for them.

What took place in the period following Prohibition seems incredible in the light of today's keen and widespread knowledge of winegrowing. But when that period began, few knowledgeable, capable wine personnel were to be found. Enology had become a forgotten trade and science during Prohibition. Only very gradually, as the American public itself became more wine-conscious and appreciative, did a number of young people start pursuing professional winegrowing careers and acquiring the necessary preparation for them.

Eventually, of course, the large distilling firms, the vast bulk-wine producers in the Central Valley, and new wineries aiming at business success learned what they needed to know, often through bitter and costly experiences. And by then they were also able to hire college-trained experts, skilled winemakers and vineyardists who simply had not existed in earlier days. New pressures from wine-knowledgeable consumers had been strong· factors in this move toward better quality standards.

In gaining mastery of the entire winegrowing operation, in time the big enterprises either adopted or invented new technologies that revolutionized many of the traditional processes. The evolution has been fascinating to watch from the sidelines in the past forty-some years. It was not, however, something that Martin Ray himself cared to participate in, because to him the high-tech, super-entrepreneurial approach to producing wine did not at all fit with traditional winegrowing not only as a fine art but also as a way of life. Which is why he made wine as he did, virtually hand-crafted; and lived and thought as he did.

A self-appointed prophet, Martin Ray foretold a grim future for California wines unless people in key positions came to their senses. Periodically he sent forth epistolary blasts against the still-permitted fraudulent varietals, to whatever recipients he hoped to influence: wine groups, wine and spirits distributors and retailers, the press—and prominent customers, of course.

Naturally he realized that from the vintners' self-interested perspective, there was little incentive to plant fine grape varieties. The vines demanded special conditions and care, were shy yielders, and proved costly to maintain. Blends, on the other hand, meant no big effort and minimal expense, especially when using Thompson seedless grapes. And surely the wine-drinking public, not knowledgeable enough to know the difference between blends and pure varietals, would be unwilling to pay more for a difference they couldn't themselves perceive.

Another flourishing winemaking malpractice in the postwar period constantly roused Martin Ray's ire. In the '40s and '50s many domestic wines, especially those produced in bulk quantities, had "grape concentrate" added to them during fermentation, supposedly to "correct" possible low-sugar content.

Grape concentrate (called "Vine-Glo" during the Prohibition years) was a thick syrup made from grape juice, canned or bottled for easy shipment and long storage. Added to water, it would ferment into wine. Initially promoted as convenient for home winemakers, the product and technique naturally was taken over by bootleggers.

After Repeal, grape concentrate made year-round winemaking

feasible to the huge bulk wineries. "Vintaging" now meant harvesting grapes and then reducing their juice to a near solid state. The process was a terrific boon to the gigantic table grape industry in the Central Valley, which could concoct this intensely sweet additive from raisin residues, a byproduct at the tail-end of fruit production that went from table grapes to raisins. These concentrates also enabled the cheap production of wines dulcetly attractive to uneducated palates. The use (and abuse) became so widespread that the BATF required wineries to list the quantity of concentrate on hand in their periodic reports, since chaptalization—the addition of sugar (sucrose) to enhance fermentation and produce higher alcoholic content—is not permissible in California wines.

Interestingly enough, during this period these concentrates were also being added to some French wines, permissible because grapes may fail to fully ripen in France. American connoisseurs became disgruntled with French wines, even those from premier producers, who were now deliberately "softening" vintages for earlier consumption.

Meanwhile, the ever-increasing numbers of Martin Ray enthusiasts were happily assured of encountering no sweet concentrate in *his* wines!

This nauseating scourge—grape concentrates—eventually would diminish as more and more Americans educated their palates to the satisfying appeal of dry table wines, before and during meals.

How could California's perverted winemaking attitudes be changed—whether coming from profit motives, ignorance, or apathy—in the interest of a great and noble cause? That was the basic problem Martin pondered. He had learned long before that anyone who spoke out against current practices would be censured or ridiculed within the trade, as well as ignored by wine writers whose positions depended on maintaining good relations with the powerful wine associations supported primarily by large-scale wine producers.

Martin Ray continued to occupy the high ground. He knew that in the late 19th and early 20th centuries a few dedicated vintners had grown small acreages of fine varieties and created from them excellent wines, whether 100 percent varietals or high-quality blends. He need not feel utterly alone, since there always had been a few perfectionist vintners outside the mainstream of California wine production. Even in earlier times they had demonstrated America's potential for producing excellent wines. Now he took pride in creating great wines that could stand alongside Europe's best and serve as models for others to come.

Martin Ray had also learned to stay aloof from the hurly-burly and politics of wine-judging competitions on any level, from county fairs to world fairs. Early on, he had found incredible the ignorance about varietal wines among the judges and so-called wine experts. Even worse could be when ordinary citizens cast their votes for the prize-ribbon wines!

When California vintners, having observed Martin Ray's astounding varietal success at Paul Masson, began labeling their blends with varietal names, they often held "tastings," private and public, to publicize their releases. But people simply did not know how to taste. For instance, in the late '30s a Wine and Food Society in Southern California heralded an all-important membership tasting. They urged Martin Ray to participate, stressing the knowledgeability of the group. So he finally set aside his misgivings enough to enter a Paul Masson pinot noir. In fact, he entered two different bottles. One was completely natural and dry, the other the same identical wine to which he'd added a touch of sugar, knowing well the public's predilection for sweet wines.

And the resulting awards? The sweetened pinot noir won the highest prize of the contest ... whereas that identical wine in its beautiful untainted state rated the lowest of all wines exhibited! That experience utterly convinced him as to the absurdity of all such events, when supposed connoisseurs could be that ignorant about fine wines.

Oh yes, another instance of that time was quite as absurd. Top officials at the Golden Gate International Exposition of 1939 had persuaded Martin Ray to enter a tasting competition, to lend prestige to this much-ballyhooed event. A prominent enologist friend of Martin's happened to be one of the judges. He was so delighted at discovering that two gold medals for champagnes were awarded to Paul Masson that he telephoned the great news at once to Martin. Then some hours later he phoned frantically to say that the officials disapproved of both golds going to Martin Ray's wines, so proposed canceling them altogether and awarding *all* contestants silver medals!

Martin was horrified at such devious behavior, and told his friend that either he would receive the two gold medals awarded him by the judges' decisions, or else he would expose the fraud. Clearly he meant it. His friend, embarrassed by that earlier impolitic disclosure, now had to dissuade the officials from altering the original plan. So Martin Ray did receive the highest awards for those two Paul Masson champagnes. (I still have Martin's gold medals from this 1939 World's Fair, encased in their impressive trappings, and smile whenever I look upon them, for they remind me well of Martin's resolute character!)

Consequently, Martin Ray never entered his wines in another tasting competition all through the years. Whereas other wine-growers depended upon medal-winning at state and county fairs and other highly visible judging events to publicize their names and products. Naturally such awards to him were meaningless.

Nor did he contribute bottles to the increasing number of "wine and cheese" events that began springing up nationwide, foretelling the Wine Revolution ahead. He simply had no desire to pursue a mass clientele for his handcrafted wines. He also did not respond when perpetually beseeched by an astronomical number of non-profit organizations, locally and around the nation, to contribute wine for fund-raising endeavors. Most of them doubtlessly supported worthy charitable causes. But he certainly could not afford to donate any of his very limited supply of costly wines. Nor could he be sure that they would even get into the right hands! Volume wineries with big inventories of course might well choose to participate, charging off costs as public relations expenditures.

Sometimes, when asked about his refusal to enter the growing number of wine "tastings" given in private and public settings, Martin might recount Paul Masson's vitriolic impatience over the very word. "Tasting? That means nothing!" he'd mimic the Frenchman's verbal explosion. "How does a wine *drink?* . . . That's the all-important thing! Many a wine may seem fine, just to taste. But maybe it doesn't *drink* worth a damn! You can't really know a wine until you've drunk it daily for a while with all kinds of food. By the time you've consumed two cases of it, you may never want to see another bottle of it again. Or you may find it drinks superbly and you like it more all the time. But just *tasting?* Bah!"

On rare occasions, however, Martin did agree to special connoisseurs' events that featured a selection of his own wines for tasting both horizontally and vertically—different varietals, different wine types made from the same grape variety, and different vintage years.

By the late '50s Martin saw an encouraging sign emerging in California's varietal wine dilemma when a few small new wineries were beginning to enter the field, particularly in Napa and Sonoma valleys and even in the Santa Cruz Mountains. Their proprietors were familiar with Europe's fine wines, so they were busily planting modest-sized acreages of the top varietals so crucially needed to improve the content of California's so-called premium wines. Then too, winemakers and managers at established older wineries no longer could ignore the public's growing demand for better quality in their vintaged releases.

Astute winegrowers now realized that as traveling in Europe

increased, particularly to those countries especially known for producing fine wines, and as postwar prosperity spiraled upwards, Americans were fast becoming more knowledgeable and sophisticated about wines. And they were beginning to expect far better wines from their own nation—which would force a radical improvement in the marketplace. So a hint of progress was in the air.

Along with accelerating demands for special information, research, and education relating to enology and viticulture, the agricultural school at UC Davis expanded its facilities and faculty as funding increased through both state and corporate support. The small, dedicated coterie of wine experts at UC Davis—Drs. Harold Olmo, Albert Winkler, and Maynard Amerine—in time was joined by other professionals, giving the department an international renown that induced even European winegrowing families to send their young offspring to attend college there. A few other universities—most notably, California State University, Fresno—developed reputable viticultural and enological programs.

Public education in wine appreciation began intensively too. The Wine Institute offered a home-education course to promote wine drinking. Colleges and universities in California and other states now responded to the growing popularity of wine. They added wine studies to their curricula, particularly in extension programs open to the community. UC Davis purveyed short courses in wine tasting and winemaking while offering practical, intensive classes for working wine professionals themselves.

But this forecast of things mostly to come in the Wine Revolution of the 1970s really gets ahead of the story of Martin's greatest fight over quality—and greatest disappointment.

Martin Ray's vigilant one-man campaign to ban fraudulent varietals had continued on through the years, waxing and waning as time and energy allowed, but most often exploding into action when his irritation level zoomed into outrage. In the early '50s, watching sales figures, he saw that low-price, ordinary French shippers' wines were increasingly undercutting sales of California's "better" claimed varietals.

During the war, Americans who liked to drink wine were for the most part cut off from imports. But by peacetime in the mid-'40s a great flood of European wines began to come in: both pure fine varietals and the traditional fine-varietal blends, as well as robust, palatable vin ordinaire, from Europe, even from South America and Australia. The surge of imports naturally had California wineries up in arms.

By 1955 this ever-mounting threat of foreign competition

prompted a concerted drive by a group of the state's "premium wineries" to keep out these shippers' wines by getting a prohibitive import tax imposed on them. But an alternative course made much more sense to Martin Ray: local wine producers, being pushed now against the hard wall of economic competition by better products, should improve their own offerings, thereby besting the imports.

When Martin was asked—rather to his surprise—to join this group of wineries in campaigning for a protective tariff on these imports, he realized this was his prime opportunity to persuade prominent winegrowers as a group to lead California varietal wines toward excellence. Only an organization like this could provide the necessary impetus for a drive that would bring about varietal improvement at last.

True to his zealous nature, Martin threw himself at once into this new endeavor with all his energy. Right off he wrote detailed letters to each winegrower invited into the group. He vetoed outright the idea of a protective tax. Instead, he urged them to acknowledge that the *only* way to triumph over foreign competition was to devise and then adopt a quality-control program. It would be patterned after the highly effective French *Appellation Contrôlée,* which dated back to the mid-'30s and therefore was already twenty years ahead of the American wine producers. (And long before that, France historically had made other strict rulings with regard to winegrowing.)

Introducing such a system—imposing rules and regulations on grape-growing, vintaging, and marketing practices, and with built-in strict inspections that would apprehend and fine violators—would *assure* the superiority, thus sales advantage, over French shippers' wines. Martin Ray also proposed that viticulturists and enologists at UC Davis help to formulate such a program, which ultimately would immensely benefit all higher-quality California wineries.

Wow! Martin Ray now blew up the biggest storm yet of his winemaking career. The owners and CEOs of wineries in the "premium" group were aghast. How had this perennial troublemaker been permitted to butt in, anyway? Now he was trying to shift the focus from preventing the entry of French shippers' wines to subscribing to a plan for imposing regulations on *them!* Furthermore, he was actually alerting the press as well as prominent wine merchants to his drive for quality control for California's top producers.

Martin Ray then had to contend with their outraged responses. In courteous but firm replies he pinpointed examples of each grower's mislabeling and false claims. "Your 'pinot noir' is no pinot noir," he wrote one of them. "And it further damages you to state on your label 'pure pinot noir,' implying 100 percent." He chastised another for labeling a chenin blanc blend as "white pinot," and shamed still another for marketing a fictitious "red pinot."

"Do you wish to be lined up on the side of such evils?" he asked them. "I think not. This improvement has to come. You will feel better as sponsors, where you belong, than on record as opposed to honest labeling." But the winegrowers made it clear that they weren't ready to face quality regulations, self-imposed or not. To give up their profitable blends labeled as varietals would mean considerable financial loss.

However, Martin Ray persisted, urging them "to think about it." As he stressed, once they launched into true and pure varietals, they'd achieve profits far beyond their present ones, and mounting with each vintage year. The premium winegrowers as a group finally agreed to consider his points, along with his proposal for Dr. Albert Winkler of UC Davis to meet with them and hopefully come up with a helpful plan that would accommodate their needs in moving gradually into quality control.

Martin was delighted when he heard that Dr. Winkler actually had set a date with them. But just before the meeting, they canceled out. And soon the ad hoc "premium" group fell apart. When informed of this backout, Martin felt deeply discouraged. He'd thought that at long last real progress toward quality was about to be made.

An even more stressful blow came to Martin in a sudden aftermath of this whole aborted quality fight: the loss of his closest friend, enologist Dr. Maynard Amerine of UC Davis. Always in the past Maynard had backed Martin's efforts to perfect California's wines, providing vital moral support and technical advice. Now, in the fracas Martin had created over trying to induce the "premium" wineries to accept quality-control measures, Maynard evidently felt that the vintners' group considered him to be in collusion with Martin Ray. So one day Maynard telephoned Martin to say that all of them had stopped speaking to him. Consequently, he must put their relationship "on ice." Martin was thunderstruck, for he had not intended to involve Maynard personally in the conflict.

Only recently, the two of them had "tasted through the cellars" to compare pinot noir vintages. "It was the 1952 and 1953 that really bowled him over," Martin wrote glowingly afterwards to a friend. "He said without hesitation that he considers them in character and quality unlike any other reds heretofore made in the country, and ranked them with the greatest French burgundies, saying, 'If no one else ever makes a great pinot noir in California, there will have been these two.'"

Now, such treasured occasions were to vanish. Martin occasionally saw Dr. Amerine in a strictly professional context, but their old friendship was never to be repaired.

How could the troubled California winegrowers fail to see that they must improve, and fast? Martin often wondered about this aloud, in amazement, to his visitors. Surely the figures told them so! Imported wines had leaped in six years from a half-million gallons in 1948 to three million gallons in 1954—heading toward twelve million by 1960. Consumption of dry table wines in America was increasing so rapidly during the '50s and early '60s, particularly in California, that it seems incomprehensible now that all premium winegrowers did not heed the obvious, and rush to plant fine varietals so as to compete with French imports.

Despite Martin's sense of defeat in his 1955 quality-control battle, over the next few years the more astute of those better-class vintners whom he had tried to influence did sense that times were changing. They were still not ready for quality controls. But they began planting some badly needed varietals, or increased their trivial acreages of them. Some did set aside, for prestige purposes, small bottlings of authentic varietals, perhaps labeled "private reserve." Not released through the usual trade channels, they were sold to select customers for private cellaring, or kept in "libraries" strictly for important tastings and winemaking reference purposes. Nowadays such early-date, authentic-varietal leftovers may yield fortunes at auctions.

Economic realism inevitably entered into the quality equation now. And signs of the public's growing interest in and knowledge of fine wines had to be factored in future projections. Whether or not quality controls were imposed, too little acreage of fine varieties existed at that time for winemakers to buy grapes for increased needs.

To provide a statistical insight into this deplorable situation: even a decade later, in 1964, only 834 acres of cabernet sauvignon existed in all of California; and that was the *most* grown of top varietals! There were only 716 acres of that prima donna of reds, pinot noir.

As for the chardonnay grape, it was such an unknown element then that the state kept no acreage statistics on it. Martin Ray alone among producers was consistently growing and selling it, though he actually had to force dealers to include it in their orders for reds and champagnes. Thereby a small demand slowly built up for this elegant dry white wine. By 1968 chardonnay's total presence in the entire state amounted to a miserable 986 acres. (Later, of course, it finally took off in extreme popularity. By 1991 some

53,000 acres of chardonnay grapevines thrived in California!)

But mounting economic pressures, first from abroad and then from within its own ranks, finally forced the California wine industry and its major wineries to rethink their strategies. Only when quality control was conceded to be financially feasible, even beneficial, did it come about. The growing popularity of "wine tastings" as social events gave varietals a widespread cachet they had never previously enjoyed. As the American public became educated about wines, many people now discerned the difference between authenticity and pretense.

In the years to come, with growing satisfaction Martin Ray would watch the new generation of small wineries spring up in California and gradually prove that improved quality made economic sense. No longer did he stand alone in maintaining this. Idealistically motivated young winegrowers who had planted or revived varietal vineyards were starting to market surprisingly good wines—greatly superior to the blends that had been foisted off as varietals on unsuspecting American consumers for years. The nation's expanding ranks of knowledgeable wine enthusiasts were impressed. And they willingly paid far more for such well-crafted products. Martin Ray's own files were bulging with ecstatic letters written by customers, retailers, wholesalers, and independent wine writers.

But wine industry moguls still strongly resented any expression of interest in Martin Ray or his wines. The press was made to understand that his name must never be seen in print—at least in any favorable context. Some reporters who sought him out for interviews intended for feature articles would enjoy a fascinating experience on the mountain and send us the draft they'd submitted. Later we'd be told that what they wrote about him was just plain dumped. Management knew that Martin Ray was a forbidden topic, for even a mention could alienate the Wine Institute and big-budget wine advertisers!

So "controversial" came to be the favored, expectable word used in labeling Martin Ray. No wonder most wine histories, whether books or articles, either do not discuss Martin Ray's contributions to progress in fine winemaking or else briefly downplay or dismiss him.

If indeed Martin Ray *was* controversial, it was not because of the wines he made, but because he was a gadfly whose accusations frequently stung their targets within the wine industry. No one else in the country agitated so unceasingly, relentlessly, and vocally—for so long—for laws to ensure authentic varietal wines and protect wine consumers from false labeling claims and other violations of the public trust.

Naturally Martin Ray would make many bitter enemies over the years—exactly as Paul Masson had predicted. Practically none of them were known to him personally, as he remained apart on his mountain, with no time or inclination to fraternize. And anyway, his damaged nervous system could never have tolerated noisy gatherings of people, long speechifying at huge banquets, endless committee meetings leading nowhere, and heated arguments.

But from the serenity of his hilltop vineyards Martin Ray periodically sent off critical blasts. The campaign was waged not for his benefit, after all, but for that of wine consumers ... and for California's benighted winemakers themselves.

Stoically he accepted enmities and counterattacks as inevitable. "If you lead a fight," he'd say, "you've got to live with opposition." He not only learned to live with it perennially, but even came to consider it favorable, since his name came to symbolize uncompromisingly high standards. (Today, public relations experts tend to agree. "For a winning combination," they say, "play up a dynamic and colorful character linked with a top-quality product. It's tremendous!")

Martin's positive, confident attitude in the face of hostility and concerted opposition startled actor Burgess Meredith when he first visited Martin—some years after the quality struggle first began. He expected to meet, as he said, a hapless guy backed against the wall, desperate for defenders. Not so. "They want people to believe I'm fighting a losing battle!" Martin laughed. As he saw it, a noble cause like this bestowed on him a certain stature in the wine world. "Mine is obviously the only defensible position," he assured the amazed "Buzzy" Meredith. For he now felt assured of triumphing in the end.

And gradually, through Martin Ray's efforts and example, increasing numbers of people *were* rallying to his side. He and his wines often made converts who helped carry on the battle; many of them he never met. Sometimes they even came to blows over him and the varietal quality cause he championed. They talked, argued in meetings, wrote letters and articles, proposed rules and regulations. But the most crucial thing they did, if they were winemakers, was to launch into making 100 percent varietal wines themselves. Or if wine consumers, *bought* only such wines from California vineyards—willingly paying for their fair value. The celebrated Wine Revolution had begun!

Of course Martin didn't devote all his time to his varietal fight. By the 1950s the vines growing on Mt. Eden's virgin soil were fully mature, producing grapes that made magnificent wines, with even more flavor and bouquet than from the old vineyards at Paul Masson. So he was overwhelmed with pleasure.

And these Martin Ray wines were unique—astounding with their pure varietal impact—in his illustrious era, which spanned the late '30s to the mid-'70s. By now they have become legendary, along with the man who made them. That lone crusader who through all those long years behind and ahead of him held aloft the banner of pure varietal wines ... all the while immersing himself in the Good Life made possible by the making of these wines.

Aerial shot, taken in the late 1940s, of Martin Ray's new vineyards and home atop Saratoga's Mt. Eden.

Eleanor frequently serenaded their guests with folk songs.

"Rusty" Ray takes a break in his cellar during the regular wine cask "topping" — to prevent oxidation in air space created by evaporation.

Family members prune winter-dormant grapevines in the early 1950s: Martin, Barclay, Peter with a friend, and Eleanor. Beyond and below them is the still largely agricultural "Silicon Valley".

Harvest time; by the mid-20th century, most regular vineyard workers were Mexican.

With a hydrometer Martin Ray tests the declining sugar content
as alcohol is produced in the fermenting wine must.

Crushing chardonnay grapes directly into the wine press
during vintage time on Mt. Eden.

An example of basket pruning in the Martin Ray vineyard.

"Just one more bottle..." Martin gets a bottle of pinot noir from the cellar at one of his long-enduring dinner parties. (Photo by Burgess Meredith.)

Martin and Eleanor Ray

36

The Good Life

M ARTIN RAY'S GREAT OLD bell, which he'd brought with him
from Masson's, fortunately had escaped both fires of the past. Now
it was installed in its destined niche next to our new house. Joy-
fully it rang in and out all our friends when they arrived on the
mountain, as in days of yore. At vintage time especially the bell
clanged almost constantly with so many comings and goings.
Some friends, though, stayed for the duration of the vintage work.

We always launched vintage festivities the day before it was
to start, with a riproaring celebrating dinner. It was repeated,
with variations, during the ensuing weeks of vintaging the separate grape varieties, lasting from late August or early September
through mid-October.

To me, the most memorable of all vintages was the vintage of
1958. To recapture it, in essence and details, I am drawing upon
what was probably the perennial favorite of all the reports I sent
out through the years to friends and clients: "Martin Ray (with
Ardent Friends) Races Storm to Bring in a Great 1958 Vintage."

Never in the history of this area has there been such a year—
revolutionary weather from beginning to end! An early false spring
brought the buds popping out, only to be hit by such cold that the
grapes bloomed very late. Then, in June it rained, something unknown in our region—and continued to rain. This meant we had
to sulfur-dust the vines (to prevent mildew) every morning for six
weeks! (instead of for a mere few days late in May).

Then an unprecedented heat wave struck, as vintage approached. We held our breath. If such heat continued, the pinot
noir and chardonnay would lose their precious acidity. But abruptly weather changed again! Autumn-crisp mornings, "sheep" in the

sky threatening rain. The delicate skins of the pinot noir berries had been sorely tried by the weather extremes. Martin felt them between his fingers, said they'd disintegrate if rain hit them. Yet sugar was not quite high enough for vintage yet. Given but a few days and nights of even warmth, the grapes might still come in at perfection. But ...?

Then we were given those few days of beautiful sunny warmth. And being high above valley fogs, the warmth was sustained overnight, built up sugar faster than we dared hope. Suddenly we were able to move up our vintage date a full week. And from all over the country our wine-enthusiastic friends rushed here to be in on the vintage—one young atomic scientist even hastening here from Geneva!

The evening before vintage, everyone gathered on the veranda for a great pre-vintage dinner at a long table there, overlooking the vineyards and valley far below. Madame Pinot Champagne 1953 launched festivities. First toast, of course, "To the 1958 vintage!"

Lights were coming on in the valley below as our dinner got under way—with candles lighted all along the lengthy table. For the entree a poached king salmon was served with heaps of just-picked watercress, and with it Martin Ray's Pinot Noir *Blanc de Noir* 1956, well chilled, that rare white so superb with piscatorial delights. Then followed roast turkey, rice Boulestin and vegetables, complemented with Pinot Noir 1948, deliciously spicy and fragrant. Martin told the story of that vintage, of the continued days of rain, and how he and Madame Pinot (Elsie, then), arrayed in slickers and boots, picked grapes themselves—spreading them on papers indoors to dry, finally covering all floors!

The only trouble with a pre-vintage celebration is that nobody wants to retire on such a happy occasion! But despite that, we were all up at dawn, ready to direct the army of hired grape pickers—far more arriving than we had bargained for. Our friends were needed, indeed, to supervise so many. All pickers had been given grape-hooks, but it was up to our friends to see that they used them properly.

"They mustn't squeeze the grapes," Martin instructed, "or juice flows and starts fermenting. See that they pick only one bunch at a time, and lay it carefully in the box, not throw it. We pay them a top rate by the hour so they won't hurry. Make sure they pick a vine clean, and keep boxes clear of leaves. You can't make a great wine unless your grapes come in at perfection, absolutely unblemished." Then he added, "I wouldn't make wine out of grapes as they're usually picked."

One doctor friend had the job of seeing that all boxes were filled evenly and stacked (all spanking-new boxes to keep grapes immaculate!). A young biochemist was seen, between tasks, racing through the vineyard with two cameras swinging from his neck—one for color, one for black-and-white—frantically shooting pictures. "What color!" he'd cry, catching the vines most ablaze with flame and gold, and those most loaded with the deep blue-skinned grapes.

The pinot noir vintage was on! For the first time in years the pinot noir grapes had ripened ahead of the chardonnay, and the crop was far larger than anticipated. Boxes were filling rapidly. By one o'clock we had hit our quota for the first two crushes, so Martin called a halt to the day's picking. It's his custom to crush after dark, to bring the grapes into fermentation at a much lower temperature and also avoid flies and bees. ("I can't have flies or I'd have to sulfur the wine like everyone else!")

So we now began to relax and enjoy ourselves at a luncheon on the sunny south veranda. By this time several other young doctors had arrived, so we lengthened the already long table. Feature wine was a chablis, Les Clos 1953, delightfully *pétillant* and refreshing with our cold cuts and salad dishes. What gaiety and laughter, what wonderful tales were told at this luncheon over which we dallied for hours . . .

Then at dusk Martin roared off on the big tractor down the slopes to haul in all the boxes of grapes up through the vineyard, with one young doctor (heart specialist at that!) perched mighty precariously on the tractor hood. By this time it was dark, Martin having to "feel" his way up through the heavy growth of the rows in the blackness, the doctor hanging on while long leafy arms of the vines brushed over him like ocean waves. "Oh beautiful ride! Oh never-ending curve!" he was heard to cry out (shades of early Robert Nathan!).

Madame Pinot as usual dumped the first box of grapes into the crusher, amid loud huzzahs for the 1958 vintage—everyone shooting pictures—and the pungent fragrance of the pinot noir exploding into the air as the berries burst in the crusher, and a rich stream of juice, seeds and skins flowed into the press basket below. All eyes were on the free-run juice being captured for the Madame Pinot champagne, and later the brilliant pink juice from the first partial press casked for the *Sang de Pinot* champagne. Everyone drank deeply of these precious juices fresh from the basket press.

Crushing and pressing went on for hours, friends taking turns dumping grapes into the crusher, swinging on the press-handle. Then about midnight we enjoyed a *coussin de boeuf* steak dinner with mammoth baked potatoes, with Martin Ray's great Third Crush of Pinot Noir 1954 to give us strength to carry on! Novices tended to fall by the wayside after this, but early morning found Martin Ray still going it with certain hardy souls, crushing the final boxes directly into puncheon-fermenters he had been preparing for the pinot noir still wine.

Half the pinot noir crop remained to be picked, but we were gambling on this much, as in 1954, letting the grapes hang on longer for chance of very *maximum* sugar for one GREAT crush! The next day rain threatened. Martin was nervous as a witch. But luckily the storm merely dipped a wing and brushed by. A warm honeyed sun enveloped the vines. And by the next weekend our pinot noir grapes basking on the south slopes had reached a magnificent 25° sugar! Again the vintage rush, the many pickers. And again the blessing of our wine-enthusiastic friends to see that the precious grapes were coming in "clean as a hound's tooth"!

Martin never did get to bed that night, for the very next day was *chardonnay* vintage, coming in right on top of the pinot noir, with not a moment to rest in between. Much preparation was needed in the cellar. But before that, we still had the enormous picking of pinot noir to crush and press during the night, and be ready with all clean boxes by early morning.

If Martin Ray is severe about picking his pinot noir clean, then he's fanatical about his chardonnay. He can't trust any hired pickers with this delicate white grape. Only family and friends will give it the necessary care, he says. First friends to arrive were a young geologist and his wife, driving up at night expecting to collapse into bed to be fresh for the morning. Instead, they were met with a staggering sight—stacks of boxes full of pinot noir grapes to be crushed and pressed immediately! But by morning all was finished, just as all our friends began arriving. A most interesting group it was, this weekend—and much fun was had in the vineyard while we worked.

At noon a long table was set on the shady porch of the guest house overlooking our first cabernet vineyard—for a brief cold luncheon featuring Holland ham with chilled pinot noir *blanc de noir* (the perfect luncheon wine, and incidentally the *only* wine supreme with ham!). By day's end everyone was ready for a shower, and dinner again on the wide veranda of the big house. Madame Pinot had prepared a huge rib roast (rare) as well as turkey, both served cold, with mammoth potato salads unmolded on huge platters, and great bowls of mixed greens. With this was served our tremendously big Cabernet Sauvignon 1947.

The young atomic scientist, quite a perfectionist, put on a singular demonstration. He presented the wine at several different temperatures, and by everyone's tasting each and checking with a thermometer it was established overwhelmingly that 82° F. was absolute *perfection* for this very big cabernet sauvignon. At that temperature (still cool to the taste) it is smoothed to velvet on the tongue, and its tremendous bouquet released.

Everyone was in great form that evening, with the happy satisfaction of the day's work. Such stories, such laughing and singing! Then a smashing climax midway in the dinner! Our Samoyed dog, Frosto, slipped his leash and suddenly appeared, like a great white wolf, nonchalantly circling the table. Martin, planning to decoy him and lead him off, held out a piece of beef in back of him, but as Martin turned his head to see him, Frosto slipped in on his other side and in one swift lunge seized the whole turkey in his jaws and leaped off into the vineyard! Various gallants tore off in mad pursuit, with fiendish cries—but Frosto and the turkey raced free of pursuit, down the slope through the vines. What pandemonium!

As dessert we held a tasting of several varieties of almonds recently harvested, everyone cracking hard-shells and soft-shells in great mountains and relishing them as we drank more cabernet sauvignon—a wondrous combination! (Martin, by the way, says almonds *must* be in shell, for they lose vital flavor-with-oil once cracked. Also, soft-shells have poor flavor *and* texture compared with hard-shells, the hard-shell "Peerless" easily outranking all others in the tasting.)

Never was there a more uproarious party than was carried on by Martin, the heart medic, atomic scientist, and biochemist to some hour like four a.m., long after everyone else retired. The whole mountain reverberated with gusty laughter, stories, and songs. The biochemist gave out dramatically with Hilaire Belloc's paean to the wonders of a great red wine. More champagne began flowing. At one point Martin was pouring champagne in a slow, steady stream into the medic's glass, while he quaffed it, sighing dreamily, "Oh beautiful wine! Oh never-ending stream!"

The night was like mid-summer—warm, too warm to crush the chardonnay yet, Martin said. The grapes would be cool enough by early morning. So they were, their temperature dropping from 80 degrees to 67 by dawn. And the crush was on! Arriving just in time for the crush were more medics, all to join merrily in the day's chardonnay picking. The heart medic had to return to The City before lunch, looked very sad. But when told we were again serving a chilled *blanc de noir,* he scowled, said, "That does it!"—and stayed on. People came and went over the weekend. All were charming and interesting and fun, and the flow of chardonnay was coming along smoothly from vineyard to boxes in the shade, at just about the same pace, though pickers changed. Martin said he never saw chardonnay come in looking so wonderful—not a single damaged berry to be seen in all the boxes! Only a little chardonnay remained to be picked on Monday. The geologist and his wife stayed over to help with the Sunday-night crush and see out the chardonnay vintage.

But suddenly we were apprehensive. Sultry heat on Monday turned to a cold wind at midday. The sun went under. Rain was certain! We seemed to pick twice as fast, bent on snatching the chardonnay before the storm. Martin knew the geologist couple had to get back to Bakersfield, but they were reluctant to go, picking just one more box, then another and another, Martin the while urging them to get over the Pacheco Pass before nightfall. "But we came to *help* you," the geologist kept insisting, until Martin finally turned on him, gently but firmly. "Now I don't want you to go away thinking you've been here to *help,* though of course you have, mightily," Martin said. "Instead, you've shared a rare experience—all the joy, work, vision, and festive mood of a vintage, with much good wine and food." Martin did eventually get the couple off and away, laden with long branches of scarlet and gold grape leaves, as well as bottles of wine, to carry the vintage mood to their family and friends. Also precious bunches of golden chardonnay grapes to feast their eyes on, touch, smell, and taste.

Then at dusk we hastened to crush and press, with a veritable gale from the west hurrying us, and intermittent drops splashing our faces. Looking off at the valley below, we could see it raining in great black streaks over Almaden. Then Monte Bello to the north turned misty with rain. But by now all of our grapes were crushed, and their juice stored in the cellar. Only the clean-up work remained to be done. Martin himself cleaned the press, removed the heavy basket and washed that. Suddenly he was very tired. Looking at the empty stainless steel tub of the press, he was tempted to lie down in it and rest for a moment. Instead, he knew he should move it out of the way. In the dark someone might run into it and get hurt. But he felt too tired.

He went into the cellar, alone finally, to check every cask thoughtfully, consider its every possible need, place "opium pipes" in those fermenting hazardously, see that nothing at all was overlooked, that everything was put away, that all was spotlessly clean and in order. When at last he turned off the lights in the cask cellar and went out, the rain was *pouring!* As he locked the door, he found himself standing deep in wet grape-leaves hurled into the cellar entrance by the storm. The leaves gave off a pungent, acrid odor strangely refreshing to him. He lifted his face to the rain, and it felt good, good. For his work was over. The wines were safe in cask. In the dark he tripped into the empty press and fell forward. It too was full of drenched leaves, so his fall into the press was not too painful—in fact, hardly unpleasant. He would just take a little rest, he said to himself happily, before extricating himself.

So it was that, several hours later, when Martin Ray failed to reappear from the cellar, he came to be found, the old winemaster himself, at vintage end, sleeping a good sleep curled up in the grape press on a bed of wet leaves, with the rain coming down over him like a benediction. A smile was on his face, as if he were delighting in the rain's coming so belatedly.

He might well be happy, for he knew that his cabernet sauvignon too would soon be put safely to bed. He felt blessed indeed to be who he was and where he was, to the point that he could relish a beatific rest, even lying drenched in the downpour.

You can see that to carry on like this over the years, you must have your own mountaintop domain, your very own kingdom, to control completely. That immense satisfaction Martin Ray learned in his boyhood, from observing Paul Masson. Tumultuous parties along with tremendous vintage work could go on all night and who could complain, as they well might do elsewhere?

But far more crucial to Martin was the independence this location gave him to *create* and sustain a life of his own design. Just as an artist selects subject and medium, so a winegrower chooses and fashions to his own standards of perfection his wines—and the environment that brings those wines into being and then carefully nurtures their maturing.

Nobody ever dared question anything Paul Masson said or did. Heaven forbid! He'd just say, "Go down the mountain and never come back!" Martin thought that just great. So when in his turn he owned Paul's mountain, and later the adjoining Mt. Eden, he followed that much-admired precedent.

People take vicarious delight in the very idea of dispatching anyone down the mountain at will, like a monarch saying "Off with your head!" So they were fascinated with Martin Ray's capability of doing this. Mostly it was just hilarious legend. Martin actually would put up with far, far more than Masson would before *he* blew his top and sent someone scurrying off. With Paul Masson there was no delayed action. He'd react instantly, with fury, at anything he disagreed with, considered an imposition or a thoughtless act. Paul would explode over a stab at his pride as well, whereas Martin would go numb with hurt—but never forget the wound.

Martin's mind kept a computer-like running index of every blooper you or anyone had ever pulled—whether inconsiderate, intentional, or plain stupid. And when some incident triggered an end to his forbearance, suddenly he'd lower the boom. For minor offenses, he'd recount to you, in order of occurrence, your every outrageous mistake, comment, act, or what-not. His play-by-play memory for such was astounding! Then he'd advise you to mend your ways.

Occasionally people ran into trouble with him because he'd seem so affable on the surface. But beware an argumentative attempt to push him around with your ideas, take some advantage of him, or challenge his authority! He'd put up with several offensive moves first, with what was extraordinary tolerance for him. Yet each infringement was mentally noted, you can be sure; added to the accumulating pressure upon his patience. If it ever snapped, he might send *anyone* down the mountain, no matter how charming or influential, or eager to order his costly wines. And the offender would never be invited back.

Most people, noting the warning look on Martin's face, immediately would cease and desist in annoying him. There was one notable exception: the sister of San Francisco *Chronicle's* columnist Herb Caen. When first introduced to Estelle as the fiancée of a close friend, Martin had found her interesting, likable. But he noted she was bossy—like me. (He often playfully claimed that I'd be the bossiest woman alive if he didn't keep me "under his thumb." Utter bosh in my case, because *everyone* gets the upper hand with me, even cats and dogs!)

This is what happened. As Estelle arrived, popping in the kitchen door, she greeted Martin. There he was, carving a huge eye-of-the-rib roast. "Oh, give me that knife, I'll show you how to do it!" she said brightly, helpfully rushing up to grab the knife from him.

Jeez, you could feel the atmosphere suddenly bulge like an overblown balloon! Was this actually said to Martin Ray, who prided himself on being one of the world's most expert carvers? He managed to retain the knife and hold himself together; just shooed her aside. But I could see she'd better watch out, for he wouldn't forget her initial transgression. If she just pulled one or two more bungles like that, they'd add enough pressure for him to blow.

Well, after we were all at table, Estelle began to direct Martin's serving. She instructed him as to what size portions should be given this person and that. Meanwhile, I wished I were seated near enough to her to give her a warning kick under the table! She also objected to his seasoning each person's serving—he didn't trust diners to add the perfect amount of freshly ground pepper.

Her fiancé noted their host's dark look and told Estelle that she'd have to learn to take it easy if she planned to join up with him. But evidently she thought he was kidding, and didn't pick up his urgently cautionary tone.

When Estelle said one more thing—perhaps her most trivial bit of advice yet—Martin set down his serving implements, then pointed over to a side table. We all looked, expecting some interesting observation, when he calmly said, "Estelle, you see your purse over there on the table? . . . Well, just pick it up and go down the mountain. And never come back."

It wasn't funny. He meant it. Even knowing he'd be losing one of his most treasured friends forever by expelling her.

This is the only time in twenty-five years I actually saw a banishment happen, though I know that stories abounded of Martin Ray's expulsions of unsatisfactory guests.

As far as I myself ever witnessed, firm-spirited Estelle caught the only brass ring on this particular merry-go-down, to get the royal bounce off the mountain!

By the late '50s our entertaining had gone into high gear, with fascinating visitors arriving from everywhere. Life on Mt. Eden was continuing so similarly to the way it had been in Martin Ray's days at Masson, that wine enthusiasts of the past hardly seemed aware of the break and transition period in his winemaking career. To them it all seemed just a smooth continuation of producing amazingly fine wines.

Some of Martin's favorite old-timers never saw Mt. Eden. Julian Street died before he could get there. Martin missed the past visits of Charlie Chaplin, expatriated in Europe now, and those jolly times when he'd be driven up in that funny custom-built Ford limousine of his. "Doc" Ricketts was gone, but Steinbeck managed to come on one of his rare trips out West. He hardly seemed the same man as of old, though; Martin worried about his lost-sheep look. British writer Alec Waugh came for a delightful vintage-time stay, with companions. And New York publishers Alfred and Blanche Knopf came often, usually separately, and on one occasion Blanche brought France's renowned Christian Dior with her.

Then there was the time we entertained a fellow who'd just come back from spending a year as a Buddhist monk in Southeast Asia. Actually, he was the wine writer Robert Balzer, whom Martin had known from his Masson period. Bob had taken a vow swearing off alcohol forever, it seems. But as he sat down at the dinner table with us and Martin began pouring samples of wines produced on our mountaintop, Bob assented to taking a taste or two of each. And then some more. For the rest of our evening together, Bob's vow simply evaporated! And apparently remained so afterwards, during his long tenure as wine columnist with the *Los Angeles Times* and other publications.

Surely our most gratifying guest of renown was Burgundy's Louis Latour, whose famous, supreme wine Martin so greatly admired. Louis was fluent in English, and during his week-long stay with us he and Martin would talk for hours each day, comparing vineyard, vintage, and cellar practices—which provided intensely interesting revelations to them both. One particular opinion pleased Martin: Latour agreed with him that a fine chardonnay (or "white burgundy") was at its very best when drunk young; and over the hill when past four years. They both cherished the fresh bloom of chardonnay wine when young.

Later, Louis Latour's charming niece, Christiane Latour, visited us, and our friend Burgess Meredith honored her with a "Midnight to Dawn" party in Hollywood, a most dramatic social event, when to her delight she was introduced to a bevy of American movie stars, including Charlton Heston and Marion Brando, then at the peak of popularity. In subsequent years, other Latour friends and relatives came to stay, and Peter Martin Ray visited the Latour *domaine* in Burgundy at vintage time from time to time, acquiring many a priceless detail for future winemaking.

Some of our happiest times in those years came when actor Burgess Meredith popped up. His visits expanded when he was appearing in San Francisco in *Teahouse of the August Moon.* He often brought other theater friends, such as Scott McKay. His tremendous gusto for living, and wine drinking, perfectly matched Martin Ray's, so their times together were irrepressibly madcap. They'd tell each other astounding stories over their wine; but enough wine was involved, over many delightful hours, that the next day they couldn't recall details so as to pass along any of these priceless tales!

To its visitors, Mt. Eden held a certain magic different from any place else on earth, with its breathtaking view of the entire Santa Clara Valley spread below, San Francisco Bay beyond, the tall forested mountains to the west, and the sunlit or moonlit vines all around us. People arrived as if on a pilgrimage to Paradise.

Part of that magic we supplied, of course, in the form of great wines and abundant, delectable foods. Yet the unique appeal wasn't just that glorious setting or the carefully planned cuisine. There was something about Martin Ray himself that tuned everyone in on the magnificence of it all. Many thus mesmerized yearned to become part of this exalted life—what Martin called "the Good Life"—forever. And said so, just as Alex Woollcott had cried out before his departure years ago from the Masson premises: "Martin, this is *it!* How can I have this life of yours?"

Our desire to find a practical way to enable others to enjoy life in this Edenic place with us ushered in the final chapters of Martin Ray's earthly career.

37

The Planting of Eden

DURING THE LATE 1950s and early '60s, when Martin Ray's lofty plan for Mount Eden Vineyards was first envisaged and then realized, wine aficionados' romantic dream of taking up winemaking as a life pursuit was still unfeasible to all but the most determined souls. The Wine Revolution—making such things possible for many—lay as yet beyond the horizon.

People inspired by Martin Ray's fine wines and way of life yearned to do much the same thing. With most it was a momentary desire that passed when realities were examined. With a few, though, the initial impulse grew into something deep and durable; some would risk, act, and even succeed. In the decades before the 1970s, however, the odds against succeeding as a full-time wine-grower dedicated to purist principles, as Martin Ray was, were nigh insurmountable. The market for premium American wines was limited, and skilled labor was in scarce supply.

Nowadays, it's far more possible for people to simply drop out of the workaday world and take up life anew as a vintner. Fine wines are in sufficiently great demand to support such a venture if sensibly undertaken, and if one can afford to wait a few years before payoffs commence. Wine-skilled operatives of all kinds are also around to help organize and successfully carry out the whole ambitious endeavor. In recent years many people of wealth or of more modest means have turned into ardent winegrowers. Sometimes they've chucked whatever they were doing before, to go at it seriously: pioneers who revive abandoned vineyards or create new ones in terrains perhaps unexplored in growing wine grapes. Others—doctors, lawyers, merchant chiefs, show-business celebrities—retain their professional careers, supporting this new endeavor as a classy pastime.

Throughout his winegrowing career Martin Ray had been

continually approached by people who proposed to "buy into" his way of life by owning a piece of his paradise. Turned on by his orchestrated magic, they wanted to be part of *his* exciting existence on the mountaintop, not off on their own somewhere. And they visualized a part-time association that would allow them to come up and hang around at picturesque turns of the year—especially, of course, vintage time. Few had any real acquaintance with the demanding labors of vineyard and cellar work ongoing throughout the year.

And Martin enjoyed having friends about him. He was making up for the lack of socializing during those last two Masson years as well as in the rugged, formative years on Mt. Eden. He loved guests' spellbound fascination with his stories as they drank wines together. He was talking, laughing, singing—carrying on into the wee hours, just as his beloved Paul Masson had done.

But entertaining friends now and then was a different story than having them around all the time. He knew that, so repeatedly turned down all overtures to associate with him in some way on the mountain. He hadn't forgotten Paul Masson's warning: "For God's sake, never allow anyone to *join* you up here! They'll all want to. If you ever let them, that's the end of your perfect life."

There was no rational reason, anyway, for getting closely involved with other people, even though they *were* friends. We had the entire mountain of 320 acres—a half-section of land—debt-free. And all to ourselves. We also had a thriving wine business. Our mountaintop life was ideal, removed from most mundane worries of the rest of the world far below us. Martin possessed everything he'd ever wanted. So he laughed off all propositions for making a permanent connection with him and his winegrowing retreat.

Yet one day, after turning down the pleas of a dear friend who wanted to buy some acreage for developing an adjoining vineyard, Martin in a remorseful mood recalled another Masson memory. Often Paul had spoken of the great advantage Romanée-Conti enjoyed prestige-wise by having five separately owned vineyard estates. This recollection set Martin to thinking. And the very act of *thinking* set in motion that tremendous organizational drive so astounding even back in college days. His creative forces were now triggered into action.

Suddenly he was inspired with a startling new conception for his mountain. Why, he could create the Romanée-Conti *domaine* of America! Yes, five separately owned vineyard estates within a single domain, exactly as it was with the French system. With his initial guidance and under his perpetual leadership. All wines would be sold under the Martin Ray Domain label, with the specific vineyard estate featured as well.

Here was his great opportunity to launch America's first *Appellation contrôlée,* he realized—the system that so benefited the high-quality French winegrowers. Just as in France, any vineyard estates on Mt. Eden must necessarily abide by strict laws regulating such things as grape varieties, planting and growing conditions, vintaging, marketing. He could institute such a system that would be self-imposed, not come from some government edict. He got right to work developing the entire plan on paper, in great detail.

When he told me about his vision, naturally I thought his brainstorm the greatest idea ever to hit the California wine world! I saw immediately how the idea offered tremendous advantages in prestige and publicity. I knew too that Martin Ray had all the inspiration, practicality, experience, and reputation necessary in transforming this grand dream of wine into dazzling reality.

Doubtless we would not have been attracted to this ambitious plan for expansion if someone within our own family ranks would be able in the foreseeable future to devote full time to carrying on Martin Ray's work. But all three of the children had taken up professions that demanded their focused attentions most of the time, and at a distance from us. For them, clearly, winegrowing could only be an avocation—pursued whenever they had time away from jobs, and while also accommodating the separate and special needs in their own family lives. (By 1958, each was married, and the first two of nine grandchildren were on their way.)

Martin had also explored alternatives. At times through the years, especially as his workload increased, he had interviewed and even taken on apprentices who could learn the trade while assisting him in field and cellar. He always hoped that eventually one would prove capable of handling much greater responsibilities, and become interested in having a permanent position here, thereby relieving him of some heavier responsibilities as he grew older. But nobody had worked out as he'd hoped.

Then too, after several frustrating attempts, Martin declined to get involved with viticulture and enology graduates. Invariably they had strong notions of their own that clashed with his methods and goals in winegrowing. Traditions that had proven right for him he understandably wished to maintain, without challenge or conflict, on his own premises. *He* wanted to do the training, not submit to the latest theories of professors! Most students, anyway, lacked the practical experience required in any small-scale winegrowing operation. They intended to become specialist winemakers—not pruners, ditch diggers, truck drivers, tractor repairers, and a multitude of other functions requiring either instant hands-on skills or the disposition to learn them as needed.

In contemplating this new dream of the winemaking life, Martin Ray saw a way to found and perpetuate a dynasty devoted to the making of fine varietal wines in America. He envisaged a large "pool" of potentially suitable successors and family commitments to draw from in shaping the future of this domain. Right away we began to consider which favored people we knew might be appropriate for sharing in our Good Life through part-ownership in the projected domain.

This budding entanglement with friends not only would end the even-paced, idyllic life on our mountaintop, but would also cost Martin Ray his very life. Or shorten it, at any rate, and bring on an avalanche of problems that ultimately would strip him of most of his mountain property.

All too late I realized that Elsie Ray would have prevented Martin's entire involvement with other people in a joint enterprise of this nature and magnitude. Far wiser than I about such matters—particularly where her husband was concerned—she never, never got carried away with enthusiasm when brakes were needed. So, without any self-protective braking, Martin Ray launched his great domain plan.

It is always much easier to anticipate and understand events through retrospection. . . . Dear reader: learn from our story, and be ever wary! Enthusiasm is fine, but caution is essential.

Martin went into swift action when planning the four vineyard estates to complete the domain (our own of course being #1). Arranging for its capitalization was an intrinsic part of the design.

For Vineyard #2—he'd call this Mount Eden Vineyards, after our mountain—he invited a number of our friends and acquaintances into a group that was rather like a select club of compatible people. Strongly oriented toward the stability of family life and its generational perpetuity so historically important to winegrowers, we decided that only married couples would be eligible to purchase a membership. To make it financially possible for certain younger persons to join, each member was expected to pay in monthly only $100 (even as little as $25 by special arrangement), toward a total investment of $10,000 for a paid-up share. We ourselves invested in one; one also was acquired by our botany-professor son, Dr. Peter Martin Ray (officially adopted by Martin some years back). Since some of these twenty-five couple-memberships were secured by well-known professional people, I saw great publicity potential here.

As to land, Martin would sell Mount Eden Vineyards (MtEV for short) some of our undeveloped land. Why not the lower quarter-section of 160 acres? He himself would clear, grade, disk, fence, lay out, and plant the vineyards for the group—with all his work given gratis. The whole domain would need a winery for fermenting, storing, and finishing wines that was far larger than the one beneath our house. So a handsome chateau would be constructed over a huge cellar. There members could gather for festivities and come up occasionally as separate couples for brief vacations. Martin could build that entire structure himself, out of poured concrete, just as he'd rebuilt Paul Masson's winery in 1941 and, later, our splendid mountaintop home in the early '50s. Since he already knew how to do it, the construction costs wouldn't be prohibitively high. And he would personally assume bank loans to subsidize all the work.

Thus was Mount Eden Vineyards conceived and created by Martin Ray. We incorporated it on April 1, 1960, sold the corporation the 160 acres as planned, on a real estate sales contract for $160,000—an enormous bargain, since nearby land, at this start of the big "Silicon Valley" land boom, was already selling at $10,000 per acre for commercial and residential sites.

Money was the least factor on Martin Ray's mind. MtEV could pay us for the land as it was able to do so, over the years. And neither of us asked for a salary—though we suspected even then that much of our time and energy in coming years would be devoted to the corporation's and members' benefit. After all, we were willing to sacrifice them for the greater glory of the domain. (Another folly to be noted in retrospect!)

So we'd taken the first big step in creating an American prototype of the Romanée-Conti domain. At this stage all was most exciting and fun and promising. Such happy get-togethers of all the members—marvelous celebrations and feast days! As when the group's first vineyard, of chardonnay vines, was being planted, fronting the chateau already commenced.

None of the members had any technical knowledge of winegrowing, but this wasn't required of them. What they all had was a keen appreciation for fine wines. Martin Ray, knowing exactly how to develop every phase to perfection, would mastermind everything and take full responsibility for its execution—charging no fee.

Martin was absolutely forthright about how it would be. As he'd assured the group at its first organizational meeting: "If any of you are accustomed to the conduct of PTA or civic group meetings where everyone has a finger in the pie and confusion and compromise reign supreme, let it be understood that we shall operate Mount Eden Vineyards through conduct of the opposite extreme! I will direct it all: development and care of the property, the vineyards, and the cellars."

Therefore, he expected everyone just to relax and enjoy what he would undertake and accomplish. And dictate. To him this seemed the perfect arrangement—never suspecting that probably only a completely dedicated wine zealot and self-styled autocrat like himself would find it so. Not for him were the windy town-hall debates, the endless legislative filibustering, and the slow-go mayhem of the "democratic way" in the larger society beyond his mountaintop.

Since it had taken ten years to develop his own vineyard estate, Martin figured on a similar ten-year development plan for Mount Eden Vineyards. Hopefully the other three projected estates would come within that time frame too.

Right off, then, having the explicit approval of all Mount Eden members, Martin Ray—with his usual zest and boundless energy, and using gigantic equipment—tore down mountain peaks and knolls, filled canyons, cleared the wilds, expanded ridges, graded, leveled, scarified and disked the soil, fenced, planted thousands of vines in 10 X 10 foot spacing, for the domain's four new vineyards. He created them entirely through his vision and own hard work, the latter of course supplemented by day laborers whom he supervised.

Our mountain workers, for both all-around vineyard and construction work, no longer were Italian, as they invariably had been in the Masson years. Out of Mexico they came, in droves, speaking mostly Spanish—entire extended families of them that often spanned three generations. They proved dependable and also delightful to have around, with their rollicking humor and seeming enjoyment of even the hardest work. As the years rolled by, we watched admiringly the younger generation grow up, and often go on to college, then move into various professional positions—having used that discipline of early acquaintance with multifaceted physical labor as a springboard to white-collar achievement. And a few are now professional winemakers themselves.

Obviously the monthly income from the MtEV group was infinitesimal against the huge development costs. As unpaid manager, Martin Ray continued to subsidize the entire operation, confident that eventually he'd be repaid. He borrowed heavily from the bank in his own name and on his credit, as the group had no established credit.

As planned, Martin arranged for MtEV to sub-sell acreage to two of its members for vineyard estates #3 and #4—bringing in helpful monthly payments. For the #5 estate, Martin sold to another MtEV member forty-three acres from our own upper quarter-section. And then, because of MtEV's acute financial need, he loaned the entire proceeds from the sale to the organization (never to be repaid).

Meanwhile, I kept the account books on these many complicated financial doings (five sets of books in all!), and paid the bills that poured in weekly. Scarcely the sort of work I enjoy, it took up a large chunk of my time for years. That, and hostessing an unend-ing succession of parties and feasts for MtEV-connected people. On top of all this I was composing and issuing monthly newsletters—my "Flashes"—about all the wonderful goings-on up at Mt. Eden.

Development work was proceeding splendidly on all projects. Martin seemed not at all concerned over not being paid as yet for the land, or our financing MtEV so heavily, or our contribution of endless hours of unpaid labor. As president of MtEV—a lifetime position, it had been agreed—he was in complete charge here! Our pride in sheer accomplishment would surely be compensation enough for our time and energy exerted. Eventually we would be repaid for all loans, he assured me, after all this development work was behind us.

And such accomplishments! By 1967 all four of the new vine-yard properties within the Martin Ray Domain had been developed into near completion. At #2, the MtEV "Chateau" vineyard planted to chardonnay, a lofty hill that originally fronted the chateau had been eliminated to create the vineyard area. At #3, Mt. Cabernet Vineyard below, a ridge had been spectacularly widened to form a mount of its own. At #4, the "East of Eden" Vineyard, planted to cabernet sauvignon, a great 40-foot-high slice was taken from a mountain peak and graded to create a glorious east-facing slope.

And at the #5 estate, beautiful Mt. Chardonnay Vineyard had been cleared from a savagely wooded mount. But while working there in removing a huge oak tree, Martin had a large limb crash down on him, smashing against his spine. He wouldn't allow this injury to halt the all-important work. (No doubt it initiated the fatal spinal complications later on). He went right on, as usual, doctoring himself with pain-killing capsules to relieve his otherwise chronic agony. He never mentioned his distress to others, for to speak of it would be to acknowledge its power over him, and that he would not concede. He was determined to hold firm control over his life—and to go on directing constant progress of the emergent domain.

The most enjoyable challenge to Martin, actually, was build-ing the MtEV chateau. First, the site itself had to be carved out of a steep hillside. Then after the great wine cellar was excavated, wooden forms were built and the concrete poured. Seventy huge ce-ment trucks, churning the eight-sack concrete mix, made their way up the narrow mountain road for the cellar alone! When the cellar structure was rock-hard, the chateau walls began to rise above it, using the cellar ceiling as the floor for the house. Thus the house was 150 feet long and 25 feet wide, with a huge kitchen added in the back on its own concrete slab flooring.

As the massive structure of the combined house and cellar was well on its way, Martin calculated that some 2.5 million pounds of concrete had already been poured! And since all was under his direction, he invariably stood in the midst of the rushing torrent of concrete—with a wide shovel manipulating it in the directions he wished it to flow, working it well into the forms, ramming it down with a rod, shouting to add more water to the mix, testing it, demanding, "More water, I want this smooth!" and sending men here and there as needed.

These pours were really exciting to witness. Each posed its own special and seemingly overwhelming problems, keeping Martin awake many nights beforehand, as he figured and refigured every detail: reviewing the steel fabrication, the stresses and strains at each point, weights involved, supports required, calculating how much concrete mix needed. (Astounding how his calculations came out exactly right every time, always just enough!)

Later we laughed over many a crisis. One, though, almost cost Peter his life. He was wading through the concrete pour of the south end of the chateau veranda, distributing the flow with a shovel, when he stepped into a big hole of liquid concrete and began sinking fast. (The hole extended deep into the ground below, to become one of the supporting pillars of the veranda, but its surface was deceptively smooth, resembling the rest of the pour.) Soon Peter would have been buried in concrete, with nobody ever knowing what had happened to him! Luckily, some worker heard him shout, and got to him just in time to pull him out.

When the interior of the chateau was completed enough, MtEV gave its first dinner inside. Hollywood's prestigious Wine and Food Society was entertained there, even before the plate glass was in the giant window frames or the vast interior was divided into rooms. At the next dinner, we dined in the big room with candles glowing on a table the entire length of the room. By then, MtEV was coming into its stride.

Martin Ray planned and presided over MtEV's events as well as our own. All the while he continued to get on his tractor and disk all vineyards himself (unless lucky enough to have Peter there). This disking, though, caused him acute back pain by tossing him sharply forward and back in a whiplash effect as he crossed mounds of hardened soil. But by doing this work he saved the vineyards' owners tremendous labor costs. Besides, he maintained that nobody could be *hired* to disk a mountain vineyard satisfactorily.

Martin went right on with all his operations: chateau finishing work; caring for all the vineyards new and old; making and watching over his own wonderful wines; and tending customers all over the country. Through the development years, we also tried to keep up some entertaining of visitors important and dear to us who were unconnected with MtEV. But we found ourselves giving up this enjoyable tradition. Our extensive domain work and MtEV activities had seemingly taken over our lives completely, leaving no time for cultivating new friends or keeping in contact with the old, and hardly any to be with our own offspring and grandchildren.

Moreover, on top of our long workdays, at least several nights each week we wined and dined until late hours some MtEV member-couple—who invariably brought various relatives and friends as well. Of course each time it would be a different bunch of people. They came to us fresh and eager to be entertained. Whereas *we* were more and more worn out—Martin particularly, in his injured condition—though he'd never admit it.

Then there were the group feasts where I did nearly all the work myself, including the strenuous cleanups afterwards. When members came to stay at our guesthouse or the chateau, I found myself serving not only as perpetual grocery-shopper and cook, but as charwoman!

Looking at this circumstance from the outside and post facto, you'd think by now we surely would have become concerned—apprehensive even. Not only about finances, having subsidized the cost of so much going on, but also about our very health and *lives*. However, we were much too busy creating this wondrous wine empire to harbor any misgivings or to sense an impending disaster. We loved it all, despite our exhaustion, and were devoted to our multiple MtEV family.

When Burgess Meredith last visited us and saw the situation, he was appalled. "These people will drain every drop of your blood, Rusty!" he exploded. "I'm not going to stick around to see it. Can't bear it!" He never sent in another $100 check, dropped out, lost his membership without even bothering to have it picked up by someone else. And dear "Buzzy" had been one of our first members, a particularly loved and cherished friend.

Buzzy's departure jarred me into trying to do something to halt Martin's victimization. I talked it over with Bill, a MtEV member always sensitive to our feelings and needs. He agreed. "Yes," he sighed, "we're killing off the goose that lays the golden egg."

Golden egg! That sparked a brilliant idea of Bill's. He had an artist create a gigantic plastic golden egg. We were centering it on the fireplace mantel one day just as Martin entered the room.

"What the hell is that?" he demanded.

"Now, Martin," Bill explained smoothly, "here's our idea: this golden egg was laid by some goose that got killed by overdoing. It's just a symbol—our way to save you from being kept up late, night after night. From getting killed off like that goose. When someone thinks it's time for everybody to leave, he or she can just point to the egg. That'll be the signal for people to clear out. No one has to say a word! I think it's a great idea. Don't you?"

Martin obviously didn't think so. He glowered at the egg. It looked preposterous to him. But he also gave an insidious interpretation to its presence: his authority as master of the house was being undermined. For after Bill left, he said, "Goddammit, nobody is telling *me* when my guests are to leave. Golden egg indeed!" Whereupon he picked up the fireplace poker and smashed the thing.

So there it was! How could he possibly be protected? Of course the egg wasn't such a smart idea anyway. It merely involved getting MtEV members to depart. How about something to prevent flocks of them from constantly *arriving!* They'd just invite themselves up, or even drop by unannounced—expecting us to be thrilled to see them and drop all else we were doing at the time, to entertain them and their friends with our usual verve.

One Mt. Eden member, a close trusted friend of ours, proposed to help. He moved to cut the number of members by buying up any shares that became available when members sometimes divorced or moved away. Because of the increasing strain, Martin permitted it, even though originally no member-couple was supposed to own more than one share.

I grew increasingly apprehensive about Martin's ailing condition, despite his gallant front. But his mind was absorbed these days on plans for launching the domain dramatically in the wine world, not on petty concerns about his person. Advance publicity stories were readied; labels designed for each of the five wine estates; special wood display cases concocted for presenting wines from each of the five estates, each bottle wrapped in a different tint of cellophane.

Martin was awhirl with exciting new ideas—always fun, always creative. He'd approved a beautiful design for MtEV wine glasses that Baccarat was to make for him in the classic style of their elegant Haut Brion; had a 300-case order lined up as a starter. The glasses were initially for members, but the next order would be for their friends too, and then for MtEV to market for all who loved superb wine glasses. Wonderful publicity for the Martin Ray Domain and its "jewel," Mount Eden Vineyards!

I continued to write, mimeograph, and dispatch my monthly news "Flashes" about the latest MtEV developments and activities of individual members. (Remember, this went on before computers and photocopier machines were available.) I also included interesting reports about the domain in Martin Ray letters going out everywhere. As before, our promotional literature was copied and recopied, circulating all around, and getting into newspaper and magazine columns. No wonder our domain and Mount Eden Vineyards were becoming the talk of the California wine world!

During the early to mid '60s the public's interest in wine had clearly awakened. The sales of varietal wines began to rise decisively. Martin Ray, taking time off from his domain-development work to study agricultural reports, watched the figures climb. Would most winegrowers now rush at last to plant varietals in their vineyards, to meet this growing public demand?

Due to increasing sales at higher prices of authentic varietals from the new, quality-aspiring wineries, the old-time better wineries were planting more premium grape varieties. In the meantime, to remain competitive, they upgraded the varietal content in their blends *if* they could buy enough premier grapes for their expanding needs.

During this period plantings of fine varietals virtually began exploding in California. In the five years between 1964 and 1969, the acreage of cabernet sauvignon increased sixfold, to more than 5,000; that of pinot noir almost quadrupled, to over 2,700. And the fast-rising chardonnay leapt from less than 1,000 in 1968 to nearly 2,500 in the following year, beginning its heady climb upwards.

Even the volume producers, noting the high prices commanded for authentic varietals, hastened to plant some top varieties that would eventually raise the quality of their blends. They needed ingredients to give some character and flavor to the Thompson seedless grapes, whose plantings continued to mount—with huge acreages and tonnages in the millions.

Martin pondered these extensive plantings of Thompson grapes. Now that true varietals finally were coming into their own, surely financial catastrophe would hit when these new vineyards really began bearing! So when a bust came to the booming wine market, he wasn't surprised. As usually happens in any supply-and-demand situation, overproduction collapsed wines sales—especially the big-volume, Thompson-seedless blends: jug-wine types. Better varietals were hurt far less, and recovered sooner. Winegrowers could read the message.

The fast-advancing trend toward producing fine wines, whether 100 percent pure varietals or blends with some fine-wine grapes— was too obvious now to ignore. Still, growers should have moved sooner to plant for quality, not high yield, as subsequent events would show. Indeed, if Martin Ray's great push for wine quality controls back in 1955 had been accepted, and implemented within a five-year period, California's finest vineyard lands would already have been transformed—in place and productive for the Wine Revolution that hit in the following decade of the 1970s.

True, as the '60s advanced, promising winegrowing changes

were in the air. Improvement now was inescapable. Martin was positive he'd see it come within the new decade. How pleased he was to learn that several wineries had actually been *fined* when caught cheating on the varietal-content ruling! Did this mean that real enforcement was on the way?

Still, he felt impatient. Why did pussyfooting authorities allow non-wine table and raisin grapes to be used in wine *at all,* but instead encouraged them to burgeon into 75 percent of the state's total wine crush? And when would the bureaucrats push the varietal requirement above that barely significant 51 percent—and also regularly conduct inspections to *verify* that a varietal wine contained what the label said it did? State and federal officialdom, he'd always noticed, invariably rallied wine producers toward maximum profit, not maximum quality, holding back wine improvement these many years.

Since Martin Ray was never profit-oriented, he was freed from the primary consideration motivating other winemakers. His sole aim was to perfect California wines to match the French ones, and even surpass them if possible. By creating wines that fully showed the state's potential for greatness, he hoped to inspire other vintners to emulate his dedication to quality. So with astounding zeal he pursued his drive, even though the California wine scene resisted change, except by slow degrees over a long period of time. It's amazing how he maintained such enthusiasm for his rejected cause . . . for forty long years.

During these seminal years of the '60s that would shape the new direction of California winemaking, Martin Ray's great domain plans were approaching their exciting fulfillment. Extraordinarily busy, he no longer maintained quite the same visible and vocal combativeness regarding varietals and quality controls. Certain that major improvements were on the way, he now focused upon quality standards he soon could exercise within his domain—by creating the first working model of a partnership estate dedicated totally to the making of fine wines, which included the very first (if self-declared) geographic appellation—Saratoga.

Nor had he time to examine closely the wisdom of his largess—in both economic assets and life energy—toward Mount Eden Vineyards. Or question our personal overinvolvement with its members.

He should have.

38

Firefall

M ARTIN RAY GARNERED MORE pure joy out of everyday life than could a hundred ordinary mortals. Naturally ebullient, with a great flair for living, he continuously rose above setbacks. He invariably imparted some of this exuberance to all who visited his mountaintop. Guests usually left us saying, "This is the greatest day I've ever spent anywhere, anytime, in all my life!"

No doubt that indomitable spirit of Martin's helped him survive all the conflicts that embroiled him throughout the years: the violently fermenting ups and downs, supreme triumphs and stark tragedies that would have completely vanquished anyone with less stamina and sense of purpose.

Through all adversity, when challenged to the limit and sometimes flagging from exhaustion or disappointment, his vibrant spirit somehow was miraculously resurrected again and again. This happened even after the almost unspeakable, ultimate tragedy—which Martin Ray survived by detaching it from his life, and not allowing one word to be said to him about it.

The final bolt that struck Martin Ray down—he who had braved many a tempest—was unworthy to be called lightning at all. It was not some chance, elemental calamity sent by an indifferent nature, but a deliberate human deed, given opportunity in this way:

In 1967 Martin Ray felt that, for future publicity and potent preeminence, it was time now to organize all five of the mountain estates into a solid permanent unit, as originally visualized. He sent out a letter to this effect to each Mount Eden Vineyards member, setting a date to meet at our guesthouse (the accustomed assembly place) to accomplish this. In it he presented his plan to make his own vineyard estate but one of the five within the domain by selling out to the combined group: not for money but a necessary controlling share—a sound procedure for future operations.

But Martin's plan interfered with that of the member he'd considered his closest associate—the one who had acquired extra shares under the guise of relieving us from excessive entertaining of members. Apparently he had ideas and ambitions of his own. So he moved instantly to halt the meeting that Martin had announced.

Having enlisted the aid of a lawyer, unbeknownst to Martin this "friend" called a secret meeting at another member's home. There he assumed control of the organization himself, since the lawyer obtained signatures of all attending members as well as some proxies: with enough votes to endorse his newly created Mount Eden Vineyards (MEV) corporate entity, which he intended to operate to his own advantage. He cleverly had persuaded enough attending members to believe they would benefit by overthrowing Martin Ray as president and instituting a supposed "democracy."

Faced with this coup d'état, both Martin and I resigned as Mount Eden Vineyards directors. All members remaining loyal to Martin Ray, outvoted and enraged at the conspiracy, dropped out too. They stopped at once their $100 monthly payments (as did we and Peter Martin), thereby losing memberships—with almost $10,000 already paid up on each share.

Thus Martin Ray's glorious dream of establishing a prestigious wine domain in America was rudely shattered, just as he was in the act of launching it. Through his later years, all his time, energy, genius, and assets (in both land and money) had been poured into this domain dream—only to be struck down in a flash. That it was stillborn and unrealized, so short of fruition in the form he had envisaged it, is forever to be lamented. It would have been a milestone achievement in furthering quality in California's wine world.

All the magic of our mountaintop existence vanished for us in a wink. Gone were all those happy days. Even our remembrances of them gave pain.

But the scheming betrayer lacked Martin's masterly hand to coordinate the remaining four vineyards into a cohesive, purposeful body. Stranded, they were buffeted by howling winds of confusion. And from MtEV's being the most joyful group ever assembled, this MEV became the angriest, fightingest bunch of individuals ever bound together. Though none of them knew anything about winegrowing, all had strong and contrary opinions about it. Their rivalries and mutual distrust grew to violent hatreds that often exploded. They fought over every decision, sometimes using their fists. Several broke down mentally or physically; one man even had to be institutionalized—which he blamed on the whole MtEV/ MEV fiasco.

So embittered did they become over the ensuing organizational shambles that they couldn't bear to meet except in factions. And of course they began suing one another. The absence of potent, effective leadership caused years of argument and litigation over control and legal ownership. These and other issues did not get resolved until the original plotter and his supporters were finally eliminated from the corporation.

Fortunately for us, we didn't have to attend these meetings! News of their warring proceedings, though, came to us second- and third-hand over months and years. And during that period we also saw their lawyers and representatives in various drawn-out and costly court proceedings.

In a court showdown in 1972, our lawyer was at the point of legally evicting MEV from the mountain. The judge was appalled to learn that its shareholders had never paid us for any land, or repaid any part of the large sums lent to the corporation member- ship by us, directly or through bank loans to Martin Ray. And he expressed annoyance that such a case usurped court time.

But our lawyer unknowingly erred, however, when he confided to Martin what MEV's wily attorney had just told him. He admitted that they "had no case." Nevertheless, he stressed, they intended just to continue on anyway. To fight it out in a higher court, on and on ...

Martin was thunderstruck, outraged. What, go on and on with this? "For God's sake, this has got to end, and right now!" he ex- claimed. He got to his feet and made his way out of the courtroom. He moved with some difficulty, as it pained him now to walk. He used a sturdy old axe handle to aid him rather than a cane. Not only did he find it more helpful, but he also considered it more fit- ting for a mountain vintner.

Now what in the world did Martin plan to do? Apprehensively, I followed him out. He had been taking such massive doses of pain- killing drugs I feared he might be all hot emotion rather than cool judgment. Unfortunately, my fear proved justified.

For what Martin did was to stop the court proceeding. He snatched the case, all set to win, from the hands of our law- yer—who glared at him as if he'd lost his mind. Martin proposed to meet the MtEV defectors in a court chamber immediately. And there he offered to buy the MEV corporation for whatever sums the dissident members had invested in its shares plus interest. We signed an agreement to that effect when they accepted. Martin thought he could safely make such a proposal because a New York real estate group had just offered him a substantial sum on a land sale. Their down payment of $350,000 would doubtless be *twice* the sum needed to buy the corporate shares. The only things that mattered to Martin were stopping further court proceedings and getting the conspirators off his mountain forever.

And then the offer Martin was counting on fell through. The New York group, which had seemed so reputable, turned out to be just a bunch of front-men promoters. (We found out later, too, that MEV's clever lawyer had flown back East to meet with them. He may have scared them out of the deal by threatening further litigation if they bought land on Mt. Eden.)

As an ex-stockbroker, Martin now realized he'd made a fatal strategic error. For one should never sign a Note unless funds to pay it are *assured;* and our signed agreement to buy the corporation for a fee was a Note. In his desperate desire to end all conflict immediately and for all time, Martin had taken the risk. Now we faced new trouble.

Martin's deteriorating physical condition interfered with his ability to devise a solution to our predicament. He was unable to organize a substitute sale to furnish the money due MEV before its lawyer got a judgment against us for the amount we'd agreed to pay for the share buyout in getting MEV off the mountain.

Our still-infuriated lawyer was in no mood to halt the judgment by exposing the huge amount of money MEV owed *us*, as major creditors. In fact, he refused to provide any legal help, even advice. And Martin certainly was in no condition to appear in court, to fight it further ... or ever to hear another word about MEV. Struck down by his fast-failing health, that inveterate fighter against elemental forces—fire, storm, and flood—finally ceased all court action. He had no money left to pay for it anyway.

So, using the judgment that prevailed, through the medium of a sheriff's sale MEV grabbed our most endeared part of the mountain: our home on the top, all vineyards and other valuable acreage over the summit. They paid us nothing at all for them, just credited a $100,000 payment against the $200,000 owed them by the Note we'd signed. Nor did they ever repay one cent of several hundred thousand dollars we had lent them over a period of time.

Like some splendid palace shaken apart at its foundation by a massive earthquake, our very existence was almost reduced to ruins. MEV at least hadn't taken the chateau property, since there was debt on it. This place then became our residence, our refuge. And remains our family home now.

After I'd planted wild shrubs all over the barren slopes fronting the chateau, and had Boston ivy greening the stark concrete exterior, it did become a charming place—overlooking our beautiful chardonnay vineyard on the slope below.

Evidently it's in my nature to cherish whatever assets one has.

For I found the closer view of the wide valley even more enchanting than the far-reaching one from above. The cold winter winds and the hot summer sun no longer came at us from all directions. And I greatly enjoyed the veranda running the entire length of the chateau. Roofless, it somehow afforded more intimate contact with the freedom of sky and surroundings. Also there was ample space all around the chateau for planting. I filled half-casks with soil so I could grow flowers and delicious year-round vegetables.

So life here from the start had many delights—until Martin's health began to fail drastically in 1975. His doctor diagnosed multiple myeloma, emanating from the site of that initial spinal injury. True to form, however, Martin bravely refused to accept the verdict, and ceased his visits to the doctor.

Due to continuing legal complications, our beautiful young chardonnay vineyard fronting the chateau was prevented from being pruned that spring, as it should have been. We could do nothing about it, since temporarily the property was legally out of our hands.

This exquisite vineyard that Martin had planted with such loving care, and given such expert attention, now was a deplorable sight—its desiccated vines dragging dead leaves over stony-hard, undisked, weed-choked ground. How tragic that over the last year of his life Martin had to endure looking down upon this frightful disintegration! As he walked slowly along our open veranda above the vineyard, he always tried to avert his eyes from the view. Sometimes when he'd forget, I'd see the awful pain and shock cross his face.

Yet despite this constant reminder of the loss of his once noble dream, it was amazing how on sunny days Martin still could join me out on the veranda at day's end. Financially shattered, suffering extreme and constant pain, and given a virtual death sentence by his doctor, Martin Ray still could lift his champagne glass to catch the sun's last rays in the bubbles, just as in former happy times. Incredibly, he seemed able to dismiss all thoughts of Mount Eden Vineyards.

He also dismissed his final calamity with a priceless rationale to bequeath posterity. "We must always remember this, goddammit," he said to me once as we sipped our twilight champagne. "We never really *own* anything in life. Everything we have is just on loan to us. Just on loan for a little while."

And then, on further reflection, he added somewhat wistfully, "And of course what we dream of accomplishing in life—that too is just on loan. Just on loan for an incredibly short time . . ."

Accustomed to being tuned to greater concerns than his own individual life, Martin escaped the usual panic and depression over approaching mortality. After all, death was no *problem,* demanding his solution. "This probably is the least difficult thing I've ever had to face—very minor, compared with so many other problems," he assured me. "It's simply a natural phenomenon, like the sun going down."

And then he recalled a phrase he'd always liked. "What is it they call out at Yosemite to hail the coming of nighttime, before the burning logs are pushed over that high waterfall? . . . 'Let the fire fall!' That's it. Just—let the fire—fall . . ."

When Martin no longer could walk, a local medic friend insisted that he be hospitalized at once. An ambulance slowly eased him on his last trip down the long, winding mountain road he'd built thirty years before.

At the Stanford Medical Center he was plagued incessantly and unmercifully with shots and tests he knew could be of no benefit by this time. "They plan to go on and on with this," he whispered to me, miserable far beyond the tortured pain of it all.

So just as he'd tried to control all else in his life, Martin decided it was up to him to end it. Late at night, with no one around, he simply removed his hospital gown, counting on the cold and damp night air to finish him off with pneumonia. And it obligingly did. He must have felt proud in taking charge thus of his ultimate destiny. For after he lost consciousness, a suggestion of a smile remained on his lips.

Martin Ray died on January 26, 1976, in Palo Alto, California, at the age of 71.

Martin Ray
Saratoga California

1950

Madame Pinot
California Champagne

Mount Eden Vineyards

PINOT NOIR
1990

ESTATE BOTTLED

Made entirely from grapes of a selected authentic strain of Pinot Noir, this wine is grown, fermented and bottled 2000 feet above the floor of the Santa Clara Valley...in part of the Union of R in the Santa Cruz Mountains

La Montaña

California
Cabernet Sauvignon

MADE AND BOTTLED BY

MARTIN RAY VINEYARDS
SARATOGA, CALIFORNIA

ALCOHOL 13% BY VOLUME • CONTENTS 750 ml (25.4 fl oz.)

Martin Ray

1982 NAPA VALLEY STELTZNER VYD.
CABERNET SAUVIGNON

VINTAGE 1941

CALIFORNIA
PINOT NOIR

Paul Masson

A Naturale red wine from the Pinot Noir grape

PRODUCED AND BOTTLED BY
PAUL MASSON CHAMPAGNE COMPANY
SARATOGA, CALIFORNIA   ALCOHOL 13% BY VOLUME

CONTENTS
4/5 QUART

Le Fruit Mûr Des Vignes Dorées

Martin Ray
1965

California Chardonnay

Epilogue

PEOPLE THE WORLD over believe that an individual human spirit, immortal and immaterial, sometimes remains in the place where in bodily life it formed close earthly attachments—more alluring than the pull of the vast universe beyond. There it oversees the welfare of loved ones and perhaps deals with unfinished business.

Often I have felt Martin at my side as I plant wild shrubs around the house, pick wildflowers along our road, or walk around the rim of our chardonnay vineyard—delighted that the old vines he planted years ago still send forth strong growth, lush with green leaves and heavy with ripening grapes.

But I've never *seen* a trace of Martin. Not yet, anyway. Maybe I'll get my turn someday. For recently someone else glimpsed him, atop Mt. Eden. I felt both astounded and envious. Why should a complete stranger be so privileged?

A visitor from the East Coast was staying at the guesthouse there—our first, dear little home together. Out on the deck, he was gazing down at the vineyard below when he noticed a man walking along slowly, stopping to examine various vines. Wondering why this fellow was studying them with such intense interest, the visitor considered joining him. But as he watched, the man simply vanished into thin air!

Jeffrey and Ellie Patterson, Mount Eden Vineyards' proprietors, when told by their shaken guest how someone clearly visible disappeared instantaneously, asked for a description of this apparition. The figure was powerful-looking, heavy-set, middle-aged . . . and wearing a broad-brimmed straw hat with a colorful band around it.

"That could only be Martin Ray," the Pattersons decided. And passed the amazing news on to me.

"Well, if Martin really does linger among his vines here on the mountain," I said, "that's the very place he'd be!" This site where he'd been spotted was where he had kept that first small section of cabernet sauvignon vines taken from three sources, to determine from comparisons which clone to use for his extensive future plantings on the mountain.

I hope that this wandering ghost of Martin Ray does more than check over a few vines. For thousands of vines—grown from clones he chose (and many he himself planted)—are growing here for him to admire, across the widespread vineyards on his mountain of old. Though he lost his domain, a Burgundian-style wine kingdom, his concept of a Mount Eden Vineyards estate at last flourishes—in others' capable hands, with years of management wrangling and financial problems finally laid to rest. His tradition of making fine, hand-wrought wines from pure varietal grapes continues on upon this mountain, his personally cherished acreage, where his memory is greatly honored.

And how Martin Ray's living persona would have rejoiced on New Year's Day in 1983! Almost a half-century after he had launched his quality fight, a 75 percent varietal-content requirement was finally decreed, with *official inspection* provided at last, to make regulation effective for the very first time. So in a very real way, it was not only varietals' vindication, but his as well.

We had celebrated earlier for Martin and his treasured varietals when announcement of the impending new rule came. It was sad that Martin didn't quite make it ... to live to see the ruling actually come about. Yet he had known it was close enough to almost grasp in his hand, this Holy Grail that he valued far more than his own personal life.

Of course Martin would have regarded this varietal "victory" as but token progress along the route to absolute 100 percent perfection. For the required 75 percent still left a loophole. The remaining 25 percent could be any wine—such as cheap Thompson seedless juice or easily grown, abundant chenin blanc. ("Would the French allow one raisin grape in *their* wines?" he'd ask, inevitably. Or maintain, "You can't blend out a pinot noir or chardonnay even one percent, or you simply don't have anything!")

Still, inspection would help enforce a varietal ruling for the first time. (Someday that minimum-requirement varietal percentage no doubt will go higher, though the trend among many premium wineries now is toward deft blending, but explicitly identifying its wholly fine-varietal contents on the label.)

Other dreams of Martin Ray's also came true in time. In the summer of 1975, while he was still alive, the BATF announced it would soon introduce an American form of France's 1855 *Appellation d'origine contrôlée* (A.O.C)—Appellation of Origin. Officially recognizing authentic "viticultural areas" in the nation would be one means of assuring quality to consumers. Applications soon began to be prepared. One came from a quality vintners' group in our own distinctive Santa Cruz Mountains, which acquired its special V.A. status in 1982. By now there are several dozen such areas just within California, and numerous others in additional winegrowing states. Ambitious vintner pioneers in such regions as the Pacific Northwest and the Northeast, previously considered inhospitable to *Vitis vinifera,* are now producing champion-class fine wines.

Martin Ray's own self-imposed winegrowing regulations, designed in 1960 for Mount Eden Vineyards (but of course never implemented), would have been far stricter, more akin to the French system. Still, Martin would be fascinated to see the extent to which some winery labels, on front and back, now detail for consummately interested consumers such things as exact vineyard origins, clonal varieties selected, farming procedures, and special picking, vintaging, and cellaring methods.

Martin Ray's innovative introduction during his Masson years of the concept of selling wine "futures" in advance of retail release is now done regularly by many premium wineries. And his desire to create a viable association for accommodating people's intense aesthetic and social interest in sharing wine and the Good Life, which led us into the disastrous organizational trap of Mount Eden Vineyards, surely proved instructive to vintners seeing enthusiasm-generating merit (with added income) in his plan. Many wineries now have special membership groups for devoutly dedicated clients. These give them not just discounts and buying opportunities, but also a warm, participatory sense of "ownership" in winemaking endeavors (including invitations to help prune, pick, vintage, and bottle), but without conferring any power. Convivial get-togethers include gourmet picnics featuring wine releases, exotic cooking demonstrations, and chamber music concerts at the vineyard's edge. Necessary limitations are set on visiting the premises.

The French *domaine* structure, which Martin Ray ambitiously aimed to emulate with his Martin Ray Domain (and Mount Eden Vineyards within it), increasingly occurs successfully in America in joint-partnership winegrowing ventures, even international ones.

Some of these changes surely would please him greatly, assuring him that all those lonely years of fiercely championing authentic varietals, for long a seemingly lost cause, went ultimately for some good, after all. He died only months before the famous blind wine-tasting contest of cabernet sauvignons and chardonnays took place in Paris, arranged by Steven Spurrier, on the Fourth of July in 1976. The top winners in both categories were Californian wines, and various others outclassed their French counterparts. In this signal "Judgment of Paris," the widely respected French wine experts who made the decisions were ill prepared for such a debacle. California winemakers were thrilled, while the rest of the world was shocked, astounded, and impressed.

Martin would want to learn about all the latest technological experiments, innovations, and equipment for both vineyard and winery. But he—who in his day questioned incessant experimentations like cold-fermenting white wines and centrifugal spinning for fast clarification—probably wouldn't have much to do with any of them. Like Paul Masson, he liked his own ways as they were. He thought nothing was better than using small, select quantities of a few fine varietal grapes ... and then taking infinite care and patience when permitting them to grow into superb wines.

Martin would be interested to note that nowadays women are increasingly becoming wine industry professionals—with some widely renowned as master winemakers. (Now what would the French male chauvinist, Paul Masson, have said about *that?*)

An incalculable legacy of Martin Ray remains his potent influence as role model. His fierce independence and purist stance as vintner, as well as the wines he made, much impressed a younger generation of like-minded winemakers. A few he himself had mentored directly. Others had their first revelatory vision of vocation when drinking one of his pure-varietal, blockbuster wines. Still more knew him only as a distant, elusive guru. And it was mostly these new winegrowers who brought on the notable economic, technical, aesthetic, and educational transformations notable in the Wine Revolution, coming in the wake of the wine boom beginning in the '50s and accelerating with the years.

Thus wine historian Charles Sullivan wrote after Martin Ray's passing, "There were few who, at this date, would not pay him the encomiums due him. For practically everything he had fought for had come to pass or was in the process. As one national wine journal put it: 'He was the catalyst for the entire wine industry, and showed others what could be accomplished if they thought big and never compromised.'"

Winegrowing as a profession has become radically different from the one Martin Ray entered in 1936 after buying Paul Masson—in that post-Prohibition period when so few Americans knew or cared anything about wine. Looking around, Martin would be impressed, surprised, and flabbergasted ... and no doubt at times outraged, offended, dismayed.

He'd certainly be pleased to see his beloved varietals, whether

100 percent pure or blended with other named fine-wine grapes, selling at prices that should enable a winegrower to be adequately rewarded for his dedicated labors. He hardly would have believed that at a much-ballyhooed fancy auction someone might actually pay $25,000 or more for a case of California wine—even if *he* had made it.

He would find mind-boggling the ever-growing list of wineries, aspiring "boutique" ones cheek-by-jowl with corporate conglomerates. He'd be amazed that chain drugstores and supermarkets have row upon row of better wines, even fine imported wines, at astoundingly high prices, that many jug-wine drinkers have graduated into drinking. (But I can well imagine his horror if seeing wine actually being poured from cardboard boxes!)

What would he think of the spate of weekly and monthly publications just about *wine*—periodicals with readerships in the many thousands, as well as coffee-table and how-to books? Incomprehensible! And he might disbelieve that the wine-tasting classes offered in many community colleges and university extensions across the nation are so popular that pupils often must be turned away.

Never a crowd-chaser, he would sedulously avoid the whole spectacle of freeloading wine tourism that abounds in most wine-growing regions. And he'd be amused, or maybe aghast, at the perpetual round of competitive wine-judging contests (in which all wines seem to receive medals), as well as community "wine and cheese" tastings that are fundraisers or come-ons for shopping malls.

On summer nights, standing in one of his own vineyards, he'd see bright lights over on the La Cresta property southeast of his own mountain, and hear faint music wafting across the canyon. For there the ever-popular concerts of rock, country, jazz, and R&B music go on from May to October within the amphitheater set up outside Masson's old Mountain Winery building that he managed to rebuild a half-century ago. And many of the attendees have just eaten elegant meals served in banquet rooms and out on the terrace of his former chateau.

If clued into the current hustle-bustle of California's wine world, Martin Ray certainly would acknowledge happily that wine has at last become a highly popular and "classy" beverage in America. And, astoundingly enough, dry wine, not sweet wine, is the great fashion.

Close to home, he'd be greatly pleased to see our children and grandchildren often working in our vineyards and cellar, and taking part in vintaging our limited gallonage of family wine.

After Martin's death, Peter Martin Ray with considerable effort managed to retrieve a portion of Rusty's land on Mt. Eden. He launched a new winemaking business as the president and winemaker of Martin Ray Vineyards. While producing new wines from fine-varietal grapes purchased elsewhere, he developed new vineyard acreage on Mt. Eden. However, he was ousted in a management takeover in the mid-'80s.

In the early 1990s, a wholly separate winemaking firm, based in Sonoma County and headed by Courtney Benham, bought the remaining wine inventory along with the right to use Martin Ray's name on wines. Many of these varietal wines, made from mountain-grown grapes, have earned high marks, honoring the heritage of the acquired label.

Someday maybe some of our offspring may resurrect the tradition of having a bonded winery here. But until such time, high-caliber wineries are eager to buy all excess grapes from the family's acreage of vineyards that our stalwart Peter farms, along with pursuing his profession as a botany professor at Stanford. Astride his yellow tractor and wearing a sombrero, in the distance he resembles his predecessor, the founding father. He too is passionately attached to this land.

If Martin's spirit ever looks down on our valley, he'll recall the days of his youth, when there were only farms and farmhouses and orchards at the base of these mountains, before Santa Clara Valley became paved with concrete, asphalt, glass, and steel—paid largely by earnings from silicon chips. On clear nights then, he could identify each light out in the vast darkness below, knowing whose farm it was. Now at nighttime, the earth below us glitters with far more twinkling lights than the sky above. The lights are beautiful in their own way, but I am glad I live above them, not among them.

Martin far preferred the simplicity of the rural past to the razzle-dazzle of urban progress. He would have liked it if Santa Clara Valley, with its fabulously deep and fertile soil, could have been saved as an agricultural preserve. Just like Napa, its perennial rival—smaller but equally beautiful—to the north. Napa County preservationists have won out in the competition in reputation for having prime vineyards. They encouraged tax-advantageous land use for grape farming and wineries by applying the state's Williamson Act, as well as through curbing urban development schemes and outlawing wide-access highways. We still have, at least, the great wine grape-growing bastion of the Santa Cruz Mountains.

Martin Ray would agree that from this great distance the view from Mt. Eden remains spectacular. Best of all, he'd revel in seeing the array of flourishing grapevines greening the slopes. For these, our last vineyards in the sky, still proclaim that age-old dream of wine.

For Further Reading

Adams, Leon D. *The Wines of America.* McGraw-Hill, 3rd ed., 1985.

Amerine, Maynard A., and Vernon L. Singleton. *Wine:* An Introduction for Americans. University of California Press, 1972.

——. *Wine and Wine Making.* University of California Press, 1976.

Balzer, Robert Lawrence. *California's Best Wines.* Ward Ritchie Press, 1948.

——. *The Pleasures of Wine.* Indianapolis & New York: Bobbs-Merrill Co., 1964.

——. *This Uncommon Heritage:* The Paul Masson Story. Ward Ritchie Press, 1970.

Bazin, Jean-François. *Paul Masson:* Le Français Qui Mit en Bouteille L'Or de la Californie. France: Edition Alan Sutton, 2002.

Benson, Robert. *Great Winemakers of California.* Capra Press, 1977.

Conaway, James. *Napa:* The Story of an American Eden. Houghton Mifflin, 1990.

Holland, Michael R., Charles Sullivan, and Jason Brandt Lewis. *Late Harvest:* Wine History of the Santa Cruz Mountains. Santa Cruz, CA, 1983.

Lapsley, James T. *Bottled Poetry:* Napa Winemaking from Prohibition to the Modern Era. University of California Press, 1996.

Lukacs, Paul. *American Vintage:* The Rise of American Wine. Houghton Mifflin, 2000.

Lyon, Richard. *Vine to Wine.* Napa, CA: Stonecrest Press, 1985.

Mabon, Mary Frost. *ABC of America's Wines.* Knopf, 1942.

Melville, John. *Guide to California Wines.* Doubleday, 1955; San Carlos, CA: Nourse Publishing, 1960

Muscatine, Doris, Maynard A. Amerine, and Bob Thompson (eds.). *Book of California Wine.* University of California Press, 1984.

Pinney, Thomas. *A History of Wine in America*: From Prohibition to the Present. UC Press, 2005

Reeve, Lloyd Eric, and Alice Means Reeve. *Gift of the Grape:* Based on Paul Masson Vineyards. Library of Western Industry, 1959.

Schoonmaker, Frank, and Tom Marvel. *American Wines.* Duell, Sloan & Pearce, 1941.

Street, Julian. (Revised by A.I.M. Street.) *Wines: Their Selection, Care, and Service.* Knopf, 1961.

Stuller, Jay, and Glen Martin. *Through the Grapevine:* The Business of Wine in America. New York: Wynwood Press, 1989.

Sullivan, Charles L. *Like Modern Edens:* Cupertino, CA: Winegrowing in Santa Clara Valley and Santa Cruz Mountains, 1798-1981. California History Center, 1982.

——. (interviewer). *Wines and Winemakers of the Santa Cruz Mountains.* Santa Cruz Mountains Vintners / David Bennion Trust, 1992-1994.

——. *A Companion to California Wine*: An Encyclopedia of Wine and Winemaking from the Mission Period to the Present. University of California Press, 1998.

Sunset Books and Sunset Magazine (eds.). *Guide to California's Wine Country.* Lane Publishing, various editions.

Teiser, Ruth, and Catherine Harroun. *Winemaking in California.* New York: McGraw Hill, 1983.

Woodward, W. Philip, and Gregory S. Walter. *Chalone:* A Journey on the Wine Frontier. Carneros Press, 2000.

Young, Casey, and Ken Dawes. *Mountain Vines, Mountain Wines*: Exploring the Wineries of the Santa Cruz Mountains. Santa Cruz, CA: Mountain Vines LLC, 2003.

INDEX

Note: In some subentries abbreviations are used: MR = Martin Ray; PM = Paul Masson, EKR = Eleanor Ray; EHR = Elsie Ray, SF = San Francisco, SJ = San Jose, MtEV = Mount Eden Vineyards, MEV = the Mount Eden Vineyards corporation (post-MR). Fictitious names given to a few persons and organizations appear in quotations marks and are identified as (pseud.).

Biographies

ELEANOR RAY was born in 1904 in Yakima, Washington. Her mother, Ina Phillips Williams, was well-known as an orator and suffragist, and became one of the state's first female legislators. In 1926 Eleanor graduated from the University of Washington, where she first got to know Martin "Rusty" Ray well. She married his best friend and business partner, Walter—whom she later divorced, after they had three children together. Under her married name of Eleanor Kamb, she made a career in advertising.

In 1951 she published *We Kept Mother Single*, her best-selling memoir that humorously depicted both the challenges and delights of single parenting. Shortly thereafter, with all of her children by then away in college, she married Martin Ray, whose beloved wife, Elsie, had died earlier. Through adroitly promoting Martin Ray wines, as well as assisting him in vineyard and cellar work, Eleanor became his invaluable partner. She hostessed hundreds of dinners given for wine-loving guests from around the world—where her culinary and social skills perfectly matched Martin's potent wines and spellbinding stories. They made many converts to the "Good Life" of winegrowing.

After Martin's death in 1976, Eleanor continued living in their chateau on Mt. Eden in Saratoga, in the midst of a chardonnay vineyard overlooking Santa Clara Valley, which by then was being transformed into "Silicon Valley." For some years she worked on writing various versions of Martin Ray's life story. Finally published, with her daughter's help, in 1993 by Heritage West Books of Stockton, *Vineyards in the Sky* garnered praise from a number of wine writers, wine historians, and vintners. A second edition, privately printed in response to continuing requests for copies, has now been replaced by this third edition, published by Mountain Vines Publishing LLC of Santa Cruz, California.

The book has helped to preserve Martin Ray's reputation, during the dismal period between Repeal and the Wine Revolution, as the prime advocate of producing 100% pure fine-varietal wines and the focused, consumer-protecting foe of fraudulent wine labeling. It also introduces to younger generations his uncompromising principles, notable accomplishments, and uniquely colorful character. Martin Ray truly serves as a model, even an icon, with a number of winemakers who follow in his zealously idealistic footsteps.

Eleanor Ray died in 2000 at the age of 96, after achieving an enduring wish of her last years: to be present at the arrival of the new millennium.

BARBARA KAMB MARINACCI, Eleanor Ray's daughter, is a book writer and editor. She has authored or coauthored ten books (including *O Wondrous Singer!* An Introduction to Walt Whitman; *California's Spanish Place-Names:* What They Mean and How They Got There; *Linus Pauling in His Own Words; Dr. Max Gerson:* Healing the Hopeless). Over the years, as a developmental editor she has worked on several hundred books, sometimes as a ghostwriter. She has also served as a nonprofit management consultant, and for three years was the executive director of a community counseling center in Los Angeles. In 1990, with her three children now grown, she moved to Saratoga to care for her elderly mother; she could then focus on preparing *Vineyards in the Sky* for publication.

At present Barbara remains living in Martin and Eleanor Ray's Mt. Eden mountaintop residence while engaged in numerous writing and editing projects— interspersed with gardening, cooking, and traveling. Currently she is producing a series of articles about Martin Ray, based largely on his own correspondence, which reveal additional or alternative facets of this complex, resolute, and charismatic vintner. They are being published in installments in *Wayward Tendrils Quarterly* (P.O. Box 9023, Santa Rosa, CA 95405).